HISTORY OF THE MAFIA

HISTORY OF THE MAFIA

SALVATORE LUPO

TRANSLATED BY ANTONY SHUGAAR

COLUMBIA UNIVERSITY PRESS / NEW YORK

COLUMBIA UNIVERSITY PRESS

Publishers Since 1893

New York   Chichester, West Sussex

Copyright © 1996 Donzelli Editore

Translation copyright © 2009 Columbia University Press

Foreword copyright © 2009 Antony Shugaar

All rights reserved

Library of Congress Cataloging-in-Publication Data

Lupo, Salvatore, 1951–

[Storia della mafia. English]

History of the mafia / Salvatore Lupo ; translated by Antony Shugaar.

p.   cm.

Includes bibliographical references and index.

ISBN 978-0-231-13134-6 (cloth : alk. paper)

1. Mafia—Italy—History.   I. Title.

HV6453.I8L8613   2009

364.1'060945—dc22   2009011765

Columbia University Press books are printed on permanent
and durable acid-free paper.

This book is printed on paper with recycled content.

Printed in the United States of America

c 10 9 8 7 6 5 4 3 2 1

References to Internet Web sites (URLs) were accurate at the time of writing. Neither the
author nor Columbia University Press is responsible for URLs that may have expired or
changed since the manuscript was prepared.

CONTENTS

FOREWORD

ANTONY SHUGAAR

In the late 1980s, when I was covering Italy's booming media business, a Milan advertising executive provided me with a subtle insight into the raucous debate then under way over the Italian government's efforts to maintain its television monopoly.

It's like a man walking his dog through a dangerous part of town, he explained. The man actually wants the dog to look completely uncontrollable so that potential muggers will steer clear.

So, even as Italian media tycoons and other aspiring tycoons were struggling to block a proposed government clamp-down, they were loudly proclaiming to anyone who would listen—especially to foreign media companies considering entry into the Italian market—that it was impossible to work with the reckless and unpredictable Italian government. (This at a time when the prime minister of Italy, Bettino Craxi, regularly vacationed with the country's most powerful media tycoon, Silvio Berlusconi, during the long August holidays; Craxi was also Berlusconi's best man at the tycoon's second wedding.)

Things in Italy, in fact, are often not quite what they seem; the real messages are often embroidered within the hems of the ostensible messages.

No study of Italian political history can ignore the existence of the Mafia, and as Salvatore Lupo explains in this important book, the existence and meaning of the Mafia are less—and more—than they appear.

Another story from the late 1990s offers an exquisite paradox: Silvio Berlusconi (who at the time had served briefly as prime minister and would begin a second term shortly thereafter) had just added the Standa chain of department stores to his vast media and real estate holdings. There was a problem, though: the Standa stores in Sicily kept burning down. Then, inexplicably, the apparent cases of arson stopped.

One of the flagships of Berlusconi's media empire was—and remains—the newsweekly *Panorama*. In this delicate period, the magazine began publishing a series of hard-hitting exposés on Berlusconi's awkward dilemma and the possibility that negotiations with the Mafia had made the problem go away.

I was interested in the nexus between politics and media and had written on the subject for the *Columbia Journalism Review*. When I called my contacts in an attempt to understand why Berlusconi's own media vehicles were focusing on allegations of his ties with the Mafia (could it have been simple crusading journalism?), I was presented with this elegant but Byzantine theorem: the editor in chief of *Panorama* was about to enter negotiations with Berlusconi for the renewal of his contract. For Berlusconi to fire him in the wake of a series of sharply critical articles accusing the media tycoon of Mafia ties would have looked embarrassing. The editor—according to this piece of conspiracy theorizing, anyway—thus greatly strengthened his hand in the ensuing negotiations.

The English term "ulterior motives" is rendered in Italian as *secondi fini:* literally, "second objectives." The sense is only slightly different, but it offers Italians the possibility of referring to *secondi, terzi, quarti, e quinti fini*—or second-, third-, fourth-, and fifth-order ulterior motives. Like the legendary 120 words in Inuit to describe snow, it seems appropriate that Italian should be capable of describing so many levels of conflicting or concealed objectives.

This book explores, first and foremost, and in admirable if exhaustive detail, the hidden levels at play in the phenomenology of the Sicilian Mafia. Lupo attempts to establish just what the Mafia is, examining various previous hypotheses that range from an inbred folk tradition to a powerful international "octopus," to use the Italian slang term (*la piovra*). In so doing he describes patterns and histories that offer eloquent illustrations of the smoke and mirrors concealing all Mafia structures.

Duplicity is the bedrock of Mafia tactics. One owner of a Sicilian citrus grove subleases it to a Mafia custodian, whose responsibility it is to prevent theft of the fruit before harvest and to negotiate the final contract with the fruit merchant who will harvest the citrus crop and sell it.

Imagine his surprise and dismay when the fruit merchant contacts the owner of the grove to complain that the Mafia custodian has allowed several other merchants to pre-harvest the grove, leaving slim pickings for him, in exchange for the full price negotiated and paid. At this point, the owner of the citrus grove tries to fire the custodian: nothing doing. He tries to sell the grove, and is clearly informed that to do so would be a fatal insult to the mafioso. The rules are ironbound, although they are grounded in a duplicitous alternate underworld.

This is the same pattern found in a Mafia boss ordering his underlings and associates—originally agricultural custodians and laborers, though the pattern persisted in the new urban settings in which the Mafia later evolved—to steal horses and cattle, so that he could first express his condolences and outrage at the brazen theft, and then offer to see if he could make an arrangement to recover the property.

Another nexus of duplicity, according to Lupo, is in the area of police informants and *omertà*, the much bruited Mafia code of honorable silence. "*Omertà*," notes Lupo, "understood as a sense of 'moral' repulsion with respect to the idea of availing oneself of the legal system, may perhaps represent a general value, an ideal model of behavior of the Sicilian populace and, in particular, of the larger criminal universe; certainly, it is no guide to the actual behavior of mafiosi, who—as we have seen over and over—collaborate with the law whenever and however it furthers their own interests." So that no one is more likely to inform to the police than mafiosi (after all, it is they who have the information), but then the doubt remains as to whether that information is a way of manipulating the police.

This shadow has, in turn, been used to cast doubts on the use of *pentiti*, Mafia turncoats who have been one of the chief tools used by crusading Italian prosecutors in the past quarter century. Sadly, it was exactly this sort of house-of-mirrors that blotted the reputation of Leonardo Sciascia, the great Sicilian author and political thinker, whose obituaries upon his death in 1989 were marred by Sciascia's contrarian statements that it had become possible to build a career as an "anti-Mafia judge."

Lupo explores an understanding of the Mafia as an underworld—this being Italy, more in the sense that the poet Virgil might give to the term than that which Eliot Ness might assign to it—in which power accrues to those mafiosi who are able to find access to powerful figures in the "overworld." Inside this strange parallel universe, the geography of organized crime is the product of evolution, and frequently a parasitical, nonorganic evolution.

The process is reminiscent of a theory from another field, that of organic chemistry and chemical evolution. Graham Cairns-Smith popularized this view in his 1985 book, *Seven Clues to the Origin of Life*. In it, he described an inorganic process whereby clays might clog a stream or silt up a pond through the propagation of crystalline structure. In so doing, the clays might cause a watercourse to dry up, and the wind might then blow the clay dust to a different pond or watercourse, renewing the choking and drying process, and so on, ad infinitum. The idea was that this inorganic process might then serve as a scaffolding upon which an organic process might well evolve, leading to carbon-based life forms.

The choking off of a stream is an evocative metaphor for the growth of the

Mafia, but a noncriminal system as a scaffolding for an opportunistic form of criminal organization is also apt. Two such systems, in the history of the Sicilian Mafia, are the citrus fruit trade and the mining of sulphur.

The citrus trade is a well-known setting for the development of the Mafia, though it is not as well known how the citrus trade with the United States helped bring the Mafia to this country. The first documented Mafia presence in the United States is in the port city of New Orleans, and that presence is clearly closely related to the substantial trade in lemons and oranges that ran through that southern port. In fact, the world of the Sicilian Mafia and southern law enforcement collided in 1891, with the largest mass lynching in American history: the victims of the lynching were eleven Italians—some American citizens, and a few Italian subjects—who had been acquitted of the murder of New Orleans police chief David Hennessy. Even though New York is, in the collective imagination, the mythic hotbed of the Mafia's presence in the United States, New Orleans remained a major center for the germination of organized crime here.

The other leading structure within which the Mafia germinated and grew is the sulphur-mining industry. Until the turn of the twentieth century, Sicily held something approaching a monopoly on the world's sulphur supply. Sulphur was a crucial component of rubber production (vulcanizing involves the addition of sulphur to raw rubber under high heat, but its name might well be a specific reference to Sicily's volcanic geology and mythological history).

It was in particular the organization of the mine crews that worked the sulphur deposits that seems to foreshadow some of the structures later found in the Sicilian Mafia. The crews were small, independently operating entities, and they stood to profit by their own production, as long as a sizable percentage was rendered to the owner of the mine. The fact that they earned by piecework is not a novel arrangement, but it was the nature of work in the mines, brutal, toxic, and violent, that made the setting such a breeding ground for the characteristics of the Mafia crew. Intriguingly, Sicilian control of the sulphur industry suddenly collapsed around the turn of the century when American technology made it possible to mine sulphur-domes in Louisiana and Texas.

As the sulphur industry began to decline, might the structure of the mining crews have served as a scaffolding for the construction of the Mafia crew as a self-motivating franchise? The sulphur mine is a recurring motif in descriptions of Sicilian life and analyses of the Mafia, from Giovanni Vergara's short story "Rosso Malpelo" (1880, from *Vita dei campi*), in which an underage boy dies in a mining collapse, all the way up to Carlo Levi's *Words Are Stones* (*Le parole sono pietre*, 1955). In Levi's account of his visit to Lercara Friddi, Sicily, during a strike by sulphur miners, he paints a remarkable picture of Signor Ferrara, the man who runs the sulphur mine on behalf of its absentee owners.

Here is Levi's description of the man, known colloquially among the towns-people as "Nero":

How can I describe him? Perhaps only a painting could adequately render the aura of that face, the atmosphere that enveloped it, the uncommon manner of his gestures. His face was impassive and inscrutable, and yet at the same time it was enlivened by grimaces expressing feelings different from those we are accustomed to perceiving: a mixture of cunning, extreme mistrust, mingled confidence and fear, arrogance and violence and even, perhaps, a certain wit: and yet all these elements seemed to be fused in that face in a way that was distant and alien to us, as if the tone of the emotions, and the very appearance of the face, belonged to another era, of which we have nothing more than an archaic, hereditary recollection.

I had the distinct impression of being in the presence of a rare representative of a lost race, not a man of today, or yesterday, or even a hundred years ago, but one of those who had lived a thousand years ago, in that period of history that has left practically no documentation at all, a time that we can only imagine.

Levi then tells how Signor Ferrara deals with the fact that he has come accompanied by a photographer:

"Of me, a photograph?" he exclaimed. "No, that's prohibited, absolutely forbidden. No one has ever taken my picture, and no one ever will. My doctor forbids it," he added, with a smile that revealed a formidable row of teeth, "and so does my pharmacist." As he said these words, he noticed that [the photographer] had his photographic equipment on a strap around his neck, ready to use; and to make sure that no one took his picture, Signor [Ferrara] rose to his feet, huge and heavy as a boulder, and placed himself, back to back, against [the photographer]: he thus made sure that he could not be surprised.

Thus the description offered by a renowned Italian anti-Fascist and socialist writer and activist. And it is impossible to separate the politics of Italy's left and right and the role of the Mafia.

Just as this book goes back to the unification of Italy in its attempt to trace the first appearance of the Mafia, the unique role of the Mafia might well be seen in relation to the anti-Risorgimento, the phenomenon of the *brigantaggio post-risorgimentale,* or brigandage. I am currently writing about this subject, and it is a forgotten but significant chapter of Italian history.

The brigand wars, as they might be called, erupted with the northern Italian occupation of southern Italy, also described in patriotic literature as the "unification" of the Italian nation.

The first three years were astonishingly violent, and more northern soldiers (Piedmontese, as they were described in the south) died in repressing the southern rebellion than did in liberating and unifying Italy in the first place. There is a remarkable letter from Lincoln's Secretary of State, William H. Seward, to the Italian government, assuring it of American support and understanding in view of their twin southern uprisings.

General Alfonso Ferrero La Marmora, a hero of the Italian Risorgimento, made the following statement to the parliamentary commission of inquest on brigandage: "From the month of May 1861 to the month of February 1863, we have killed or executed by firing squad 7,151 brigands. I know nothing more, I can say nothing more." One French newspaper decried the Italian campaign of military repression, comparing it to the eradication of the Native Americans then under way in the United States.

The brigandage continued, at a lower boil, for a solid twenty years after that, until 1880, and its ultimate repression coincided with the beginning of mass Italian emigration to the United States and to South America. The historian and Italian prime minister Francesco Saverio Nitti coined the phrase "O emigrante o brigante" ("Either emigrant or brigand"), summarizing the options available to starving peasants in southern Italy.

What the brigandage did in the context of this history, however, was to clearly emphasize to the ruling class in Rome that, while disorders broke out in Calabria, Campania, and other parts of the mainland south, there was a reliable organization in Sicily that managed to keep the peasants under solid control.

The collegial understanding that developed between government and Mafia was shattered with the advent of the Fascist regime, which successfully repressed the Sicilian Mafia by quasi-military means. Sciascia, in fact, probably was thinking of the anti-Mafia campaign of Mussolini's prefect in Sicily, Cesare Mori, when he lamented the antidemocratic dangers lurking in the wholesale repression of the Mafia. Sciascia in fact quotes one of the Mafia bosses sent to prison by Mori. The elderly boss addressed the court famously with these words: "Your honor, with all the murders that I have committed, that you should send me to prison for a killing of which I am innocent . . ."

It was, in fact, the techniques used in eradicating the brigands that Mori adopted during his rule in Sicily.

His suppression of the Mafia was effective but short-lived. When World War II came to an end, the Mafia returned to power in Sicily all the faster because they alone had no compromising dalliances with the Fascist regime.

The commanding officer of Allied occupation forces in Sicily after the war was none other than Colonel Charles Poletti, former governor of New York State (very briefly in 1942; he had previously served as lieutenant governor under Herbert Lehman), and his driver and interpreter was Vito Genovese, who had left New York in 1937 to escape prosecution.

With the end of the war and the fall of Fascism, the Mafia returned to Sicily.

It is understandable that in the years of left-wing turmoil in Italy, when terrorist groups like the Red Brigades named themselves after formations from the Italian anti-German Resistance movement, the Mafia was identified with the "imperialist occupation" forces, such as NATO and multinational corporations like AT&T.

Paradoxically, when a Christian Democratic politician named Ciro Cirillo was kidnapped by the Red Brigades, the party turned to its contacts in Neapolitan organized crime (Camorra, not Mafia) to see if they could arrange Cirillo's release.

The intersection between the Mafia as an organized crime system and its legend as a Robin Hoodish mutual aid society may be a dynamically moving boundary, part of a process that evolves over time, making the goal of an understanding of the nature of the Mafia even more of a moving target.

Suffice it to extrapolate from some of the political organizations that we have watched metastasize from revolutionary forces into crime cartels: Sendero Luminoso, FARC in Colombia, the Irish Republican Army (as so memorably portrayed in the 1980 film *The Long Good Friday*), and others. At one point, a colonel in the Cuban army was found to have been in cahoots with Manuel Noriega in trafficking drugs in the Caribbean.

It is easy to theorize a socially responsible Mafia protecting peasants in the early days, long before the beginning of documented Mafia history, and then degenerating into its present cancerous form.

Ultimately, by the end of the Cold War, there was no clear political alignment of any sort with organized crime in Italy. As strong as the ties with the Christian Democrats had been, the loss of a unified anti-Western force in Russia and China deflated the rigid alignments in countries like Germany, Italy, and Japan. As Italy moved out of its ideological phase and into its second boom period of the late twentieth century, the idea of pro- and anti-Mafia political alignments began to seem superficial. In the corruption fever that culminated in the Tangentopoli investigations, bribe-takers made sure that payments were divvied up equally among the parties. And in that context, the Mafia declared open war against the Italian state.

As an American living in northern Italy, I was fairly removed from direct contact with the experience of the Mafia dominion. Only once did I happen upon the aftermath of an execution-style murder—a man had been shot as he sat in his car in the Via Vetere, off Corso di Porta Romana.

But the one time I really came in contact with the stark menace of the Mafia was in Palermo, in the years following the maxitrial against the Mafia, but still prior to the murders of judges Giovanni Falcone and Paolo Borsellino.

I went to pay a call on Michela Buscemi, a woman who was one of only two civil plaintiffs in the gigantic trial of nearly 500 Mafia defendants. I rode a bus from the center of Palermo out into the countryside. The bus tooled along highways, and finally came to a stop in a barren piazza, the end of the line. From there I followed the directions I had been given, through narrow streets, and past a small open piazza where an Apecar, the small, Vespa-built, three-wheeled pickup truck that is the workhorse of Italian farmers, sat, loaded over the cockpit roof with gigantic, surreal bright purple cabbages. The driver sat inside, speaking in a whiny sing-song into a microphone wired to a loudspeaker, describing the virtues of his merchandise in an echoing wail that sounded like a muezzin's chant. I finally came to the street on which Michela Buscemi lived. It was literally the last street in the last hamlet of Palermo. And across the way was an empty lot that swept upward into the mountains. There were cactuses and rocks, and nothing more.

Inside, Michela sat with her small family and told me about how one of her brothers had stumbled upon a Mafia killing, and had then been lured away and killed. After a short time, "they" came calling for the other brother, yelling his name night after night. And then he too was gone.

She knew more than anyone should know about how her brothers had died: hog-tied, tortured, partly dissolved in a barrel of acid that proved to be defective.

And when she decided to turn civil plaintiff, something analogous to state's witness, a badge of infamy in the Mafia-ridden society of Palermo's poorer neighborhoods, her own mother had spat in her face.

"They call here, on the phone, late at night," she said. "Sometimes they don't talk, other times they threaten to kill us." She stopped, panting slightly. Sitting in the dark living room, she pointed to the window, through which could be seen the Martian landscape of the red-rock mountain. "That's the mountain where the Bandito Giuliano lived," she resumed. "Can you imagine how long it would take the police to get here?"

Her solitude and exposure made her courage all the more remarkable.

Fear of the Mafia is reasonable, but ignorance of what it really is only makes that fear worse. This book provides invaluable documentation on just what makes up that mysterious essence: the Sicilian Mafia.

PREFACE TO THE ENGLISH EDITION

TRANSLATED BY ANTONY SHUGAAR

This book, now available in English, was first published in Italian in 1993; it came out in an expanded edition in 1996. The research upon which it is based, however, began in the mid-1980s, a time when my own conscience, like that of many other Italians—whether or not they were born in Sicily—was shaken by a horrifying series of events: a ferocious internal gang war pitting Mafia factions against one another, reaping a grim harvest, in the Palermo area alone, of many hundreds of deaths: the assassinations of numerous politicians, magistrates, policemen, and journalists, most of whom were fighting on behalf of the rule of law and of democracy itself. It seemed to me at the time that historians, hitherto reluctant to consider the Mafia to be a culturally significant subject for study and debate, had the duty to pose themselves this question: how could an entity, a system that had been dismissed in the past as *traditional,* not merely survive the advent of modernity, but even attain so dramatically within the context of modernity the role of protagonist?

In the meantime, between 1986 and 1987, Palermo witnessed the "maxi-trial," the result of the findings of the pool of investigating magistrates. Looming large in that pool were the heroic figures of Giovanni Falcone and Paolo Borsellino. The Mafia, the court declared in its verdict, was a powerful secret society, known—as it is in the United States—as Cosa Nostra, with its own dynamics and ritualized rules, involved in a huge and valuable volume of business affairs, extending from the local scale to the national and the international stage. Only a short time later, both Falcone and Borsellino paid with their lives for the heavy sentences inflicted as a result of that trial upon hundreds of mafiosi, ranging from *capos* to civilian allies (*affiliati*) and Mafia soldiers. In reaction to those murders, the Italian state engaged in a vigorous new attack on the

Mafia, resulting in the arrest of the "superboss" Salvatore Totò Riina and a large number of his confederates. The country was rocked by the indictment of the leader of Italy's powerful Christian Democratic party, Giulio Andreotti, on charges of aiding and abetting Cosa Nostra.

By showing that the Mafia must be understood rather than simply deplored, the maxitrial offered decisive encouragement to scholars. Certainly, outside of the courts of law, it was necessary to employ the tools of the social sciences. In the process of researching and writing my book, I have done my best to free myself from the stereotypical depictions that inevitably proliferate in the context of public debate. I have tried to write a work of history based upon reliable sources, reasonable hypotheses, and original research. I am greatly encouraged by the fact that my work has met with public and scholarly appreciation. I am even ultimately flattered by the fact that my work has been so nonchalantly plundered by certain of those scholars and writers who enjoyed it, with the results published in English before my own book could come out in the English language.

A great deal has happened since 1996. Riina is still in prison, along with his successor, Bernando Provenzano, and virtually the entire leadership of Cosa Nostra; more complicated, on the other hand, has been the story of identifying high-level complicity. For instance, Giulio Andreotti, at the end of an exceedingly lengthy judicial process, was acquitted in 2004, but the juridical motivations for that acquittal were such that they left an indelible stain on his honor. In any case, considering the successful efforts of investigators on the far shore of the Atlantic Ocean—in America, that is (here, too, beginning with trials held in the years 1985–1987)—we can now say that the two Mafias are currently in a state of crisis, and that the organized crime systems that were once shrouded in complete secrecy are nowadays open in an unprecedented manner to investigations and to law enforcement. It is hard to say whether, at some future time, we may truly hope to be rid, in both Palermo and New York, of their malevolent and cumbersome presence.

Salvatore Lupo
Palermo, Sicily

HISTORY OF THE MAFIA

CHAPTER I

INTRODUCTION

ABOUT THE NAME AND THE CONCEPT

Among the growing mass of printed materials concerning the Mafia, it is rare to find history books.[1] And yet historians need to provide answers to a number of crucial questions and not just questions about the origins of the Mafia, which are too often reduced to a quest for a mythical point of origination, in opposition to a depthless present day. When, how, and why did the array of factors that we can define as the Mafia emerge from the larger complex of Sicilian history? What, in this phenomenon, has changed with variations in the historic context, and what in contrast remains (relatively) stable? Along what lines does the past project itself into the present?

The word "Mafia" has appeared continuously from the mid-nineteenth century to the present day in political debates and journalistic commentary and reporting, in judicial investigations, in fiction, and in studies conducted by anthropologists, sociologists, jurists, economists, and historians. It is a term with multiple meanings, however, referring to different events depending on the context, circumstances, and intentions and interests of those who use it. It is difficult to identify a topic, a typology, or a succession of reasonably homogeneous phenomena that can safely be clustered under the heading of Mafia. It is equally difficult to avoid the impression that it is precisely this latitude of application and looseness of definition that have made the term so popular.

Giovanni Falcone once wrote:

While there was [a] time when people were reluctant to pronounce the word "Mafia," . . . nowadays people have gone so far in the opposite direction that it has become an overused term. . . . I am no longer willing to accept the habit of speaking of the Mafia in descriptive and all-inclusive terms that make it possible to stack up phenomena that are indeed related to the field of organized crime but that have little or nothing in common with the Mafia.[2]

Falcone's polemic was directed against those who freely and indiscriminately blend a criminal superelite originating in western Sicily, which today is widely known as Cosa Nostra, along with its equally renowned counterpart in the United States, with organized crime in general and even, in some cases, with ordinary crime. According to the most commonly accepted definition, Mafia corresponds to the regional criminality of Sicily, and Camorra corresponds to the regional criminality of Campania. In order to establish a sense of symmetry, the mass media have recently begun to use a comparable term for Calabria: the *'ndrangheta*. We might add to this list a Chinese Mafia, a Turkish Mafia, a Colombian Mafia, a Russian Mafia, and so on. This, however, is only the first stage of the confusion of languages, because the term also takes on much broader meanings, even outside and quite distant from the field of organized crime. It can be used to refer to the influence of lobbies, secret associations, and deviant state institutions.[3] It can also be used to indicate a close relationship between politics, business, and crime, a diffuse atmosphere of illegality, dishonesty, and corruption taking the form of favoritism, clientelism, election fraud, and an inability to apply the law impartially. There has been some discussion, for instance, as to whether the political and profiteering group that a few decades ago was headed by the Ligurian socialist leader Alberto Teardo could rightly be classified as a Mafia *cosca* (Mafia family), despite the fact that it was not accustomed to the use of violence. This dilemma is anything but neutral and scholarly, because since 1982 the judiciary in Italy has had the right to find individuals guilty of "Mafia conspiracy."

At this point, we should mention a factor that negates what most observers generally find. It is not true that Sicilian society has always drawn a curtain of silence over the Mafia phenomenon. With the possible exclusion of the 1950s, there has always been an abundance of discussion of the Mafia in Sicily, and the epithet of mafioso or protector mafiosi is one that everyone (including many mafiosi) attributes to their rivals, political opponents, and various public officials. In Palermo in particular, but also in many other cities on the island that have no real history of a problem with the Mafia (suffice it to mention Catania in the late nineteenth century), every reform movement, or quite simply all political opposition, has defined itself for the past hundred years as part of the struggle against the Mafia. The reader should also consider that on many different occasions the Mafia has served as a metaphor or a pretext for battles relating to the national political system: notably, in 1875, with the special public safety laws and the transition from the Italian right to the left; in 1926, with the Mori operation and the establishment of a totalitarian regime in Italy; in the years following the Second World War, when the massacre at Portella della Ginestra announced the hegemony of the Christian Democrats over the political forces on the Italian right and indeed over the entire nation; with the first parliamentary Anti-Mafia Commission and the advent of the center-left government; and today, when the Mafia is used to uphold the image of a parasitic Mezzogiorno, or southern Italy, or else as shorthand for a dilapidated and corrupt system of government. None of this should come as a surprise. The political struggle bends to its own purposes a conceptual tool that lacks all precision, while all of the various factors cited above share a sufficient number of commonalities to confer a certain legitimacy on use of the term in a looser sense. But this clustering together of only relatively homogeneous conceptual factors does little to help make the battle against the Mafia easier or more effective, nor does it help produce a clearer understanding of the situation. In some cases, "the superstructure of words feeds upon itself, enveloping in a form of metastasis the structure of the facts and killing it."[4]

The concept of the Mafia thus loses all solid anchorage, both spatial and chronological, since the categories of corruption and clientelism can be variously applied to sharply different phenomenologies, times, and places. Thus, if everything is Mafia, then nothing is Mafia.

A return to the original use of the term may seem to be a good antidote to the conceptual ambiguities. Nonetheless, in the primordial broth of post-Risorgimento Sicily, when the word "Mafia" first came into use, these ambiguities were of a far vaster scale. The first known mention of mafiosi appears in 1862–1863, in a highly popular play intended for a broad audience. The play was entitled *I mafiusi di la Vicaria,*[5] and it was set in 1854 among the *Camorristi* imprisoned in the Palermo prison. In April 1865, a secret document signed by the prefect of Palermo, Filippo Gualterio, mentions the "maffia, o associazione malandrinesca" ("Mafia, or criminal association").[6] As early as 1871, the law of *pubblica sicurezza*, or police law, made reference to the "lazy, vagabonds, mafiosi, and suspicious individuals in general." In the fifteen years that followed, the term *Mafia* coexisted with its counterpart—camorra—with no consideration of regional characterization, whether Sicilian or Campanian, and without any substantial conceptual distinctions. The word "camorra" referred more specifically to illicit systems for the control of markets, auctions, competitions for contracts, and voting. In some cases, the sources attribute the term to urban settings, while indicating that "Mafia" was more proper to rural settings. We also find opposite usages, however: the protagonists of *I mafiusi di la Vicaria* are, for instance, city-dwelling artisans, and the prefect of Palermo in 1874, Gioacchino Rasponi, described the Mafia as *malandrinaggio di città,* or "urban brigandage."[7]

The officials of the *Destra storica* (historic right wing) used the term *mafiosi* to describe both brigands and draft evaders, the notables in control of the municipal political parties and the small-time criminals, opponents to the existing political order and those trying to subvert the existing social order, the businessmen operating the sulphur mines and their employees, and both landowners and peasants. Among these various subjects, so different one from the other, the only common trait was the context in which they operated in the broader sense. They operated in a milieu consisting of a violent, barbarous, and primitive society, at both the lower end and the upper end of the social hierarchy, a society in which prefects, *questori* (administrative directors of the district police), military commanders, and *delegati di PS* (or police inspectors) believed that it was impossible to find a reasonable social counterpart and interlocutor for the liberal state—what the language of the time referred to as the middle class but can be better described as an upper class of aristocrats and notables. The Sicilians are viewed (in the Gualterio report) as excessively troublesome, factional, and determined to manage the commonwealth as if it were private property. To govern "this sort of a populace . . . with English- or Belgian-style laws and ordinances, which presuppose an educated and moral people, like in those countries, or at least like in the northern section of the Italian peninsula," means taking on the challenge of "a hazardous and terrible experiment," inevitably destined to end in chaos and violence. That at least was the opinion of the prefect of Caltanissetta, Guido Fortuzzi, whom we could describe as the last of the men of the right.[8] In substance, however, this idea also guides the first substantial volume to explore this topic, a work by Leopoldo Franchetti (1876).[9] This discovery of the island's sociocultural diversity, this first version of the Mafia as a metaphor for backwardness and underdevelopment, for that matter, joins neatly with the difficulties that post-Risorgimento moderates encountered in identifying a political interlocutor or counterpart in western Sicily, in a Palermo where public opinion tilted toward Republicans, "regionalists," and exponents of the moderate left rather than toward the governing party. The political intention that underlies the Gualterio report is to characterize the "maffia" by its ties with the most extreme parties—republicans and Bourbons; and identify the key personality as General Giovanni Corrao, the leader of the radical Garibaldian group and, after he was assassinated (1863), his successor, Giuseppe Badia. The prefects make their "discovery" accidentally, to the extent that this serves to explain their impotence to create a substantial consensus and their inability to demonize the opposition.[10]

Just twenty years later, the word "Mafia" made its first appearance on American shores. It was used to describe a mysterious organization dating back into time, an organization that was thought to be directed and controlled by a headquarters still in Sicily, commissioning its affiliates and members everywhere around the world. This vision of the Mafia served to stigmatize it as an alien conspiracy, a foreign plot carried forward by "socialisti, nazionalisti o quant'altro" (socialists, nationalists, or whoever else).[11]

There were also suspicions that the Italian government might have had a certain complicity, as in the satirical cartoon from the late nineteenth century in which a magic Pied Piper leads the filthy rats of the Old World—including a mafioso rat—across the Atlantic Ocean, to the jubilation of the crowned heads of Europe and the despair of Uncle Sam. This is one of the ways in which white, Anglo-Saxon, Protestant America expressed its fear of those who were different, demonstrating an ethnocentric rigidity in the face of the "second wave" of emigration. It also served in practical terms to support an argument in favor of limiting entry visas for Italians trying to migrate to the United States (in particular southern Italians). Italians were accused of trying to reproduce in the New World the worst aspects of the society from which they were emigrating: diseases, ignorance, superstition, and of course criminal behavior, which was greatly feared, exotic, and mysterious.

The first appearance of the term *Mafia* in Italy and its first appearance in America have various points in common: the Mafia is a metaphor for something irreconcilable with the values affirmed by the nineteenth-century state. As such, it appears to be darkly intertwined with political subversion, and most importantly, it reflects a fear of the obstinate survival of the obscure and distant past, of a cultural context that is profoundly hostile to modernity. This motif was destined in various forms to reappear periodically throughout the twentieth century, just as a singular and paradoxical contradiction in the attitudes of the public authorities recurred over the same period. The public authorities simultaneously denounced the incapacity of Sicily's traditional culture to grasp the sovereign nature of the law, and yet they also made extensive use of that very pathology they were denouncing as an *instrumentum regni*, or tool for governing. This justifies the fact that the opposition should have turned the accusation against the governing party and should have inaugurated another theme, that of the links between the Mafia and political power. After 1860, liberal Italy made use of a strongly authoritative approach to governing in the distant Sicilian province, based on "exceptional" methods, but especially—as we shall see—in the more everyday management of law enforcement, this government made use of criminals. And that is not to mention the use made of mafiosi as electoral canvassers even during times of greatly restricted suffrage. Here, too, we see a certain parallel with what was happening in the United States, where the establishment—the police, the political machines, and entrepreneurs—made use of mafiosi (as well as exponents of other ethnic forms of organized crime) as intermediaries with the alien universe of immigration.

Already, in this early phase, just as would happen later, the individuals, the business and cliental groups, the Sicilian community, and the Italian American community in the United States—in short, all those who were targeted and accused of forming part of the Mafia—responded in court, or in the press, or in the chambers of Congress, with two basic arguments. On one hand, they declared that "normal" criminality existed everywhere, while in contrast the Mafia itself did not exist at all. The other, more sophisticated argument, however, overturned the thesis, accepted the description of Sicily as an archaic society along with the denunciation of the communications gap between Sicily and the Italian state, but then proceeded to reverse its significance in a polemical turnabout. This argument claimed that only a thinly disguised persecutory intent could then apply to the sphere of the upper classes a concept that was so typical of the cultural universe of the working classes, viewed with paternalistic condescension (or with ideological involvement?) as the chivalrous remnants of a traditional world and as a robust barbarism that was in the process of dying out through natural historical evolution. Only an inability to understand Sicily could translate that into the idea of a secret, criminal conspiracy. It is natural enough that the original formulation of such an argument should have been the work of an ethnologist, indeed one of the leading European ethnologists of the nineteenth century, the Palermo-born Giuseppe Pitrè. It is natural, too, that it should have come in the wake of the discovery of both the word and the concept in the 1880s. And so, as Pitrè wrote, the Mafia "is neither a sect nor an association, it has no rules or statutes, . . . a Mafioso is not a thief, he is not a brigand . . . ; the Mafia is an awareness of one's own being, an exaggerated concept of one's own individual strength, . . . hence the intolerance of superiority and, worse still, of the arrogance and bullying of others." The other key word—omertà— was said to derive from the root "uomo," and therefore it signified man, par excellence, a man who responded independently and in a manly fashion to all offenses, without availing himself of state-administered justice.[12]

Pitrè claims that the term *Mafia* was regularly used even before 1860 in the working-class quarters of Palermo as a synonym for "beauty" and "excellence," and that therefore a *mafiusu* would be a man of courage, and *mafiusedda*, a beautiful and proud young woman. This is supposedly a term of "old" Sicily, which after 1860 lost its "original" and positive meaning, and took on another significance, murky but in any case negative, close to that of brigandage, Camorra, and *malandrinaggio*. Moving in this direction, Pitrè mischievously comments that we reach something that is almost "impossible to define." The thesis tends to converge, in the apologetic and regionalist intent, with the apparently opposite thesis of the linguists Traina and Mortillaro, according to whom the term was unknown on the island prior to 1860 and would therefore have been introduced by the ill will or the misgovernment of "continentals" or mainlanders.[13]

It is as if the protagonists, faced with the rapidly growing popularity of the word, believed that it would be enough to provide an etymology to solve the mystery of the concept, finding an original and truer meaning in that way. In reality, the philological approaches already prefigured the interpretative ones, and there is an overlap between those approaches and the choices of alignment, which could hardly fail to encompass the American sector, of course. Those who failed to understand the practical vested interests implicit in the various interpretations of the Mafia therefore wound up indiscriminately blending together the various points of view of the accusers, the apologists, those hopelessly compromised and implicated, the totalitarians, the Sicilianists, and the anti-Sicilianists. The result was the distinctively repetitive dynamic of Mafiology whereby, as if in a series of grotesquely deforming mirrors, the stereotype became all the more unquestionable the more remote and mysterious the location in which it was first formulated. By opposing this vicious cognitive cycle, the book I have written will avail itself of the most classic tools of the historian, archival and judicial sources, as well as the documents of parliamentary investigations, in all cases, rigorously telling the stories of human beings who actually lived, and not the stories of characters out of novels thinly disguised as sociological stereotypes. The dialectic of the interpretations of past and present, those of Franchetti, Pitrè, Mosca, and Sciascia, those expressed in the press or in the halls of justice, will be considered as one of the possible tools for garnering information and understanding. From this one can begin with the awareness that the issue of whether one or the other of the two options prevails forms an integral part of the historical episode and that definition of the respective prosecution and defense camps helps, in the broadest possible sense, determine the outcomes of the struggle for and against the Mafia.

If we schematize, to the greatest degree, possible lines of interpretation that in reality are more often blended together, we can distinguish a few fundamental areas: the Mafia has been viewed as a mirror of traditional society, with a focus on political, economic, or—more frequently—sociocultural factors; as an enterprise or a type of criminal industry; as a more or less centralized secret organization; or as a juridical ordering that is parallel to that of the state, that is, as a sort of anti-state.

THE MAFIA AS A MIRROR OF TRADITIONAL SOCIETY

Investigative journalism, sociological and anthropological investigations, even the reports of the Anti-Mafia Commissions, all attempt to establish a context for phenomena and forms of current and relevant behavior, making use of the history of the past hundred years and even beyond that. Unfortunately, however, these sources often use an outmoded approach to historiography that describes nineteenth- and twentieth-century southern Italy (the Mezzogiorno) as a semifeudal society. The region is depicted as entirely agrarian and organized according to the latifundium, or large landed estate, economically and socially inert and immobile, swept by only a single impulse of reform: the peasant movement. In this context, it seems logical to assume that the Mafia served essentially to ensure the subordination and obedience of the peasants to the ruling classes, even though this function does not appear clearly until the years following the First World War and the Second World War—that is, in certain specific moments of the long story of the Mafia. In other cases of *latifondismo* (that is, an economy based on large landed estates), both in Italy and elsewhere, there is a distinct absence of such a phenomenon, which clearly is not comparable with the theme of the private armies used by feudal landowners and *fazenderos* to uphold their power around the world. For that matter, the mafiosi who were most specifically considered to be representative of the traditional model, Calogero Vizzini and Giuseppe Genco Russo, were hardly the blind and subservient tools of the agrarian power. Rather, they were organizers of cooperatives and won much of their power base by serving as intermediaries in the transfer of land from the large landowners to the peasants, and therefore by placing themselves firmly astride the collective movements precisely in the postwar years following the First World War and the Second World War. Therefore, they were not the *guardiani* (rural watchmen), but rather the undertakers of the *feudo*, or large landholding class, and they played a role that could not be imagined outside of the great political and social modernization processes of the twentieth century.

One might very well wonder why the latifundium, or large landholding, is the context that is almost universally discussed, while it is instead fairly obvious that, from the beginning, there has been a compatibility between the Mafia and the fragmentation of large landed estates, and a high degree of integration between the Mafia and prosperous international—and even transoceanic—markets, in the sulphur-mining industries of Sicily and along the coastal areas of the Palermo regions, the Trapani region, and the region of Reggio Calabria, on the mainland side of the Strait of Messina:[14] sectors and periods of economic and social dynamism that southern Italy, however underdeveloped it might have been, still offered in considerable abundance. Fascinated by rural and "primitive" settings, scholars have often forgotten the island's "capital" and its urbanized countryside, even though many nineteenth-century sources identified those as the center of the Mafia infection. According to Antonino Cutrera (1900), it was here that "the true Mafia is based, the legendary Mafia, the Mafia of the great criminal trials, which has aroused such terror with its great murders . . . a unique feature of the history of crime in Sicily."[15] We do not necessarily agree with the concept of a "true" Palermo-based Mafia, in contrast with the Mafias of the Trapani or the Agrigento areas, but unquestionably the majority of the most spectacular Mafia crimes and episodes occurred in an area that roughly coincides with the province of Palermo. This area extended from the city's hinterland, the "rich" agricultural zone of the Conca d'Oro, to the rest of the coastal strip that pushes all the way to the Trapani district, the inland area of the province, the latifundium zone, which established links to the city in the nineteenth century, and to a lesser extent in the twentieth century, by the chains of rent, by the movement of revenue from the interior toward the city, and often by the movement of management (administrators), *gabellotti* (renters and sublessors of parcels of farmland), and *guardiani* in the opposite direction. In our history of the Mafia, which focuses on a vast area centering on Palermo, we will find a disconcerting continuity of the groups, places, experiences, and sectors of activity. The power of the Grecos in the *borgata,* or the outlying suburb, of Ciaculli, and of the city's mafioso hierarchy has lasted more than a century. In this hundred years, everything has changed in the economy, in society, in politics—everything, one might venture to say, except for the continuity of this territorial control. In particular, in what in the nineteenth century was called the *agro palermitano,* or Palermo territorial countryside, midway between city and countryside, in the *borgate* and in the villages of the hinterland, the Mafia groups established a system of control over the territory that set out from the dense network of *guardianìe* (custodianships). They ultimately seized control of both legitimate and illicit business, cattle rustling, smuggling and contraband, and the early commercial intermediation of citrus fruit and other products of the area's rich agriculture. In a more recent era, the same area proved to be the more or less natural marketplace for the expansion of real estate and for speculation in that field—age-old locations and age-old power bases finding new opportunities for profit. The Mafia's introduction into a transoceanic migratory network and its involvement with long-distance trade, such as the citrus fruit business, simply laid the groundwork in terms of mentalities and abilities well suited to smuggling tobacco and narcotics.

The idea of equating the Mafia with the latifundium, along with the other equivalency—equating small landholding with social progress—represents a way of analyzing the phenomenon as a relatively feudal residue of the past, projecting it toward an obscure past and liberating the future from its murky claim. In the history of the various interpretations that have been offered of the Mafia and of the battle against it, the idea cyclically resurfaces according to which "modern" changes (agricultural land reform, industrialization, education, and the development of more liberal sexual ethics) ought ipso facto to destroy the phenomenon, together with the broth that nourishes. The Italian left wing has put forward such a mind-set and propagated it in good faith ever since the end of the Second World War, and over time, with some instrumental manipulation, nearly everyone has adopted it, with the objective of winning more public funding, more resources to control. Similarly, in the United States, the Mafia has been described as a holdover from a "peasant" culture destined to die out once the Italian community was absorbed into the upper ranks of American society. But it is possible to look further back in time, when the Italian liberals still identified "feudalism" and Bourbon mismanagement of the government as the causes of all the ills of Italy's south. Many believed that the Mafia would vanish once the sound of locomotive whistles echoed through the villages of the desolate Sicilian hinterland. They were completely unaware that people would still be talking about the Mafia long after the whistle of train engines, the sonic booms of jet planes, and the beep of modern computers had sounded.

Today, more than thirteen decades after the unification of Italy, the context that was once simplistically decried as archaic has changed in all its various components. Yet we are still faced with something that we call Mafia, as we attempt to understand how this phenomenon that at first glance is typical of a "traditional" universe has managed to survive the process of modernization. It is clear, therefore, that the modern does not overwhelmingly clash with a Mafia type of phenomenon, as demonstrated by the case of America and the south of Italy in recent years. Nor does the category of immobility adequately explain either the phenomenon itself or its context. The Sicilian Mafia has remained in the spotlight for over a century, though it remains to be proven that the phenomenon described by this name truly presents, inevitably and universally, a significant degree of homogeneity. The Camorra presents itself in specific moments of history, as if in a series of flash photographs, encompassing the era following Italian unification, the Giolitti regime, and the post–Second World War period.[16] In Calabria, for a brief time the *picciotteria*, which emerged suddenly and was harshly repressed at the turn of the twentieth century, revealed a dark history that was largely overlooked in the debate of the time, and it is no accident that only recently has it become the subject of historical analysis.[17]

In any case, the Mafia was traditionally a geographic phenomenon characteristic of Palermo and nearly all of the Palermo province, Naples and certain districts of the Neapolitan hinterland, the province of Reggio Calabria, part of the province of Trapani, the inland Sicilian area of the sulphur mines and the large landholdings, with the exclusion of the eastern section of the island. Only in the past thirty years has the infection spread until it covered with some homogeneity three Italian regions, or states—Sicily, Campania, and Calabria—as well as a fourth region, Puglia (Apulia).

This evolution, or perhaps we should say, this regression, calls into question not only the explanation based on the notion of socioeconomic archaism, but also its sociocultural counterpart, which makes Mafia behavior a direct consequence of the anthropology of the Sicilians or, in general, of southern Italians. This culture is said to be characterized by a mistrust of the state and therefore by a habit of taking justice into one's own hands, by a sense of honor, by clientelism, by a familism that exempts the individual from a perception of his own responsibilities in the face of a larger collective than his immediate surroundings.[18] These characteristics ought to be relatively homogeneous throughout all of southern Italy. It is therefore impossible to explain the uneven distribution of the phenomenon in the past. Nor is it clear how this phenomenon, ostensibly a product of a traditional culture, has been able to extend and become diffused well outside its original territory, in parallel with the modernization of the country, even though a sociocultural hybridization was in fact a crucial and constituent element of the historical transformation.[19]

It should not appear that we are attempting to expunge the cultural element from the explanation of this (and from any other) social phenomenon. If we accept the notion that the depiction of southern Italian anthropology offered here is credible, we should then attempt to distinguish the phenomenon from its context by investigating the way the Mafia organization appropriates cultural codes, instrumentalizes them, modifies them, and turns them into an adhesive to ensure that they remain intact. Let us consider the rejection of the concept of the impersonal nature of the law, the scorn for the police and for those who collaborate with them—traits that were quite prevalent among the common folk, the bourgeois, and the aristocrats in nineteenth- and twentieth-century Sicily, but that the Mafia reutilized for its own purposes. Or let us reflect on the image of a moderate and protective Mafia, unfailingly offered by the mafiosi, either through their representatives or directly in person. We shall see the great Mafia capo of the postunification period, Antonino Giammona, described by his lawyer as a *uomo d'ordine* (literally, a man of order), unwilling to submit to arrogant abuse; we shall also see the defense lawyers of the Amoroso brothers (1883) insist on the lower-class origins of their clients, who were ignorant perhaps but conditioned by an anthropology made up of iron-bound codes of honor, a furious attachment to solidarity, and family hatreds.[20] In 1930 Vito Cascio-Ferro's lawyer stated that the Mafia, in the person of his client, represented "an attitude of distinctly bold and fearless individualism, devoid of squalor, evil, and criminality."[21] In a broad array of contexts, the Mafia always defines itself in the same terms. As we read in the epitaph engraved on the tomb of Ciccio Di Cristina, Mafia capo of Riesi in the years following the Second World War: "His Mafia was not criminality, but respect of the law of honor, defense of all rights, and great-heartedness." "Are we interested in defining what the judges and governors call Mafia? It is not called Mafia, it is called *omertà*, that is, men of honor, who help rather than profiting off of the weak, who always do good and never do evil," is written in a text confiscated from Rosario Spatola,[22] a Mafia entrepreneur and a leading money launderer of profits from the narcotics trade in the late 1970s.

Therefore, it is first and foremost the Mafia that describes itself as a way of life and a form of behavior, as an expression of traditional society. Every eminent mafioso makes a point of presenting himself in the guise of a mediator and resolver of disagreements, as a protector of the virtue of young women. At least once in his career, the mafioso boasts of the rapid and exemplary execution of "justice" against violent muggers, rapists, and kidnappers. We are, in any case, in the presence of a power group that expresses an ideology meant to create consensus on the outside and coherence and compactness on the inside. In that ideology there is a certain degree of self-persuasion, a great deal of overweening ambition, and an even greater degree of propaganda destined to clash in the great majority of cases with a far different reality. The ideological scheme was at the time saved by a reference to a new Mafia. By this point, it was nothing more than common criminality, which no longer embodied the sense of respect and honor that characterized the old Mafia. Nonetheless, the argument appears suspect when one considers that it appears as early as 1875 in the reports from the *delegato di PS* of Monreale[23] and, in a different form, in the writings of Pitrè as well (the word indicates a concept that was once good but has now lost its virtue). It has resurfaced periodically throughout the entire period of history in question—in the years of the First World War, when the old-school mafiosi were supposedly replaced by ferocious criminals; in the wake of the Fascist repression of the 1920s, at a time when (according to the recollections of the Sicilian American Mafia capo Nick Gentile) there "died in Sicily an honored society, the Mafia which had its laws, its principles, an organization that protected the weak and . . . its place was taken by . . . people without honor, people who robbed without restraint and killed for pay";[24] in the United States in the 1930s when, according to the New York Mafia capo Joe Bonanno, the old Sicilian tradition began to give way to the toxins of the New World;[25] during the 1950s, when the honorable old agricultural Mafia supposedly yielded to a ferocious urban gangsterism; and finally, last but not least, upon the advent of the Corleonese, when—according to Buscetta—Cosa Nostra lost its age-old virtues and was disfigured by violence and greed. Greed and ferocity, as will be documented in the pages of this book, are intrinsic characteristics of the Mafia of both yesterday and today, and both Mafias are and were capable of slaughtering innocent people, women and children, in defiance of their codes of honor. The varying quantity and quality of the violence are linked, rather, to political situations (for instance, the years that followed, respectively, the First World War and the Second World War), or to the various generational shifts that brought new leadership and new cadres, giving birth to internal conflicts of a cyclical, rather than an epochal, nature.

THE MAFIA AS A BUSINESS ENTERPRISE

The distinction between the old Mafia and the new Mafia, even though it has a merely ideological or rhetorical substance, continues to resurface because it represents an excessively facile conceptual shortcut in the face of the complex cross-breeding of old and new detected in this field. Thus, Pino Arlacchi, in his famous book *La mafia imprenditrice* (Italian edition, 1983; English edition, *Mafia Business: The Mafia Ethic and the Spirit of Capitalism,* 1987), did his best to preserve the figure of the old mafioso as he might have borrowed it from Anton Blok, Jane and Peter Schneider, and especially Henner Hess. Indeed, Arlacchi reduced the Mafia figure to that of the country notable, poor and in any case scornful of wealth, eager only to win social consideration. Arlacchi contrasted this figure with a modern entrepreneurial Mafia, a creation of the 1970s, eager to amass wealth and especially focused on drug trafficking, as ferocious as the previous Mafia was moderate. We find this excessively clearly delineated conceptual contrast unpersuasive. As for the past, it should be said that the *gabellotti,* too, were entrepreneurs; though not particularly innovative ones, still they were definable as "speculators, who use gunpowder and lead as a means of speculation"—in the words of a nineteenth-century landowner[26]—or, to use the words of Franchetti, as "industrialists of violence." It is indicative that Arlacchi's misleading description of Calogero Vizzini should derive once again from the mafioso's intentionally minimizing self-description as a poor, ignorant bumpkin ("I don't say much because I don't know much. I live in a village, I come to Palermo only rarely, and I don't know many people"),[27] while instead the sources depict Vizzini as "a gentleman, a knight of industry, a multimillionaire."

These sources describe him as working among other places in London in 1922, with other "industrialists" of the sulphur sector, with high executives of the Montecatini Company, with the elite of the world chemicals industry, in negotiations for the foundation of the international sulphuric acid cartel.[28] In the other camp, that of the present-day Mafia, Arlacchi placed excessive emphasis on Mafia entrepreneurship, a supposed "Schumpeterian" characteristic that is both creative and innovative. In the area of the legal economy, it is questionable whether the mafioso can show entrepreneurial abilities that are much more complex than those needed for operating a traditional farming concern, which (leaving aside the great difference in contexts) finds its present-day counterpart in building and commerce, while the introduction into large-scale financial activities, such as that of laundering "dirty" money, makes the mafioso not an entrepreneur but a *rentier*. In general, the clientelistic structure of the Mafia *cosca*, which is required to carry out a continual redistribution of funds among its ravenous members and which involves an endless fragmentation of corporate structures with a view to concealing their activities, hardly seems to resemble the rational and vertical structure of the capitalist corporation.[29]

It is evident that a far more substantial continuity in the phenomenon exists. The learned quotes that Luciano Leggio offered from Pitrè, the writings of Spatola, and the statements of *pentiti*, which included those of the most recent generation, clearly show that there is no fundamental transformation that, with the passage of time, drives the enterprise syndicate to renounce its image, and its protectionist and traditionalist ideology. Yet this does not prevent it—and never prevented it—from seeking money and displaying ferocity. Sicilian and Italian American mafiosi continue to declare their hostility to drugs, which destroy the sociocultural ties of the community, even when they are caught red-handed dealing narcotics.[30] From the prison in which Nitto Santapaola—boss of the Mafia of Catania—was finally confined after an extended run from the law, Santapaola depicted a city that no longer enjoyed security, and therefore, prosperity, because it had been deprived of the safety he and his friends had guaranteed. "Where is the flourishing Catania, where are the businessmen, the shopkeepers who could live and work without fear?" he wondered, forgetting the cost in tears, blood, and corruption caused by the safety and security he had provided.[31]

Taking into account elements of this kind, recently Diego Gambetta again proposed, in a different and far more rigorous context, the theme of the Mafia-as-enterprise, or enterprise syndicate. He stated that a mafioso sells a specific "product," protection—in a historic context, the protection of Sicily or southern Italy, where trust and confidence are lacking.[32] As the reader will see in the present history of the Mafia, such a concept is evident from the very beginning, in every phase of the story. It has been adopted by magistrates, policemen, scholars, novelists,[33] and—once again—even the mafiosi themselves, who set themselves up as protectors from criminality. In this sense, the heart of the problem, the basic function of the Mafia, can be identified in the racket that protects a legal institution, the business enterprise, using violence to ensure a monopoly for itself—specifically, the verbal and physical intimidation of thieves, traitors, witnesses, and competitors. Mafia wars are largely waged among aspiring protectors. It seems open to question, however, whether Gambetta is not underestimating the extortion factor as opposed to the protection extortion factor.[34] The *Mafia d'ordine* (order-keeping Mafia) always presupposes a disorder that needs to be organized and kept firmly under control, whether during post-Risorgimento Sicily or during the more recent process of criminal escalation. It is therefore, to a considerable degree, the Mafia itself that helps to create the widespread sense of insecurity on which it battens and which it exploits. Thus, it is reasonable to say that its sole function is a self-determined one, given that ordinary criminals constitute the base from which the *cosche* (Mafia families) recruit their members. Frequently, the threat is amplified, or even created ex novo, in order to ensure that the insurance policy is purchased. It often happens that in linking the party that explicitly makes the threat and the party that is willing to provide protection to the target of that threat, there is a prior arrangement to play these specific roles, that of extortioner and protector. The division of labor is made within the context of the same organization in order to persuade entrepreneurs, in the past and today, to subscribe to this "insurance" service. The Mafia, as we have already mentioned, is a power, nor does the fact that its blend of violence and ideology that creates consensus prove anything about the substance of its claim that it provides a service. "They act, therefore," Gaetano Mosca noted as early as 1901, "in such a way that the victim himself, who is actually paying a tribute to the *cosca*, can flatter himself that this is actually a gracious gift or the price paid for a service rendered, rather than an extortion exacted through the threat of violence."[35] The same reasoning applies to that sort of ex post facto protection that offers intermediation to arrange for the recovery of stolen objects, an intervention "apparently on behalf of the victim of theft" but that in point of fact is undertaken by organizations featuring nothing more than a "division of theatrical parts," played by thieves and intermediaries.[36] Then there is the interplay of protection and intermediation artificially fomented in order to modify the power relationships among the factions within the Mafia. Let us think, for instance, of the case of Vito Ciancimino, the corrupt politician with whom a great many mafiosi aspired to establish close contact, but who happened to be in "the hands" of Totò Riina: it was impossible to establish contact with Ciancimino except through Riina. Pippo Calò, one of Palermo's Mafia capos, suggested to Leonardo Vitale the idea of kidnapping Ciancimino's son, not only to make a little money, but also to attain another goal: "It was expected that, given their relationship, Ciancimino would then turn to Riina and [Calò] would himself be able to play the role of the intermediary, while in reality serving our own interests."[37]

We should not think that, as in the perfect market of classical economics, supply and demand for protection intersect and that all subjects are on an equal basis. In a class-driven society like that of the nineteenth century, the asymmetry of power among the negotiating parties is at a maximum, though it tends to diminish over time. In any case, both in the past and today, it is difficult to hypothesize a freedom of choice, and therefore any real advantage, for the peasants, the small shopkeepers, or the entrepreneurs who were not in on the game, being forced out of the market or else obliged to limit artificially their range of activities. If any deal exists, it is that of the lion with its prey, and therefore is null and void, as jurists might say. On the other hand, as for both past and present-day large-scale entrepreneurs, the contract for protection actually can be considered to be advantageous. Particularly respectful of the clauses of those contracts were the "continental" companies that came to do business in the infected zones. Such is the case, for instance, of the Standa-Berlusconi group, which the investigating magistrates of the Catania district recently judged especially reluctant to reveal to law enforcement forces the terms of its understanding with local extorters and protectors.[38] The logic of collusion, then, is common to northerners and southerners alike. Indeed, we can say that the outsiders, in not forming part of the local networks of clientelism, tend to offer greater space to their representatives, much as did the old large landholders who lived in Naples, Rome, or even Madrid, since they had never actually seen their lands and gave their administrators the authority to do as they wished. This was the opinion of the economist Carlo Rodanò, who provided an insider's account of the penetration of the Mafia in the Chimica Arenella, or Arenella chemicals plant, the crown jewel of Palermo manufacturing since 1911, which was owned by a German group and run by a German:

> His behavior was that of a man unfamiliar with the area. Pure-blooded Sicilians, even when they were obliged to have dealings with mafiosi, unless they were complete fools took care not to allow that contact to become very close, because while those good fellows stood out for the agreeable way in which they offered all their potential clients an apparently altruistic form of protection, it remained true that, with the passage of time and the growth of the friendship, they would inevitably find a way of appropriating

100 percent of the possessions that their new protégé had avoided losing by acquiring that protection; ordinarily, the mafioso would also take a substantial chunk of what was left over.[39]

The local governing classes' skill at "establishing and keeping their distance" points to situations that are still typical of an elitist society. With the passage of time, the associations established to provide services to the dominant class become autonomous, and the cases of major Sicilian entrepreneurs of more recent periods who availed themselves of Mafia protection (the Salvos, the Cassinas, and the Costanzos) point to a much closer relationship to the Mafia network itself.

Finally, the basic element that distinguishes the type of protection linking the Mafia with the establishment is the factor of reciprocity. Just as the *questore* (administrative director of the district police) of Palermo, Ermanno Sangiorgi, stated at the turn of the twentieth century, "the *caporioni* of the Mafia are under the protection of senators, members of parliament, and other influential figures who protect them and defend them, only to be protected and defended by them in their turn."[40] Even today—just as in the past—it is the "protection industry" that is obliged to ask politicians and public institutions for protection from the rigors of the law.[41] The truth is that the intertwining of Mafia and politics cannot be reduced to a straightforward "economic" logic, and it is rather futile to try to force that point. Within the physiological and variegated relationship of give and take with the machinery of politics, but especially in major historical turning points such as Italian unification or the post–Second World War years, this interlinking process profoundly determined the very structure of the Mafia. It might also be that the Mafia seeks to condition the government, as has happened in Italy in recent years. The history of the Mafia cannot be reduced to a single scheme, applicable in all situations and all periods.

Protection, however, is not the only "industry" controlled by the Mafia; indeed, protection inevitably constitutes a sort of bridge leading to other activities. The person who holds the keys of security, whether it be the friend of mafiosi or a mafioso himself, is best suited to enter a market such as the nineteenth-century marts of the *gabella del latifondo*—that is, the market of commercial mediation in the citrus-growing districts in the area around Palermo—or in the construction subcontracting of the twentieth century. As in the past, when the threat of brigands was used to induce the large landowners to entrust to the mafiosi the management of the agricultural enterprise, so it is today that shopowners are threatened by armed robbery, extortion, and loan-sharking to accept mafiosi as partners. We thus see the transition from the protection business to full control of a company; this is an intrinsic part of the phenomenon. On the one hand, we have a continual transformation of mafiosi into profiteers, and on the other hand an ongoing transformation of "clean" companies into companies—generically—corrupted or "in contact" with the Mafia. This twofold process was not determined by the intrinsic characteristics of the commercial activities in question, but rather by the Mafia groups' degree and level of control of the territory. From this power base, the mafiosi went on to control other illegal lines of business (large-scale smuggling and drug trafficking) that in and of themselves have little to do with the protection business and control of the territory.

The twofold nature of the Mafia's activities corresponds to a twofold organizational model. On the one hand—in the case of Palermo—we see a series of organizations that take their name from the territory in which they operate, that finance their activities through protection/extortion, in some cases paying salaries to their members, and that pay for legal expenses and subsidize the families of those who have been arrested. On the other hand, as Buscetta explained, we see a business network that cuts transversely across the organizations and in which the various affiliated members can participate, under certain favorable conditions, but still risking their own funds and earning money as individuals.[42] To distinguish the first organizational model, based on extortion, from the second organizational model, which is more fluid and profiteering, we might examine the distinction between a power syndicate and an enterprise syndicate proposed by the American historian Alan Block, although that distinction was made in an interpretative context that was somewhat different from the one explored in this study.[43] The two functions, as will become evident, interact, clash, and in any case tend to be linked together. It therefore becomes impossible to distinguish the mafioso from the trafficker, with the mafioso considered the protector (intermediary, guarantor) and the trafficker the protected,[44] in the presence of an opposite or reverse process of the inclusion of entrepreneurs, smugglers, and drug traffickers into the Mafia organizations, within which the roles tended to overlap. It might happen that a *camorrista* like Cutolo should demand the payment of a *pizzo* from the Nuvolettas, who were the Neapolitan affiliates of Cosa Nostra, and that in fact they continued to pay that protection fee until they felt they were ready to wage war on Cutolo. This, however, has more to do with the shifting relationships of power between the two alignments, and certainly not with any fundamental difference in their natures.

THE MAFIA AS AN ORGANIZATION

Police and judicial sources are every bit as rife with ulterior motives as other sources. Those who make use of them immediately venture into a gallery of mirrors involving the battling truths of the prosecution and the defense, of the reputation and the infamy that make up the role of the mafioso. For many years administrative measures (*ammonizione*, a special security regimen, or *domicilio coatto*, an obligatory residence) have been based on public rumor and opinion as interpreted by police and magistrates as well as on the judicial efforts made by the liberal governments, Fascism, and the Italian republic to attack the phenomenon of the Mafia. There has never been anything spontaneous about that public rumor and opinion. It has been instrumentally guided and created by a number of Mafia factions as a way of combating the opposing factions; and then, when the interests of criminal politicians or ordinary politicians pointed toward a repressive crackdown, it was instrumentally adopted by certain state agencies. Credit should be given to the judges of Palermo (Chinnici, Falcone, and Borsellino) for shifting this age-old mechanism to the interior of the structure designed to protect civil rights within criminal prosecution and trial, and for ensuring that through the evidence and testimony provided by those willing to collaborate with the law we have finally obtained a source of information from within. Such sources are no longer filtered—as was the case during the Liberal era or under the Fascist regime—through police reports or the executive branch of the government.

In this case we are faced with a point of view—that of the Mafia determined to surrender and *pentirsi*, or repent—that cannot exempt us from the need for sophisticated analyses, full-blown reconstructions, and references to broader issues than those that the protagonists themselves, both mafiosi and investigators, have been concerned with or have been willing to present to us. However, taken as a whole, the confessions of Joe Valachi (1962), the memoirs of Nick Gentile (1963), the revelations of Leonardo Vitale (1974), and those of Tommaso Buscetta and so many other mafiosi following in his footsteps have shown us a Mafia that is clearly a secret organization and that as such would subsequently be taken to court and be found guilty.

Evidently, the first of these accounts, by Joe Valachi, focuses on the counterpart of the Sicilian Mafia, located on the far shore of the Atlantic Ocean, in the heart of world capitalism. The leadership of the "five families" of the New York Mafia, which took form in the early 1930s with the creation of the so-called Commission, included individuals nearly all of whom had come to America at very early ages. The one exception was Salvatore Maranzano, who arrived in 1927 at the age of forty-three and who immediately became a boss, certainly because of a power base that he had already built in his hometown of Castellammare del Golfo. American sources indicate that the 1920s was a time of a significant immigration of mafiosi, with the arrival of no fewer than 500 criminals fleeing the prefect Mori.[45] Can we therefore speak of a sort of transplant?

The fact that the Sicilian-born leaders of the six families (Bonanno, Luciano, Gambino, Reina, Lucchese, Profaci) all came from corrupt areas of the western section of the island would seem to favor that interpretation: three of them came from Palermo, and the other three came from Lercara, Corleone, and Castellammare. Or was the U.S. Mafia basically new, considering that it took on an interregional character without counterpart in Italy, and that among the heads of the families we find two Neapolitans (Genovese and Gotti) and two Calabrians (Costello and Anastasia)?[46] Powerful bosses like Joe Bonanno painted themselves as direct descendants of a "Sicilian Tradition," but that may be nothing more than the product of the well-known ideological self-portrayal.[47] Bonanno himself believed that the "purist" line was defeated with the "Castellammare war" of 1930–1931, in the face of the overwhelmingly evident process of Italian American cross-breeding in which he was personally involved in a leadership role; and that is not to mention the decisive role played in these developments by such Jewish criminals as Meyer Lansky and Benjamin Siegel.

In the United States, the basic unit of the organization, described in nineteenth-century Sicily as a *cosca, nassa, partito* (party), *società* (society or company), or *fratellanza* (brotherhood), was called a family. In actual practice, both in Palermo and in New York, the Mafia family rarely corresponded to the blood family, and in America just as in Sicily, both today and in the past, it may well happen that—in open defiance of the familistic ideologies—in infra-mafioso conflicts, parents and children and brothers and sisters often find themselves on opposite sides and wind up murdering one another.[48] The emphasis on the family appears to be little more than a tribute to the traditionalism found in radically different fields and typical of Italian Americans. It also seems that the name used to designate the organization as a whole—Cosa Nostra—comes from America. As far as can be determined, the name was previously unknown in Sicily and certainly calls to mind an immigrant on a quest for a *cosa "nostra"*— something of "our own"—clear and understandable, to be preferred to the incomprehensible *cose "loro"*—their things. This terminology refers to the Sicilian component only among present-day *pentiti* and can lead us to overturn the customary thought that Sicily exports its archaic ways, leaving us to wonder to what degree a flow of the archaic is engendered in America and then reexported to the Old World. Here we find an interaction of models, which followed the travel patterns of individuals moving not only from Sicily to America but also from America to Sicily. In this respect, the best known episode occurred after the end of the Second World War when U.S. authorities sent back to Italy sixty-five "undesirables" of Italian nationality, with the intention of returning a group of foreign criminals who had infiltrated American society in an earlier period. In contrast, the Italians saw these deportees as ambassadors and propagandists of a way of life, or of a typically American criminal organization, which they considered to be far more dangerous than the local Mafia. However, a far more frequent and continuous series of movements occurred along the circuits of returning emigrants. For the present let us consider a single case: Nick Gentile built his career in America, where he first arrived from his birthplace of Siculiana in 1903, at the age of eighteen. He returned to Sicily in 1909, 1913, 1919, 1925, and 1927–1930, and then, for good, in 1937, managing all the while to take part in election races in his homeland and various forms of the import-export business, as well as to organize murders, be arrested, and then released, thanks to his contacts and ties among various officials, including those in the Fascist regime.[49] This introduces the theme, which we'll come back to later, of international profiteering activities, including drug trafficking, "operated by this association [the Mafia] in the United States and in Europe." Apparently, a document mentions the existence of the New York Commission prior to the revelations of Valachi, Gentile, and Bonanno: a report dated 1940 from the Italian financial police, the Guardia di Finanza, addressed to the U.S. Customs supervisor of New York and to the Federal Bureau of Narcotics.[50] This document, sent from Italy to inform Americans about an American event, indicates the intensity of the trans-Atlantic relationship, even though it came at the end of a historical phase, the period between the two world wars, when migratory flows from Italy had completely collapsed.

Of course, this does not mean that the U.S. Mafia was not clearly distinct from the Sicilian Mafia. First and foremost, the U.S. Mafia was profoundly modeled on American society, as is emphasized by a number of studies (prevalently democratic and Italian American in nature) that focus on the criminalizing elements of the American society into which these immigrants were introduced, in contrast with the traditional WASP thesis of a foreign conspiracy. This praiseworthy effort to overturn the racist idea that Italian Americans had a predisposition to engage in crime, however, ultimately points toward a model of the Mafia that was nothing more than a form of clientelism in its society of origin— "a system of godfathers and clients exchanging favors, services, and other benefits," perpetuated by the immigrants when they arrived in the New World, and destined to die out once the Italian American community was fully integrated into the upper ranks of U.S. society.[51] According to the anthropologist Francis J. Ianni, the mafiosi of the Lupollo family were "modest, taciturn people, . . . men of honor" deserving of "sympathy and admiration," linked together in a "family business" in which legal activities gradually replaced the illegal activities that had once been necessary for advancement for those who came from a world where there was neither law nor justice.[52] In short, theirs was "a vanishing way of life"[53]—yet another variation on the theme, inevitably refuted by events, of a modernity destined to automatically dissolve the archaism of the Mafia. The vertical and highly structured organization described by Valachi was therefore basically a paranoid invention of the authorities and the WASP power structure. The Mafia, as Hawkins asserted, is like God: to believe in it is tantamount to a profession of faith that cannot be sustained by empirical evidence.[54] We should point out, however, that Ianni's study was based on documents provided by the Lupollos themselves and certainly reflects their point of view; whereas Hawkins, without knowing it, formulated the same equation, Mafia = God, that had already been set forth by Pasquale Sciortino, the lieutenant and "intellectual" of the Giuliano gang, in a polemic with Girolamo Li Causi.[55]

The Americans' unwillingness to consider the Mafia as a criminal organization, especially (though not only) during the years that followed Valachi's revelations, profoundly influenced the sociological and anthropological debate concerning the Sicilian Mafia that took place between the 1960s and 1970s. In both cases, the only aspect considered worthy of study was "Mafia behavior," identified as that of the traditional Sicilian way of life, whereas "the Mafia," inasmuch as it was a structure independent of that mode of behavior, was not thought to exist at all, since the Sicilians were only capable of identifying with their families and their clientele. These were "natural" and personal aggregations that required no further bonds of association, such as a special oath or a specific ritual. Characteristic in its obstinate persistence in this direction is the work of the German sociologist Hess (1970),[56] who believed that the *cosca* corresponded to "a series of paired relations that the mafioso establishes with people otherwise unrelated to one another." The *cosca* was unstable and was established on specific occasions for specific purposes; the *cosca* coalesced around the boss's personal charisma and network of relations, and it died with the passage of those elements. "We are not in the presence of a static association of conspirators," Arlacchi wrote a few years later, in a paraphrase of the Schneiders' more balanced formulation, "but rather of a group of friends and relatives that, like any other organization of the sort, often gets together to play cards, go hunting, or to celebrate a birth or a wedding, or to enjoy a *schiticchio* [banquet among men]."[57]

Once again, we can point out how the effort to reduce the entire subject to the context of Mediterranean anthropology tended to coincide with the interpretation that mafiosi had and offered of themselves; they were content to portray themselves as innocuous country cousins rather than members of dangerous criminal associations. The old boss of Ribera, Paolo Campo, unhesitatingly acknowledged certain forms of behavior and declared himself to be a mafioso, but—as usual—he criticized the mafiosi of his day (1985) who had become nothing more than "common criminals." Most importantly, he took great care to deny that he had ever become an "associate" with a formal induction (the oath of loyalty): "I never committed criminal acts, nor did I ever associate myself with others to do that. I have to say that I was born mafioso and that I will die mafioso, if by Mafia you mean, as I do, to do good to one's neighbors, to give something to those who are in need, and to find work for those who are unemployed."[58] It is a typical defense strategy in Mafia trials, a strategy that, as mentioned earlier, coincides with the emphasis on traditionalist factors: already, during the nineteenth-century trial of the Amoroso brothers, the defending lawyer described the charges of conspiracy or association as "a chimaera," "a contrivance," "a mysterious anomaly." Similarly, Cascio-Ferro was described as an "individualist." Interpretative schemes like Hess's, which included references to Pitrè, the "true and unrivaled sage who understood the Sicilian soul," find their precedent in the theorizing of the lawyerly culture of the nineteenth and twentieth centuries. According to this theorizing, the traditional Sicilian, a man of the people, a "man of the countryside," would be incapable of founding an association as complex as the one described by the police, since he was an individualist or, at the very most, a familist.[59]

In 1965, in the aftermath of Valachi's confession, Robert T. Anderson attempted to preserve the traditional thesis by describing the path that led from Mafia to Cosa Nostra. Originally, Anderson stated, the Mafia was supposedly a coalescing of family groups, but in America, once it came into contact with modernity, it adopted "impersonal" organizational models, centralized governing institutions to prevent a primitive internal violence, primarily because that would be bad for business. The Sicilian organization, Anderson maintained, also followed this path, when confronted with the demonstrated effects of the American model and the similar processes of economic development.[60] Here we encounter the usual opposition between the old Mafia and the new Mafia, in which a naïve and all-inclusive model of modernization relegates culture, clientele, and blood family ties to the traditional world, placing in the world of the present "impersonal" organization, while instead the problem lies in understanding the complex interactions that exist, past and present, between the former elements and the latter institution.

Today, in the wake of the investigations of the last thirty years in Italy and America, nearly everyone is willing to recognize that Mafia organizations are characterized by a level of continuity extending beyond the life spans of the individual members, by a hierarchical structure, and by a membership that is carefully filtered, in accordance with the definition offered by official American institutions.[61] In accordance with Anderson's approach, however, it is often said that these characteristics have been acquired only recently, whereas it would be more accurate to say that they have only been recently acquired, not so much by the Mafia, as by the mafiologists, or at least by the majority current in that field, because from the very beginning, there have always been those who described "Mafia associations" of this sort. This is the case, for instance, of the two policemen and criminologists, Giuseppe Alongi and Antonino Cutrera, between the end of the nineteenth century and the early twentieth century, who made use of the investigative findings of the *questura* of Palermo in the three decades from 1860 to 1890—analyses that Hess summarily dismissed as "erroneous."[62] The methods of the division of territory and coordination among the *cosche* revealed by that documentation were very similar to those on which Buscetta insisted. In particular, in the years between the end of the nineteenth century and the early twentieth century, there existed a command structure composed of representatives of these groups, whose acts and rules (as we shall describe below), in the wake of the previously mentioned *questore* Sangiorgi, resembled the New York Commission as well as the organization in Palermo, which from the 1960s on oversaw the activities of Cosa Nostra, until the further centralizing crackdown of the Corleonese. This does not mean that the Mafia groups of the Palermo area have remained under the control of supervisory institutions from Italian unification to the present day. Indeed, those institutions are unstable, fully exposed to the stress of internal divisions, and have probably had their ups and downs. Moreover, in recent history, the territorial extent of their authority (the city? the province? the region?) has shifted according to various circumstances. However, the relative success of the efforts at centralization in Palermo (as in New York) is likely the result of this age-old proclivity for coordination, since these tendencies are universal in the realm of organized crime but do not always achieve results. In Naples, for example, the attempt in that direction with the Nuova Camorra Organizzata (NCO, or New Organized Camorra) under Raffaele Cutolo ended in a bloodbath, and prevailing today at Reggio Calabria is a horizontal model, or a "swarm model."[63] In the Caltanissetta and Catania districts, the groups linked to Cosa Nostra have been unable to take full control because of the continuous emergence of new gangs. And the affiliation of the Palermo families with eminent personages of the *'ndrangheta* or the Camorra, tending to reinforce business ties established in the context of cigarette and drug smuggling, failed to bring about the expected centralizing effects.

In short, one should avoid falling into the trap of the idea of the Single Great Conspiracy, eschewing the popular image of a *piovra* (octopus, a term used colloquially in Italy to describe the Mafia—*translator's note*) with one head and a thousand tentacles, with omniscient and omnipotent leadership, a notion that has been simplistically foisted on the public by authorities in both America and Sicily, in particular during the course of the first investigations and inquiries in the nineteenth century. The mafiosi are involved in business dealings that link them with subjects who neither belong to the Mafia nor could they ever do so: intermediaries, criminals of every kind and every nationality, Turkish or Chinese drug traffickers, bankers. In their role as protectors—a role that as we have seen is highly ambiguous—they interact with landowners, entrepreneurs, and shopowners. In their necessary connections with politics and public institutions, they make deals and agreements with notables, professional politicians, policemen, and judges. As we shall see, the individual mafiosi carry on conversations with the outside world, in some cases independently of the Mafia as an organization. This helps us to see, among other things, that the concept of the Mafia as an anti-state is overstated and misleading, and it points us to the theme of the ties linking the Mafia and official power.[64] This field should be carefully considered and entails in fact current implications both in the judicial field (I am referring to the penal category, recently introduced into Italian legislation, of external involvement in Mafia conspiracy) and in the political field. Let us consider, for instance, the attempt to distinguish between the political responsibility and the penal responsibilities of public figures involved in various ways in relationships with organized crime. Stefano Bontate, the Grecos, and other eminent leaders of Cosa Nostra have deemed it useful to find a venue for meeting with their partners from the worlds of politics and economics in the more-or-less secret Masonic lodges. In scholarly terms—as well as political and judicial terms—it is useful to wonder how these fluid and varied networks serve as parallel and overlapping structures to the organization that ties the mafiosi together.

THE MAFIA AS A JURIDICAL ORDERING

The relationship between the Mafia and freemasonry extends well beyond the occasional presence of Mafia bosses in the ranks of the Freemasons. The current diffusion of "anomalous" Masonic lodges in Sicily, and even more important, the fact that throughout the liberal era Sicily was the Italian region with the highest Masonic presence,[65] represents a contextual element when we consider organizational models and the tendency of power to be managed in a non-transparent manner. In order to explain to outsiders the logic that drives mafiosi to gather into an association, it comes naturally to Nick Gentile to compare it with freemasonry.[66] In effect, the function of Masonic solidarity between professionals and businessmen is comparable to the Mafia solidarity linking individuals with ties to different or even opposing groups, based on different continents, which creates a field for communication, knowledge, and influence that represents a comparative advantage for this type of criminality. Most importantly, this is what preserved the solidity of the ties between Sicily and the United States. During the maxitrial, Buscetta responded sarcastically to a lawyer who was making a point of his doubts about Buscetta's description of the Mafia oath of membership: "I read in the newspaper that a lawyer, present here in the courtroom, in his youth foolishly decided to join the Freemasons, and he laughed and laughed at their oath. It is a facsimile of our oath."[67] It is natural that the mafiosi chose to adopt this reference to a sectarian logic with the "protective" themes that are typical of their ideology: hence the reference to the tradition of the *Beati Paoli*, a mythology made up of secret societies that defend the weak and engage in shadowy rites, which were frequently mentioned among the broader audience in Palermo through a famous adventure novel written by Walter Natoli.[68]

Moreover, both a historical and functional link exists between the Mafia and freemasonry. The rituals and oaths of the Mafia are entirely identical in the descriptions found in nineteenth-century police archives, in the old books by Cutrera, Colacino, and Lestingi, as well as in the confessions of Valachi, and in those of Buscetta, as well as in the "bugged" tape recordings of the FBI. These rituals express not only the generic symbology of blood found in so many organized crime milieux, but also the overwhelming documentation of a centuries-old continuity of a type of secret organization developed out of the model provided by freemasonry and *carboneria* (or Carbonarist movement), which, as we shall see, was freely available in Sicily in the mid-nineteenth century. In his work, Hess refused to admit even the "possibility" of such rituals,[69] perhaps because they in fact point to mechanisms of politico-criminal mobilization that were somewhat more complex than those he had hypothesized and because the very idea of the initiatory oath contradicts the assumed identity of Mafia and general culture. By crossing the threshold, the inductee became a culturally new individual.

> The neophyte in liminality must be a *tabula rasa*, a blank slate, on which is inscribed the knowledge and wisdom of the group, in those respects that pertain to the new status.... They have to be shown that in themselves they are clay or dust, mere matter, whose form is impressed upon them by society.[70]

Polygenesis makes a criminal into an honored member of society. "Following the decline of [the] hereditary aristocracy there arose the aristocracy of murder, acknowledged, embraced, and honored."[71] The concept of honor, borrowed from aristocratic language, ideally serves as an expression of the pride of membership in an elite, criminal though it may be, with an emphasis on distance from ordinary people. A man is honored precisely to the degree that many others are not so honored and cannot hope to be. This results in an amplification of the effect of identification in a system of norms that expresses "the internal language of the organization and not that of the external legitimization,"[72] even though it is preferable that such language should at least formally echo common language. In the nineteenth-century organizations of freemasonry, even outside of Sicily, the informer was termed *infame,* or infamous.[73] From the Masonic concept of humanity derives the Camorristic concept of humility—that is to say, subordination to the wishes of the organization. Hence, according to one interpretation, by converting the "l" sound to an "r" sound, which is typical of the Sicilian dialect, the word *omertà* is derived.[74] This interpretation is far more plausible than Pitrè's version (*omertà*=virility), if we are interested in distinguishing a generic subculture from a criminal infrastructure ready to kill its enemies, or if we are equally ready to denounce its enemies "with anonymous letters or through highly secret channels to the police. This is the humility of the Mafia"— thus the authoritative definition offered by the bandit Salvatore Giuliano.[75]

To obtain its goals, the Mafia as an organization regulates the relations within each individual group; prevents competition among groups with the principle of territorial jurisdiction and with a series of clauses and codicils in cases where such a principle may not be applicable in certain concrete situations; and calls for ad hoc agreements or less unstable structural confederations in cases where the set of rules in place is no longer adequate to keep the peace. In the descriptions of a great number of *pentiti,* the mafiosi actually seem to be obsessed by "regulations and statutes," in contrast with what was claimed by the followers of the frequently cited Pitrè. And in contrast with what they claim, we might set forth the interpretation formulated as early as the post–First World War years by another Palermitan, the great jurist Santi Romano:

> It is well known that, under the threat of current laws, associations often thrive in the shadows whose organization might be said to be almost analogous, on a smaller scale, to the organization of the state: they have legislative and executive authorities, tribunals that settle controversies and order punishments, agents that inexorably administer punishments, elaborate and precise statutes, comparable to our laws. And they therefore set up an order all their own, like the national state and the institutions sanctioned by law.[76]

According to Romano, the Mafia therefore was a "juridical ordering," one of the many de facto orderings that organized groups adopt in the folds of the

larger social fabric. In some cases, these orderings are declared illegal—"A revolutionary society or a criminal conspiracy will not constitute rightful organizations for the state that they aspire to overthrow or whose laws they violate,
just as a schismatic sect is declared unlawful by the Church"[77]—without alter-
ing in any substantial manner their substance and without changing the ethical
judgment, positive or negative, of the objectives and methods of the groups in
question. In other cases, again according to Romano, the state will be indiffer-
ent to other orderings, considering them neither harmful nor competitive to
its own ordering. This explains why interest in the Mafia's rituals and internal
forms of adherence (in contrast with the crimes committed by individual mafiosi), which was so powerful among the police authorities during the course of
the postunification nineteenth century, gradually ebbed in the subsequent era,
up to the present point at which membership in a Mafia family—beginning at a
particularly stark point in the Mafia emergency (1982)—became a crime in and
of itself.

Giuseppe Guido Lo Schiavo, a highly placed magistrate in Sicily following
the Second World War, took theoretical arguments from Romano for his praise
of and emphasis on the *Mafia d'ordine* as an aid to public institutions in the fight
against banditry. Lo Schiavo clamorously expressed this praise in his funeral
eulogy for Calogero Vizzini, where he offered the hope that Vizzini's "authoritative successor," Genco Russo, would lead "the occult political clique . . . on the
path of respect for the laws of the state and social betterment."[78] In other words,
a less juridical ordering was supposed to converge with its greater counterpart
in the logic of peaceful coexistence, or perhaps of complicity based on mutual
self-interest, in keeping with the practice of the Christian Democratic regime.
This, however, did not mean that the realistic acknowledgment of the ordering
of the Mafia necessarily led to an accommodation with it, as has been recently
stated, using a substantial dose of unilaterality.[79] Even Lo Schiavo himself had
been one of the leading men in the group of magistrates who had fiercely battled
against the Mafia during the Fascist regime, considering it, again with reference
to Romano's theories, to be a criminal conspiracy. The general prosecuting attorney of Palermo, Luigi Giampietro, the great prosecutor in the trials of the
1920s and 1930s, simultaneously used the economic paradigm (the Mafia is "an
insurance policy" taken out by "landowners and businessmen" to protect "their
possessions and their persons") and the paradigm of the parallel state or anti-
state.[80] The theory, so fertile in terms of knowledge and understanding, was
neutral in terms of its practical applications in that truly the state could recognize or not, as it chose, depending on political circumstances, the ordering of
the Mafia as an adversary. Fitting into this tradition was Cesare Terranova, a Communist magistrate and member of the Italian parliament who was murdered by

the Mafia. An inflexible adversary of both the Corleonese and the Palermo Mafias, Terranova reiterated in his verdicts during the 1960s that there existed "only one Mafia, neither old nor young, neither good nor bad," but "efficient and dangerous, divided into clusters or groups or 'families,' or more accurate still, '*cosche*.'" The existence of this coherent organization would ultimately be demonstrated at the beginning of the 1980s by the investigations carried out by the pool of magistrates of Palermo. In its own territory, Cosa Nostra regulates business, levies taxes, or, in other words, collects bribes, produces legitimacy, and defines as illegal, establishing rules and exceptions, judges, absolves, and punishes. As Falcone stated, once again echoing Romano, it "is a society, an organization, that is, in its own way, juridical."[81]

The fact that the Mafia wishes to be a juridical system does not, however, signify that it actually succeeds in regulating the relations within it and outside of it. The very processes of centralization provoke harsh conflicts, and violence becomes part of the process, a resolving element, forcing any assumed general rules into compliance with the vested interests of individuals and groups. This should come as no particular surprise, considering that the violation or self-interested exploitation of rules forms part of the historical reality of political systems that are far more complex than that of the Mafia. I do not believe that we can say that Mafia capos have a higher level of "public" ethics than their counterparts in the world above. Valachi, Gentile, Bonanno, Buscetta, and Calderone all portrayed themselves and their friends as wise men who applied the rules, who sought to mediate conflict, and who avoided illegal violence, turning to bloodshed only as a last resort, in order to apply the rational and carefully weighed deliberations of the organization. At the same time, they depicted their enemies as treacherous individuals, unwilling to respect the laws of (their own) society, always ready to engage in betrayal, killing at the drop of a hat, and verging on the brink of sadism and insanity. We can believe that the self-portrayal of the *pentiti* is a sincere one, yet if their adversaries were to speak, they might well tell the story from a diametrically opposed point of view. In fact, the Catanian false *pentito* Ferone and his obstinately irreducible adversary, Santapaola, mentioned earlier, recently accused one another of the same crime—that is, of not respecting the rules of the feud, of killing women and innocent victims. In short, they are described as trending toward an animalistic and uncontrolled violence.[82] In reality, such internal conflict—such as the contrast between the old Mafia and the new Mafia—is an integral part of the Mafia's ideology. It is an expression of a mediocre and obscurantic vision of the world. If we step outside of that vision, it becomes necessary to acknowledge that such a system of governance is in and of itself ineffective because it is unjust and inevitably leads to the worst perversions of justice. The "war of all against all"—*bellum omnium contra omnes*—that was supposed to be warded off instead looms inevitably, tragically, over every deliberation of the Mafia Commissions, far more than upon the sentence of the courts of the official power, the resolutions of parliaments, or even international bodies.

It is within this contradiction that we should place the greatest discontinuity in the more than one hundred year history of the Sicilian Mafia, which beginning in 1979 became the protagonist of a ferocious terroristic escalation directed against magistrates, policemen, and honest politicians and corrupt politicians alike. Thus, it broke with its past behavior of prudently blending into the shadows of social and institutional powers, toward which it had previously deemed an attitude of collaboration both advisable and normal, perceiving those institutional powers as unquestionably superior to it. In recent years, this aggressive approach distinguished Cosa Nostra from all other types of criminal organizations, at least those operating in Italy. Was this perhaps an effect of the fragmentation of the state, which had become a weak network of informal relations that created a vacuum to be filled by a compact clandestine structure? Or was this merely a shortsighted and arrogant decision, at the far extreme within Mafia ideology itself, with which the Mafia ordering finally revealed itself as antagonistic to that of the national state, whereby this underworld finally wound up rendering itself as distinguishable from the overworld, and therefore subject to attack from it?

CHAPTER II

THE REVELATION

PROTO-MAFIA

It is not particularly meaningful to know where the word "mafia" comes from[1] or whether, and in what context, the word may have been used before 1860. However, it is crucial to note that after that date the term entered into very general use to refer, however vaguely, to a pathological relationship among politics, society, and criminality. Thus, the very moment of Italy's foundation as a nation and a state coincided with the first, generic, and exceedingly ambiguous perception that a problem of this sort existed. *Esse est percipi* ("To be is to be perceived"): it is proper to start here. By contrast, the very idea of a mafia implies the existence of a state that ensures freedom of opinion and trade, equality before the law of all citizens, government by the people (or, in this early stage, by the wealthy and powerful) and the rule of law, and a transparent and formal process. Both the word and the thing itself are a product of the gap between promise and reality, a gap that can in part be blamed on the same *Destra storica* (historic right wing) that claimed to abhor the Sicilians' total lack of respect for the law. The fact that Sicily never experienced a large-scale outbreak of pro-Bourbon brigandage did nothing to prevent the government from extending the Pica Law of 1863 to Sicily, establishing martial law on the island as well. The measures General Giuseppe Govone and the prefect-general Giacomo Medici took to round up the numerous men avoiding the draft called for general sweeps of whole provinces in western Sicily: towns and villages were surrounded and occupied by armed soldiers, and the relatives of those avoiding the draft were persecuted, in line with the concept of collective community guilt in the eyes of the military authorities. But by theorizing and implementing these systems, the generals succeeded only in achieving the opposite of what they hoped, swelling the already vast ranks of draft-dodgers and deserters (26,000 in 1863) with a huge number of individuals who had become fugitives from justice precisely in the wake and as a direct result of the army's actions (it would be no exaggeration to call them terrorist actions). "I have been reliably informed"—an anonymous Palermitan wrote in 1867—"that in one village in this district, there were thirty-four fugitives from justice in proportion to a single draft-evader."[2] As a moderate writer named Diomede Pantaleoni noted as early as the end of 1861, political isolation led the representatives of the government to rely on "Bourbons and pro-Bourbons" and even on the "stabbers"—the so-called *pugnalatori*— to the point of employing political assassination.[3] In fact, in the years that followed, it seems quite plausible that the pro-government party made use of that tool—as in the case, for instance, of the murder of the previously mentioned Garibaldian "general" Corrao—as well as employing a sort of forerunner of the approach that in more recent years was known as the *strategia della tensione,* the strategy of tension. The strategy of tension relied upon terror to usher in stronger government: consider the still shadowy episode of the *pugnalatori* of Palermo of 1863.[4] This strategy had the aim of encouraging divisions among the left wing, by criminalizing the most extreme leftists and bringing about a useful collaboration among the more "moderate" groups.

In other words, the term *mafia* itself proposes its own periodization, and it does us no particular good to slide backward in time, pursuing an endless chain of supposed links of causation based on the concept of a meta-historical Sicilian diversity. Leaving aside the many authors who have ventured as far back as the thirteenth-century uprising against the French known as the "Sicilian Vespers" and even further back to Gaius Verres (Roman magistrate, notorious for his misgovernment of Sicily—*translator's note*) and to the alleged ethnic dialectic between the western, Carthaginian section of the island and the eastern, Greek section, most scholars take as a point of reference the rule of the Spanish viceroy, a specific application of the larger nationalistic polemic against the corrupting Iberian influence and the *preponderanza straniera,* or foreign domination.[5] If we trace the line of continuity linking nineteenth-century Sicilian history with that of previous centuries,[6] we can identify in the events of seventeenth- and eighteenth-century Sicily links between political power, social power, and criminality comparable to what came later.[7] We must, however, remember just how different the contexts were. In a society of the *ancien régime* (and not just in Sicily), personal relationships tended to prevail, as codified by law, and not merely in practice. Subjects were not equal, and jurisdictions differed in accordance with the qualities of persons and groups. Some had the right to use force, whereas others did not. The concept of *mafia* cannot be applied to this historical context, precisely because the very relationships that in the present period seem so pathological, so scandalous that a specific word has emerged to describe their illicit nature, were a physiological part of it. And that term emerged precisely at this point.

The most useful point of reference for those who wish to investigate the culture medium in which the Mafia developed, a sort of "proto-Mafia," is the nineteenth century prior to the unification of Italy, which marks the origin of the concept of *camorra*. The abolition of the feudal system, which was ordered by decree in Sicily in 1812 with a number of provisions that differed from the law governing the mainland of southern Italy (*Mezzogiorno continentale*) in 1806, and then completed in the 1830s, destroyed a number of the fundamental cadres of the *ancien régime*. As early as 1875, Leopoldo Franchetti identified this as a decisive point in triggering the process of "democratization of violence," whereby the right to use force, originally the exclusive privilege of the aristocracy, was legally transferred to the state, while substantially remaining in the hands of private citizens, progressively involving new social groups and spreading beyond any rigid hierarchies of order or class.[8] But I would not adduce the introduction of private ownership, which supposedly leads to the Mafia, in Sicily in the early nineteenth century and in Russia today, as a paralegal structure protecting this new institution.[9] Like all explanations relying on a single cause, this one begs a few simple objections. Why did the laws abolishing feudalism lead to the creation of the Mafia in western Sicily but not in eastern Sicily? Why don't we see the same sequence of events in the many parts of Europe, where laws abolishing feudalism were put into effect during the Napoleonic occupation and the first part of the nineteenth century?

On the other hand, in eighteenth-century Sicily, private property and land ownership already existed to a very large degree, both in the narrow sense (allodium, or "land freely held, without obligation of service to any overlord") and in the sense that the *feudi,* or estates, were basically managed and operated as private landholdings. Following the reforms, most of the feudal lands, awarded to barons, remained in the hands of their long-standing holders or were shunted onto the general real estate market. The ultimate effect of this array of measures, both before and after the unification of Italy, was to encourage the commercialization of a considerable volume of lands, both feudal and ecclesiastic, and to give free rein to the nineteenth-century trend toward intensive agriculture with the abolition of the various rights and other encumbrances caused by the indebtedness of the nobility. In one case that is known, that of the Duchy of Nelson (near Bronte), the process was pushed forward by the ducal administration through a series of determined juridical and political demands; the populace responded in kind to what they viewed as a series of ducal "usurpations" and, then, dramatically, reacted with full-fledged insurrections in 1848 and 1860.[10] Generally, the most violent conflicts over the basis of land ownership, that is, the disputes over state-owned land, took place in eastern Sicily, where there was no mention of the Mafia. The western section of the island, the preferred territory of the Mafia phenomenon, preserved a structure that was more directly under the influence of the "feudal" past.

The legislative and administrative measures of the early nineteenth century take on a more complete significance when we connect them to the administrative reforms carried out under the Bourbons, in response to the demands that emerged during the Napoleonic period in Sicily as well. Given the differences in political history, the reforms came later in Sicily than in the mainland of southern Italy (*Mezzogiorno continentale*)—positing for the first time the idea of a modern state[11] and thereby inaugurating the historical context in which we can set the theme of the Mafia. This change led, among other things, to the establishment of a professional magistracy and a police force. The magistrates, drawn from the ranks of the local elites, allied themselves accordingly, paying the merest lip service to the idea of blind justice that they were being asked to administer. The police could either be identified with the new gendarmerie, centralized but scarcely able to maneuver among groups and factions, among the bandits and the prominent citizens who protected them; or else with the *compagnie d'armi* (literally, companies at arms), composed of men selected by the village worthies from among the "rough and ready" young men of the district. Their mission was not to pursue criminals but rather to recover goods stolen in their jurisdiction by negotiating with the thieves. Many believe that there was a prior understanding between the company at arms and the thieves.

A perverse dynamic thus developed between the company at arms, prominent citizens, and local criminals. This ensured the landowners and property holders that their assets would remain intact, and their lands untroubled, through a very specific type of control exerted by the captains of the companies at arms over the local criminals. The practice of negotiation between victim and robber allowed the victim to regain some of his possessions, and it permitted the criminal to escape punishment and keep part of the loot. The captain would receive a "prize" for his role as an intermediary, practically an honest broker named by the seller and the purchaser in a public transaction.[12]

The debate in the Bourbon period was similar to the one that took place in the period following the unification of Italy. On one side were those who supported a system for maintaining the public order that was substantially outside the law, first through companies at arms and later with *militi a cavallo*— militiamen or soldiers on horseback. On the other side were the supporters of a state-run corps (respectively, the *gendarmi* and the Carabinieri). The second parties considered the first system disastrous because it provided a forum for connivance between landowners and criminals; after 1860 they used the word "mafia" to describe it. We should also mention the early nineteenth-century debates concerning the practice of inciting the murder of fugitives from the law, sanctioned by law and rewarded with cash, on the part of the turncoat and well-paid comrades of those same fugitives. These incentives were present in the decrees of outlawry and were also destined to create a bridge linking criminals, prominent citizens, and the authorities. We find an echo of this technique, following unification, in the continual negotiations among bandits, mafiosi, and the police force, which often culminated in the murder (this time, illegal) of a gang leader. As Giovanna Fiume, in emulation of Franchetti, claimed, there are two aspects to the matter. On the one hand, banditry represented an instrument in the factional fights between the new small-town elites and was an outgrowth of their clientelistic networks. On the other hand, it was the progressive consolidation of a new idea of legality that delegitimized the traditional forms of behavior of the local elites and the state itself, calling into question a form of "justice" that lay somewhere between the public and private spheres.[13]

It was from among the members of the small-town elites that *gabellotti* (renters and sublessors of parcels of farmland) were recruited, along with administrators to oversee the sulphur mines, the large landholdings, and the orchards and olive groves. During the course of the nineteenth century, both before and after Italian unification, these new elites attempted to take the place of the former feudal aristocracy, which was slowly but surely loosening its grip on the Sicilian countryside, breaking up and redistributing their social power along with their own possessions. But a requisite condition for that power seemed to have been control over a military force. Military force was not only required to manage the labor force but, in more general terms, to protect the sulphur mines and the farms, as well as to ensure the personal safety of prominent citizens, who were constantly at risk of kidnapping. That same military force could also come in handy during the frequent clashes among the clientelistic and family groups that constituted the municipal "parties" in nineteenth-century Sicily. The military force in question was that of the *campieri,* or private guards of farmland, a private militia that, much like the pseudo-public militias of the companies at arms, the soldiers on horseback, and the *guardie municipali,* or town gendarmes, was meant to keep order in the countryside. Like the other forces mentioned, they were usually recruited from among former bandits capable of intimidating ill-intentioned and suspicious characters in language they would understand, or, when necessary, work out agreements with them in the spirit of good neighbors. These people could do their master's dirty work, or entrust that dirty work to some outlaw with whom relationships of patronage had already been established in the past.

The *gabellotto* performed a function relating to social order and control that extended well beyond the boundaries of the large farms practicing extensive agriculture. The *gabellotto*'s staff of *campieri* and *sovrastanti* (local superintendents) took the place of the feudal militias of the eighteenth century, worked alongside the city and town militias of the nineteenth century, and covered the areas left unguarded by the control of, first, the Bourbon state and, later, the liberal state. Already Emilio Sereni, writing many years ago, considered the Mafia less as a feudal holdover and primarily as a tool of an "aborted" bourgeoisie, the bourgeoisie of the *gabellotti*, which over the course of the lengthy breakup of the feudal economy and powers developed a capacity for intimidation that was exercised both upward and downward along the social hierarchy.[14] Although the holdings of the old aristocracy were breaking apart, the factions of the local community were trying to intercept these streams of wealth, using violence, internally and externally, to compete for the chance to lease or purchase land. From the towns, through the *gabella*, or subcontracting of farmland leases, the new ruling classes went on to gain influence over larger geographic areas. This class was most distinctively represented in central and western Sicily.

Here, even in the years following unification, agriculture as a sector of the economy was necessarily practiced on a large scale, in order to allow the land to lie fallow, through alternating seasons of growing wheat and pasturing. Generally, the land was cultivated by the wealthier farmers (*borgesi*) on small plots, while cattle breeding was managed directly by the leaseholders. Moreover, in the absence of stall-based livestock rearing, the pastures had to be located at various elevations, which meant that the herds had to move over considerable distances. Thus, even though the aristocratic landholdings were breaking apart, economic unity was often preserved intact through the system of what were known as *condomini*, under the control of the major operations.[15]

In 1866, Antonio di Rudinì, a young aristocrat who would enjoy a great career in politics, declared that the absence of security had produced the following phenomenon: those who moved to the country and wished to live there must become brigands. There was no alternative: in order to defend oneself and one's property, one was obliged to seek the patronage of robbers.[16]

It seems, however, that the problem of protection and safety had more to do with the farming business, especially where livestock was concerned, and less with the property itself. As we said earlier, the ability to control criminals was a prerequisite for obtaining and managing the *gabella*, or long-term lease, and it tended to eliminate rivals who enjoyed no such control. Throughout the nineteenth century the question of cattle theft remained a central issue in the

overall debate: it was primarily as a cattle breeder that the *gabellotto* acted as
an entrepreneur, and his herd of cattle constituted not only his primary capital,
but also the easiest capital to steal. It was in this crucial area that, under the
Bourbon regime, the practice of the *componende* (negotiated settlements) developed. These were negotiations between the victims of theft and the thieves
themselves for the return of the stolen goods and livestock, and they were conducted under the supervision of powerful criminals, respected professionals,
or prominent citizens. At the beginning of the 1840s, the *sottointendente* of Termini, Puoti, described a three-level system, with those who actually committed
the crimes on one level, the negotiators on the second level, and finally the organizers, who "stayed on their own lands, corresponding one with another, over-
seeing and controlling operations . . . receiving the animals on their lands . . .
deciding who had deserved death and who would do the killing."[17] In 1838, according to the magistrate Pietro Calà Ulloa, "the populace has come to a tacit
agreement with the monarchs" through "unions or brotherhoods, a sort of
sect that they call parties," which, under the command of "landowners" and
"archpriests," serve as "little Governments with the Government," through the
componende, thereby depriving the law of the power to prosecute crimes, and
through other conspiracies against public officers.[18]

Calà Ulloa attributed no "political color or purpose" to these brotherhoods,
but the term "parties" shows what Calà Ulloa (who would later be a leading figure in the pro-Bourbon reaction) saw as the problem. Puoti was more explicit
when he stated that "the thieves in Sicily, without meaning to, are the means to
a revolution and they will be the instrument for an uprising that will redound to
the benefit of those who now protect them."[19] As in the period following Italian
unification, the discovery of the proto-mafioso scope of criminal activity was
prompted by the concern that the "new" state authority felt toward the general
sense of political and social insubordination, on the part of commoners and
the ruling class. Officials of the Bourbon monarchy, however, knew that they
had a much more broad-based process of political mobilization to fight against,
which was and remained their primary concern, given the program set forth by
Ferdinand II just one year before Calà Ulloa's report: "The first thing to which
Sicily must become accustomed is obedience."[20] In this case, to a much greater
degree than in the case of liberal Italy, social discontent, increasing criminal
activity, and political opposition appeared to be an inextricable whole, both as
perceived at the time and in actual fact.

From 1815 until 1860, the periods of peace were just brief intervals, punctu-
ated by the uprisings of 1821 and 1848, in an alternation of revolutions and resto-
rations. Of course, there was no open war between Sicily and the "Neapolitans";
rather, a substantial part of the ruling class, especially in Palermo, had an

anti-Bourbon preference, which in thousands of local contexts amounted to a smoldering civil war. Here, as in so many similar situations in the nineteenth and twentieth centuries, individuals used history at large for how it could best help them deal with the history writ small of their villages, their families, their lives. Violence served as a midwife to new equilibriums, if not a new civilization. The revolutionary process defined political conflicts and social conflicts, and implemented private vendettas, factional infighting, and grabs for wealth and power. In Marineo, the insurrections of 1821 and 1848 were marked by massacres carried out by one "party" upon another. In Castellammare del Golfo, the popular uprising of 1862 turned against the neo-bourgeois group of the *Cutraras*. In Bronte, in Biancavilla, and elsewhere, in 1848 and in 1860, the question of state-owned lands further inflamed the bloody insurrections and fierce repressions.[21] Individuals and groups became accustomed to resolving disagreements violently, linking them to broader contexts as suggested by the direction of "large-scale" politics, and arming, making use of, and keeping under control what the sources of the time generically refer to as the class of the "ruffians."

Clearly, it is impossible to distinguish between the social and institutional disorder unleashed by the reforms of the early nineteenth century and the political disorder. The synchronic character of the two upheavals gives each a radical and uncontrollable nature, so that with each new shock it seems that behind the revolution or the reaction the broken fragments of the *ancien régime* were boiling. "What is happening in Sicily is what happens everywhere following a revolution," declared one of the witnesses heard by the Parliamentary Commission in 1875. "In revolutions, wealth moves around, and some become rich, some become poor. Our country has yet to find its center; that is the cause of all this social upheaval."[22] A typical case of juxtaposition and overlapping among political, social, and criminal elements is that of the military organizations that incited the insurrections in Palermo—that is, the guilds, insurgents, civic militias (1821),[23] squads, countersquads, and the *Guardia nazionale* (1848 and 1860). In contrast to what was happening on the mainland of southern Italy, the populace at large did not tend toward *Sanfedismo* ("Holy Faith"; a popular anti-Republican movement that mobilized peasants of the Papal States against the Parthenopaean Republic in 1799, culminating in the restoration of the Bourbon Kingdom of Naples under Ferdinand I of the Two Sicilies—*translator's note*) and instead followed the example of the bourgeoisie and the aristocracy, which at first favored independence and later became liberal. This, however, did nothing to ensure social order, as we see from the stark clashes internal to the revolutionary front in 1821 and, especially, in 1848, when the actions of the *guerriglie* (guerrillas or insurgents) and the popular squads triggered the counterrevolutionary terror of the countersquads and the *Guardia nazionale*.[24] In each case, according to the historiography of the Risorgimento, the revolution was pushed back by the reaction (or, at least, as in 1860, the moderate stabilization) caused by the explosion of a "class struggle" among its members. In reality, it is not always clear precisely who was involved in this struggle. Often, the depiction of anarchist squads thirsting after plunder conflicted with an opposing depiction of squads linked to the aristocracy by the traditional bonds of fealty and vassalage, or by a salary that amounted to 6 *tarì* (a small medieval coin struck in Italy, Sicily, and Malta; also, a corresponding unit of value).

It is natural to think that the political violence of the Risorgimento, especially the squads, represents the cultural medium in which the phenomenon of the Mafia developed.[25] Many writers at the time, whether pro-Bourbon or liberal-moderates, suggest this view. One such author, the prefect Filippo Gualterio, identified the following as accomplices of the Mafia: the liberals during the revolutionary phases, the pro-Bourbons during the restoration phases, and above all, the Republicans of his own time. Playing the game like some sorcerer's apprentice, in a style reminiscent of the Bourbon police, in September 1866 the *questore* (administrative director of the district police) Felice Pinna remained willfully inactive in the face of the first warning signs of an uprising that was destined to throw Palermo into uproar. His goal was to provoke a full-fledged insurrection, which he could then crush with a wholehearted repression,[26] and he still gave credence to the alleged mysterious conspiracy among clerics, supporters of the Bourbons, Mazzinians, and the "Mafia." The revolt took place according to the well-tested tactics of previous city insurrections. The center of Palermo, at the agreed hour, was invaded by squads pouring in from the *borgate,* or outlying suburbs, and the surrounding villages and towns (Monreale,[27] Bagheria, and Misilmeri), while the urban "plebs" also began to move. At the climax of the revolt, on 19 September, there were 12,000 armed rebels in the city, 1,200 of whom had come in from the countryside, and "two thousand citrus gardeners, peasants, and *carrettieri* (teamsters), and the most ferocious of them all, who live in the *sobborghi,* or outlying districts, and in the *casolari,* or farmhouses," surrounding Palermo.[28] "There were members of the Ciaccio squad who told me, and I heard the same thing from many people, that the squads of 1866 were the same as those of 1860, and that many from 1848 also took part."[29]

"Long Live the Italian Republic," cried the rebels of 1866. That cry hearkened back to a collection of experiences (a certain time and certain events), an array of symbols borrowed from the *sinistra azionista* (the left of Mazzini's *partito d'azione,* or action party—*translator's note*), and preserved in this context, as is shown by the insistence on an "Italian" republic, chosen over what might have seemed more likely some regional reference. "Revolutionary republicanism was doing its work. The armed *malandrinaggio* (bandits) of the countryside around Palermo became its armed flag-bearer and the people chose to follow, chanting its cries of revenge."[30] This was the situation of the forces in the field, except that none of the parties was capable of taking command, and in truth none really tried to do so, as if the lower section of a network of political relationships had been stripped of its upper framework, constituted by the liberal aristocracy and its conspiratorial tradition. This is the theory set forth by Duke Gabriele Colonna di Cesarò: "The first thing that the rebels did was to go in search of the men who had led them in 1860: Pignatelli Monteleone, Riso, Turrisi, Torremuzza. . . . Of course, they wanted nothing to do with it, whereupon the ranks of the ruffians fell into disarray."[31] I am not sure that I am willing to rely entirely on sources that tend to describe the upper classes as "intelligent," thus implying that other classes are devoid of intellect, reducing all their actions to a lust for rapine and plunder. The problems of postunification Palermo were massive, and, to a great extent, since they were bound up with the loss of its status as a postfeudal capital, different from the problems of the rest of Sicily, especially the eastern part of the island.[32] This was the source of the essentially political passions that brought 20,000 or 30,000 people into the streets, combatants and noncombatants, and about whom we know very little nowadays. Nor do we know much more about the military organization that was making its last effort at this point.

The problem of the "ruffians" arose in 1866 just as it had in preceding years. A well-known example is that of the *giardiniere* (leaseholder on citrus groves) of Monreale, Salvatore (Turi) Miceli, *caposquadra* (squad chief) in 1848. Miceli was inducted into the Bourbon police by Maniscalco, was once again a rebel in the uprising of 1860, and was arrested as an accomplice of bandits but freed, mysteriously, through the intervention of the *questore,* Pinna. Clearly, Miceli was unable to complete under the liberal regime the game he had already begun to play with the Bourbon regime: that of using as a *uomo d'ordine*—a man of order—the skills of professional violence acquired in the school of politics. Indeed, he died in 1866, leading an attack on the prison where Giuseppe Badia was being held. Badia was a former commander under Garibaldi, who succeeded Corrao as the leader of the radical group, a future internationalist, and a "wealthy industrialist" with relationships with leading mafiosi of the Conca d'Oro. Among these mafiosi was the Amoroso family whose members participated in the "anarchist" uprising[33] and also reappeared at the head of the Piazza Montalto *cosca* (Mafia family). However, not all the ruffians took part in the revolt. Those who led the assault on the *palazzo* of the prince of Sant'Elia were repelled by "countersquads":

Here is an example of the practical utility that the landowners of Sicily obtain by protecting their *coloni* (tenant farmers). The Prince of Sant'Elia has removed a great many men from the ranks of the insurrection and has turned their weapons, I would not say against the brigands, because they themselves were brigands, but towards his own rescue. . . . This system also saved the lives of a few other squires in Palermo.[34]

A few of the leading figures from the revolution adopted positions in defense of law and order. As we shall see, this was the case, for instance, with Antonino Giammona, as well as Salvatore Licata, whom the *questore* Rastelli described, indulgently, as an old *maffia* capo. Born around 1805, "he [Licata] performed some actions in 1848 worthy of a good patriot; the same was true in 1860 and in 1866. He is said to have committed some murders as well, but the law has been unable to touch him." Perhaps giving up all hope of touching him, in 1861–1862 the authorities named him as one of the mounted soldiers, while his son Andrea was named commander of the *guardie campestri,* or rural and agricultural police, of the Piana dei Colli, located in the heart of the Conca d'Oro. Salvatore Licata's son Andrea attained so high a rank that he was described as "a second *questore.* Two other sons of Salvatore, in the meanwhile, were sentenced to house arrest and prison as dangerous criminals."[35]

In short, whether they took one side or another in 1866, the mafiosi of Palermo were products of the revolution. As the duke of Cesarò also said, "if we go to look at the most respected *maffiosi* the only names that we find are the Licatas, Cusumano, the Di Cristinas . . . in other words, precisely those who were most effective in the fighting of 1860, those who were the most loyal and devoted to the intelligent party,"[36] that is, to the liberal aristocracy. In contrast with what the duke says, the (reciprocal) loyalty, the network of patronage, did not break in 1860.

NETWORK AND ORGANIZATION

Caltanissetta Province, 1861. Don Giuseppe Lumia, the former mayor of Montedoro, owned and operated "in economia" (meaning the owner also operated the mine himself) a sulphur mine. He employed numerous laborers, including some from the neighboring town of Sutera. One day, as he was traveling to Sutera to hire more laborers, two of his former employees, with whom he had quarreled over wages, saw him as he passed by. One of these two laborers was widely known by the eloquent nickname "lu ringhiu" ("the snarl"). Just outside the town, the pair took Don Giuseppe by surprise, murdered him, and left a playing card on his dead body: the five of *aremi* (Sicilian dialect for the suit of coins). A few months later, the two laborers were themselves found murdered in the countryside; it was widely rumored that Don Giuseppe Lumia's widow had insisted on revenge.[37]

The Lumia family, along with the Caico family, to which it was bound by close family ties, formed part of the developing "bourgeoisie" in the towns of the Sicilian interior. Over the course of the nineteenth century, in the wake of the tremendous boom in sulphur, the Lumia family had attained rank in the ruling class. It had its beginnings in the rental or sale of state-owned lands. We are talking about a power based on a measured display of prestige and wealth, the sort of display that led the Caico family, during an especially good year in the sulphur business, to pay their employees entirely "in gold" on the Feast of Our Lady of the Rosary. Their power, in order to be exercised, required the entourage of the *campieri*. A romantic description of that entourage was provided by Louise Hamilton, an English girl who married a scion of the family and who had special need for an escort of bodyguards because of her strange custom of taking long rides on horseback through the desolate countryside of the Caltanissetta region. As we know, Don Giuseppe, his wife, and the Lumia-Caico family used the *campieri* primarily to lay down the law among sulphur miners, bandits, and cattle thieves, without being obliged to rely on the law of the state.[38] Here we encounter a great many of the elements and actors that we have considered typical of the Mafia, even if they could all be connected to the more general theme of the exercise of class-based power in the context of large landholdings. If we were to consider the episode involving Don Giuseppe Lumia narrated above from the point of view of the sulphur miners, we could similarly refer to a very primitive form of class struggle, an episode of social banditry. In this episode, it is difficult to distinguish a specific phenomenology, called *mafia,* or, in particular, a path linking it with the Mafia of the present day.

If, instead, we return to Palermo, we will see something emerge more clearly that will allow us to find more-salient links between past and present. Let us begin with a cluster of relationships that extend from the capital toward its vast province, a chain that linked together a number of individuals. For the first link of the chain, we have Antonino Giammona, who seems to have been the leading figure in the Mafia of nineteenth-century Palermo. We will encounter him again time and again in our account, at the command of the *cosca dell'Uditore*— the Uditore Mafia family from the 1870s until the end of the century. Giammona was born in the *borgata,* or outlying suburb, of Passo di Rigano around 1819 and matured in a revolutionary climate. He was "extremely poor" until 1848, but, "dabbling in brigandage—*briganteggiando*—under the banner of the revolution," over time he became a leaseholder of *giardini*, or citrus groves, the owner of land and buildings purchased in the sales of state-owned property in the period following unification, as well as the proprietor of a sheep-farming operation. Around 1875 his worth was estimated to be on the order of 150,000 lire. In a time when suffrage was quite limited, he controlled a bloc of about fifty votes. His career enjoyed a turning point in 1860 when, as a captain in the *Guardia nazionale,* he distinguished himself as one of the protagonists of the "return to order" (*ritorno dell'ordine*) in the hinterland. He took a stand in favor of law and order again in 1866. From this time forward, stated his lawyer, Francesco Gestivo, with a certain indulgent pride, "amidst an absolute vacuum of official public safety," Giammona made use of his "moral authority" to take the helm of a "league of property-owners against the property-less."

> Now in the area around Palermo a sort of *Guardia nazionale* has been formed, and Giammona, like other owners of *giardini, gabellotti,* and others who are in the same walk of life have banded together, and their association has been so successful that there have been no more killings, robberies, usuries. And what has the result been? The result has been that they have earned the hatred of those who were not able to do what they did; and so reports against them, depictions as ruffians, mafiosi, suspicious individuals.[39]

From Giammona, three threads are seen to extend: downward—criminals; toward his peers—the other leaders of the Mafia; and upward—the prominent citizens who protect him and whom he protects. In fact, he could offer "shelter and protection" in his area to various fugitives from the law, but when confronted with an attempt by Francesco Paolo Morana (brother of a member of parliament) and Baron Dionisio Maggio to extort money, he felt no hesitation in carrying out a full-fledged massacre among his unruly guests.[40]

But the thread that led upward from Giammona wound its way in particular to Baron Nicolò Turrisi Colonna, a leading landowner of relatively recent status, forward-thinking and enlightened in the way he ran his businesses, a student of agricultural science, a patriot even before the unification, and thereafter a prominent member of the moderate left wing, as well as a senator, and the mayor of Palermo.[41] Turrisi Colonna constitutes the second link in our chain. As we have seen, the duke of Cesarò named Turrisi Colonna as a reference point for the patriotic mafiosi. In 1860 he commanded the civic national guard (*guardia nazionale cittadina*) in which Giammona served as an officer. In the years that followed, the relationship between Giammona and Turrisi Colonna lasted right up to the letters of appreciation the senator wrote in 1875 on behalf of the Mafia capo who had run afoul of the law for the first time. For that matter, in Castel-buono, the inland village where his father had been a *gabellotto*, Turrisi Colonna made use of outlaws: at least three of his *campieri*, or private guards of farm-land, were mentioned in a list of mafiosi compiled by the subprefecture of Ce-falù. The authorities searched one of his estates in 1874 for a gang of wanted men, though he protested loudly that he felt he had been the victim of political persecution. Following this episode, the prefect Rastelli told Franchetti that he understood that "he would have to leave Palermo . . . because he had made the error of touching the *campieri*" of the senator.[42] A few years later, Domenico Farini, president of the Senate, recalled that in 1876 Members of Parliament Morana and La Porta had told him in private that Turrisi Colonna was the "head of the Mafia."[43]

In 1875, Andrea Guarneri admitted that it might have been a mistake to "base the police on the *maffia*," as was done in 1860 in Palermo. However, he also pointed out that it would have been difficult to do otherwise in a former capital city with a population of 200,000, riven by intense political and social tensions. In situations like that of the territory around Agrigento, where he had been pre-fect in 1860, it was possible instead to establish directly a "police force of the landowners."[44] Other sources also tell us that in the Palermo district of Termini and in the adjoining district of Agrigento, the postrevolutionary return to nor-mality had been achieved at the hands of armed groups under the command of a few prominent citizens, including the Nicolosi family of Lercara and the Guc-cione family of Alia, mayors, landowners, and (the Gucciones) leaseholders of entire latifundist "states" in various areas of the province of Palermo.[45] Here, too, however, the processes of revolutionary mobilization, especially the up-risings of 1860 and 1866, constituted turning points in the lives of such notori-ous brigands as Leone and Valvo, as well as for various mafiosi. The name of Giuseppe Brancato, a physician and the Mafia chieftain of Ventimiglia, harks back to a history of anti-Bourbon conspiracies, especially the insurrection of 1859 in which the Baron Bentivegna lost his life when he was abandoned by his squads, including the one commanded by Brancato himself.[46]

Similarly, Angelo Pugliese, known as Don Peppino il Lombardo (the Lom-bard), the greatest bandit of the years following unification, met up with the insurrection of Palermo in 1860 when it freed him from the prison in which he was serving a life term. In that same prison, he claimed to have met many promi-nent Italian patriots, including Silvio Spaventa and Luigi Settembrini, who tried to convert him to love of country. That may be why he chose to describe himself as a *garibaldino*—or follower of Garibaldi—during the time he was an outlaw. After his escape from prison, he hid out in the Uditore *borgata*, and it was there that he made the acquaintance of a gardener (an operator of the citrus groves) named Giammona, who can probably be identified as the Mafia chieftain himself. This Giammona recommended Don Peppino to a prominent citizen, Angelo Palazzolo, who procured him a position as a *sovrastante* (local superintendent, something more than a *campiere,* or private guard of farmland) with the Guccione family. This marked the beginning of the former life-sentence convict's career as a brigand.[47] The Nicolosi family and the Guccione family were described as being interested parties to Don Peppino's exploits. They obtained comrades and confederates for Don Peppino from their own networks of dependents and followers, who helped to launder the earnings from the economy of brigandage.[48] In exchange, the bandit agreed to keep his hands off their assets and property and to make life difficult for their rivals. Two landowners from Prizzi, Giuseppe Valenza and Luciano D'Angelo, took direct part in the gang's illegal actions in order to increase their own revenues, carry out vendettas, and earn reputations as violent men. In this way, they were able to remain the leaders of the two opposing factions of their native town over the years that followed. It also allowed them to carry on a relationship, occasionally friendly and at other times ferocious, with the small-time criminals of the area.[49] The Guccione family, the Nicolosi family, Valenza, and D'Angelo were all identified in the *propalazione* (confession) made during the preliminary judicial investigation by Don Peppino himself, but later retracted during the trial. All the same, they emerged unscathed from the 1868 trial. In contrast, lengthy sentences were handed down to the core group of outlaws, "a few ragged paupers sent to expiate in prison the crimes that they committed in league with the rich, who went unpunished!" as noted by the royal prosecutor Giuseppe Borsani, future chairman of the Parliamentary Commission of Inquiry of 1875.[50] This marked a major watershed. Right up until the 1920s, in fact, we find the name of the Guccione family at the center of all the debates over complicity between landowner's and brigands, and we will see how Don Peppino's brigand networks would spring back to life in the immediate years that followed, giving rise to Leone's and De Pasquale's bands and engendering other bands right up to the end of the nineteenth century.

The chain, then, has four main links: the Mafia capo Giammona; the brigand chief Angelo Pugliese; the major *gabellotti* Guccione; and the prominent citizen and landowner Turrisi Colonna. They were surrounded by myriad *guardiani* (rural watchmen), thieves, extortionists, brigands, and policemen. There was also a lawyer, of course; in Gestivo's case, the lawyer was also a politician who was responsible for providing an ideological justification for the Mafia. That task was one that Turrisi Colonna chose to turn down; he looked at the world from his elevated point of view. The police chiefs closed, or when necessary, opened their eyes. They could also direct a brigand's flight from the law or prompt the establishment of *cosche,* or Mafia families. This was true, as we will see, of the police chief Albanese, who in turn took his inspiration from the post-1848 model of the notorious chief of the Bourbon police, Maniscalco, who claimed to have administered "with successful results . . . by persuading the Mafia capos to safeguard public security."[51] This network, provincewide in scale, had little in common with the network of loyalties among relatives, clients, and friends, which many social scientists[52] identify with the village *cosca,* the only possible form of mafioso organization.

Even the police, who were naturally inclined to see conspiracies on every hand, wavered and continued to waver at great length between the two ideas of a murderous but informal solidarity, on the one hand, and a single pyramidal structure, on the other. When set in opposition in this manner, those two ideas are both contrived and misleading. The prefect Gioacchino Rasponi spoke of the Mafia in 1874 as "a sort of tacit understanding [which] has no precise rules but which operates in an instinctive and habitual form, so to speak." At the same time, Rasponi referred to a "permanent link" between countryside and city. In particular, he described the degrees of initiation and the hierarchies[53] of an organization that he and his colleague in Trapani, in another feeble attempt to express a slightly different nuance of meaning with a different word, described as *camorra.* As the events of 1848, 1860, and 1866 faded into the past, the Mafia increasingly differed from the type of association that nearly everyone had in mind, a subversive political association ("a criminal class considered with suspicion and aversion by the entire liberal juridical culture").[54] What kind of political context could be imagined for the array of confederates and protectors surrounding Don Peppino il Lombardo, including the partisan of Crispi, Valenza, along with the supporter of the Bourbon regime, Nicolosi? But in terms of organizational models the great upheavals of the Risorgimento were destined to have their influence, however indirectly.

Important evidence is provided by none other than Turrisi Colonna. In an essay that was published in 1864—two years after the play by Mosca and Rizzotto, and one year before the Gualterio report—Turrisi Colonna offers a clear-headed analysis of the problem, beginning from the period of the Risorgimento, which for him, as a liberal and a Sicilian, was not materially different from an analysis of the Bourbon and Neapolitan officials. In fact, without expressing a view either for or against, Turrisi Colonna describes the Bourbon belief in a link between the ruffians and the liberals. With regard to his own views, he states that ever since 1848 the revolution needed anyone capable of bearing arms, and that in 1860 "the entire sect of old thieves was bearing arms . . . ; weapons were in the hands of all the young men who practiced the profession of *guardiani rurali* (rural watchmen or custodians), and of the numerous body of smugglers in the countryside around Palermo."[55] Smuggling was a major element in the Palermo Mafia, as it was for the Neapolitan *camorra*. This harks back to the Palermo regime, which "let such smuggling carry on undisturbed, provided that there were no robberies on the public roads, extortions, or anything of the sort; and the renowned *caporioni* of the *maffia* took this responsibility upon themselves."[56] In this venue, tolerated in the liberal period as well, a series of transactions were carried out among ruffians, businessmen, and the municipal administrations. Smuggling became intertwined with the *guardianìa* (the business of providing custodianship), since the guards could choose whether or not to allow the contraband to pass freely through their *giardini,* or citrus groves. It also fell under the purview of another public corps of the police, that of the *guardie daziarie* (customs police), who were often accused of turning a blind eye to the doings of mafiosi and smugglers.

In Turrisi Colonna's essay, we do not yet see the word "mafia," but crucial importance is attributed to the concept of "sect." The sect was originally made up of cattle thieves, "necessarily including the membership" of smugglers and *guardiani* of Palermo, the *campieri,* and the *gabellotti* of the large landholdings, smugglers and dealers of all kinds. The sect controlled the island, scorned the law, offered protection, and received help.[57] Alongside the word "sect," the baron Turrisi Colonna mentioned other key words: *camorra,* infamy, and humility:

> Humility entails respect and devotion to the sect and the obligation to refrain from any act that could harm its members, directly or indirectly. . . .
> Anyone who has lived for any length of time in the countryside around Palermo knows that often the sect gathers in large assemblies to discuss the behavior of this or that member. . . . The assembly, after hearing all the participants, comes to a decision.[58]

Actually, I doubt that *just anyone* would be likely to know about the operations of these assemblies-qua-courts, which we will encounter again in the course of our history. In addition, I am very much persuaded that Turrisi Colonna must have had first-hand information about them. He depicts himself as an opponent of a government that is incapable of performing its proper function of defending law and order; as a liberal who recalls with a certain fondness the Bourbon companies at arms; as a scholar who views with detachment, as if from without, the events in which he has personally taken part and continues to take part; and as a modern landowner who is obliged to negotiate with criminals on behalf of the higher interests of agricultural production, the first in a long series of theorists of the state of necessity of the ruling class in Sicily.[59] I believe that he was not the chief of the Mafia, but rather the protector of a number of the most important mafiosi, the representative of a social and political group that established a connection with the ruffians and then decided to make use of them even after the revolution.

During the conspiracy of the Risorgimento, there existed a clandestine network inspired by freemasonry through its local version, the *carboneria*. According to Giuseppe Giarrizzo, following 1824, the network of Carbonarist sects had already begun to "lose their cultural or political motivations" and to calcify into "local or parallel power structures."[60] Actually, for the entire period extending from the Restoration to 1866, the rampant diffusion of ordinary and political violence makes it daunting to distinguish clearly among revolutionary mobilization, activities designed to seize control of the management of local power, and mere criminal activities. The entire process can be summarized in the phrase coined by Franchetti—the "democratization of violence"—if we accentuate the political and revolutionary aspect that was absent in Franchetti's analysis. In any case, we should also remain keenly aware of the fact that, in terms of its complexity, substance, and liberating significance, the revolution could not be considered as a mere forerunner of the Mafia. Rather, the Mafia should be considered a by-product of this process, and it appears as such precisely when the revolution ran out of steam, between 1861 and 1866. Similarly, we can say that the mafioso ritual represents a by-product of the rituals of freemasonry or *carboneria*. According to a document dated 1818,[61] the distinction between freemasonry and *carboneria* was the openness of the *carboneria* movement to the lower classes, to the "good craftsman, [to] the honest farmer," perhaps even to the "common riff-raff." The revolutionary military organization in Sicily, as is well known, was not based only on the *Guardia nazionale,* which mobilized according to status and class, because among the various bourgeois and aristocratic factions, which were often openly fighting with one another, both in the villages and in the great melting pot of Palermo, the populace also took arms, and not only the "honest" and "hard-working" citizens. The sworn oaths described in the sources, whereby the populace promised to follow the leadership of the "civil" class without indulging in plunder or thefts, seemed to have been designed intentionally to mobilize the ruffians, while keeping them in rein. After 1861, the ruling class would begin to organize on its own behalf in the context of freemasonry; the ruffians, on the other hand, would reproduce the structures of the sects (factions) in their own fashion.

The earliest description, of which I am aware, of the mafioso oath of membership (which, as we have pointed out, corresponded to the present-day oath of Cosa Nostra in Sicily and America) can be found in a report by the Palermo police on the *cosca* of the Uditore *borgata* commanded by Giammona. The godfather pricks the index finger of the aspiring mafioso, uses the blood that issues from the finger to stain a sacred image, and then burns the image "to symbolize the annihilation" of any member who might think of betrayal.[62] As Nino (Antonino) Recupero has noted, the bloody threats against all traitors, "the blindfolded entrance into a secret room (symbolic of rebirth), the oath sworn with one's own blood and over a flame . . . are a crudely emphasized version of certain aspects of Masonic rituals, adopted precisely by the Carbonari."[63] There were also rites of recognition. A member who meets another member whom he does not know and who belongs to a different group, will complain of an ache in a *scagghiuni* (tooth). There follows an exchange of phrases that serves to identify the *cosca* to which they belong, accompanied by weird theological references: "—Who did they say to worship?—The sun and the moon.—And who was your God?—An *Ariu*.—And to what realm do you belong?—To that of the index finger."[64] The "Grand Orient of Monreale," the local *stoppagghieri cosca*, or clan, for which the police reported rituals identical to those of the Uditore, was also described in the press as a pseudo-lodge that decreed life or death for its members and for its enemies.[65]

We are, then, as Turrisi Colonna would say, in the presence of a sect, or an array of sects sharing the same rituals. This standardization of different organizations that presented themselves as local can be explained with a certain political experience, but also with the house arrest of Ustica and Favignana and with the Palermo prison of the Ucciardone, which constitutes a "University of Crime," or—according to what the Marchese di Rudinì declared in 1866—"a sort of Government"[66] of the *cosche*. It was here, as we shall see, that Salvatore D'Amico, the future *pentito* of the *stoppagghieri*, took his oath and was initiated into the secrets of the organization. Moreover, during the Bourbon period prison was already a meeting place for political and ordinary prisoners, which takes us back to the intersection between criminals and the Risorgimento, as well as the advent of the very concept of mafia, in the play by Rizzotto and Mosca. In the play, a great patriot (perhaps Crispi, in a sense not unlike what had happened to Spaventa in Don Peppino's confession) warned the ruffians to turn their organizing impulses toward good deeds, especially toward founding a mutual aid society.

The Mafia is linked to the far broader phenomenon of popular associationism, which was often sectarian and conspiratorial in its early days. When faced with secret associations such as those of the *posa*, or millers, which used terrorist methods to induce the laborers in Palermo's mills to band together in order to establish monopolistic control over prices and wages, the Palermo *questura* (police administration)—in actual reality, and not in the playacting done for public consumption—encouraged them to set up a mutual aid society. Moreover, on more than one occasion, in the years that followed, the *cosche* would become intertwined with more formally established institutions, typical of a growing tendency to form social and civic associations, that is, public associationism: the Fasci Siciliani, the agricultural cooperatives (and not to mention, in the United States, labor unions). In some cases, more traditional organizations, such as the confraternities, played a role. But the geographic area in which a "popular" Mafia can apparently be identified is the area around Agrigento and Caltanissetta, where the context of large landholdings overlaps with the sulphur-mining industry, the people running the mines, and, as noted earlier, the sulphur miners themselves.

The nineteenth-century *picconiere* (pickwielder, literally, a manual laborer; ditchdigger), moreover, was not so much a member of the proletariat, subject to a corporate discipline and hierarchy, as he was a crew chief (*capo-ciurma*) who subcontracted (in some cases, in partnership with others) the exploitation of a tunnel, with *aiutanti e carusi* (assistants and apprentices) working under him. For this very small-scale entrepreneur, the capacity for violence was a professional attribute. "Murder in the workplace . . . was itself an occupational hazard": indeed, it was used to contain rivalries among the "parties" that were competing to work the mineral deposits.[67] Sulphur miners constituted a majority of the membership of the *Fratellanza*, or "brotherhood," of Favara, placed under judicial investigation as a *cosca mafiosa*, or Mafia family, in 1885. It, too, was distinguished by the rituals found in the Uditore and in Monreale, and here they were described by an investigating magistrate as a "strange mixture of mysticism and cabala, holy concepts and empty vulgarity."[68] Significantly, it was in this area around Agrigento that Luigi Pirandello was to set a 1910 novella about a peasant league that made use of cattle theft—with the customary *componenda*, or negotiation, for the return of the loot—as a tool used in salary negotiations with the large landowners. It seems like an application of Eric Hobsbawm's theory of the Mafia as a primitive form of class struggle. But the Sicilian author Pirandello displays a slightly greater sense of realism than Hobsbawm, the English historian. In Pirandello's view, there was no socialist salvation destined to redeem these archaic mechanisms in the context of the dawning of modernity. On the contrary—with the waning of any political motivation and the self-dissolution of the *Lega*, or "league"—the mafioso mechanism took hold and wound up operating under its own power, in keeping with its own logic of protection-qua-extortion.[69]

The *Fratellanza* case shows that the organizational models of the Mafia were already spreading on an interprovincial scale in the years between the 1870s and the 1880s. Favara and other villages of the Agrigento area would also constitute centers for diffusing the phenomenon in the future, even if they remained—in my view—less important than the villages around Palermo and the city of Palermo itself. In the sulphur-mining area, we also find a "lower" social characterization of the mafiosi than is found elsewhere. It is meaningful that Franchetti should have developed the definition "ruffians of the middle class," precisely with reference to the social condition or status of the Mafia chiefs of the Palermo area, in part with reference to their greater ability to operate as intermediaries between common criminals and the upper classes. In the Palermo area, because of the "extraordinary clustering" of *cosche*, that is, their ability to cover the territory and operate in reciprocal relationships, we can already identify the structures of a horizontal-type organization, defined by the system of Mafia affiliations. This does not exclude, indeed it entails, a series of vertical links connecting the mafiosi to the landowners, the underworld to the overworld, and it binds together subjects of diverse social standing, ineluctably marked by the principles of authority and class power.

In conclusion, from Palermo, the aristocracy of the nineteenth century, a more-or-less new class, dominated the large landholdings of western Sicily and controlled the market of leases. Yet in the towns and the outlying areas of the capital itself, that class was obliged to take into account the vast underworld of the ruffians. In the aftermath of unification, there developed a clear contrast—a contrast that later took root in the general understanding of the status quo—between the eastern and the western sections of the island, the eastern being "peaceful," and the western "criminal": the bulk of the western sections was represented by the province of Palermo, which, in 1871, supplied 1,265 of Sicily's total of 1,877 fugitives from justice.[70] Palermo was the "city of the revolution," but it was also a city where—according to the malicious interpretation of Bourbon functionaries—"there live 40,000 proletarians, whose survival depends on chance or on the whims of the powerful."[71] These "powerful" forces attempted to manage the revolutionary process and to negotiate their own positions in the new state—without, and often in defiance of Catania or Messina, and also without, and often in defiance of the eastern section. As was evident in the revolts of 1820–1821, but also in the uprising of 1866, Palermo came to personify the interests of the Sicilian nation. The relationship between ruffians and the large landowners of Palermo was the decisive element, in any historical characterization of the origins of the Mafia, in situating the Mafia in the western section of the island.

PUBLIC ORDER OR PUBLIC DISORDER?

Over a period of 130 years, the Mafia has often been described as an "extraordinary" problem. This is an error of perspective. Viewed as a whole, the various allegedly extraordinary events fit together into a cyclical pattern, made up of politico-criminal emergencies during the course of which the Mafia emerges from its subterranean dimension and presents itself to the view of one and all.

The first of these emergencies occurred in 1875, when the government asked the Italian parliament to approve a bill that would allow the executive branch, whenever it saw the need, to apply "extraordinary measures for the public safety"[72] at times and in areas especially plagued by crime "or where there existed associations of brigands, *malandrini* (bandits and criminals), stabbers, *camorristi, maffiosi.*" In practical terms, only Sicily was discussed. The bill would have allowed the government to order, without the approval of the judicial authorities, arrests of suspects, searches in homes, and the dissolution of associations that might not fit into the precise prescriptions of the body of the law. Moreover, after a certain period of time, those arrested could be handed over to the ordinary courts of law or ordered into house arrest, by verdict of a special commission.

The prime minister, Marco Minghetti, appeared before the Italian parliament in an especially weak position. The proposed law had already been rejected in committee, with a report from the leader of the left-wing opposition, Agostino Depretis, but it was proposed again with practically no modifications. The documentation (which was published) does provide a clear depiction of the gravity of the situation in terms of public safety. Although the military authorities favored the proposed solution, the prefects expressed misgivings, and among them Rasponi, the *primus inter pares,* or first among equals, among the officeholders in Palermo, actually wound up submitting his resignation in protest. The only one who showed any enthusiasm for the idea was the prefect of Caltanissetta, Fortuzzi, who, as mentioned earlier, blamed political liberty itself for the 550 murders committed in the province of Palermo, "as many as might result from a particularly bloody battle, but one that took place every year." Fortuzzi lingered on the subject of the "moral perversion of this populace that considers the ideas of justice, honesty, and honor as so many dead letters, this populace that is therefore predatory, violent, and superstitious":[73] an astonishing example of a prefect (according to the opposition parliamentarians) accustomed to "slandering en masse the populace of which he is in charge."[74] From the point of view of many Sicilians, he was only the latest of the many "continental" (meaning from the mainland of Italy) public officials who had been holding forth since 1861 about how unworthy Sicily (or the Mezzogiorno, as southern Italy was called) was of becoming part of modern civilization. The minister of the interior, Girolamo Cantelli, hobbled by fear of wounding Sicilian sensibilities, remained undecided whether to institute a general provision or one specifically limited to Sicily, and so he wound up adopting a solution that seemed certain to make everyone unhappy. The government at large, however, used none of the minister's prudence when it decided to take as a model the English approach in Ireland, showing a very odd conception of national unity amidst the parliament's protests.

It was in vain that the Imolese count, Giovanni Codronchi, one of Minghetti's followers, urged a distinction between "the political question" and "the question of public safety," since he lacked credibility, having been the chief proponent of the repressive approach that just a few months previously had led to the arrests of Republicans at Villa Ruffi. Given the drop in the number of crimes in the 1874–1875 period (following the peak in 1871–1872), there was ample fodder for the arguments of those who insisted that the truly exceptional nature of the situation in Sicily was to be found in the forty members (of a total of forty-eight members from Sicily) elected to parliament for the left-wing opposition. The direct opposition between the Italian government and the Sicilian parliamentary delegation suggests a settling of accounts from a lingering dispute that first began in 1861 with the brutal liquidation of the Garibaldi-led uprising and marginalization of the democratic forces. It was Francesco Crispi, the most authoritative leader of that undertaking, who exclaimed: "Be certain of this: we are still experiencing the consequences of a revolution that was never laid to rest, that was never quenched in the hearts of the Sicilians." For his part, Ferrari said: "I would like to know what memories Palermo has of the General Govone who deprived the city of water, and of the Legislature that supported General Govone. The question is political, and politics penetrates everywhere."[75]

The experience of a fifteen-year military government, the denial of legal rights, and "Piedmontese" administrations therefore gave the opposition every reason to believe that the draft law of 1875 represented nothing other than one final and cynical attempt to force an entirely antigovernmental Sicily to "knuckle under." On the left it was noted that from 1860 on, the island had been under special rule, with only a few brief intervals. Furthermore, given the fight against crime, the Law on Public Safety of 1871, requested by none other than Giacomo Medici, already gave broad powers to the government because it facilitated the special security regimen of *ammonizione*, which was intended to counterbalance the alleged unreliability of the island's courts and, especially, juries. For that matter, the Depretis Commission observed that too often this tool (i.e., *ammonizione*) was used in place of the courts of law. "The verdict . . . of public opinion, pronounced and often guessed at behind closed doors by agents of the government, cannot serve as the foundation for a judgment or the justification for a sentence."[76] The *ammonizione* was based on a purely police mentality, even though from 1865 on, it could only be imposed by *pretori* (police courts).[77] It could entail a legal conviction because violation of its provisions could be punished with a prison term or house arrest. Note, for instance, the way in which the instructions that Medici provided to his underlings at the time accentuated the basically antijuridical nature of a vicious cycle, based purely on the suspect's reputation and the public official's whim:

> Since it is a violation of [the special security regimen of] *ammonizione* for the person so warned to continue arousing suspicion, possessing an evil reputation, and that entire set of circumstances that gave rise to the report in the first place, it will be sufficient, in order to catch them in violation, to surprise them in an act or situation that is such as to revive the suspicions against them.[78]

The numerous clashes between the two state powers were also the product of the magistracy's legitimate caution with respect to political trials, which casts a different light on the accusations of leniency leveled by *questori*, prefects, and military commanders on the question of *malandrinaggio* (or brigandage). As early as 1865, the Catanian patriot Gabriele Carnazza had resigned the magistracy to defend a few local leaders in the pro-Bourbon party from what was clearly an infamous attempt to frame them.[79] This helped to prove that an alliance between the "red" and the "black" (or the left and the right) could more easily take the form of a defense of threatened liberties, rather than culminate in the possibility of insurrection which was feared (or devoutly wished for?) on the right. The left-wing Neapolitan member of parliament Diego Tajani treated this theme in the debate of 1875. Using a rich array of details, he described the differences that he had experienced between 1868 and 1872, when he served as royal prosecutor in Palermo, dealing with the prefect general Medici and the police chief Albanese: "One day the priests, the reactionaries, and the members of the independence movement are conspiring together and are ready to launch an attack; a week passes, and no one has ever heard of conspirators, reactionaries, or priests; one day the brigands are swarming over the countryside, and practically pounding at the city gates; the next day no one mentions brigands at all."[80] Tajani went on to describe various abuses: the misuse of the special security regimen of *ammonizione* in order to intimidate the opposition, the protection of criminals and their release from judicial control, or else arbitrary detentions and arrests even after official acquittal in a court of law. Only someone who "knew absolutely nothing about all these things" might have considered voting the government bill into law.[81]

Considering these prior abuses, one might well wonder about what grounds the government had to demand the concession of special powers and what assurance the government offered that it would not use them for political ends. Fortuzzi, leader of the prefectorial extremism, was one example of the danger of manipulating criminal issues, as seen in the case of Baron Angelo Varisano, an old follower of Mazzini who faced charges of *manutengolismo,* or abetting of the Mafia, only to be acquitted after a groundswell of public indignation throughout the province, a groundswell in which the young Napoleone Colajanni participated.[82] The measures passed by a very narrow margin, amidst a crescendo of outrage that was stilled in Sicily only with the collapse of the Minghetti government in March 1876.

In response to the thousands of questions raised by the great conflict between the right and the left, which also amounted to a bitter regionalist debate, a Parliamentary Commission of Inquiry into the "social and economic conditions of Sicily" was established and was chaired by Giuseppe Borsani.[83] Thus, although political considerations seem to have outweighed criminal aspects throughout the debate, it does offer extremely valuable documentary material that casts a first light on the phenomenon of the Mafia. Alongside the minutes of the parliamentary debate, and the abundance of documentation attached in regard to presentation of the law on public safety, there were a great number of interviews and the final report of the Commission of Inquiry over the signature of Romualdo Bonfadini. At the same time, in open contrast with that report, Franchetti and Sonnino published the volumes that emerged from their "private" investigation, while other essays and books were published on the subject as well. We should mention in particular Pasquale Villari's two *Lettere Meridionali* on the *camorra* and the *mafia.*[84] In the course of two short years, 1875–1876, we finally find full recognition of what the Mafia is and its role in the politics, economics, and society of the new Sicily and the new Italy.

Let us begin with the findings of the Bonfadini report. What is useful is not so much the unimaginative definition of mafia as an "instinctive, brutal, self-interested solidarity, which brings together, to the detriment of the State, the Law, and the regulatory institutions, all those individuals and those strata of society that choose to earn their livings and their luxuries from violence, rather than from hard work," but rather the distinction among "three types" of threats: a general predisposition to "crimes of blood" found throughout the island; "the *malandrinaggio* in the countryside," practiced especially in the provinces of Agrigento, Caltanissetta, and Palermo; and the "associations of criminals," which were "especially common" in Palermo.[85]

A few Sicilian intellectuals tried to fob off banditry as an imported phenomenon, using the pretext of the Calabrian origins of the first and the most famous postunification brigand, Angelo Pugliese, known as Don Peppino il Lombardo, who was captured and tried in 1868. Many of the later brigand gangs were splinter groups that had spun off from his original group.[86] In fact, however, banditry has deep historic roots in Sicily as well as elsewhere in the Mezzogiorno. It also shows considerable continuity between the Bourbon period and the postunification period in terms of methods, characteristics, and areas of influence, which extended from the western part of the island to the eastern region only in the surrounding districts. Among those, the most active were the Rocca-Rinaldi group, operating between Cefalù, Mistretta, and Nicosia; the Leone group, between Termini and Cefalù; Capraro–De Pasquale, between Sciacca, Corleone, and Termini; and Vaiana, between Agrigento and Bivona. The Vallelunghese and the Valledolmese groups worked in the areas surrounding the towns—Vallelunga and Valledolmo—after which they were named.[87] The brigand bands were therefore few in number and apparently quite small (three to ten persons), but they swelled "with the arrival of peasants who hurried to join them to take part in a particularly rich piece of plunder and then, after hanging their rifles back on the wall, they would return to their work in the fields." Others, "while not taking direct part in the commission of the crimes, might prepare the instruments in the shadows, conveying messages and reports, guarding and protecting the hideouts, keeping a lookout and standing guard."[88] The brigands moved through areas that were to a greater or lesser degree under the control of the forces of the state, the *guardie a cavallo* (mounted police), and the private militias. They committed robberies, stole cattle, and kidnapped people; they needed contacts who could safeguard or sell their booty and loot and victims. In some areas, they openly swept armed through the countryside; in other areas they carried out their negotiations and laid low. This was the case, for example, of the outlaws commanded by a blacksmith from Favara, a certain Sajeva, who, according to the military authorities, "had come to an understanding, tacit or explicit, with the people of the town of Favara . . . ; their crimes were committed in the townships of Grotte, Racalmuto, and Canicattì, as far away as Licata and Girgenti (Agrigento), but . . . if they ever harmed anyone from Favara, it was only to carry out a vendetta on behalf of Tom, Dick, or Harry, i.e., some unspecified person."[89]

Thus, "in contrast with Neapolitan"—that is, mainland southern—brigandage, the Sicilian variety "did not exist on its own"[90] but necessarily existed in a dense network of relationships among outlaws and the population at large, which could be variously interpreted as open complicity, as relationships of dependency and interest, or merely the relations of good neighbors, either as an indicator of caution or terror—a welter of relationships that the authorities described, taken all together, as *manutengolismo,* or abetting of the Mafia. *Manutengoli* (or abettors) might be both the individuals who provided logistical support to the bands and received benefits therefrom, or the poor peasants who were forced to give shelter to the bandits or who might simply be reluctant to provide information to the *forza* (slang for police—*translator's note*). *Manutengoli* might be prominent citizens, landowners who maintained relationships with ruffians out of a justified fear for their lives or their belongings, out of cowardice, or in order to demonstrate that the source of their authority lay far above the law that governed ordinary men. The elements of the exchange were universally known: the prominent citizen would shelter the bandit in his farms, he would provide him with information and supplies, or in any case ensure that his employees or his leaseholders supplied information and supplies to him. In exchange, the bandit would refrain from hostile acts toward the family members, the clients, and the interests of protector-protectee. Indeed, by performing hostile acts against the prominent citizens' adversaries, he would perform a welcome service to those prominent citizens (directly or indirectly). As at Favara, it might happen that the brigands would intervene in municipal conflicts as the armed force working on behalf of one of the factions. For instance, in the feud between two prominent families of Partinico, the Scalia family made use of the brigand Nobile to kill a son of the notary Cannizzo; Cannizzo, in turn, hired killers from Monreale in order to take his revenge.[91]

In its vagueness, the word *manutengolismo,* or abetting of the Mafia, reflects the nature of events and relationships, the countless ambiguities of an environment that made it difficult to distinguish between coercion and free choice. Prefects, *questori* (administrative directors of the district police), *delegati di PS* (or police inspectors), soldiers, and officials at both low and higher levels from the period of the right wing, all accused the landowners of cowardice, if not of actual complicity. The left wing and a considerable swath of public opinion turned the accusation around, leveling it at the authorities themselves, noting that they had been incapable of safeguarding the most basic rights and had indeed criminalized the victims of extortions and intimidations. To combat both the Mafia and brigandage, many called for armed self-defense among the landowners, who were of considerable significance to a class-based state that had recently been founded and had an uncertain future. Medals and praise were showered on those who, "armed to the teeth," went in pursuit of the bandits, as in an episode in 1873 that involved the Matrona brothers of Racalmuto.[92] Unrealistic hopes were placed in the military forces fielded by the large landowners, as revealed by the words of an official from the mainland who stated that "if Sicily were obliged to defend itself against a foreign invader, it could assemble an army of men perfectly armed for mountain warfare, with breech-loading rifles and double-barreled shotguns, and all of them crack shots."[93]

Clearly, however, the logistics of private self-defense entailed the same negotiations between *malandrini* (criminals) and landowners, as one powerful entity to another, that constitute one of the crucial aspects of the question.

> The antibrigand option (*opzione antibrigantesca*) for the local prominent citizens [wrote Mangiameli] became a major test of loyalty to the State. . . . And yet acknowledgment of the state's monopoly on violence is merely theoretical both on the part of the elites, and on the part of the government functionaries themselves: the state demands and appreciates involvement in the antibrigand operations, and therefore invites an armed vigilance that in point of fact reproduces the problem of a diverse array of sources of power whose legitimacy also depends on the use of violence.[94]

The idea of the sovereignty of the law made only halting progress, encountering obstacles in the form of the spread of private forces and the same cyclical theorization and practice of extraordinary governments. Moreover, the very same officials who were willing to request freedom-crushing measures against criminals were also willing to make nonchalant use of the same criminals, namely, the Mafia, as an instrument of "local government."

This was the observation Tajani made in the parliament and hurled into the face of Italian public opinion, provoking an enormous uproar, greater than that triggered by the speeches of the leaders of the left, Crispi and Depretis. Members of the opposition, using a certain amount of rhetoric and displays of indignation over the slandering of Sicily, focused on the illegality of the government's actions and more or less overlooked the Mafia. In contrast, Tajani openly admitted that in Palermo especially, but also in Agrigento and Trapani, to deny the existence of the Mafia was like trying to "deny the existence of the sun" and that the Mafia was something "that you could see, you could feel, you could touch":

> There, crime is nothing more than an ongoing negotiation, an extortion note is written that says: I could burn all your crops, your vineyards, I won't burn them, but give me something that corresponds to your wealth. There is a kidnapping, with the same mechanism: I won't kill you, but give me a certain amount and you will remain unharmed. You can see *capoccia* (chiefs) of the Mafia who take up a stance in the middle of an estate and tell you: I assure you that there will be no thefts, but give me a certain percentage of your harvests.[95]

Transactions, then, were between landowners and mafiosi, and also between mafiosi, outlaws, and the authorities. Chief among these latter transactions was that of providing the brigands with safe-conduct passes so that they could eliminate other brigands in whatever way necessary. This system was frequently used during Medici's tenure and often with disastrous results, as in the case of the bandit mentioned earlier, Di Pasquale, "whom the police, with the *best* of intentions, *tossed* into the midst of civil society,"[96] and who constituted one of the most serious threats to law and order in the 1870s. According to Tajani (and many confirm his statement), the authorities had already started down this dubious path immediately following 1866, when the ineptitude of the police chief Pinna, produced by the "usual ignorance of local conditions," had triggered an uprising. Medici had then named Albanese as police chief; as we know, Albanese was an admirer of Salvatore Maniscalco, the notorious Bourbon chief of police after 1848. Following that model, Albanese had, among other things, secured the cooperation of a certain Salvatore Marino from Monreale, "a dreadful individual, who . . . had relationships with four or five false Republicans on the one hand and with the clerical party on the other, and at the same time served as one of the leading secret agents working for the police." Indeed, in 1869, Marino provided the accurate information that led to Mazzini's arrest as he stepped off the boat in Palermo.[97] But the connivance between revolutionaries and the police, between guards and thieves, went much further than that. The following year, the efforts of the district attorney, along with his own private group of investigators and possibly the Carabinieri, led to the discovery of a gang that had carried out daring and spectacular thefts, with the direct involvement not only of Marino, but also of various police officers, including a personal aide to the immediate cabinet of the *questore* (administrative director of the district police), a certain Ciotti at whose home a portion of the loot was recovered.

The involvement of the police force in criminal activities was common practice, especially in the case of *militi a cavallo*—militiamen or soldiers on horseback. Like the *guardie rurali* (rural guards) of the townships, the *militi a cavallo* were obliged to reimburse, up to a certain sum, any losses incurred by landowners through thefts in their jurisdiction; they therefore had a strong interest in either preventing thefts or, if possible, ameliorating the damage. There was less interest in capturing the thieves, especially if they could be encouraged to decamp to other jurisdictions outside of the militiamen's jurisdiction. The reader should note the similarities with the state, municipal, and private watchmen, who all performed their institutionally prescribed responsibilities through an ongoing process of negotiation with criminals. Indeed, these guardians were also criminals themselves, people with prior convictions—as

Albanese confessed nonchalantly—who "although they were also abettors [they had] here and there affiliations and therefore [commanded] respect."[98] Their position in the network of relationships among institutions, landowners, and criminals varied from case to case, and in many circumstances they were suspected of actually prompting or threatening the crimes.

Beginning with Italian unification, the corps of mounted soldiers or militiamen was repeatedly reorganized, suppressed, and revived. Filippo Cordova and others on the left demanded that it be abolished, while the right wanted it to be reformed. Among the shortcomings of the institution and its usefulness given the inefficiency of the Carabinieri, police agents, and the army, Bonfadini took his position, pointing out that the greatest successes in the fight against banditry had been the work of the militiamen:

> The *milite a cavallo* (militiaman or soldier on horseback) . . . represents, in the current phase of public feeling, the only force capable of breaking through that layer of mistrust that exists between the populace and the authorities. The militiaman is not from the mainland, he does not embody odious functions . . . he does not lend his vested authority to fiscal confiscations. The information that it would take a Carabiniere *brigadiere* (a rank corresponding to sergeant—*translator's note*) a week to obtain, and that a Bersagliere captain might never obtain, a militiaman can gather in fifteen minutes of private conversation with the housewives and matrons of his village or with the tipplers at the local tavern.[99]

This description is quite saccharine, inasmuch as the soldiers or militiamen did not learn what they knew from matrons and tipplers, but from bandits and *campieri,* or private guards of farmland. And it is difficult to make clear distinctions between public safety and private security: Pietro Landolina, baron of Rigilifi, for example, boasted that he had once prevented the kidnapping of the Baron Sgadari through information supplied to him by a mysterious *Signor A.* and through Landolina's ability to mobilize soldiers under the command of a great friend of his; on a second occasion, he had been foiled in a comparable attempt by the thick-headed interference of none other than Fortuzzi.[100] The soldiers or militiamen could therefore calibrate the efficacy of their efforts, in accordance with pressure from political (the prefect) or social powers (the landowners) for the capture of a bandit or for the protection of a target. The absence of strong opposition also formed part of the system of relationships linking landowners, bandits, and *guardiani* (rural watchmen). It happened in Misilmeri in 1874 that, when the *corpo delle guardie campestri,* or corps of rural and agricultural police, was disbanded, the crime rate plummeted, but in general, the guards warded off such occurrences by protecting the members of the faction that ran the government of a town, while declaring open season on the members of the opposing faction.

This is what was happening in Monreale, where it was openly stated that crimes were being committed with the approval of a certain Lo Biundo, the commander of the *Guardia nazionale,* and of a clique composed of persons occupying strategic positions for the defense of "law and order." In 1869, two fugitives from the law declared that they were willing to denounce what was going on; but before they could be interviewed by judicial authorities, they were killed in an ambush, apparently at the hands of Lo Biundo and his men. In agreement with Tajani, the *pretore,* or police magistrate, Salvatore Barraco, began investigating them as persons under suspicion, but he was summoned for a meeting with Albanese and asked not to pursue that line of inquiry because the two men who had been killed were "extreme ruffians," and so "considerations of public safety had led the authorities to order that they be killed."[101] This episode led to a warrant for the arrest of the *questore* (administrative director of the district police) for ordering a murder, and his acquittal, but only for inadequate evidence, as well as the resignation of the prosecuting attorney, who later, in the debate of 1875, would denounce these connections between the Mafia and public authority. The *questura* (police administration) authorized the activities of individuals such as Lo Biundo, and when they went too far, "called them *caporioni* and said: 'All right now, enough is enough, keep your promises.'"[102] Leaving aside the question of whether they were found guilty and sentenced to prison, a very solid thread linked Lo Biundo, Marino, Ciotti, Albanese, and Medici.

Even before Tajani's speech, Rasponi judged that the system that had "endured in Palermo from Maniscalco to the *questore* (administrative director of the district police) Albanese" now "absolutely [had to be] abandoned." He claimed that when Minister Cantelli ordered him to take over the prefecture of Palermo, Cantelli had entrusted to him the task of restoring the police force there to the standards of "civilized peoples," that is, to eliminate the *maffioso* elements.[103] Was the Mafia a sort of "secret police"? This term was used. The phrases "Mafia ufficiale" and "alta Mafia" ("official Mafia" and "high Mafia") reveal the widespread perception of a link to purposes of maintaining law and order, or at least controlling the existing disorder, that had marked the fifteen years of right-wing government.

It has been stated by certain newspapers that we were opposed to the extraordinary law because we were friends to the Mafia, or in other words, that we were abettors—said Cordova— . . . Well, gentlemen of the

Government, the center of the Mafia lies in the ranks of your law enforcement institutions, and, of course, without knowing it, you yourselves are the abettors.[104]

UNDER FRANCHETTI'S LENS

The Commission of Inquiry chaired by Borsani and Bonfadini, though controlled by moderates, was not sufficient to cancel out the defeat that the right had suffered in 1875. The Commission aimed at healing the internal divisions of the ruling class, focusing on the demands of the Sicilian left, which wanted to discuss ports, railroads, and the requirements of a society experiencing considerable economic progress.[105] The subjects of *malandrinaggio*, the Mafia, and the police and judicial systems remained the focus of public attention, but the wealth of documentation assembled was not published, and Bonfadini's report constituted a fairly unassuming venue for that array of material.

The opinions expressed in 1875 by right-wing public officials remained undefended and apparently undefendable; the compact opposition of the *classe "d'ordine"* (literally, the class in favor of law and order) to measures designed to ensure law and order in and of itself seemed to constitute a condemnation. The response, rather than coming from any official inquiry, emanated from the "private" investigation carried out by two young Tuscan intellectuals, Leopoldo Franchetti and Sidney Sonnino. These right-wing sympathizers were convinced that in the wake of the inevitable defeat of Minghetti's government, it was necessary to reframe matters conceptually. They were, moreover, convinced that it was possible to prove "scientifically" that the Sicilian ruling class was absolutely inadequate and that therefore the same was true of the southern left wing that through its victory at the polls in 1874 had poised itself to govern the nation. Sonnino explored the condition of the peasants, criticized the agricultural contracts as unfair, and proposed the Tuscan institution of *mezzadria* (sharecropping) as the only alternative certain to reduce the level of violence and conflict in relations among the classes.[106] Franchetti did not specifically examine the problem of the Mafia, but instead discussed the general problems of local politics and administration, of a ruling class accustomed to considering institutions as tools for bullying, incapable of rising to the modern understanding of the public weal or commonwealth in which the exercise of power is filtered through the impersonal institution of the law, and the selfishness of the upper classes is tempered by a paternalistic concern for the interests of the subordinate classes. Given the belated and incomplete way in which Sicily emerged from feudalism, the island was truly unable to adopt such a conception wholeheartedly, even though it was formally in place from 1860 on, with the imposition of a juridical ordering deriving from a higher level of historical evolution: hence the reciprocal functionality between the two themes—political and institutional on the one hand, and economic and social on the other, in the volumes of the *Inchiesta* (Inquiry).

The term *mafia*—Franchetti declared—found a class of violent men and ruffians ready for it, looking for nothing so much as a noun that could describe them, and who, by their special character and importance in Sicilian society, had earned the right to a different name than that given vulgar criminals in other lands.[107]

The term, however, does not represent a "complete social phenomenon," but only the "partial manifestation" of a more general cultural manifestation, that is, "*mafioso* behavior," the true "manner of being of [this] society." In linking the adjective *mafioso* not necessarily to a criminal, but to any ordinary individual who wishes to "ensure that his rights are respected, regardless of the means utilized to achieve this end," the young Tuscan scholar was simply relying on the general understanding of the term in Sicily, which was "the ultimate authority on this subject." Consider, in fact, the Marchese di Rudinì, who in this same period made a distinction between one or more criminal and "malignant" *mafias* and a "benign *maffia*, . . . a spirit of bravado, that unidentifiable determination not to be put upon," which is thought to be a common heritage of all Sicilians.[108] Pitrè, for his part, reduced the Mafia to an "intolerance" of "arrogance from others" and mischievously allowed the topic to wander away from the specifically criminal aspect and toward the notion of a more diffuse culture, which was, moreover, viewed quite favorably. Basically, however, the adjective "benign" employed by Rudinì also betrays an attempt to water down the relationship between the general condition of the island of Sicily and the existence of mafioso organizations, even though in the 1860s both Rudinì on the right and Turrisi Colonna on the left had placed their existence at the center of the picture. Clearly, the harsh clash of 1875, or else improved relations between the ruling class and the criminals, led to this (instrumental?) manipulation of the analysis, to the condensation of what Pezzino called the Mafia "paradigm."

In Palermo, someone went so far as to tell Franchetti that he himself was a mafioso, in the sense of a man with a strong self-awareness. I learned this from Franchetti's travel notes, which were recently published.[109] These notes cast light on many aspects, particularly on the fact that the "opinion of the Sicilians" that he had gathered was not merely the views of the ruling class—which appears obvious—but to a large extent was the opinion of the Mafia itself—that is, of the characters who were most directly in collusion with the Mafia. During their travels toward the interior of the island, the two Tuscan gentlemen,

Leopoldo Franchetti and Sidney Sonnino, spoke in Alia with Guccione and at Valledolmo with Runfola—that is, with the two most important *gabellotti* abettors. Both had much to say about the inadequacy of public safety and about the relations between the Mafia and brigands. In Palermo, Raffaele Palizzolo, the parliamentarian who, as we will see, was at the heart of the closest relationships between the Mafia and politics, confessed that he had no problems with brigands in his lands near Alia, thanks to the good relations maintained by "his brother." He boasted of his friendship with Medici, and he described Albanese as a scoundrel. He, and everyone else who was interviewed, considered Albanese responsible for Tajani's accusations.[110] But the chief source for the inquiry was the lawyer Gestivo, whom we have already seen to be an apologist for Giammona. Gestivo described Albanese as a mafioso, but Medici as merely dishonest. Gestivo placed the activities of the two men in the more general context of postunification history, beginning with the assassination of Corrao and continuing on to the uprisings of 1866, which he considered the matrix of all the government's illegal behavior. Gestivo was far less emphatic in his defense of Giammona than he had been in his statements to the Parliamentary Commission. Gestivo said that Giammona was a target for the authorities because he was the chief "elector" (ward heeler) of the left wing in Monreale and because he was an enemy of Licata in the territory of the Conca d'Oro. Here—Gestivo admitted easily—was a fertile profusion of mafioso arrangements for the monopolistic management and operation of both *gabella* (lease and sublease) and *guardianìa* (custodianship), endowed with "*statuto e affigliamento* (statute and affiliation). Many of those in Palermo extend their operations to Termini or at least correspond and have understandings with similar *società* (associations or gangs) in that town."[111] Absolutely valuable and interesting was the depiction of the social origins of the brigands, who came from the middle class, as well as Gestivo's view of the nobility, "the true foundation of the *maffia*." None of this was in contrast with the idea that *gabellotti* and the Mafia served to hinder the landowners' freedom of action.[112] Finally, there was a wholehearted denunciation of the relations between the Nicolosis and Don Peppino il Lombardo, and of the political and judicial conspiracy that succeeded in saving the Nicolosis and condemning il Lombardo.[113]

Clearly, no one denied the existence of the Mafia, in contrast with what a fairly superficial common sense might lead one to expect. Each person provided the travelers with their own interpretation, self-interested to a greater or lesser degree: the Mafia was a harmless cultural code, or else it was a dangerous organization, but encouraged by others, especially by the government. According to the two men from the moderate left, Turrisi and Gestivo, Licata and

Albanese were mafiosi, but not Giammona; the Nicolosi family members (formerly pro-Bourbon and later close to Medici) were abettors, certainly not the landowners who were "forced" to provide assistance to the brigands. This only confirms my idea that from its origins to the present-day *pentiti,* the Mafia has always offered, either directly or through its protectors, an interpretation of itself. Often, implicit in that interpretation was the idea that the absence of the state demanded the organization of a mafia—benevolent, defensive, and protective—in contrast with the evil, lawless, bloody mafia. The picture that emerges in this nineteenth-century phase is rendered even more complex by the remarkable capacity of a Gestivo and—even more—by a Turrisi Colonna to judge from outside, as it were, a phenomenon in which they were instead profoundly coinvolved.

I do not know to what degree Franchetti was aware of the role played by those with whom he was speaking in the Mafia phenomenon, which he was asking them to interpret for him.[114] Certainly, Franchetti the traveler was fully aware of the instrumental aspect of each analysis that was proffered. Hence he believed that, in the Sicilian context, morality and law could only be based on force. In opposition, another force might well arise, but inevitably linked to individuals, factions, or clientelism. And so he adopted the thesis that he was being offered, whereby the essence of the Mafia is a form of behavior but devoid of the customary indulgence toward the supposedly benign form of that behavior. And so his reasoning takes on its extremely personal character. Assuming something of the structure of a theorem, departing from premises and reaching consequences with great clarity, his reasoning scorned empirical data and proved convincing even when (or perhaps precisely because) it clearly took them to extremes, as in his description of the actions and loyalties of the brigands. This, then, is a fundamental text for all later sociological and anthropological explanations. Moreover, all those explanations remained well under the level of the model, incorporating the idea that there was a *consequential* link between the mafioso cultural background and the phenomenon of the Mafia, but failing to make the necessary *distinction* between the two. For Franchetti, on the other hand, the crucial element was the existence of a "class with its own activities and interests, a social force unto itself,"[115] the criminal class.

In Franchetti's view, the dialectic between mafioso behavior and the Mafia explained the ideological solidarity that linked *malandrini* (criminals) and the populace at large in opposition to the authorities, including that class of property owners (or middle class) that constituted the foundation of strong liberal institutions throughout Europe. Why did Sicilian landowners not rise up in revolt against a state of affairs that, in the final analysis, diminished their power when, at least in appearance, they needed to do no more than to "act in concert for three days running in order to eliminate brigandage?"[116] This was the crucial topic of the debate of 1875. Franchetti's analysis of the "democratization of violence" basically shows that he was perfectly aware that the keys to the question were no longer entirely in the hands of the traditional ruling class. In fact, he focused his analysis on the provinces, on the role that was played in postfeudal and postunification Sicily by a small-town elite that relied on its control of local resources, both economic (state-owned lands and former privately owned estates) and political (national and municipal systems of elections). Concerning these topics, Franchetti wrote with such clarity that his writings constitute a *locus classicus* of the debate over southern Italy, from Turiello to Salvemini. In this context, however, we are in the presence of a generally southern Italian phenomenon, difficult to link directly to the Mafia.[117] On the other hand, what is perhaps a more specific feature of central and western Sicily is the role of certain small-town and village elites in controlling both the *gabella*, or subcontracting of farmland leases, and brigandage.[118] From this fact may emerge a profit-sharing arrangement, a rather more intimate relationship than that of reciprocal protection that links so many landowners, aristocratic or not, to the ruffians. "Great fortunes are being assembled almost in the public eye with *manutengolismo*, or abetting of the Mafia, and by taking part in cattle theft,"[119] noted Franchetti, without mentioning the names of those who were his sources, the Gucciones and the Runfolas, or even the Nicolosis, members of this ruling class in the fullest sense, at the level of both town and province. As Mangiameli now confirms,[120] this left the pages of criminal activities to reappear in the pages of political history as an interlocutor of General Medici or, perhaps, the opposition.

The relationships that Franchetti was trying to analyze were not those linking a puppet with its puppeteer. It was true not only of the aristocrats of Palermo, but also of the prominent citizens of the countryside, who were taking the aristocrats' place in the ownership and working of the land. Even among them the great abettors identified as the executive leadership of the Mafia could only successfully perform their functions provided that they preserved a proper relationship with the hot-tempered, violent society in which they were trying to operate. We thus see a series of social powers—that of the prince of Sant'Elia, that of the Gucciones, that of the Valenzas, that of Don Peppino il Lombardo, and the more elusive power that resides in each link of the chain of protections on which the brigand relied. These powers were distributed unequally, and they operated in diverse ways, but they were all linked together in a network of negotiations and equilibriums that could not be swept away at the whim of any one of them, even if he were the most powerful of them all.

This articulation of powers was thus clearly defined only in the province of Palermo, where the most spectacular phenomena were in fact concentrated. Franchetti stated that "mafioso behavior" was common in this and other "criminal" provinces, as well as in the "quiet" provinces of eastern Sicily. This was a knotty point in his thesis. The claimed link of causality between a cultural prerequisite and the criminals' abuses of power was in fact called into question by a comparison between the two sections of the island. There was still no explanation of why the ruling class in eastern Sicily had succeeded in "preserving its precious monopoly on force and preventing, until this writing at least, that a number of ruffians who had scrambled up from the lowest classes in society, should succeed in gaining a share in the monopoly, even if it were in the service of that ruling class"[121]—that is, the bravos and cutthroats who had originally been in the service of feudal power and had later gained independence from it. In fact, it would not seem that the landowners showed any superior military skills to their counterparts in the Palermo area.[122] Nor was the author in question willing to posit that in the areas around Siracusa (Syracuse) or Catania a closer connection might have been attained between state and society, or that there might be a social hegemony based on anything other than force. His unwillingness to adduce the socioeconomic differences among the various areas— for instance, the different impacts of the latifundium or large landholding (which was clearly a factor for Sonnino) or the tradition of desmenial cities, as an explanation for the zonal diffusion of the Mafia and brigandage—appears paradoxical in an intellectual who was so keenly interested in the ways in which the feudal system was breaking apart. But the paradox was, in fact, only apparent.

Franchetti was laboring to assemble an intellectual construct that, as is so often the case, is great because it is unilateral, if not actually sectarian. In this construct, the Mafia must appear as the revealing element, alarming and repulsive, of a social context that is entirely unsuited to the liberal principles on which the civil world was founded. He thus reveals himself to be an adherent of the old right wing, which could preach the theory of "administrative decentralization" and self-determination of landowners, while still opting for centralism because it was persuaded of the immaturity of the ruling classes, especially in the south.[123] That immaturity was especially evident in 1874–1875, when these ruling classes made their bid for a full partnership in governing the nation. The Inquiry, therefore, constitutes a variation on a different level of the same elements that appear in the laws on public safety. With this difference: Franchetti did not propose extraordinary "remedies" for Sicily, but instead, not unlike Fortuzzi,[124] a different form of government, clear-eyed and terrible, like every reactionary utopia. He observed that "Sicilians of every class and order . . . are equally incapable of grasping the concept of the Law." They are like sick people who complain but "fail to understand the why and wherefore" of their illness; indeed, they cannot "understand the ultimate purpose of the measures that are taken or need to be taken." The state should not make use of any channel of communication offered by this infected society. It should not recruit its staff from among the Sicilians, at any level. And, of course, "in order to bring Sicily to the condition of a modern people," the government must not, "in any case," take into account the desires, suggestions, and especially, the protests of Sicilian public opinion and elected members of parliament.[125]

These supposed "remedies" ran the risk of leaving the debate at the same point as in June 1875. In Sicily, the *Risposta all'orrendo libello di Leopoldo Franchetti*[126] could hardly be anything other than hostile, not merely because of a conservative spirit or an adherence to the "values" of the mafioso culture, but also because the author's evident political goals appeared to be the culmination of the long process whereby criminality was instrumentalized, a process first established by the Italian right wing. Anyone who began to think about the problem of the Mafia could easily be swept away by the ideological superinfusion of the topic, as was the lot of the *delegato di PS* (or police inspector) Giuseppe Alongi. When describing his thoughts on the matter to a *pretore,* or police magistrate, Alongi found himself being criticized as a follower of Franchetti's "fanciful novel," even though he had never heard of Franchetti.[127] And yet at certain points, Franchetti's analysis comes quite close to Tajani's, such as in their recognition that systems like that used by Albanese tend to undermine the foundation of the credibility of institutions that were already ill adapted. However, the two authors accentuate their views differently, in accordance with their political intentions. Franchetti claimed that there was a collapse of state ethics in the face of the negative influence of the regional collectivity, hence the unrealistically radical proposal of a general quarantine. For Tajani, the Mafia, a dangerous but beatable enemy, became invincible once it was made a tool of the government. Franchetti considered the original infection to have come from society, whereas Tajani saw politics as the origin.

The situation evolved in a direction precisely opposite to that which Franchetti had hoped. The right wing lost power, and its place was taken by a southern, landowning left wing that achieved a preliminary standardization of the ruling class among the various regional sections, transcending all the divisions of the post-Risorgimento period. The Italian south, or Mezzogiorno, finally had its state. In particular, an era was beginning in which the Sicilian political class would enjoy growing influence, reaching its apex from 1887 on, when Francesco Crispi, the leader of Sicilian democracy from the Garibaldi-led invasion, took office as prime minister of Italy. But the turning point, for our story as well, came in 1876 with the foreseeable decision of the new Depretis government not to make use of the law on public safety. Over the course of the year, however, the state of law and order in western Sicily deteriorated still further, with added international complications due to the kidnapping of the English merchant John Forester Rose by Antonino Leone, the heir to Don Peppino il Lombardo in the *Almanach de Gotha* of banditry. At this point, Minister of the Interior Giovanni Francesco Nicotera, one of the leaders of the southern left, summoned one of his trusted men, Antonio Malusardi, to become prefect of Palermo (December 1876).

MAFIOSI AND BANDITTI

At first glance, there is not much difference between the methods used by Malusardi and Gerra, the last right-wing prefect: the special security regimen of *ammonizione* and house arrest, large-scale military operations, illegality, and beatings. "What the Honorable Gerra was hindered from doing on a daily basis by the party, the Commendatore Malusardi was able to do with full freedom,"[128] wrote Giacomo Pagano, a leading member of the right but an admirer of the new prefect, in order to cast light on the inconsistency of the left wing, which suddenly was no longer an inflexible defender of the rules. In fact, there were heavy protests this time as well, and over the course of 1877 they resulted, among other things, in a hundred or so judicial proceedings against police officers, including no fewer than fifteen against the detective Michele Lucchesi, the prefect's right-hand man. These, however, were primarily reactions from local potentates such as the Baron Antonino Li Destri from Gangi, placed in an uncomfortable situation through ordinary police work, rather than any uprising over political and other issues.[129] After the "parliamentary revolution," there was a first cleansing of the toxins that, during the era of right-wing rule, had made it impossible to establish any solidarity around the institutions.

Malusardi was thus able to display his tactical skill by completing the government's counteroffensive, which was already undertaken in the middle of the 1870s and had resulted among other things in the capture, the killing in open combat, or the murder of the bandits Capraro, Valvo, and Di Pasquale. The effectiveness of the operations of the first seven months of 1877 was unprecedented: the elimination of numerous gangs and the killing of five of the most renowned brigands, including Leone.

These results were attained through a strategy of encirclement. As Pagano further noted, given the structure of Sicilian *malandrinaggio*, the chief target "could not be the destruction of the brigands, who would from time to time control the countryside, but the destruction of the network that allowed them to operate."[130] According to the police, this network corresponded to the Mafia proper. We can get a better idea of this by comparing the lists of mafiosi prepared in 1877 for the districts of Cefalù and Termini, including, respectively, 123 and 96 individual files.[131] The alleged abettors in the list were quite numerous and were active in receiving stolen goods and providing logistical support to the bandits, as well as in occasional participation, along with the bandits, in robberies, cattle thefts, and kidnappings. In this sense, the list for Termini, an area of intense gang activity, is clearly defined. It features, for instance, forty accomplices of the brigand Leone, as against the eleven accomplices in the other district. In general terms, the criminal identity of those included in the list is clearer, which we should keep in mind when recalling the possibly arbitrary nature of the compilation of such lists, based on the reputation of the suspect, the good (or bad) intentions of the official, and especially the relationship—of the official himself and the government that he represents—with the local parties: this element was often decisive in the decision of whether to include individuals on the lists or to exclude them. From the accompanying information, we can gather the specific ways in which the alleged mafiosi, during the course of their lives, came into conflict with state repression, and especially with the special security regimen of *ammonizione* and with house arrest, given that the ordinary jurisdiction, on the whole, in any case, had gone AWOL. A majority of those appearing in the police records of Termini had been the targets of public safety or police administrative measures at least once, while among those of Cefalù, less than a quarter had been the targets of such measures, while more than a third of that list, though reputed to be mafioso by "public renown," had never had any run-ins with the law. This might mean that in Cefalù the information was less reliable, or else that the phenomenon was more fully concealed in the nooks and crannies of society, especially considering the greater seriousness of the phenomenon of brigandage in Termini, where in fact the same "public renown" attributed on average more serious crimes to the mafiosi.

Up to this point, we have made reference to the mafiosi considered to be "second rank," distinguished by those compiling the lists from those of the "first rank" with this criterion. The higher level in the criminal hierarchy corresponds precisely to the higher level in the social hierarchy, so that the first rank included landowners and leaseholders, prominent citizens, and professionals of all sorts. The choice is interesting, and it offers a response to the debate over the "Alta Mafia" or the "Mafia in guanti gialli" (kid-glove Mafia), though it is also reasonable to point out that the higher the status of those included in the lists, the greater the likelihood of ulterior political motives in the accusations of *mafiosità* (literally, "mafiosity"). Of course, the social standing of the second ranking tended to vary more broadly, accommodating a range of criminality covering an array of different classes and orders, in which an individual's dangerousness was often evaluated by the compilers in accordance with their supposed capacity to "influence" other members of their own class, or a generic crowd of followers. Only in a few isolated cases do we find ideological descriptions, such as "reactionary" or "internationalist." Here too we encounter landowners and professionals, such as the notary from Cerda, even though it had never been "possible to find and cite criminal actions attributed directly to him," even by insistently questioning the usual *vox populi*, or public opinion.[132] There are, of course, *campieri* and *sovrastanti* qua abettors, in some cases emerging from the ranks of law enforcement, We also find the *guardia municipale*, or municipal police force, with prior convictions, and an *ammonizione*, or the man ordered under house arrest in 1865 and later enrolled as a *milite a cavallo* (militiaman or soldier on horseback), discharged summarily in 1875 as a *manutengolo*, or abettor, but who in the meanwhile had become a landowner and a subcontractor of the consumption tax, also in Cerda.[133] Since sudden wealth seemed to have come to many of those included in the lists, it would appear that crime paid, at least in the eyes of policemen accustomed to consider two specific symptoms as significant: "change in status" and ease of movement through a countryside that was generally unsafe.

Let us take as an example a certain Giuseppe Sansone, also known as *Chiariano*. Sansone was a contractor for public works in Termini Imerese, who, according to our informers, was "a true *mafioso* in the most complete meaning of the word." In 1863 he was arrested and then acquitted on charges of robbery. He later came under suspicion of involvement in a string of kidnappings. Through these activities (or perhaps through other activities), he accumulated "considerable property." "He is often seen traveling through the countryside, in a suspicious manner, where we are assured that he carries on relationships with criminals, some forming part of bands, others operating on their own." His company employed "many suspicious individuals." He concealed fugitives from the law, and he worked with the gangs as a crucial link in the process of recruiting new members. It was said that he had publicly "promised to protect those *mafiosi* who were enjoying successful careers, adding that the *mafia* was great and that he would do his best to establish an association between the gang chief Leone and a certain Matteo Neglia, a dangerous fugitive from justice."[134] Here we are clearly in the presence of "profiteers" and middlemen, who move between the countryside and the small town, between one small town and another, establishing arenas of activity that generally extended beyond the merely local, as was the case with the cheese merchant from Termini who often traveled to Palermo, both for his own business and "to interact with the Mafia capos of that city and perhaps also to lay in a stock of false banknotes that he would then pass in various places."[135] As we will see, printing counterfeit paper money was a major activity of the Palermo Mafia.

If we compare the two lists, we see that the list from the Termini district cast light on a higher sector of the social pyramid: more *borgesi*, fewer peasants and laborers, more merchants (manufacturers, contractors), more city folk (clerks and professionals), even if we cannot fail to notice in the list from Cefalù the eight priests who, once again, raise doubts of instrumentalization, given the hard line that Malusardi took toward the Catholics. The "first rank" accentuated the socially elevated characterization of the Mafia of Termini, since this list (in contrast with the list from Cefalù) included such personages of great status among the notable class as the Guccione, Nicolosi, and Torina brothers.

Malusardi was exerting intense pressure on the Mafia's infrastructure, as is shown by the great number of names belonging to the "second rank" on Termini's list that, over the course of 1877, were either arrested or were forced into hiding. Giuseppe Torina became a fugitive in order to escape the effects of the special security regimen of *ammonizione,* as did Giovanni Nicolosi. According to the *delegato di PS* of Caccamo, Torina and his brother represented "the party of the *alta maffia*"; they were abettors on whose estates Leone "found shelter and any help needed" inasmuch as the members of his gang had been "shepherds or *curatoli* for the Torina brothers." In town, municipal contractors and clerks joined forces with *campieri* and *borgesi* to form a group that clustered loosely around the Torina brothers and controlled the town government. Thus, we find an aggregation of business, local politics, clientelism, and crime. Interestingly, the offensive against the Torina brothers originated in Rome, with Nicotera himself. And surprisingly it was Nicotera, citing "highly secret information," who informed his subordinates in Palermo about who "the capo of the Mafia in Caccamo" was.[136] The objective was not only to prevent contamination of the public institutions, but also to increase the government's bargaining power: the government ordered the special security regimen of *ammonizione* of Giuseppe Torina and threatened to order the special security regimen of *ammonizione* of Raffaele Palizzolo, the two rivals in the electoral district of Caccamo in the rerun of the political elections scheduled for the spring of 1877, after the elections of November 1876 had been invalidated due to fraud:

"Haste is in order"—wrote Malusardi to the subprefect of Termini,

because the indictment that the *pretore*, or police magistrate, will issue for Torina will influence Raffaele Palizzolo to make a public withdrawal of his candidacy . . . since it is the Government's wish that neither one nor the other [neither Torina nor Palizzolo] should be elected to parliament, because the election of either of these men would not be an expression of the legitimate will of the voters, but rather an expression of the [illegible] and the bullying arrogance of the Mafia.[137]

Palizzolo was a member of the Palermo regionalist group, but he had interests in Caccamo, both as a member of the provincial council and as a leaseholder on the former S. Nicola estate, property of the arch-episcopal seminary that was broken up into shares as a result of postunification laws. Palizzolo's contacts in the area were such shady characters as Domenico Nuccio, a small landowner who had already been indicted once for murder, subjected to the special security regimen of *ammonizione* twice, and was an abettor and a "colleague" of Leone, who was prosecuted by Malusardi for kidnapping and who ultimately fled to New York. Here is a description of Palizzolo's arrival in the town of Ventimiglia:

[F]ollowed by some 50 men on horseback . . . , all people who claimed to be good citizens, led by the famous Domenico Nuccio and his family, who had offered Palizzolo hospitality, and whose entourage was nothing more than a motley assortment of *maffia*, bravos, and petitioners, each of them out for their own ends. . . . The purpose of Signor Palizzolo's visit to Ventimiglia and Ciminna was to beg for votes, so that he could be appointed a member of the provincial council.[138]

In 1877, Palizzolo gave up his candidacy to parliament, thus warding off the threat of the special security regimen of *ammonizione* and a direct clash with the government. Nor was the government, for that matter, interested in a direct fight. Some understanding of the dynamic can be gleaned from the case of Giuseppe Anzalone, a landowner in Lercara, formerly a *manutengolo* (an abettor) of Don Peppino, and the only prominent citizen held in prison on charges of ordering a murder. If Anzalone was acquitted, noted the author of his personal file with some concern, it would be best not to make him the subject of the special security regimen of *ammonizione*. Rather, it would be wiser to send him home immediately under house arrest, keeping him from fleeing to the countryside and "becoming the leader of bands of criminals, which would certainly be disastrous for the countryside, already plagued by brigandage."[139] Here, aside from the repeated statements on the "moral" perils of *manutengolismo*, or abetting of the Mafia, it is quite clear that the authorities' greatest fear still focused on militant brigandage. Malusardi and Nicotera's goal was not to reinforce the bond linking brigandage and prominent citizens; rather, it was to break that bond. They were not trying to change the ruling class, but only wanted to persuade that class to swear an oath to law and order, and to seal that oath by handing over the brigands. This was nothing new. Nor were the landowners, even the most compromised ones, at all reluctant to collaborate. The Li Destris in Gangi, the Cannizzos in Partinico, and even the Valenzas in Prizzi always insisted on their commitment to the fight against brigandage, their particular variety of control over criminal lawlessness. That explains how Palizzolo, accused of being a *manutengolo,* could be remembered many years later as a "champion of morality, a champion of the league of landowners, who organized to resist brigandage" by Member of Parliament Salvatore Avellone,[140] an individual who was himself the subject of much talk. As we can see from certain of the personal files, in clear conflict with any supposed code of *omertà,* even the "second-rank" mafiosi did their best to avoid the special security regimen of *ammonizione* or to ruin some rival or other by confiding the secrets and misdeeds of their village or town to the *delegato di PS.* Obviously, the same would be true of the leading prominent citizens, who needed to be on good terms with the authorities if they hoped to continue to exercise power. Leonardo Avellone, a relative of Salvatore Avellone, mayor for life of Roccapalumba, and clientele-chief and protector of mafiosi, "in several instances performed very useful services for law enforcement."[141] Giovanni Nicolosi, who, according to the police, protected criminals and organized crimes during his term as mayor (1875–1876), in several cases "took the trouble, however, to give the authorities advance notice so that the hapless criminals could be caught in the act, and so he appeared to have performed a signal service for the police."[142] The Gucciones, for whose arrest a warrant was issued in 1875, "by making facile promises that they would arrange to have brigands fall into the hands of the Law . . . succeeded in having the warrant rescinded."[143] All those who wanted to capture Leone appealed to the province's ruling committee, consisting of the Nicolosis, the Gucciones, the Cerritos, the Runfolas, and the Torinas.[144] Behind the special security regimen of *ammonizione* against Giuseppe Torina and behind the pressure on Palizzolo was the demand for Leone's head.[145] The most spectacular of the many episodes involving Lucchesi during the course of the year 1877 took place at the Guccione home, where the superdetective was careless enough to be found during a raid by the Carabinieri:[146] this took place in the context of a plot that, after leading to the murder of Di Pasquale at the hands of Leone, culminated with the killing of Leone himself by the police.

This marks the end of the history of the gangs in the years following unification. In 1877, the state simultaneously accentuated its capacity to carry on relations with local society and to remain autonomous from that society. We should not underestimate the spectacular signal of a watershed contained in dissolving the corps of soldiers on horseback and the decision to place one hundred of them under house arrest. "The classic brigandage is finished, once and for all," wrote Alongi in 1886,[147] but that was not true of the Mafia. In the face of the new harmony between the government and the ruling classes, kidnappings would decline practically to zero; kidnappings had been the crime that best symbolized the conflict between ruffians and the upper classes. The Mafia retrenched and focused on the *gabella* and *guardianìa* of *feudi* (estates) and *giardini*. Moreover, as we will see, even with respect to this type of activity, after the mid-1870s, the state would display a capacity for control or even attack that was much greater than it had shown in the past. The citizens of San Mauro Castelverde expressed their thanks to Malusardi for the "return to peace" that freed them from the bloody whirlpool of factional fighting and feuds: "Brigandage here was a myth, to which we submitted more easily than to any established force. Now the myth has vanished."[148] The expression of thanks may have been heartfelt, even if San Mauro was to remain a center of brigandage of primary importance. More in general, Pezzino pointed out, "it is clear that not much had changed," noting how the bursts of applause directed toward the prefect included the enthusiastic participation of prominent citizens who had been involved in the most notorious Mafia crimes.[149]

Twenty years later, in a speech before parliament that was not very cryptic, after all, Palizzolo himself offered his interpretation. The "facile" charges of *manutengolismo,* or abetting of the Mafia, he claimed, were only a way of covering up "ignorance" of the state of things in Sicily, where the police must maintain "extensive and friendly relations with every class of citizens" as long as they are "supporters of law and order and the institutions." By so doing, the prefects "were able to obtain at all times invaluable information, reports, and services."[150] This is an example of the theorization of a practice and an autobiographic passage that, if it refers to Malusardi, nonchalantly overlooks the energetic methods with which that collaboration was carried out. For that matter, Palizzolo did obtain something in exchange for his services: among other things, the protection of several individuals who were linked to Leone and who in Caccamo perhaps represented the "third rank" of *manutengolismo,* so that he was able to create and reinforce a new and different network around his own authority. In February 1876, he contacted the local *delegato di PS* in order to protest the expulsion order issued for Pietro Rini, "since I have already entrusted quite a few of my lands, on leases or on a sharecropping basis, to Rini, and if he were to leave, I would not know who would be better to work with." Once the uproar of early 1877 had passed, he turned directly to the *questore* (administrative director of the district police) for the opposite purpose—that is, to ensure that his protégés (Filippo and Salvatore Pesco, and Matteo Filippello), previously indicted for murder and subjected to the special security regimen of *ammonizione* as *manutengoli,* should be allowed to move freely from Caccamo toward Monreale and the countryside around Palermo, along the provincial extension of his interests.[151] In any case, relations between Palizzolo and the authorities were not always rosy. In 1896, Palizzolo would make a retrospective reference to those officers who (perhaps as a consequence of a political change) failed to respect the function of the prominent citizens, thus exposing to the "wrath of the brigands" the mafioso faction that had once governed, which thereby "had its livestock massacred, its houses burned, and its crops burned to the ground." Moreover, it was an absurdity that, in the alternating sequences of cabinet ministers and prefects, the "deserving" collaborators with the authorities should have been "hounded, subjected to the special security regimen of *ammonizione,* and deported" by those same authorities.[152]

The provincial Mafia began to emerge in 1877, at the end of the lengthy upheaval of the Risorgimento, with increased emphasis on its order-preserving role and displaying the complexity of its structure. Those who focused on the community dimension as the sole context for this phenomenon were running the risk of a very basic misunderstanding, especially if they thus failed to look beyond the boundaries of the township. On the one hand, there were places from which the infection spread, otherwise it would be impossible to explain how towns like Alia or San Mauro could produce brigands at such an unparalleled rate and with such remarkable continuity. Even though different individuals may have been involved, brigands from San Mauro were active from the end of the 1860s until the end of the 1920s. On the other hand, there were areas in which the gangs expanded and operated, determined by the need to avoid or the utility of interacting with the various territorial systems of state or landlord-managed security. As a folk saying advised, "brigands are born in San Mauro but they grow up in Gangi." "What is the meaning of this?" wondered Cutrera. "It means, quite specifically, that in Gangi brigands found powerful protectors," such as the barons Sgadari and Li Destri, whose names appear with such regularity in the chronicles of nineteenth- and twentieth-century *manutengolismo.*[153]

In short, if the township actually represented the site of the schism between factions, the problem of the Mafia should be correlated with forces that were operating on at least a provincial or district scale: large landholdings and, therefore, large leaseholdings, the market for land and for the *gabella,* which created a meeting ground for communities and a forum where the members of the communities might compete; and the political and administrative system, which extended beyond the level of the township and reached the level of the electoral district and the provincial delegation, an institution in whose control many mafiosi/prominent citizens (Palizzolo, Torina, Francesco Nicolosi) were involved. Finally, as we have seen, came the field of gang activity, which implies an equivalent extension of the networks of *manutengolismo*. Suffice it to consider the way in which Palizzolo moved his mafiosi. In the district of Termini, this network of relationships appeared in an especially salient manner to be endowed with the qualities of stability and extraterritoriality. Was the strong presence of brigands the cause, or was it rather the effect? Let us consider the mechanism whereby gangs descended one from another, from Don Peppino to Leone, as noted by the reporter and magistrate Giuseppe Di Menza. Let us compare it with the mechanism that appears in the lists, whereby many individuals aided and abetted the entire succession of groups that, over the course of time, took power and were then routed by the authorities, or collapsed due to internal squabbling and betrayals. Both the minor and the major *manutengoli* linked to Leone were, at least in part, the same individuals who had been involved in the affair of Don Peppino il Lombardo. And, too, let us recall what we said earlier about the brigands as an expression of the local parties. In fact, instead of seeing the brigands as members of the (municipal) parties, we have a case here of a party (subprovincial) of the brigands, a mafioso network that constituted the single stable element (and it mattered little whether inherent or derived) that police and thieves had to take into account. Behind the slowdown in the brigands' attacks in 1874–1875, viewed as an attempt to deflect the extraordinary police laws, behind the successful appeal to the high leadership of the *manutengolismo* for the elimination of Leone, we can detect a mechanism that defies classification as part of the Mediterranean anthropology of the winks and nudges that the mafiosi supposedly use to communicate, at least according to the opinions, for once unanimous, of mainland observers and Sicilian accomplices.

MIDDLE-CLASS RUFFIANS

As Palermo gradually lost its identity as a capital of the *ancien régime*, it became an increasingly powerful engine for the transformation of the hinterland. The process had begun in the eighteenth century with the city's expansion outside the old defensive walls and the *grande villeggiatura*—"grand resort living"— that is, a new and concerted investment in construction and real estate by the aristocracy. Around the aristocratic villas, or on either side of the roads that led into town, *borgate* formed. As early as 1861, these *borgate* housed 27,000 of the 200,000 inhabitants of Palermo and provided manpower for the intensive agriculture of vineyards, vegetable gardens, and *giardino*, that is, the citrus grove, which prevailed wherever water could be found or transported.

Partinico, Bagheria, and Monreale all underwent the same process of transformation. The immense expanses of farmland around Monreale, in particular, represented a direct extension of the countryside surrounding Palermo.
The countryside, perennially verdant, began to take on a distinctive appearance, with irrigation facilities, the houses for the guardians protecting the
farms and the collection of the harvests, the welter of narrow lanes wedged
between the high enclosure walls surrounding the *giardini,* which, significantly, became known as the *firriato,* or the iron grate.

There was then a remarkable contrast between the arid, large landholdings,
pressing in on all sides, and this verdant oasis, transformed in a way that would
have been inconceivable if the city were not nearby, and specifically in the absence of the market that the city itself represented. Also, only a major commercial center and port complex could have allowed goods such as citrus fruit to
reach their distant destinations, even in the era of sailing ships and later in
the time of steamships: Northern Europe and, especially, the United States. The
Conca d'Oro thus accentuated the image traditionally presented to travelers:
a Garden of Eden, beautiful and bountiful, created by nature and by human
labor.

> Let us take care, however [Sonnino noted sarcastically] lest we be swept
> away by excessive enthusiasm, let us examine these wonders with a more
> clinical eye, because while we are out enjoying a pleasant stroll we might
> just be shot by mistake, despite the many stations of the Carabinieri and
> the many patrols, we might fall afoul of a bullet fired for vendetta or *chi-
> accherìa* (literally, "conversation," an ironic description of gunshots designed
> to warn or intimidate—*translator's note*) in the direction of the landowner
> by a simple farmer crouching behind the enclosure wall surrounding those
> shaded *giardini*. . . . For this is the domain of the Mafia, whose dens are lo-
> cated in the cities and the *borgate* that ring Palermo, in the district of the
> Colli, in Morreale (Monreale), in Misilmeri, in Bagheria.[154]

The contrast is vivid and would evoke the image of a paradise inhabited
by demons if it were not for the fact that this paradise had been built by its own
inhabitants. Here the widespread presence of the Mafia appears to be in contrast with the unmistakable presence of a fertile and "blessed" land where
people could find honest work, whose products could be easily sold at high
prices and into a vast market, where the lands had a unit value fifty times as high
as the price of dry (unirrigated) lands, those large landholdings that in the eyes
of the nascent field of positivist sociology, by their very existence, instead justified the social malaise that led to criminality. You can read the give and take

in the debate between Senator Simone Corleo, mastermind of the imposition of a real estate tax on church possessions, and Carlo De Cesare, member of the Commission of Inquiry of 1875 and a pioneer of the social sciences in Italy. Corleo claimed that large landholdings, a barbaric holdover from feudalism, the dwindling population of the countryside, and the increasingly proletarian masses all contributed to the spreading infection of the Mafia. He was forced to admit, however, that the situation in the Palermo countryside constituted "an exception." De Cesare, in exasperation, replied: "Listen, Professor, these theories work just fine in science, but things happen in Sicily that shake your belief in science. . . . In Monreale almost everyone is a landowner, everyone owns a little plot of land. But there is no place where the public safety is in worse condition." In response, Corleo, honest positivist that he was, could only say that "this troubles the mind of science," and indeed men of greater intellectual stature than Corleo, such as Pasquale Villari and Napoleone Colajanni, were equally perplexed.[155]

But some observers were unwilling to accept the notion that Sicily simply constituted an exception to the "laws" of society, or, as superficial thinkers were willing to have it, that the phenomenon of the Mafia had no social root causes at all.[156] Tajani made a distinction between the economic vitality and the "moral" crisis of the years following unification.[157] Franchetti preferred to believe that Palermo reflected the array of problems that plagued postfeudal Sicily, and he attributed a logical priority to the situation on the interior of the island. He went on to note, however, that there were alluring sources of nourishment for the "industry" of violence[158] in those opportunities for profit and social mobility that were so rare throughout most of the Italian south, or Mezzogiorno; opportunities that were especially attractive to the city of Palermo, which was faced with dwindling prestige and wealth in the wake of unification due to the "shift of interests" adduced by contemporary thinkers to explain the revolt of 1866.

"Palermo . . ."—stated the prince of Sant'Elia—

was the capital for every category of affairs, and thus every sort of fictitious life battened [off] the earnings of the other provinces of Sicily. This was the industry of Palermo in times gone by: beg the king for a position and pray to God for a winning lottery ticket. Events turned out unfavorably for this industry: the clerks were placed on waiting lists; revenues from other provinces ceased to flow in to the coffers; taxes were levied; poverty spread everywhere.[159]

In this context, control of the farms of the city's hinterland came to constitute an extremely important vehicle for upward mobility, especially for those mafiosi who were involved in custodianship, *gabelle,* or subcontracting of farm-land leases, and commercial intermediation. We have already explored the case of Giammona. "Respectable individuals, the sons of landowners," was one ad-mittedly exaggerated description offered of the Amoroso brothers, mentioned above; the Licatas were described as well-to-do. We can easily identify all these individuals as "ruffians of the middle class," to whom Franchetti refers in delin-eating a typical model of the Palermo Mafia capo.[160] The term "middle" clearly meant they were therefore representative of a far more varied social setting than that found further inland, a social environment that was formed by aristo-crats and *gabellotti,* true, but also by merchants, intermediaries of every sort, professionals, peasant tenant farmers, and numerous other types. These were "marginal" individuals, just as the very property regime was marginal and of-ten extremely muddled given the ancient emphyteutic leaseholdings; the com-plications attendant on disputes over inheritances and successions, with a re-sulting fragmentation of agricultural corporations; and the usurpation of the property of the numerous religious and charitable institutions. The Palermo countryside, Misilmeri, and Monreale were a few of the relatively rare areas where the redistribution of the ecclesiastical and state-owned landholdings that followed unification was successful and "redounded to the benefit of pri-vate and public wealth,"[161] but not with the expected effect in terms of social harmony—indeed, with a sharpening of conflict. In Monreale, the authorities were unable to collect the fees due from long-term leaseholders' emphyteutic leases, nor could they distinguish between abusive leaseholders and legiti-mate leaseholders, or for that matter, the rightful landowners. Prince Pietro Mirto Seggio was faced with a permanent "revolution" carried out by the *villani,* or peasants, who claimed the right to work 500 *salme* (a *salma* is a mea-surement of land area) of the former Renda estate, once owned by the Benedic-tine monastery. In the end Mirto chose to enforce order through two former brigands and "their frightful Mafia." Mirto was the liberal mayor whom the authorities considered politically acceptable in a town full of "usurers, pro-Bourbon sympathizers, and Septembrist (referring to the Palermo uprising of September 1866—*translator's note*) reactionaries." He was also the only large landowner who spent some of his time living in town, and his status was far higher than that of a group of middle-class ruffians who sat on the town coun-cil, including Giuseppe Cavallaro, the son of the Mafia capo Simone Cavalla-ro.[162] And the capo of the other Mafia faction, Pietro Di Liberto, was a well-to-do landowner, as well as the administrator of the holdings of the *Mensa Arcivescovile,* the endowment of the archbishopric.

Even before the reforms of 1882, when suffrage was limited, Giammona con-trolled some fifty votes; the Amorosos and the Badalamentis during the political elections worked for Member of Parliament Valentino Caminneci, and during the provincial elections (apparently) for Palizzolo. In his villa at Malaspina, Palizzolo employed one of the few members of the Amoroso group who was acquitted in the trial of 1883, Giacomo Lauriano, known as Jacuzzo:

> I later learned that he had been arrested and tried on several occasions [explained the notorious yet prominent citizen, called as a witness for the defense in that trial] but since, on each occasion, the prosecution released him with a recommendation against proceeding to trial, and since he always possessed [a] license to carry a weapon, I assumed that he was simply the target of some campaign of harassment.[163]

The reasoning seems paradoxical at best, since it was none other than Palizzolo who intervened, in various hair-raising episodes of Lauriano's career, to obtain the reissue of his permit to carry a weapon and other favors.[164] This was the classic exchange that involved large landowners, corrupt politicians, and prominent citizens of all sorts. Don Michele Serra was the editor-in-chief of *L'Amico del Popolo,* a left-leaning newspaper that was also taking payments from Medici, who "was very influential at Piana dei Colli," especially serving as intermediary between mafiosi like the Biondos and the *questura:* "The *Alta Maffia* is in command"—wrote a person excluded from this network—". . . With the protection that they enjoy, either they hit us with an *ammonizione* (special security regimen), or else they send us to an Island [internal exile], but more likely they will kill us."[165] Relations between the men of the public institutions and mafiosi could be even more direct. Andrea Licata, through his special relationship with the *questore* Biundi, succeeded in obtaining *ammonizioni,* or orders for a special security regimen, house arrests for his enemies, and impunity for his father and his brothers.[166] Giacomo Pagano, a typical professional and landowner, turned to the same *questore* to complain of thefts being carried out in his citrus grove, and he was promised that Licata the *guardia* ("guard") would intervene, promises that seemed especially bewildering to him when he discovered that the thefts were the work of the "criminal" Licatas. He concluded that "neither the *questore* nor the police officers, nor any of the law enforcement personnel [has] very clear ideas about the criminals,"[167] but he knew perfectly well that if he had a solid relationship with Biundi or with Licata himself, the problem would go away. It is clientelism that ensures protection; it is clientelism that determines whether or not the ruffian should take on the garb of an enforcer of law and order or maintain the garb of a bandit. Moreover, the negotiators were not always leading figures, such as Turrisi and Giammona; in some cases, the parties to the transaction were situated in a subalternate area of the network of relationships. In those cases, the landowners were obliged to "lose something in order to keep from losing more":[168] give up the direct administration of the *giardini* and rent them out, even though citrus prices were high; subcontract the custodianship of facilities and crops, putting up in the meanwhile with an acceptable level of theft. And, finally, even the thieves were obliged to accept self-imposed limitations and to agree to abide by the rules of a complex and, above all, mercurial game, because each and every mutual warranty involved a number of ruffians, a number of landowners, and a number of officials, while excluding others, those that (to use Gestivo's words) "had been unable to do what they had done" and who might be discontented with the state of affairs. Conflict always lurked beneath the surface.

Let us examine a concrete case. In 1872, Gaspare Galati, a respected physician and a well-to-do landowner, began to take an active interest in the operation of a 4-hectare (10-acre) *giardino,* "largely" owned by his sister-in-law Marianna Fiorentino and located in Contrada Malaspina, a rural district near the Uditore *borgata*. A citrus grove of that size was already a business concern of some substance, equipped, among other things, with a steam engine that was used to pump water to the surface. Therefore, Galati was perplexed at how little revenue it produced. He was able to establish that the *guardiano* Benedetto Carollo was embezzling freely, especially when selling the citrus fruit produced. In 1874, the physician believed that he had found a good opportunity to rid himself of the "unfaithful" *guardiano,* and he finally fired him. But his problems were only beginning. Carollo, in fact, was a member of the Uditore Mafia, the chief of which was none other than Giammona. After the traditional series of threats, the new watchman was murdered, and another watchman who took his place was wounded and frightened into quitting. Galati himself had to flee to Naples, taking his family with him, after appointing yet another watchman.[169]

On numerous occasions, Galati had asked Biundi for help, inevitably with less than satisfactory results. Clearly, Galati was not a member of the right network, in terms of either institutional relationships or local relationships, since there were grounds for squabbling with a landowner in Malaspina linked to the Giammona *cosca*, the notary Francesco Sardofontana. Sardofontana, in fact, was the stepbrother of Marianna Fiorentino, and his mother had written him out of her will, thus depriving him of an inheritance that would have involved, among other things, the *giardino* that had served as the backdrop for all these dire events. In this and in similar cases, there was reasonable doubt about who rightfully held title of ownership, since it was generally thought that Galati himself had been the source of the "suggestions" that persuaded the mother to disinherit her son as punishment for his relations with the Mafia of the Uditore *borgata*.

We have here two correlated conflicts, opposing the landowners on the one hand and the *guardiani* on the other, each against the other. But things are not always so clear-cut. The initiative can spring from the lower reaches of the inter-class "party" of the landowners / officials-*guardiani* / ruffians, following the logic of the rackets, or else in a quest for monopoly where the struggle pits competitors one against another. It was precisely this competition over the *guardianìa* (the business of providing custodianship) that so bloodied the countryside around Palermo, causing thirty-four killings in 1874 in the Uditore *borgata*, with a population of eight hundred, and triggering murderous gang wars like the one between the Badalamentis and the Amorosos. The conflict that divided these two groups, which had previously belonged "to a single brotherhood," initially arose out of a series of reciprocal thefts and with the bloody punishment of the respective thieves, as if each of the two sections of the order-enforcing structure wished to prove that it was more efficient than the other. This flummoxed the politician Caminneci, who had no idea which faction he should side with, as it did the *questore* Sant'Agostino himself, who in 1880 even went so far as to underwrite a peace negotiation involving the leading figures of the two "parties," within the official precincts of the *questura!*—"Transactions, and certainly not honorable ones, with people that just the day before, and again the day following, it [the *questura*] denounced as dangerous lawbreakers."[170] In another case, Don Michele Serra attempted to broker a negotiation between rival groups and persuade the *curatolo* (or guardian) of a citrus grove, Andrea Ajello, to hand over the property to the competition, if he wanted to save his skin. The story had a tragic end all the same, with the *curatolo* murdered in an ambush ordered by Giuseppe Siino, lieutenant to Giammona and custodian of a Turrisi Colonna citrus grove.[171]

In any case, Ajello was no saint. His sons were in prison, and he himself had searched for a paid killer to eliminate his enemies. All of the custodians and *curatoli* were members of the world of the ruffians, since there existed a filter to keep out any outsiders. The conflict arose later from the governance of reciprocal relations. The sources tend to cover up this aspect, providing a simplified version in which a few brave citizens were persecuted by ferocious delinquents. Thus, once again, the authorities wound up supporting one faction against the other, if only in ideological terms. The *guardiano* Sedita, murdered by the Amorosos, was described as an honest man who had stood up to the plots and intrigues of the Mafia. In reality, Sedita was a member of the Badalamenti group. Antonio Lo Cascio, the first of the *guardiani* hired by Galati, was not a respectable person; otherwise, "he would not have wanted to take the place of Carollo."[172] Gaetano Cusumano, the second *guardiano,* was the brother of the Giovanni Cusumano who had been murdered by Giammona and is thought to be the same Cusumano mentioned by the duke of Cesarò among the patriotic mafiosi. The third *guardiano,* Francesco Paolo Mazzara, was also a dangerous individual, "previously convicted of smuggling, and mutiny" and a member of "a powerful Mafia group" willing to recognize Giammona's authority but capable of threatening to kill him during a tense summit meeting between the two factions.[173]

Galati, Pagano, and the authorities were more or less conscious parties to these struggles; but it was part of the logic of competition that the monopoly proved to be uncontrollable. Whether closely intertwined or independent one from another, the conflicts managed by the landowners and those managed by the ruffians were different in form and outcome. This aspect, though it passed unobserved in the debate at the time, nonetheless seems absolutely crucial. The landowners who were not in collusion were subjected to intimidation and damage; they were not allowed to choose whom to hire, and they were obliged to rent their *giardini* to certain individuals and, in some cases, to sell them, but only because they had become the object of a sort of boycott that isolated them. It was others whose lives were in danger. That explains why a phenomenon would have survived the political watershed of 1875–1877 that was harmful to the interests of individual landowners but was considered almost harmless to the ruling class taken as a whole, especially when compared with the practice of kidnapping, which (even if it too could fall into the context of clientelistic conflicts) ran the risk of triggering a direct clash between the world of the ruffians and the world of the landowners. The mafiosi of the Palermo area, many of whom had prior convictions for precisely this type of crime (kidnapping), were generally reluctant to engage in it. When someone suggested to the Amorosos that they kidnap the landowner Catalfamo (1879), they replied that operations of that sort were too risky and not sufficiently profitable; they would do nothing to hinder the kidnapping, but they had no interest in taking part directly.

Hence, we see that middle-class public opinion underestimated the dangers of the Mafia, which they viewed as an internal problem affecting only criminal groups, an opinion that we find again in more recent times, and which was skillfully exploited in the closing summation of the lawyer Lucifora, who argued in defense of the Amorosos in the trial of 1883:

> What does it matter to reputable people like us if the Amorosos and the Badalamentis cut each other's throats? What do we care . . . if two rival

parties in a district fight for supremacy? . . . If there were property damage or if people were hurt, then we have an interest in the matter, our property would be at risk, our loved ones at risk, everyone would be in danger from the killer's rifle or dagger. But, in fact, victims and killers in the Orto Botanico district were all brigands, they were only killing one another.[174]

PUBLIC JUDGMENT

The protection of illustrious figures and a reputation as a citizen who had never had the slightest brush with the law did little to keep Giammona out of the newspaper crime reports after a career of nearly thirty years and to move him toward a peaceful bourgeois respectability, after he made it through the difficult transition of 1860. There was a mechanism at work that we shall see again in radically different periods and circumstances. These mafiosi served as intermediaries between ruffians and the political and social authorities, doing their best to satisfy both sets of interlocutors, but at every step they ran the risk of being dragged into the criminal arena: first, through conflicts with other groups, and then through the protests of those excluded from the network of patronage, protests that could outweigh the inertia and protection that the Mafia enjoyed in outlying areas by mobilizing the center of the political system, especially in a general context of movement and change, like that of 1875–1876.

In the face of the passivity demonstrated by the Palermo *questura* and magistrature, it fell to the minister of the interior to take advantage of the memoir that Galati published, in August 1875, *I casi di Malaspina*. It took the minister to point out that the killings at the Uditore had prompted no judicial proceedings of any kind and that they had not even been deemed worthy of reporting, "even though, as serious and numerous as they were, they constituted a totally abnormal situation, to which I certainly should have been alerted."[175] Under the supervision of a skilled Roman policeman, Ermanno Sangiorgi, the investigation finally got under way, quickly identifying situations that in all likelihood were already well known. The response followed a well-tested script. An attempt was made to discredit Mazzara, who was even arrested on a false charge of avoiding the draft. There was a nighttime raid on the *giardino* in question, and numerous oblique messages were sent, such as the time that Benedetto Carollo asked permission to go hunting in the *giardino* in the company of the Commendatore Schiavo, the first presiding judge of the Court of Appeals of Palermo, "while no one could fail to be aware of the whole murderous sequence of events that occurred on the land in question . . . at the hands of none other than Carollo himself." The Mafia vaunted its network of protection: for that matter, if the prosecution was basing its case on "reputation" and "public opinion," the defense would be obliged to make a similar and opposite case, adducing the reiterated trust of highly respected figures. Serafino Siino, who was a candidate with the others for the special security regimen of *ammonizione,* traveled the length and breadth of Palermo's hinterland, in the company of his protector Nicolò Morana (brother of a member of parliament), gathering signatures attesting to his "well-known" honesty. "Out of respect for Signor Morana, on the one hand, and out of fear of Siino, on the other, everyone quickly agreed to sign."[176]

Giammona tried another tack. Through Member of Parliament Morana, he informed Codronchi that "he would be willing to offer revelations" in order to ward off the special security regimen of *ammonizione.* The deal was not consummated because Gerra, despite Codronchi's encouragement, was unwilling to accept the idea that "a member of parliament should be involved in recommending people who had been subjected to the special security regimen of *ammonizione.*"[177] And so Giammona also presented a collection of signatures of powerful individuals whose destinies we have seen intertwining with Giammona's: the barons Turrisi and Di Maggio, Member of Parliament Morana and his brother Nicolò, and other landowners and "shopkeepers." A brief for the defense was drawn up by Gestivo, who, as usual, placed the problem of the Mafia in a context of class-based self-defense, with a leitmotif of victimization. In this scenario, Giammona and his son Giuseppe were both being persecuted for "the twofold and unforgivable crime of living on the fruits of their own labor, and taking care not to allow others to rob them nor take advantage of them."[178]

The *questore,* the prefect, and the body of magistrates of Palermo wished to go no further than the special security regimen of *ammonizione* that was issued against the Giammonas in December 1875, while Gestivo challenged them to bring the Giammonas to court "without distracting them from [their] natural judges." The provocation should be acted upon, opined Minister Cantelli, well aware that the tool available to a state based on the rule of law was public judgment for the crime of Mafia conspiracy, without which the Mafia could neither be understood nor attacked: "The idea of a trial for conspiracy among wrongdoers . . . is my own. It is not absolute, but rather suggested as a way of cleaning up, if possible, that countryside at a single blow. . . . it is important that, in the face of a relatively unusual formal request for support from the authorities, they should not appear impotent."[179]

Therefore, this was an attempt to respond to a (supposed) demand from public opinion and to the situation in the field, not only in the district of the Uditore, but also in a similar situation found on the other end of the Palermo countryside, in Monreale, with the "sect" of the *stoppagghieri,* for which—according to the version provided by the authorities—we have a date of birth, 1872, and a father,

Giuseppe Palmeri from Nicasio, a follower of Mazzini. Giuseppe Palmeri had a brother, Paolo, who was the local *delegato di PS*. Seeing that Paolo was exposed to the intrigues and dangers of the Mafia, Giuseppe decided to found "a counter-party (a sort of counter-Mafia)" whose membership encompassed "all the most terrifying and squalid elements that [were] moving about in the underworld." At first, they provided "a few useful services to law enforcement," and then they degenerated into the commission of robberies and murders.[180]

Stoppagghiere was, in fact, a pejorative term used in prison to describe a spy[181] (the members of the "sect" called one another "compari"—a term similar to god-father). The police admitted that they had founded a *Mafia d'ordine* (order-keeping Mafia), that they had applied the principle of *"similia similibus* used in homeopathic medicine"[182] in the same town of Monreale where, the reader will recall, Albanese had done much the same thing at the end of the 1870s with the members of the *Guardia nazionale*. They were the members of an "old *maffia* known as the gentleman's *mafia* . . . who had enriched themselves through their shadowy machinations," and were in conflict with "young men, also *maffiosi*, who wished to win themselves a position with the same arts."[183] A point of contact was found in Marino, the false "Republican" and informer for Albanese who reemerged as one of the *stoppagghieri* and who became a fugitive from the law, though not before arranging for his file in the court of Palermo to vanish.[184] The "old" Mafia had every interest in regaining the support of the authorities, perhaps by accusing its adversaries of being "internationalists." Here, too, we see some of the peculiarities of Monreale, which beginning in 1848 was the primary center of politico-criminal mobilization: certain of the *stoppagghieri* took part in the uprising of 1866, and as late as the 1870s, signs appeared in town with messages somewhere between anarchistic and legitimist. The *delegato di PS* Negri, who took Palmeri's place, attempted to obtain more information about Marino from a certain Caputo, another member of the sect whose inquiries were, however, brought to a sudden halt by a blast of buckshot. This was the dramatic turning point. With Negri and with his replacement as *delegato di PS* Bernabò, the "old" mafiosi once again became friends of the institutions and collaborators, while the "young" mafiosi returned to the ranks of common criminals, devotees of the steeliest *omertà*.

Giuseppe Palmeri responded to the charges with subtle irony, displaying a social quality that was ill-suited to involvement in police frame-ups: "I have no need to waste my time and test my conscience in order to satisfy my needs. I live on my investments and I do not have to work for a living, and by nature and education, it has never been in my nature to get mixed up in matters as serious, or tawdry, or deep as the story told by your pulp novelist."[185] And so his brother would have been an unusual composite of *delegato di PS* and prominent citizen: I know of another example in the figure of Stanislao Rampolla from Tindaro, who belonged to Albanese's staff at one point, and who also boasted a cardinal in the family.[186] In more general terms, in a town like this one, the succession of *delegati di PS* represents a decisive factor in determining local equilibriums.

The *stoppagghieri* affair was a confused welter of possible lies and possible truths. Bernabò claimed that it was originally a mutual aid society that included 150 members in town, organized into sections, and that expanded over time to the neighboring *borgate* and villages, but none of that is borne out in the documentation. Indeed, his fellow *delegati di PS* tended to note that "every town has its own local *mafia*." Moreover, the officials reported Mafia associations in Misilmeri ("Fontana Nuova"), in Bagheria ("Fratuzzi"), and in other locations, and "no one questions, in good faith, that relationships exist" among the members of these groups whereby they managed individual deals and business.[187] Other aspects of Bernabò's "theorem" are based on more substantial evidence, and specifically on the testimony of a *pentito* (or turncoat), Salvatore D'Amico from Bagheria, a relative of Caputo who was therefore involved in the internal divisions of the organization. Indeed, D'Amico, with a prior conviction for murder and time spent in the Palermo prison, had once been inducted into the sect by means of a complex ritual "in the presence of respected representatives of the *malandrinaggio* of Bagheria, San Giuseppe, San Lorenzo, Altarello, Misilmeri, Borgetto,"[188] and, of course, Monreale.

D'Amico never made it to the witness stand during the trial held in Palermo in May 1878: he was murdered the month before. Only twelve people were brought to trial and found guilty of conspiracy and for individual murders, and the alleged capo, Di Liberto, was not among them. A technicality resulted in a retrial, and the venue was shifted to Catanzaro *per legittima suspicione* (meaning the court and indeed the venue were recused—*translator's note*) in 1880, resulting in acquittal for all the defendants. The trials of the members of the Fratuzzi clan in Bagheria ended quite differently, especially the trial of the Piazza Montalto *cosca*, the last in the series (1883), with a guilty verdict for Mafia involvement and no fewer than twelve death sentences for murder.

The Amorosos and their followers had already been questioned in 1875, but in 1878 something new happened. A certain Rosario La Mantia from Monreale, with a prior conviction for robbery, came to the office of the Italian consul in Zaragoza, Spain, on his way from America, and stated that he was willing to reveal very important information. After negotiations guided by Tajani, who was at this juncture the minister of justice, La Mantia was brought to Rome and was subjected to questioning there. He told his questioners that in New Orleans he had met a *compaesano,* a man from his hometown, Monreale, who was a fruit vendor. After they had been acquainted for a certain period of time, he confessed to La Mantia that he was Salvatore Marino, "that he had been obliged to leave Italy and travel abroad . . . but that he had left comrades behind who continued to execute all his orders." In the meanwhile, Marino had contracted yellow fever, and on his deathbed he begged his compatriot to burn a number of his letters, a request with which La Mantia did not comply. And so the letters made their way to Palermo: they had been written by such prominent individuals as Michele Amoroso and Giuseppe Giammona, and investigators viewed several obscure phrases as planning for crimes.[189] Neither documents nor witnesses were used in the second trial of the *stoppagghieri;* instead they were brought into play in the preliminary investigation of the Amoroso trial, in part in connection with the revelations of another *pentito,* who this time actually succeeded in testifying. The La Mantia affair only reinforced the thesis of the close coordination among the *cosche* that Franchetti had already linked to the "remarkable clustering" of mafiosi in the Palermo area.[190] Salvatore Di Paola and Giuseppe Maraviglia, members of the group of Piazza Montalto, traveled to Marseilles to intercept the informer and kill him, which renders less believable the story of his chance meeting with Marino. La Mantia must already have long been privy to the secret affairs of the Mafia and the *questura* (police administration). After being in the pay of the investigators for a couple of years, he vanished abroad just when he was scheduled to testify.[191]

The supervision and manipulation of the police appear glaringly in every phase of the *stoppagghieri* and the Amoroso trials. Here we see the retraction of the testimony of another defendant who had confessed after a month of secret and illegal detention in the *questura* (police administration). When the defense objected, the *questore* Taglieri responded simply: "salus patriae suprema lex esto"—Latin for "Let the Safety of the Fatherland Be the Supreme Law."[192] Witnesses belonging to opposing factions had opposing opinions of the defendants' "capacity to commit crimes" and of their good or evil reputations, but none of them had anything decisive to say about the crimes in question. The accusations were documented by government functionaries, who recounted what had been confided to them in secret. We therefore see evidence of a polarization that was destined to remain a typical feature of Mafia trials, where the police served simultaneously as witness, plaintiff, and prosecution, with *delegati di PS,* who considered that they had obtained their results when they succeeded in court in "upholding so well the case of the prosecution that they convinced the jurors of the full culpability" of the defendants.[193] In particular, proof of the crime of criminal conspiracy remained an issue of public opinion and reputation and the way in which the institutions of public security interpreted public opinion. In a subsequent trial brought against a modest Palermo gang of thieves, it was noted as an exceptional case that "evidence . . . was derived not only from the minutes of the testimony of the officials and agents of *Pubblica Sicurezza,* or police officers, but also from explicit statements made by private citizens."[194] Such testimony was generally absent in Mafia trials; but the credibility of police functionaries was also dubious, as they absolutely refused to reveal the sources of their crucial information. In the case of the *stoppagghieri,* as well as in the case of the Amoroso clan, the court protected that "official right to secrecy," which closely resembled the "state secrecy" that had been applied in the trials for massacres in the 1960s and 1970s by the officers of the Italian intelligence services, opposing the defense's demand that Bernabò be indicted for perjury or incomplete testimony and the objections to Taglieri.[195] The matter came to a high point of absurdity when the *questore* himself admitted that he had been led by the hand through every step of the investigation into the Amorosos by an authoritative individual, who was "above all suspicion or objections," whose name he was of course unwilling and unable to disclose.[196]

And so the trials concerning the reputations of mafiosi were transformed into judgments of the reputations of policemen—that is, their credibility and that of their mysterious informants, who were all obviously lashing out at one person to protect another. There was always and inevitably a sole protagonist of the Mafia war: if the association of the Amorosos was a criminal conspiracy, wondered the lawyer Marinuzzi, "then why not charge the Badalamentis as well?"[197] The *stoppagghiere* who killed Simone Cavallaro (in some cases identified as the capo of the "old Mafia," in others as an *eccellente galantuomo,* or respected gentleman) was in turn murdered that same evening; but we learn nothing about that, nor are we told about any of the other murders committed by his faction. We do know for certain, however, that the *delegato di PS* Cicognani, sent to monitor the trial in Catanzaro, intervened to apply pressure on the jurors.[198] The functionaries lacked credibility, as did the government that paid their salaries. The defense attorneys, of whom the most important (Cuccia, Lucifora, and Marinuzzi) were present in both cases, set forth this thesis in particular for the *stoppagghieri* trial. They had good cause to do so, given that in two different cases, in the times of Albanese and Palmeri, the police admittedly encouraged the formation of associations of "wrongdoers." Marinuzzi's summation during the trial in Catanzaro began with the crimes denounced by Tajani and linked them to the more recent ones, dismissing the charges against the *stoppagghieri* as part of a right-wing attempt to provide justification for the special police law. The summation concluded with a Sicilianist peroration that fully won over the Calabrian jurors whose verdict delivered "another stern and richly deserved lesson to those who, sons or guests [of] our beloved Sicily, oppress and reject her with impunity."[199]

Recourse to a regionalist approach adopted by Marinuzzi, the follower of Crispi, and even more shamelessly by the all too familiar Gestivo, was not successful. In fact, it was not even attempted during the course of the Amoroso trial just three years later, though in a very different climate. The chief judge of the court noted that the association in question was not political in nature, "as some might think,"[200] warding off all misunderstanding in the name of liberal protection of civil rights. The objections focused on the existence and nature of an association established to kill but not to rob, founded in 1874 and inactive for four years, since the first murder attributed to it dates from 1878. This was a curious fact, Cuccia argued, "since when criminal conspiracies exist they must necessarily be active."[201] In this case, Taglieri's response appears persuasive: "the foundation of the criminal association" was *guardianìa*;[202] the association—I would add—does not threaten private property but rather defends it, and the murders are committed in a time of conflict in relation to the supply of protection.

The *guardiani* did not always live on the estate, since their reputation was often enough to discourage potential wrongdoers. Remaining in the *borgate* or in the city, they could form part of a network that could engage in business as well. In fact, the *guardiano* performed functions of some substance in the complex and frantic circuit of trade, which to some degree distinguished this Mafia of the *giardini* from the Mafia of the large landholdings. The "thefts" against which they stood watch, for instance, were often connected to the purchase and sale of citrus fruit, during the course of which an agreement between *guardiano* and purchaser could prove damaging to the seller. Carollo, *guardiano* for Dottore Galati, demanded for himself 20 percent of the price that he had set with the purchasers, "since this is a customary *camorra* [or form of extension] of the Mafia in general." Far more serious was the fact that he arranged for a number of other clandestine rake-offs from the fruit crop "already purchased and paid for" (but not yet gathered) to the serious damage of the purchaser, "which damaged the credibility of the estate and scared away future purchasers of the citrus fruit." In this case, the custodian-dealer wound up sabotaging the very mechanism he had been hired to protect. Galati attempted to get rid of him by renting the estate, but he received no offers because Carollo discouraged potential renters by declaring, in threatening terms, that "this orange grove would never be leased, nor sold."[203] There also existed another *guardianìa*, that of water, entrusted to the so-called *fontanieri*, or water administrators, who could, if they so desired, reduce in critical periods of the growing season the supply of water channeled through the irrigation pipes and surreptitiously sell the remaining water supply, causing the destruction (or rescue) of a crop, the ruin (or fortune) of a farmer. For an intensive form of agriculture like that of the Palermitan countryside, water was an irremediably scarce resource, strategic in nature, a typical monopoly asset for the owners of the wells and for the *fontanieri* who physically managed that trade. For the citrus growers, "there is no way to summon them to their duty . . . legally, because justice has a cost, not an economic cost, but because they are dangerous and compromising thugs."[204] Still, the Mafia as an organization could do so, especially in cases where the *guardiano* supplied water to the wrong group, as did Felice Marchese, who (according to Bernabò) was murdered at the orders of Di Liberto.

The *fontanieri*, noted the economist Ferdinando Alfonso, "are in an ideal correspondence," not with the landowners, but with the *giardinieri*, or keepers of a citrus grove, that is, the *gabellotti* and their intermediaries, those who—in the context of the boom of the postunification citrus market—"were purchasing all the fruit of the *giardini* owned by the landowners, and then joined together and drove up the prices" paid by the large-scale exporters, who then sent the merchandise to the distant American shores.[205] This conjunction of high prices and low production led the competition toward increasingly early purchases, creeping steadily ahead of the natural cycle of seasons, as well as advances of substantial sums by intermediaries, with the likelihood of threatening demands for their money back in case the risky transaction turned out badly for them. The contracts for the purchase of citrus fruit were framed in an intentionally ambiguous way, in order to leave room for a "genial" agreement that would protect the continuity of business and general coexistence, in order to ensure that there would be an authoritative interlocutor for both of the parties involved, both producers and middlemen. Thus, control of the mediators who evaluated the production, who served as both guarantor and in many cases guardian of the product in the aftermath of the stipulation of agreements, was one area of operation open to and occupied by the Mafia.[206] The Amorosos were known equally as *giardinieri* and dealers; many of the murder victims, such as Caputo or Gaspare Amoroso, were lured into the discreet penumbra of a *giardino* with the excuse of purchasing a batch of citrus fruit. "All, by the basic nature of things, are speculators who use, as the medium in which they speculate, both gunpowder and lead."[207] And so, setting out from the original demand for public and private security, through the narrow "correspondence" between *guardiani, fontanieri, gabellotti,* and intermediaries, through the fiduciary relationship with the landowners, which transformed the ruffians-qua-custodians into profiteers and landowners, the characteristic of the organization is delineated:

In contrast with other organizations that have been subjected to the rigors of justice (for instance, the organization of the *Posa de' mugnai e carrettieri*) [this one] was not founded to ensure the forced monopoly over a given industry, the forcible taxation or arbitrary hiring of laborers; rather it attacked in general all sources of ownership, all economic manifestations of wealth, industry, and labor.[208]

This opportune distinction between a monopoly over a sector and a monopoly over a territory should not be taken too literally. The activities controlled were undergoing a period of transition in the *borgate* (cattle rustling, smuggling) or a period of departure (citrus trade) in which the members of the organization played a role of business intermediation in contact with other mafiosi or with subjects extraneous to the world of criminals. It was within the *borgate* and the villages of the hinterland that a system was created that tended toward a model of territorial monopoly, beginning from the area of custodianship of the infrastructures, harvests, and water. The two aspects, which should be considered separately in conceptual terms, overlap in practice, neither of them exclusive of the mutual relationships among Mafia families that are still configured as business relationships, or as recognition of the respective territorial seigniories.

Compared with the 1860s, the period of trials for criminal conspiracy in 1875–1883 had the benefit of shedding light on this reality with greater intensity of focus on the principles of juridical civilization, even though within the context of an enduring illegality, in the clientelistic relationship between pieces of the Mafia and pieces of the state.

CHAPTER III

GUARDIANI AND PROFITEERS

MAFIA AND POLITICS

On 1 February 1893, in a railroad car traveling along the Termini–Palermo line, Emanuele Notarbartolo di San Giovanni was murdered. Notarbartolo was a scion of one of Sicily's most respected aristocratic families. Although he had political affiliations with the *Destra storica* (historic right wing), he was widely viewed as a man who rose above party politics, and he was universally respected for the moral rectitude and administrative skills he had displayed while serving as Palermo's mayor (1873–1876) and as the general manager of the Banco di Sicilia (Bank of Sicily) (1876–1890).[1]

This was not a case of political terrorism like those that had blighted the years following Italian unification. Investigators rapidly discounted the possibility that this had been an assault by ordinary lawless brigands. A major factor in their reasoning was the "modern" and reassuring setting: a railroad passenger car. In fact, the victim had felt sufficiently safe to let down his guard, abandoning the precautions he had carefully employed since his kidnapping in 1882. He had unloaded the rifle he carried with him, and he had taken the opportunity to sleep during the train trip. ("Between brigands and the railroad there is a total incompatibility, a profound anachronism.")[2] The murder was committed with a knife, the sort of weapon commonly used in crimes of passion, not in murders carried out "at the orders of others" ("Hired killers invariably . . . use firearms").[3] This was not a killing that belonged to the struggle among equals for control of the *gabelle* (subcontracting of farmland leases) or *guardianìa* (custodianships). We know that it was not customary for the mafiosi of the Palermo region to murder landowners, much less citizens as eminent as Notarbartolo. Nonetheless, the *vox populi* buzzed with rumors that this had been a Mafia murder. In fact, the public prosecutor Gualtiero Sighele declared, this was a murder ordered by "the highest ranks of the Mafia hierarchy."[4] Sighele named the killers—two members of the *cosca* (Mafia family) of Villabate, Matteo Filippello and Giuseppe Fontana—and the man who had ordered the killing as Raffaele Palizzolo. "In public gathering places, in the streets, everywhere, the refrain was: this must have been the work of Palizzolo."[5]

The murder of Notarbartolo marked a qualitative change, but it stood alone, an isolated benchmark pointing to developments that lay far in the future. Let us put the murder into perspective: this case was the only time in nearly eight decades that the Mafia dared to strike a blow at such a highly placed individual. Notarbartolo's dead body was the first *cadavere eccellente* ("excellent cadaver," in the sense of social elevation; see Alexander Stille's *Excellent Cadavers*), and it was also the last until the killing of public prosecutor Pietro Scaglione in 1971—the only such murder since Italian unification. The scale of the crime prompted an equally outsized reaction. A state of Mafia-related emergency reigned not only in Sicily but throughout Italy. In fact, on the grounds of what Italian law terms *legittima suspicione,* or recusal of the court, the three trials for the Notarbartolo murder were held in other venues, first in Milan (1899–1900), then in Bologna (1901–1902), and finally in Florence (1903–1904).[6] Not only were the trials held far from Sicily, but the Italian press gave ample and prominent coverage to the proceedings. The media thus "nationalized" the dark subject of the Mafia, a distinctly Sicilian phenomenon, bringing it to the attention of the Italian public to a far greater extent than the parliamentary debates of 1875 had succeeded in doing. Beginning on what the Marchese di Rudinì described as the "spotlit stage of Milan,"[7] all Italy watched spellbound as if witnessing a sensational spectacle that featured hundreds of witnesses who had traveled north from Sicily, garbed in outlandish costumes, speaking in an incomprehensible tongue that required the intervention of court-appointed interpreters.

In the first trial, only two defendants were summoned to appear, the railroad employees Garufi and Benedetto Carollo. It was evident from the mechanics of the events that they had been accomplices to murder, not the killers themselves. No charges were brought against Palizzolo and Fontana (the original evidence against Filippello had proved too slim). This approach prompted outrage from the Notarbartolo family. In particular, the self-restraint of the victim's son, Leopoldo, was sorely tested by the timidity and the contradictions that had characterized the preliminary judicial investigation. Now, in the "free air of Milan,"[8] he electrified the courtroom by openly accusing Palizzolo.

"I can hardly convey the thrill of concern, the astonishment of the magistrates, the members of the jury, and the audience when these words were spoken," wrote the correspondent of *L'Avanti!* "An overwhelmingly heightened state of attention, acute and verging on painful, bound the entire courtroom to the rapid, incisive, and confident speech of that twenty-eight-year-old youth who was standing forth, demanding revenge upon his father's alleged murderer, a man of great power."[9]

Driven by pressure from the civil plaintiff, the trial was transformed into a "public preliminary investigation"[10] that stood in sharp contrast to the official preliminary investigation. The police detective Cervis accused his colleague Francesco Di Blasi, manipulated by his master, Palizzolo, of having steered the investigation in the wrong direction and of concealing important evidence. Di Blasi was placed under arrest in the courtroom. An investigation undertaken by the prefect of Palermo unearthed a note in which, just one day after the murder, Di Blasi, on his initiative, asked to be put on the case and suggested preposterous "leads." The Palermo prefect concluded his report with these words: "His close relationship with Commendatore Palizzolo offers solid grounds for suspicion that he had ulterior motives for wishing to have access and control of the threads of this intricate skein in order to protect his friend and master."[11]

Cervis insinuated that the Palizzolo "party" was treated with indulgence, if not full-fledged complicity, by the *questore* (administrative director of the district police) of Palermo in 1893, Ballabio. When Di Blasi and Ballabio were brought together face-to-face in court, Ballabio was unable to control his temper and berated Di Blasi, calling him "a liar and a coward [who] has brought dishonor upon the *questura* (police administration) of Palermo."[12] General Giuseppe Mirri, who served as minister of war in 1899 in the Pelloux government and was head of the police in Sicily during the state of siege, accused the magistrature of "the greatest imaginable lassitude, negligence, indeed, criminal neglect."[13] The subsequent *questore,* the former detective Michele Lucchesi, was equally emphatic: "A magical hand, mysterious yet powerful, has manipulated this trial! How else can we explain the fact that it is only taking place after an interval of six years, even though four months would have been quite sufficient time to prepare."[14] All these witnesses, and a great many others, testified to Palizzolo's "propensity for criminal acts" and his ties to the Mafia.

As we shall see, both General Mirri and the *questore* Ballabio had various matters on their conscience and thus contributed in turn to a scandal that was "so broad and murky," as Pelloux and Sonnino observed with concern, that it called into question the larger political equilibrium.[15] In the Milan court, the content of the debate was so subversive that the local military command found it advisable to prohibit officers from attending the sessions of the trial.[16] Despite that cautious measure, the press served up a distressing picture: lawyers accusing the public institutions of complicity with the Mafia, politicians and police officers charging one another with involvement, to the disgust of respectable citizens and the delight of subversives. The respectable citizens were forced to admit that there was "mysterious and subtle poison [at work . . .]: under the façade of the Mafia the power of politics was at work, and under the façade of politics the power of the Mafia was at work."[17] The subversives, on the other hand, were able to point to the squalor of the Italian state, which had deigned to condemn them: "Let's not talk about 'sloppiness,' however grave, nor about 'negligence,' even enormous negligence, in all this. More than 'guilt,' there is a larger organized crime in the administration of justice, justice is complicit with and protective of murderers, there is infamy, shame, and dishonor."[18]

Concerning certain episodes, the Milanese public prosecutor admitted, judgment should be left "to public opinion, which is right more often than not, and which rightly assigns praise and blame."[19] And public opinion found magistrates, *questori,* and prefects all guilty, a guilt that tainted the governments under which the investigations had been led into various dead ends.

Among those governments, oddly enough, was the government led by the Marchese di Rudinì, a personal friend of the victim, Emanuele Notarbartolo, and head of Notarbartolo's political party, the *Destra* (or right). These were the years (1896–1897) of the *commissariato civile* (special but nonmilitary government) for Sicily. Rudinì assigned Giovanni Codronchi to that post. Codronchi's official task was to attack clientelism; his real assignment, as Sonnino sarcastically noted, was to create a "Commissariato elettorale" that would disintegrate the party of Francesco Crispi and recapture that party's moderate wing, restoring it to a pro-government position.[20] And Codronchi was the right man for the job: a member of the right wing, and therefore scorned by Sicilian democratic forces as far back as 1875, but in 1889–1890, when he served as the prefect of Naples, the faithful executor of Crispi's policies.

In April 1896, even before he was officially appointed, Codronchi expressed his intentions: "We all know who carried out the crime, who gave the orders. Justice was reluctant to take on important people who were close to Crispi. . . . I told Rudinì that I had no intention of respecting even his friends, representative Palizzolo, to mention just one name. Rudinì answered: 'That's fine, Palizzolo is a rogue.' "[21]

Codronchi overestimated his own importance. The fact that the case was reopened was probably the result of instructions from Rudinì; those instructions, however, proved difficult to execute, as the chain of evidence led not to the supporters of Crispi, as had been hoped, but rather to Palizzolo. "Rogue" though he might well be, he constituted one of the mainstays of the Sicilian right wing. On the other hand, the member of parliament, Palizzolo, absolutely needed government support. Alongside the suspicions accumulating in connection with the Notarbartolo case, there was growing and troubling evidence concerning the murder of a certain Francesco Miceli, which Palizzolo attributed to the persecution of Giolitti—hence the feigned commitment to the defense of civil rights on which his support of the project of a *commissariato civile* was based:

> As soon as a major crime takes place anywhere in the province, and the first judicial documents are being drawn up in the office of the prefect, the prefect is willing to accept the advice of some Byzantine adviser, who might be a ministerial political candidate for the upcoming elections. . . . They always consider the opposition candidate to be responsible for every crime, and the more-or-less necessary accomplices are his friends and supporters.[22]

It should therefore come as no surprise to us to learn of the unpleasant situation that faced Leopoldo Notarbartolo, when he found out that Codronchi was in cahoots with Palizzolo.[23] In the months that followed, there was a daily correspondence between the pair, in which Codronchi, the count from Imola, imparted instructions for the high-level political decisions, and Palizzolo, the parliamentarian from Palermo, oversaw local operations: the dissolution of municipal administrations, the parceling out of state-owned land, the extension of terms for the debt of various companies, the selection of pharmacists summoned to provide medical services for Palermo's poor, the recruitment of the corps of tariff and customs police.[24] Palizzolo was especially attentive to the selection of police officers. He objected to the transfer away from Palermo of the *delegato di PS* (or police inspector) Olivieri, calling him "my loyal constituent who could provide great assistance to me," while, in contrast "you have chosen to leave in place in this [province] and in my own district other officers who wish me no good at all!" He intervened on behalf of a former *delegato di PS,* a certain Francesco Saitta, and in this case Palizzolo prompted outrage from the high commissioner, who wrote: "This Saitta has been found guilty, sentenced, and expelled from his office; and now you are recommending that he be appointed chief of the *Guardie Campestri* (or rural and agricultural police)!" Palizzolo expressed particular interest in obtaining appointment as city police commissioner in the clerical-moderate administration, under the leadership of Senator Amato-Pojero. Thanks to Codronchi's string-pulling, that administration took power in 1897 in the Palermo city hall: "I have numerous friends whose rights and considerations have been trampled underfoot, and they are fully determined that I, if only for a month, become a member of the executive power [*sic!*]. . . . Amato should have depended upon Your Excellency's learned advice, as well as that of the friends without whom he could not last for forty-eight hours in the office of Mayor."[25]

If we wish to understand what "friends" Palizzolo was talking about, let us note that, in view of the coming administrative elections in Palermo, the island's capital, a reform of the electoral system was put in place that gave the candidates put forth by the *borgate*, or outlying suburbs, an outsized importance. According to De Felice, individuals with strong Mafia ties were thus elected with dozens of votes, while in the center of town opposition candidates were rejected who had obtained more than a thousand votes. Among others, there was Salvatore Licata, son of the same Andrea Licata whom we encountered in the 1870s.[26] No one but Palizzolo could control individuals of this sort. We should not be surprised, then, to learn that in 1897 Codronchi declared that he was confident of Palizzolo's innocence and, instead, that he had his suspicions concerning the Crispi followers Paolo Figlia and Francesco Tenerelli.[27]

Lucchesi was the *questore* of Palermo. The high commissioner considered Lucchesi to be "a highly capable man, [who] knows everything and everyone," though the high commissioner expected he would have to expel him from office at some point, because he was a "scoundrel."[28] In fact, Lucchesi was a fine-edged tool of police work, who was fully knowledgeable concerning the various "toxins" (*veleni*) of Palermo at least as far back as the Malusardi years. On one occasion, when he had been caught in friendly conversation with a notorious mafioso, he is said to have cried: "You see what I'm forced to do? This individual deserves to be clapped in handcuffs, and I would be only too glad to march him straight into prison myself."[29] Of particular note were the instructions that the *questore* gave his subordinates in the summer of 1896. He ordered them to ignore all complaints against the mafiosi of Villabate "lest individuals wrongly accused of serious crimes [should go into] hiding, thus endangering the conditions of public safety."[30] This was the man in charge of reopening the case with the new public prosecutor, Vincenzo Cosenza. He decided to focus on the "rumor-mongering" of a convict, a certain Bertolani, who claimed to have heard Fontana (at the time in prison in Venice for distributing counterfeit banknotes) boasting that he had murdered Notarbartolo. Bertolani identified as the man who had ordered the killing—interpreting in the most expansive manner imaginable the wishes of his guardians—no less a personage than Francesco Crispi himself.[31] As a result, the judicial investigation was modified, and Garufi and Carollo were indicted. In the new bill of charges, Fontana was no longer a suspect; his alibi now seemed ironclad, but this was in part because Cosenza failed to bring Lucchesi face-to-face with the railroad employee Salvatore Diletti. Diletti had told the *questore* that he had recognized the mafioso Fontana as the man who had been present aboard the train on the day of the murder. Left unprompted, Diletti retracted his testimony, and it was not until the trial was actually under way that he once again leveled his accusations against Fontana.[32]

As we can see, in 1896–1897 a number of mechanisms were at play that differed sharply from those put into operation in 1893 by Palizzolo's supporters. Codronchi was determined to identify the man who had ordered the killing, and then, when all evidence pointed toward Palizzolo, he wound up focusing on Fontana alone. That target was missed as well owing to Cosenza's reluctance. On the other hand, both the high commissioner and his even higher political mastermind would remain convinced that their former ally was not guilty, or at least that he was not alone in his guilt: "I do not offer any warranties for Palizzolo," Rudinì wrote to Codronchi in December 1899. "The body of opinion that has formed against him says that he is a man who is capable of committing crimes. But . . . the ferocity shown against him, in the first preliminary investigation, shows, practically, that a special effort was made to send justice in the wrong direction, misdirecting the investigators."[33]

The letter called for cool and collected behavior during the frantic days of the Milan trial, when everyone was trying to establish their distance from Palizzolo. Rudinì continued to insist that the only real scandal was the failure of the state to indict Fontana, and that therefore, "if there is something rotten," it should be searched for among the ranks of the magistrature.[34] Codronchi was forced to make limited admissions concerning Palizzolo's "willingness to commit crimes." In contrast, Lucchesi thundered accusations against the magistrates but also against the member of parliament, Palizzolo, without realizing that he was causing embarrassment for his protectors. "This behavior of his," Rudinì commented once again, with some irritation, "strikes me as astonishing!"[35] The explanation for the behavior of the former *questore*, according to the prefect of Palermo, Francesco De Seta, was quite simple: "He gauged his behavior in terms of his own personal interests: it was opportune to attack Palizzolo violently, even though in different times the two had been close friends."[36]

In Palermo, the progress of events was a cause of considerable concern for the magistrature, which had been the target of such devastating accusations. Cosenza protested at the forum that the Milanese court was providing for the airing of the "ignoble and nauseating spectacle of . . . a personal vendetta."[37] This anomalous procedure was justified by the civil plaintiffs as a "revolutionary" act of force in the face of Palizzolo's undue influence over the public prosecutor, who has "provided grievous evidence that we have no reason to hope for the victory of truth and justice at his hands."[38] While Palizzolo placed his reliance on the machinery of Palermo's judicial and police apparatus, the Notarbartolos utilized their network of contacts and relations in the moderate and aristocratic camps, especially during the months of the Milan trial. In particular, support was provided by none other than Humbert I (Umberto I), king of Italy, at the behest of the prince of Camporeale, and was redoubled through the personal ties that linked Leopoldo Notarbartolo's uncle, a major in the Italian army and a baron, Gaetano Merlo, to the prime minister, General Luigi Pelloux.

"We clearly saw that the Ministry was supporting us," wrote Notarbartolo, Jr. "If something was too intricate or jumbled, my uncle . . . would take the train to Rome and obtain from his friend Pelloux whatever we wanted. And so we managed to secure on behalf of the institutions of justice highly confidential documents of the Banco di Sicilia, of the *questura,* and of the high command of the Royal Carabinieri of Palermo, and even documents from the Ministry of the Interior."[39]

The whole affair, however, was also the venue for an unprecedented mingling of this bloc of traditional and moderate forces with the far left. The extreme left played an important role, first and foremost, in the management of the trial. Leopoldo Notarbartolo hired two socialist lawyers, Carlo Altobelli and Giuseppe Marchesano. Marchesano came to constitute a link with the Palermo-based socialism of Aurelio Drago and Prince Alessandro Tasca di Cutò. During the year of the Italian banking scandals (1893), this convergence was less paradoxical than it might otherwise have seemed. Between the right and the left there existed a point of contact in the general denunciation of the blending of opportunism and profiteering, politics, and the administration, as well as a general critique of the systemic degeneration that led to utilization of the Mafia: "Just what should the government do?" Drago wondered. "Fight the Mafia? Then who will run the elections? And so the Mafia must be organized. And the government organized it, armed it, and paid it."[40]

Socialists and radicals, for that matter, needed to get back into the political game from which they had been expelled by the state of siege of 1894. And so, taking a shared anti-Crispi position, they attempted to establish ties with the followers of Rudinì who had previously been allied with Codronchi. Their advances, however, were spurned. Hence the violent accusations that in 1899 Giuseppe De Felice Giuffrida, the Catanian socialist who had once been a leader of the *fasci,* would in particular level against "the former viceroy of Sicily." "We two are the favorite targets of the famous De Felice," Lucchesi wrote to Codronchi, "because you as a sincere monarchist competed against him in the election, and I put him on trial and sent him to prison."[41]

The trial in Milan came in the wake of the violent repression of the uprising of 1898 and the early phase of parliamentary obstructionism in opposition to the "freedom-murdering" laws proposed by Pelloux (June 1899). The last two months of 1899 and the beginning of 1900 were a time of a left-wing offensive against a government that had shown itself to be exceedingly harsh toward the socialists and equally pliant toward the mafiosi. As Leonida Bissolati put it, Italian politics "has two faces, and on one face is the symbolic figure of Palizzolo, on the other face we see the image of the representatives De Ambris, Chiesi, and Turati, under surveillance by the state police." In the wake of a particularly strident speech by De Felice, one of the leading figures in the obstructionist movement, Pelloux was moved to admit that Milan was offering "a lesson, a bitter lesson for us all."[42] The shock wave of the exploding scandal, for that matter, also struck the government in the person of Mirri, who was forced to tender his resignation when the public prosecutor Venturini, whom Mirri had violently attacked in Milan at the trial, handed over to the newspaper *Il Tempo* a number of letters dating from 1894 in which General Mirri had demanded the release from prison of the mafioso Saladino, who had close ties to Crispi's followers.[43] On 8 December, while rumors were spreading that Palizzolo had fled the country (in fact, he was still in Sicily), Pelloux blocked all telegraph lines between Rome and Palermo and, trampling on proper legal procedure, managed to bring about an immediate vote in the Italian parliament authorizing Palizzolo's arrest, which was promptly carried out without a magistrate's warrant.

This was a significant problem, considering the Palermo affiliations of the now jailed member of parliament, Palizzolo. As had been the case so often in the past, there was a clear disconnect between the police and the magistrature, which (as the *Giornale di Sicilia* noted) "rather than serving as the natural ally and supporter of the police, actually hinders its action, rendering it powerless and ridiculous."[44] The *delegato di PS* Lancellotti—indicted for abuse of power after the members of the *cosca* (Mafia family) that he had investigated were all acquitted, "as usual," for lack of evidence—revealed that one of those mafiosi said openly to him that he felt much safer as long as Judge Pezzati, a friend of Palizzolo, was in Palermo.[45] Palizzolo, from prison, repeatedly stated that he placed "all his hopes, all his trust" in the public prosecutor.[46] The resistance that Cosenza was displaying in response to the pressure of the minister of justice of the new Saracco government, Emanuele Gianturco,[47] threatened to foment a clash between the executive power and the judiciary, especially once the public prosecutor decided to himself undertake the bill of indictments, since he did not trust the prosecution, which clearly thought the defendants were guilty. In the end, Cosenza was forced to bring Palizzolo and Fontana to trial, but the charges were such that they constituted a sort of impassioned plea on their behalf. In this atmosphere of divisions, pressures, paradoxes, and new and far more serious suspicions, the trial of Bologna got under way.

THE HONORABLE PALIZZOLO

"Palizzolo was good-hearted, kind, affectionate, a poet in his spare time, a little vain, quite loquacious, incapable of keeping a secret, and hence incapable of ordering someone to carry out a murder."[48] This is the portrait that Palizzolo's defense team painted of him. In fact, he was a colorless individual, who indulged in old-fashioned oratory that veered off into almost ridiculous effects, at least to the sophisticated ears of a Milanese journalist who listened to him speak at the Bologna trial: "He speaks leaning on a chair, with a tragic stance, abounding in gestures, modulating his voice, sometimes sweetly, at other times gravely, and occasionally impetuously, with an evident attempt to achieve dramatic effects." The defendant's tone became gentler when he explained his own degree of influence: "I was the only member of parliament accessible to my constituents. . . . I lived among the people and came down to their level, doing my best to be their adviser and friend. And the people felt gratitude."[49]

As the defense had little or no reluctance to admit, Palizzolo, the administrator of charitable organizations, the member of a countless array of civic commissions, and member of town and provincial councils, had created a network of clients that included people from every walk of life. Among them, therefore, were also a number of mafiosi of whom he made use "in the elections,"[50] not unlike any number of other parliamentarians. In certain points, this interpretation converges with that of Gaetano Mosca, who handed it down to posterity, sanctifying it with the seal of approval of a great intellectual:

> He was exceedingly popular, if popularity consists of being easily accessible to people from every walk of life, every class, and every sort of morality. His house was open to everyone; it mattered little whether they were gentlemen or swindlers. He welcomed them all in, made promises to all of them, shook hands with everyone, and chatted tirelessly with one and all; to everyone who came he would read his poetry, described his oratorical triumphs in the Chamber of Deputies, and, with skillful allusions, conveyed to all his visitors how many powerful friends and acquaintances he boasted.[51]

In Mosca's view, then, we are not dealing with a criminal, but rather with the typical product of expanded suffrage, one of the *homines novi* (new men) who take up politics as a profession, accustomed to winning the consensus of the constituents with a practice of performing small favors for a small-scale clientele. In practical terms, Mosca downgraded the family capo to clientele capo, in order to render more acceptable the evident collaboration between him and Rudinì and Codronchi. He thus depicted Palizzolo as one of those petty bourgeois parvenus against whom the marquis of Rudinì, his political mentor, often railed.[52]

Palizzolo in fact had created for himself a sizable fortune through the purchase of state-owned property. Still, he was not a "new man," as we can divine from the aristocratic attribute of *cavaliere* that was frequently used in accompaniment to his surname. He became a member of the Italian parliament in 1882, a date that was emblematic of the expansion of Italian suffrage. Still, he was no pro-Crispi democrat. Instead, he was a regionalist, a leading member of the Palermo party that, as we know, was focused on the general issue of the post-Risorgimento "perturbance." The investigation that was conducted into his career takes us back to the crucial years of 1876–1877 and flatly contradicts any sugary portraits of his loyalties. Instead, we clearly see him as a *manutengolo,* or abettor, of the brigands Valvo, De Pasquale, and Leone, and an unwilling collaborator of Lucchesi and Malusardi. In later years as well, Palizzolo proved to have been involved in episodes of brigandage, among them the kidnapping of Emanuele Notarbartolo (1882).[53] Many threads of evidence lead to this member of parliament. It was a client of Palizzolo's who obtained for the bandits the *bersagliere* uniforms in which they disguised themselves. After the ransom had been paid, the bandits hid out on farmland adjoining one of Palizzolo's properties in Villabate. Through a mysterious intuition, it was none other than our old friend, detective Di Blasi, who uncovered their hideout. According to Girolamo De Luca Aprile, it was the usual mechanism at work: Bardesono, feeling the pressure of public opinion as well as that of Depretis, must have "bared his teeth at Palizzolo,"[54] persuading him to cooperate.

The *manutengolo* was a certain Giuseppe Fontana (son of Rosario), who in 1882, in Villabate and "over a certain expanse of territory that extends all the way to the boundaries of the adjoining province [Messina] . . . exercises uncontested mastery." In 1866, he was subjected to the special security regimen of *ammonizione,* and in 1873, he wound up in prison for murder, where he waited confidently for his liberty to be restored through the efforts of "individuals of distinguished social standing." In the 1880s, he was sent into internal exile, once on the island of Ventotene and twice on the island of Ustica, where Palizzolo came to pay him a visit and succeeded in obtaining his liberation.[55] Fontana was a cousin of Giuseppe Fontana (son of Vincenzo, identified as the killer of Notarbartolo). Another link between Palizzolo, the member of parliament, and the *cosca* (Mafia family) of Villabate was Filippello from Caccamo, formerly a *manutengolo,* or abettor, of Leone, who was ordered to move there in 1875 by none other than Palizzolo. Nearly all of them were previously identified as supporters of brigands. The members of the *fratellanza* (brotherhood), said by the police to hold meetings between Villabate and Ciaculli, devoted themselves to extortion, robbery, cattle theft, murder of alleged spies, as well as political activity carried out on behalf of the mayor Pitarresi—as well as Palizzolo.

The sphere of operations and influence of this association of wrongdoers is not, however, restricted to the territory of Villabate alone. Instead it extends over the neighboring *borgate* of Palermo, to Ficarazzi and to Misilmeri, and its numerous offenses nearly invariably went unpunished due to the terror that the organization inspired in witnesses and in the victims as well who, rather than exposing themselves to certain death, preferred to suffer their losses in silence.[56]

Responsibility for the 1882 kidnapping can be assigned in accordance with this territorial logic, inasmuch as the location of the kidnapping itself (Caccamo) and the place where the brigands holed up after collecting the ransom (Villabate) had only one thing in common: the patronage of Palizzolo. In 1892, this area was not part of his electoral district. In particular, the Albergheria, a quarter of Palermo where he boasted an especially fervent constituency, is located in the historic center of the city. Both Mosca and the defense team cited that location with special emphasis in a bid to debunk the idea that he had any ties to the Mafia, which of course is located primarily in the *borgate*, while in the older urban quarters, the criminality tends instead to assume the configuration of *ricottaro*, or exploiter of prostitutes, that is, pimp.[57] The argument points us instead to the time when Palizzolo first ran in Caccamo, and in any case it may implicate connections quite different from mere electoral ties. In Caccamo, just as in the area to the southeast of Palermo, in Mezzomorreale, Ciaculli, and Villabate, Palizzolo owned land, and therefore had relations in the milieux of the *guardiani* (rural watchmen), the *gabellotti* (renters and sublessors of parcels of farmland), and the *fontanieri* (or water administrators). Here we might well point to the more general category of the bond linking mafiosi and landowners, were it not for the fact that Palizzolo was not a sufficiently large landowner to employ—as, however, he did—numerous full-time salaried employees, "all ready and willing to commit crimes . . . , even though, as at Inserra, the revenue of the estate was insufficient to pay the salary of the *castaldo*, or agricultural administrator: we might say that he maintained these patches of land for no other reason than to give work to convicts!"[58]

In this connection, the Miceli murder can provide some illumination. Palizzolo was charged in this murder as well as in the Notarbartolo murder.[59] The scene of the crime was the enormous "Rocca di Monreale" estate, whose owner, Marianna Gentile, died in 1873, leaving as the principal (but not sole) heir her nephew: a highly intricate situation, because there were no fewer than five hundred interested relatives, some of them receiving sizable bequests, while others contested the validity of the will. Palizzolo acquired the rights to a substantial number of shares of the inheritance and invested a disproportionately large sum, given the loss-making operations of the farm, the modest income, and the generally chaotic conditions of its workings. Nonetheless, he failed to complete his sweep of the inheritance on account of "the costs of . . . administration and legal representation, the greed of many who had already laid hands on their inheritance, and the shortage of resources."[60] He therefore altered his tactics, working to achieve an agreement of some sort and striving to prevent the intro-duction of Francesco Di Liberto into the estate. Di Liberto had been appointed a *gabellotto* by the court-appointed administrator. In consideration of the "many affiliations" of the member of parliament, Palizzolo, Di Liberto withdrew "in the interests of quiet living."[61]

Working to block his ambitions was Francesco Miceli, *fattore* (overseer) of the Villa Gentile, an individual who was "courageous, strong, and industrious in his attempts to keep farmers honest." By family tradition as well he was not the sort of man who could be easily intimidated. He was the son of Turi Miceli, leader of the squads of Monreale of 1848, 1860, and 1866. Palizzolo stated that he had no fear of "Miceli's Mafia" and announced that he "would bring people to the estate to keep him in his place."[62] Among those "people" were a pair of rough customers named Nicolò Trapani and Filippo Vitale, the latter a convict sen-tenced to internal exile serving under Malusardi, capo of the Mafia of Altarello di Baida. Miceli continued to bring criticisms of the management of Palizzolo and his protégés, persuading along the way some of the heirs not to sell their property. Nor did he show any signs of fear when Palizzolo, member of the Ital-ian parliament, boasted of his past relations with the bandit Leone. Miceli also failed to soften his position when a revolver bullet narrowly missed his head. He only gave up when a shotgun blast struck him dead on 17 July 1892. After his death, Palizzolo's men had free rein and turned the Gentile estate into a key point in the network of tobacco smuggling and cattle rustling, along the route that ran from the interior to Palermo. For instance, animals stolen from Sciara, about 30 kilometers (20 miles) from the capital, Palermo, were found there in 1889. Also, a girl who was kidnapped and then released through Palizzolo's mediation was brought to Sciara.[63]

This may help explain the lack of economic sense in Palizzolo's business affairs, and it may also help us to understand why Francesco Paolo Vitale, who was born into a well-to-do family, was willing to live and work there as a modest *guardiano* along with his cousin Filippo. This was not so much a farming opera-tion run with mafioso personnel as it was a strategic marshalling point for crim-inal activities. Palizzolo did not deal with mafiosi as a landowner or a politician. Rather, he viewed property and politics as links in the relations among the *cosche*

(Mafia families), making him a large-scale coordinator on a subprovincial scale. Already for some time, the police had considered it a solid piece of information that Palizzolo was the "patron of the Mafia of the Palermo countryside and especially the southern and eastern sectors."[64] But it was during the trial in Milan, and to an even greater degree, during the Bologna trial, that his role emerged most clearly, with no uncertain outlines. Aside from the initiative by the civil plaintiffs, the credit for this outcome should go to Ermanno Sangiorgi, the one-time persecutor of the family, or Cosca dell'Uditore, who in August 1898 Prime Minister Pelloux appointed *questore* of Palermo, alongside the prefect Francesco De Seta, to wage the battle against the member of parliament, Palizzolo, and the Mafia.

In the *questura*, the anti-Palizzolo faction reared its head once again. Sangiorgi arranged Palizzolo's arrest even before the recalcitrant Cosenza issued a warrant. Sangiorgi also cut through the delays in taking Fontana into custody; Fontana had been hired by the prince of Mirto to challenge the depredations visited on that aristocrat's inland properties by the brigand Varsalona, and Sangiorgi summoned the noble gentleman to his office and even threatened to jail him if he failed to produce Fontana. Fontana thereupon turned himself in, but to the gentleman and not to the police. In other words, he surrendered at the Sangiorgi home (and not in the *questura*), turning up in the prince's carriage, accompanied by his lawyer. The ritual was described in the press as the sort of negotiation that is carried on "between equal powers." "That prince has properties and large landholdings in many different provinces across Sicily, and arresting Fontana would have been a very difficult undertaking," De Seta said in justification. "Here it is no source of shame for a landholder, even an honest landholder, to garrison his property with guards and extend his protection, with this end in view, to individuals linked to the Mafia."[65] Once again, it was the *questore*, in both Milan and Bologna, who testified to Palizzolo's "willingness to commit crimes" and who extracted from the archives of his office documentary evidence of the pressures exerted by the member of parliament, Palizzolo, on behalf of a great number of mafiosi. Those documents became the strongest argument available to the civil plaintiffs. Meanwhile, both *questore* and prefect dissolved all "commissions and administrative boards of which Palizzolo was a member" and managed the political elections of 1900, in which the convicted member of parliament ran for office, "at the behest of his numerous and eager clientele," and victoriously supported the lawyer Giuseppe Di Stefano Napolitano, a candidate who had all the right qualities: "He was young, wealthy, respected in the courts and throughout the city, and new to politics."[66]

The *vox populi* had for some time "insisted that there were links" between the Notarbartolo case and other murders, "both typical and characteristic," speculating on how to explain all the various elements "without relying upon the idea of an association, or at least a network of criminal interests."[67] The old *questore,* Farias, had already begun investigations; the new *questore* reached out for old contacts and, "under the seal of professional secrecy," obtained information about a plant for the production of counterfeit banknotes; he identified its location, raided it, and confiscated the equipment and arrested the counterfeiters. The same informer at this point provided a key with which to solve the interpretation of other crimes.[68] There reappeared, as during the time of the Amorosos and the *stoppagghieri,* a *deus ex machina,* the superinformers, the anonymous "reliable source" who "can and must be trusted implicitly."[69] This informer led the authorities by the hand and painted a picture of the "shadowy partnership" operating behind the individual crimes. The occasion offered by the Notarbartolo case led Sangiorgi to attempt to demolish with a single grand blow the mafioso power, providing elements of understanding that by their character of completeness and detail are unparalleled. In thirty-one handwritten reports, totaling 485 pages, composed between November 1898 and February 1900, the *questore* laid out a description of a major organization, focusing on its hierarchies and its crimes:

> The countryside around Palermo . . . is sadly plagued, as are other sections of this and neighboring provinces, by a vast association of criminals, organized into sections, and divided into groups; each group is governed by a capo, known as the *caporione.* . . . Over this association of lowlifes rules a supreme capo. The selection of the capos is done by the members, and the selection of the supreme capo is done by the *caporione* gathered in an assembly.[70]

The names, well known to us (and to Sangiorgi), of the Giammonas, the Siinos, the Bonuras, and the Biondos, represented the leadership of the organization. We find Gaetano Badalamenti, who was already a leading figure in the feud with the Amorosos. The "mastermind" remained Antonino Giammona, "who provides leadership in the form of advice, grounded in his long experience as an old ex-convict, and instructions on how to commit murders and create defensive positions."[71] The operative management was placed in the hands of the younger members, Giuseppe Giammona for Passo di Rigano and Francesco Siino for Malaspina. Francesco Siino also served as the capo, or boss, of the organization as a whole. Apparently, it consisted of some 670 members, scattered among the "groups" established in the *borgate* that surrounded the capital to the southwest (the Conca d'Oro, to use the official name), while the *questura* was unable to prove that it extended its authority into the provinces. Neither did the capos of the *cosche* in the area that runs from southeast of Palermo to the sea participate in the summit meetings, nor were they involved in the bloody wars within the organization itself. In particular, the followers of Palizzolo were left out: the mafiosi of Villabate and the intermediaries of the significant reconciliation between Palizzolo himself and the Mafia boss of Settecannoli, Salvatore Conti, yet another of Codronchi's town councilors of 1897 who, having attempted to break free, wound up being forced to kiss the hand of the member of parliament, Palizzolo. Their names are Salvo Saitta, Francesco Motisi, Filippo Vitale, and Salvatore Greco.[72]

It is in any case worth noting the degree of acrimony with which "Calpurnio," a hack writer guided by Palizzolo, covered the roundups and arrests of 1900: "Throughout Palermo, it was with horror that we recall the trial that implemented a vast criminal conspiracy stitched together by Sangiorgi! Hundreds of unfortunates languished in prison, and when they had been reduced to poverty and they had served the few months of their sentence, what irreparable ruins they found once they set foot once again in their homes, back among their loved ones!"[73]

As De Seta put it, "the Mafia . . . was reduced to silence and inaction."[74] The trial for criminal conspiracy that was held in 1901 ended, however, with a great many acquittals and a few very light sentences. This result prompted a comment from Sangiorgi, pointing to circumstances and relationships that are, however, unfortunately all too obscure to the modern reader. "It could not have gone otherwise, if those who indicted them in the evening rose in their defense the following morning."[75] In the absence of a *pentito* willing to provide sworn testimony in court, the associative nature of the Mafia remained a thesis impossible to prove to a jury.

THE SHADOWY PARTNERSHIP

According to Sangiorgi, we are in the presence of a centralized organization. Perhaps we should actually speak of a federation among the *cosche* of the *borgate*. Here, too, it would be appropriate to wonder whether the police officials behind this depiction of matters were not exaggerating their information in order to accommodate the laws concerning criminal conspiracy, with a view to increasing the alarm already spreading among the government authorities. However, the judicial sources did not provide much greater assurances of objectivity, but for the opposite reasons, given that the obstacles to bringing *maxiprocessi* (maxitrials) to trial might well lead the magistrates to prosecute individual crimes and to refrain from investigating more complex and subterranean structures.[76]

In fact, the *questura* might perhaps have been overstating the case in claiming that the Mafia's infrastructure extended to a provincial scale; but there was no exaggeration in pointing out the ties linking the various groups in the western Palermo area. That linkage is evident from the overall array of circumstances documented and from the very history of the Mafia of the *borgate,* extending back to 1875. There are those who might question the highly formalized nature of these criminal organizations: the "members," who regularly pay cash dues and who assemble in regular meetings to make especially important decisions; the fact that in some cases suspected traitors were offered an opportunity to defend themselves before those same assemblies;[77] the ritual nature of murders, which whenever possible were to be perpetrated collectively; the election of *capi, sottocapi,* and *capo supremo*—bosses, underbosses, and overlord. The natural response would be to point out the resemblance between this structure and the structure described in the descriptions provided by the various *pentiti* (Buscetta, Contorno, Calderone, and others) for the 1860s, 1870s, and 1880s. Judge Giovanni Falcone and the *questore* Sangiorgi—separated by a full century in time—were both able to state that there existed ties of coordination between the leaders of organizations with the same territorial base. The Mafia leadership required a proxy from its membership, and therefore an electoral mechanism and a body of laws. Of course, the balance of equilibrium governing such a structure was highly unstable, and this particular juridical system, more than other such systems, was liable to be subverted through the use of raw force. Consensus and conflict constituted two cyclical phases, one organic and the other critical, in the life cycle of individual *cosche* and, to an even greater degree, in the context of the coordination among a number of *cosche.* Here, too, the processes that operated at the end of the nineteenth century worked pretty much like those at play in the 1970s. Mafia wars brought about new states of equilibrium, shattering age-old alliances: in the case at hand, the alliance between the Giammonas and the Siinos.

The conflict came to a head in December 1896, when the discovery of a first clandestine printing shop created economic difficulties and reciprocal mistrust. Nor was the situation resolved by the vicious and blind vendetta carried out upon the young daughter of the suspected spy, the tavern-keeper Giuseppa Di Sano.[78] The reputation of Francesco Siino began to decline, and the Giammonas, the Biondos, and the Bonuras, capos, respectively, of the *cosche* of Passo di Rigano, Piana dei Colli, and Perpignano, began to question his leadership— "since they were all well-to-do people with substantial reputations within the Mafia, they were unwilling to accept Siino's superiority." Siino, in turn, during a general meeting held in January, exclaimed: "All right then, because I am no longer accorded the respect that is due me, let each group think as it wishes and fend for itself."[79] This marked the beginning of a phase of recurring territorial violations and reciprocal provocations. "Among the laws of the Mafia," noted Sangiorgi, "there is the rule of respect for the jurisdictions of others, and infraction of that rule constitutes a highly personal insult."[80] Once all attempts at peacemaking (we have no idea how sincere those efforts might have been) had been exhausted, there began an "unequal battle for resources and power," in which the Giammonas were victorious, as a result of their superior economic and military resources, the greater number of adherents to their faction, and the unidentified protection in high places that they were said to enjoy. "We counted our own numbers," Francesco Siino was forced to admit following the murder of his nephew Filippo, "and we have counted the numbers of the others: there are 170 of us, including the *cagnolazzi* (aspiring mafiosi), and there are five hundred of them. . . . We must make peace."[81] The surrender took the concrete form of the Siinos' renunciation of the "front" of the *guardianìe* that they had formerly controlled, and the flight to Livorno of Francesco Siino himself, the clan's capo.

The concluding phase of the Mafia war was intertwined with the police roundups and sweeps that hit the Giammona faction especially hard. Some of the information that Sangiorgi possessed, for that matter, could have come from nowhere other than the interior of the Mafia, which illuminates the methods whereby "the *questura* . . . silently penetrated into the organism of the Palermo Mafia."[82] The identity of the mysterious informer leads back to the usual factional structure that involved sectors of the Mafia and sectors of the state. From the very beginning of their disagreement, the Giammona group accused Siino of being "in league with the *questura*." One mafioso shouted, immediately following his arrest, "I know that the cause of the persecution of so many sons of good mothers is none other than that infamous cop-lover Francesco Siino, but, by the blood of the Madonna, we shall not rest until we have exterminated him and all his ilk."[83]

The war was not especially bloody: four dead and several more wounded, all on the Siino side, and only a tiny portion of the murders attributed to the organization by Sangiorgi. Those murders formed part of the everyday activity of the *cosche,* which consisted of a total control of all economic transactions carried out in the territory of the *borgate* in order to impose "*castaldi,* or agricultural administrators, *guardiani* , labor, *gabelle,* prices for the sale of citrus and other products of the soil."[84] Among the 218 mafiosi documented in close detail in the Sangiorgi Report, the most sizable group was that of the full-time, salaried employees in charge of guarding and supervising agricultural operations: there were forty-five of them, an assortment of *giardinieri* (or keepers of a citrus grove), *custodi* (custodians), *curatoli* (guards), and *castaldi* (agricultural administrators), and to them we should add the six mechanics who were in charge of the steam engines used to pump water. We then find twenty-six landowners, who owned *giardini*, or citrus groves, land, and rural estates, who had in many cases only recently attained the status of landowners (an element that here as elsewhere was emphasized by the *questura*); that is to say, they were of the civil class and had received academic diplomas. Another twenty-five individuals could be classed under the heading of intermediaries: dealers, smugglers, middlemen, businessmen and manufacturers, and *gabellotti*, while there were twenty-seven laborers, farmers, and herders. The eleven goatherders and the seven teamsters represent a typical category, providing links between the town, the hinterland, and the countryside. Then there were small businessmen and wage earners of various sorts: innkeepers, bakers, pasta makers, haberdashers, cobblers, shop porters, bricklayers, masons, stone carvers, and so on. A comparison with the provincial Mafia of Termini and Cefalù not only shows the obviously greater presence of urban characters, but especially the greater specialization in protective roles (for instance, the category of *campieri,* or rural custodians, and watchmen). We might say that the rural Mafia more generally reflects the social structure; in fact, I have been obliged to remove from the comparison the "first category" of grand notables present in the provincial lists, as they would not have had any counterparts in the Palermo organization, which was more compact, both in social and in functional terms.

"Ordinary people, in the countryside and the city"[85] were the individuals whom the Notarbartolo affair brought (or brought back) to public attention. Once again, the social hierarchy corresponded to the criminal hierarchy, and custodians and dealers/smugglers, landowners, and *gabellotti* formed something close to the entire governing body. According to Mosca, "the social status of the most influential members of the *cosche* is somewhat more elevated than that of the poorer sector of the general Sicilian population; only rarely, however, does that ruling class of the Mafia reach the level of the middle class."[86] Here, as is his custom, the political scientist did his best to defuse the issue in a display of a certain ideological prudishness in the face of a concept like that of the middle class, a concept that was so crucial to the symbolism of moderate liberalism and for that very reason employed by Franchetti previously with specific and polemical intent. This was indeed a middle class, though it had only recently risen to that standing and its elevation remained suspect.

Even in the ancient center of Palermo, among the "alleys and lanes of the Castro and Albergheria quarters" (the heart of Palizzolo's electoral constituency), "ancient and stratified" organizations operated, composed of beggars, thieves, and pickpockets and cutpurses, often underaged, burglars, prostitutes, and pimps or *ricottari*. "Parallel to the hierarchy of persons is the hierarchy of crime," and the leadership belonged to those who ran bordellos and gaming houses, the fences and receivers of stolen goods who operated flourishing businesses based on "self-proclaimed lending agencies or pawn shops."[87] A few years later, a vast organization was reported, diffused throughout the city, and devoted to robbing coach drivers.

On the whole, this street variety of criminal operations appears to be quite distinct, by social makeup and by function, from the Mafia of the *giardini* and the *borgate* with its hierarchy of landowners, smugglers and dealers, *guardiani*, and *fontanieri*. Only a closer examination can show the differences between the western sector of the hinterland (the Conca d'Oro) and the eastern sector (Villabate, Mezzomorreale, etc.). First, it would appear that in the former case (street Mafia) the powerful organizational bonds controlled by the Mafia itself represented a different reality than that constituted in the second case by the large-scale political broker. It is true, of course, that the emergency of the Palizzolo case led to a closer focus on local politics, which, in the western sector, more extensively examined by Sangiorgi, led only to a generic disdain for the protection that "members of parliament, senators, and other influential individuals" provided the mafiosi, "and subsequently, in exchange, were protected by them and defended."[88] In any case, it should be noted that Villabate and Monreale, in contrast with the *borgate*, were independent townships where the Mafia party could directly engage in the takeover of local power, while in the context of the larger city of Palermo, the Mafia as an organization was obliged to take into account more complex interests and political aggregations. The groups from the eastern sector of the hinterland then displayed a lesser degree of territorial and criminal specialization, making use of more extensive networks of relations, at least along the line running from Caccamo and Sciara to Palermo through Ciaculli and Monreale. These towns not only subsisted on prosperous and intensive agriculture; they also constituted the portal to the interior of the island, while the immediate point of reference for the entire Conca d'Oro was the city of Palermo. A comparative analysis of the crimes committed by the two criminal organizations, respectively, to the east and the west of the capital, shows that on the east there was a greater abundance of "common" crime (robberies, kidnapping, cattle theft), while in the west what prevailed were functions of "order-keeping" (*guardianìa;* commercial brokerage).

We should not overstate the case, of course. Even on the eastern side of Palermo we find the typical murder of a middleman. Fontana provides favorable rates for the repayment of a debt, thus preventing the forfeiture of his brother-in-law's *giardino*.[89] Filippello can put on the appearance of a proponent of law and order, not only in the defense of his patron Palizzolo but also that of such individuals as Gaetano Focher, the inspector from the *monte di pieta* (charitable lending and pawn institution) of Palermo, who sent him to Altavilla to take possession of property from a bourgeois who was clearly reluctant to pay his debts. The former *manutengolo,* or abettor, of Leone does no more than explain to the former landowner that there is such a thing as downward mobility, urging him "no longer to avail himself of the funds of Focher that had been seized, because otherwise things would turn out badly for him." Then he left the village, having impounded the estate, leasing it for the benefit of the local Mafia capo.[90]

On the other hand, smuggling and passing counterfeit bills, robberies, and extortion letters were all crimes extensively practiced in the Conca d'Oro as well. However, and this may be no coincidence, it was neither Siino nor Giammona who killed Notarbartolo. The events described in the Sangiorgi Report depict a Mafia that stayed "in its place." We will not speak of a "plebeian" criminality, as does Marcella Marmo, depicting a nineteenth-century Neapolitan camorra that attempted to "caccià l'oro de' piducchie" (literally, "dig gold out of lice"), meaning that it exploited the commercial transactions of the poor and skimmed a take from salaries. Percentages skimmed off of small-scale business activities, the *componenda* or kickback for resolving such cases of extortion, and for obtaining the return of petty thefts, also existed in Palermo, but for the most part they involved the quarters of the inner city.[91] The Mafia of the *borgate,* the terminal point of a wealthy economy, lived on the relationships among small-scale criminality, the middle class, and the upper classes, an interstitial phenomenon in which contact between the world of criminals and the world of the highest classes was limited to certain milieux. There was never a case of a member of the upper classes being murdered. Or rather, there was one case only, in which a lawyer who attempted to obtain compensation for unpaid *gabelle* was wounded by a rifle shot.[92] The response to an excessively independent-minded landowner was always that of a general boycott and ostracism, or else a chain of murders that created a vacuum around him. When Senator Eugenio Olivieri appointed a cousin as overseer to reduce the depredations of the mafioso *curatolo,* the *cosca* did its best to discredit the interloper through various means and worked to ensure that for years he was unable to hire a *guardiano,* but it never physically harmed him. If he had been a *giardiniere* (or keeper of a citrus grove) instead of a townsman, the outcome would have been far different. Even the distinctive "message" sent by the damaging of trees could only be conveyed once for each *giardino* because, if it were repeated, it would constitute an insult to the landowner, and no longer to the *gabellotto* or the *guardiano.*[93] This subtle aspect of the ritual once again points to the caution and prudence with which intermediaries interacted with the upper classes.

The men who drafted the report said that they were certain that the function of the Mafia as an organization was to restrict the right to private property. Still, they could not conceal the fact that it was precisely the defense of private property that served as the underlying motivation for most of the murders committed by the Mafia. For instance, that was the case with the four individuals murdered around the end of 1897, whose corpses were made to vanish in order to hinder the investigations and contribute to the myth of the Mafia's omnipotence. There were also refined grace notes of misinformation, with eyewitnesses volunteering accounts of having seen the murdered men alive and well in Tunis, and letters from the vanished men arriving, again from Tunis, until finally the corpses were uncovered. At the time, the current Mafia term, *lupara bianca*, literally, "white shotgun," meaning a Mafia murder in which the corpse is made to disappear, was not yet in use. Instead, the case was known as the *caso dei quattro scomparsi* ("case of the four vanished men").

The first of the four was the baker Tuttilmondo, executed for stealing from his master. The second was Antonino D'Alba, innkeeper and member of the *cosca* of Falde. This time, we are talking about an individual who possessed a "small degree of authority," based on "two strategic points"—one of the many inns or taverns in which the mafiosi meet, and a warehouse in the Arenella, "a neighborhood that might well have been designed for smuggling."[94] The innkeeper was the cousin of a certain Francesco D'Alba, who worked for Eduardo and Samuele Hamnett, important citrus merchants who belonged to the British colony that had transplanted itself in Palermo. The Hamnetts suspected their employee of being the author of certain "begging" letters, as well as the dynamite attack in September 1897 that targeted their home, as well as the homes of other manufacturers of allied products. This may have been an indicator of the tensions that in this period divided the various operators in the citrus fruit market.[95] In order to protect themselves, the Hamnetts mobilized a relative, Francesco Serio, *gabellotto* of the civil class, "who maintained relations of patronage and clientelism with the Mafia." But when he entered into contact with the bosses of the Falde group, they realized that Francesco D'Alba was given information by his cousin: a betrayal that cost the innkeeper his life.[96]

Last of all, there were Vincenzo Lo Porto and Giuseppe Caruso, coach drivers affiliated with the *cosca* of the Olivuzza. In the *borgata* of the Olivuzza stood the renowned villa of Ignazio Florio, the great shipowner and financier, scion of a business family who had married into the crème de la crème of Palermo's aristocracy. Both halves of Florio's personality—both the aristocratic half and the bourgeois half—aspired to tranquility and security; the *guardianìa* of the villa was entrusted to Pietro Noto, who with his brother Francesco was the capo of the local *cosca*. In the summer of 1897, relations between Lo Porto and Caruso and the Noto brothers—all at one time "close friends"—were rapidly deteriorating because, according to the coach drivers, the Notos had taken the lion's share of the profits from the sum obtained by a "begging letter," or extortion, that had been sent to Joshua Whitaker, another major British merchant and entrepreneur.[97] The two coach drivers decided to undertake a spectacular and provocative project: they would steal from Villa Florio a number of artworks of great value. Once again, the theft constituted above all an insult, a way of heaping scorn on the credibility of the organization and its capos, and possibly bring about a new leadership. This shows how the instability of the Mafia hierarchies exposed the members of the dominant classes, who wished to be in contact with an "order-bringing" Mafia, to involvement in criminal deeds that were hardly compatible with the quality of their status and reputations. Ignazio Florio, "surprised and indignant" over what had happened, personally demanded an explanation from Pietro Noto as the head of security for the villa and, more generally, of the quarter of Olivuzza. "The objective that the two coach drivers had set out to obtain, the humiliation of their boss and underboss, had been attained."[98] And the Notos were obliged to undertake a negotiation that resulted (perhaps following the payment of a ransom) in the recovery of the loot, which mysteriously reappeared in the Florio villa, in the exact location from which it had vanished.

There followed a feigned truce between the coach drivers and the Notos. In reality, the Notos had called a summit meeting with the city coordinating committee, with the attendance as well of mafiosi from the province. During that meeting, the disrespectful rank-and-file mafiosi, who were habitual burglars and thieves, were accused of having operated outside of the control of the "society," and in particular of having failed to contribute the percentage of the take that was due to it. The pair were sentenced to death, and, on the night between 24 October and 25 October, they were lured into an ambush and executed.

This time the organizational strategy, an astonishing collective execution carried out by some thirty individuals as an internal warning to the members of the *cosche* and the affiliated and neighboring structures, a shrewd mixture of true and false information in order to disorient the authorities, was unable to fully attain the desired goal. This was in part because *omertà* was more of an ideal model than an actual model of real-world behavior that could be relied upon in all circumstances. Caruso's father, "without reluctance, both in private and in public," explicitly denounced the responsibility of the Mafia for the killing and threatened to go to Rome to demand justice from the national government "if the local authorities failed to render justice in the face of such horrible murders."[99] It took new and unmistakable intimidations to persuade him to moderate his protests. More interesting in this context, however, was the reaction of two women, the widows of Lo Porto and Caruso, because their story unveils the crucial point, the relations between the world of the violent and the upper classes.

Toward the end of November, roughly a month after the murders, Agata Mazzola, the widow of Lo Porto, walked up to Donna Giovanna d'Ondes Trigona in Florio (meaning Florio was her married name—*translator's note*), the mother of the two young brothers, Ignazio and Vincenzo. Donna Giovanna was walking from her villa to the convent of the Sisters of Charity. Agata Mazzola asked her, in that context, for a little charitable assistance on behalf of her orphaned children and herself, now deprived of any means of support. Sangiorgi believed that the widow knew nothing of the theft from the villa. Perhaps, however, it is more plausible that the woman wished to clear up the situation with a desperate provocation. Signora Florio, however, remained unperturbed and brusquely replied: "Don't bother me, because your husband was a thief who came to steal from my palazzo together with Caruso."[100] Later, when Donna Giovanna emerged from the convent, the discussion resumed, this time with the participation of Caruso's widow as well. The two widows claimed that their husbands had been murdered for refusing to take part in the Notos' proposed plan to kidnap the young Vincenzo Florio, and therefore, not because they had insulted the illustrious family, but instead because they had insisted on showing the highest respect for the Florios. This was a blatant attempt to capture the proud matron's benevolence, raising the stakes still more in the game against Pietro Noto and invoking the suspicion triggered by the violation of the villa's security: "The thieves," claimed Agata Mazzola, "were employed in your palazzo, where outsiders cannot think of entering."[101]

This singular and public exchange between the widows of two coach drivers and the most renowned matron of upper-class Palermo shows a paradoxical fact. Of the two parties to the discussion, the party that was most accurately aware of the actual nature of the criminal act in question was not the widows of the two thieves, but the noblewoman. She was so fully involved in the order-keeping function of the Mafia as a structure that she considered the murderous punishment of the theft to be a normal course of events, provided that the two coach drivers had actually committed the theft for which they were murdered. The widows, on the other hand, could do nothing more than to deny that their husbands were guilty of that theft, and they never questioned the proper devotion of the lawless class to the upper classes in the society in which they lived. The unfortunate Sangiorgi was unable to place these relations within the context of the articles of criminal law, and specifically how to discuss a person of such great prestige and wealth:

> Signora Florio is a religious and pious noblewoman, and it is impossible to say which is greater: the enormous wealth at her disposal or the outstanding virtues of her most noble and well-born soul; it is therefore reasonable to suppose that, if she is invited to testify under oath, she will not and indeed cannot conceal from the investigating agents of the law her meeting with the widow.[102]

THE INTERMEDIARIES' CLIMB TO POWER

Two eminent men of late nineteenth-century Palermo, Notarbartolo and Palizzolo, were both involved with the sordid mafiosi of Villabate in a grand plot involving murder. Why was the former director of the Banco di Sicilia murdered? The answer to this question is a decisive one, and not only for the straightforward solution of the murder investigation. This episode marked a fundamental turning point in the history of the Palermo Mafia: the involvement of an authoritative member of the ruling class in the violent dealings that had heretofore been reserved to the reciprocal relations among criminals implied a watershed transformation, and perhaps a shattering of the filter that had until then separated the two worlds, or perhaps we should call it the valve that had governed communications between those two worlds. For that matter, Palizzolo already represented a case that in his own time was unusual in the realm of relations between politicians and mafiosi. What remains to be identified is the common ground shared by these two radically diverse figures—the notable, famous for his moral integrity, and the politician, "much discussed" for his relations with brigands and criminals. That common ground was one on which Notarbartolo, who boasted that he had never had private dealings with Palizzolo, to the degree that he had refused to frequent social gatherings where he was invited,[103] was forced to set aside his haughtiness as a great aristocrat and, let us say, a respectable individual.

First of all, there is the field of the representative public institutions where, in fact, the first clashes between the two did take place in 1873, at the point of transition in the city government of Palermo between the clerical-regionalist coalition, in which Palizzolo was the commissioner of the food administration board, and the liberal administration led by Notarbartolo. At that point, the new mayor brusquely demanded that the former commissioner pay the sum of 3,625 lire that he owed the administration in relation to a purchase of flour.[104]

But, beginning in 1875, Notarbartolo was the director of a major publicly owned bank, apparently sheltered from the most treacherous currents of the political system. He was placed in this office by the last of the right-wing prefects, Gerra, and was left there even after the "parliamentary revolution" because of his distinguished achievements in restoring the bank, in serious difficulties, to financial health.

As soon as he took office, the new director analyzed the reasons for this financial crisis according to the formula of an old-style moderate, in contrast with the blithe approach to finance seen elsewhere, and in support of a prudently deflationary line: "Perhaps the scale of credit issued [was] greater than needed, hence the fever for risky speculations of all sorts, which rather than helping, actually undermined the true and productive types of commerce."[105] Later, modifying his judgment, he aimed instead at the excessive concentration of finances provided to two companies at risk, "La Trinacria" (a Palermo shipping company) and Genuardi (an Agrigento sulphur-exporting company), on account of the presence of individuals involved in these companies on the supervisory staff of the bank itself.[106]

According to the bank's charter, a government-appointed general manager served alongside a fifty-member general board of directors composed of representatives of the provinces and the chambers of commerce, an institution that theoretically represented the interests of a civil society and that established itself as a political and clientelistic counterweight to the powerful administrative structure of the bank. As Notarbartolo wrote in an 1889 letter to the minister of agriculture in the Crispi administration, Luigi Miceli, it had become increasingly "difficult if not impossible to administer and securely safeguard the interests of the institution," because the general board of directors intended "to subjugate the executive management and the discount committees, . . . intrude into every field."[107] The members of the board of directors had no banking expertise, but it was they "who were most active in the provincial, town, and commercial elections." Indeed, "the aim of succeeding in obtaining a chair on the boards of directors and the discount committees of the Banco di Sicilia was the source in Sicily of electoral battles." Even a "diplomatic" evaluation, offered in private to his son, Leopoldo, described a board composed of a few *galantuomini* (gentlemen), profiteers such as the Catanian Senator Tenerelli, and protectors of mafiosi and criminals such as the Messinese Orioles, and the Palermitans Figlia, Muratori, and Palizzolo.[108] "They consider," he confided to the prince of Camporeale, "the Banco di Sicilia as a *res nullius* [ownerless property]."[109]

The general manager's concerns grew in the wake of 1887, when in southern Italy the economic crisis hit the publicly owned banks working on behalf of the land reform and indirectly hit the Banco di Sicilia and the Banco di Napoli (Bank of Naples), institutions that ensured those banks of rediscount. This meant the risk of returning to the plight of 1875, with the difference that now there was not a single major debtor affecting the available choices, but rather a number of small banks in trouble, a few of which had members of the board of directors, such as Todaro from Agrigento, Palermo from Messina, and even Muratori, as officers or shareholders, and therefore in the dual role of controllers and controllees.[110]

A few days after the first letter, Notarbartolo returned to the topic in a second letter to Miceli: "The general board of directors is leveling a personal opposition that cannot be described in any other terms. The more-or-less feigned battle has been going on for many years now. . . . Actually, of the four elected advisers on the Central Board, three (Marchese Ugo, Commendatore Palizzolo, and Figlia, Esq.) always voted against the proposals of the administration."[111]

Notarbartolo achieved a reform of the charter that would reduce the importance of the board and change the way its members were appointed, while in contrast emphasizing the group of officials that he had created. On the other hand, the support offered him by Miceli, a cabinet-level minister in the Crispi administration, might not necessarily have been enough to allow a supporter of Rudinì to ward off the influence of such faithful followers of Crispi as Figlia, Muratori, and even Tenerelli. In fact, Notarbartolo was forced to suffer considerable political isolation. On 23 April, two "personal" letters were pilfered from the minister's desk, and through Palizzolo's efforts they reappeared as copies in the 19 May session of the general board of directors, in the absence of the chairman. Since Tenerelli asked to see the originals, it was Muratori, after some hesitation, who showed them to him. At that point Palizzolo "attacked Notarbartolo, saying that he was incapable of judging himself and his colleagues, criticizing him as an abuser of his office because of the accusations he had made against board members who had been on the board for years. He suggested a vote of confidence, which was in fact taken under consideration."[112] The vote of confidence was annulled by the minister (the general manager did not serve at the pleasure and confidence of the board of directors), and a criminal investigation was begun into the theft of the letters. Nonetheless, the measures asked by Notarbartolo were not adopted. In fact, on 6 February 1890, after months of uncertainty, Crispi ordered the dissolution of the administration of the Banco di Sicilia (Bank of Sicily), along with that of the Banco di Napoli (Bank of Naples).

The conditions of the two banks were, considering the period, fairly good; the government order was therefore perceived as unforeseen and unjustified. Girolamo Giusso, chairman of the Banco di Napoli, told the Italian chamber of deputies: "I feel as if I have wandered into a village of brigands, and as if I had just been stabbed in the gut. . . . Those decrees look to me like crimes!"[113] Crispi eliminated two members of the old right wing, Giusso and Notarbartolo; it was paradoxical that they should have been charged with loading the banks with excessive exposure when it had been the government in the first place that had pushed the banks not to reduce their lending or issues.[114] In other circumstances, for that matter, the two southern banks had offered their support, as in the case of the plan, much cherished by Miceli, of an Italo-British shipping company that would give southern Italy's agricultural products access to the British market, following the breaking off of relations with France.

Notarbartolo had encountered some difficulties in managing this operation in August 1889: "The events of May and all that followed," he wrote to Minister of the Post Office Pietro Lacava, "offer full grounds for the fear that the assembly is no longer willing to obey the minister's wishes."[115] The issue, for that matter, was hardly likely to increase the chairman's popularity in his hometown. In Bari, Catania, and Naples, the project had demonstrated the government's attention to the exporting interests, but in Palermo the fears of the Navigazione Generale Italiana (NGI) over establishing a government-sponsored line outside of the monopoly that it held on a national scale were to provoke quite a different effect, as shown by the virulent attacks that immediately targeted the Banco di Sicilia; those attacks came from the press linked to the shipowners' trust.[116] Because of his support for Miceli, Notarbartolo found himself in front of the opposition to the city's far more powerful lobby, a lobby that extended from the broad base of support of Casa Florio in the aristocratic and bourgeois circles, extending through the labor bloc and based on the shipyards and the Oretea foundry, constituting a transverse party that included nearly all of the municipal political world: the followers of Crispi, first of all, but then the entire conservative front, and even Colajanni and the "Florio-brand" socialists.

This lobby, which extended its tentacles from Palermo toward Genoa and everywhere else that Navigazione Generale Italiana had any interests, employed Raffaele Palizzolo as an instrument, along with the follower of Crispi, Rocco de' Zerbi (another questionable individual), both in the parliamentary battles for state funding and against the antimonopoly reforms that were periodically planned and proposed. Those reforms had their most authoritative supporter in the person of Giolitti.[117] In this case, Palizzolo, a sworn enemy of the Palermitan followers of Crispi, found himself aboard a ship that was helmed by none other than Crispi; this is in contrast with Mosca's simplistic view, but also in contrast with the depiction of the southern Italian politician—or *ascaro*—described by Salvemini, given the ability to place himself in the intersection between the small-scale and large-scale circuits of political life.

Upholding the interests of the NGI in Italy's parliament, with a mixture of historical references and learned quotations, Member of Parliament Palizzolo acquired the nationalist and labor party tones so typical of many other pressure groups. In 1885 he recognized "Florio and Rubattino as meritorious individuals who have performed immense services for the Italian fatherland." He praised their altruism; he emphasized their contributions to the defense of the nation; and he defended their right to obtain public funding: "It is wrong to say 'there is not enough money.' One less battleship, the cry goes up all over the land, but don't deny the merchant marine the aid it so greatly needs, this great national force, this great industry of our nation."[118] In February 1893, a few days after the murder of Notarbartolo, Palizzolo took the floor again on behalf of state support for NGI, painting an apocalyptic picture of the results of blocking them: "Should this contract fail to receive approval, we shall see in the course of a single day one hundred six steamships lowering the Italian flag, and six thousand families, that is to say, twenty-four to twenty-five thousand individuals, left without food to eat, while millions and millions will cease to travel to our homeland; . . . it would constitute a national disaster."[119]

Perhaps success for the Italian-British shipping company would also have been a disaster (but for whom?). Fortunately, following the expulsion of Notarbartolo, the Banco di Sicilia's attitude toward the company gradually became increasingly chilly (certainly a contributing factor in its bankruptcy), especially once Giulio Benso, duke of Verdura, a loyal follower of Crispi and a shareholder in the Navigazione Generale Italiana, took over as director of the bank (February 1891). From that moment forward, relations between the largest bank in Sicily and the shipowners' trust became increasingly close and frequent. In July, while the bitter political debate over the extension of the maritime conventions was under way, the new general manager began buying up shares, for the very substantial sum of 1.8 million lire (equal to dozens of billions of lire, or, today, tens of millions of Euros or dollars), and actually purchased 6,950 shares of NGI stock in order "to sustain the share price in the markets of Milan and Genoa."[120] The first lot of shares (3,000 shares) was purchased on behalf of none other than Florio, who, however, did not make the transaction legal with a written order until the beginning of the following year, after one of the government-appointed board members, the duke of Craco, expressed the concerns of the various officers, who considered this sort of speculation illegal for a publicly held bank. In any case, this was the group that had been assembled by Notarbartolo and that had remained loyal to him, as the victors of 1889 knew full well. Since then, they had roundly criticized the "Notarbartolo faction," made up of bank employees who were "arrogant and vain, elevated to the highest ranks of the bank by the favoritism of the late director."[121]

It was they who had informed Notarbartolo of the new developments in the NGI affair: the purchases of 1892 were no longer being made on behalf of Florio, but, without any real collateral, on behalf of other, less illustrious individuals, such as a certain Salvatore Anfossi. Then a secret report was sent to Minister of the Treasury Giolitti, followed by an inspection entrusted to Commendator Biagini (the same one who three years before had uncovered the misdeeds of the Bank of Rome), who was rightly believed to be "guided by Notarbartolo"[122] and who began to bring light to the intricate affair. Anfossi, an intimate of Palizzolo, served as a front: Member of Parliament Palizzolo, as an administrator of the bank itself and intimately acquainted with the NGI, was deeply involved with the operation of driving up the value of company shares and decided to turn the already shady affair, conducted with public money by Florio and by the duke of Verdura, to his own advantage. Biagini's inspection threatened to ruin everything; behind that inspection loomed the shadow of Notarbartolo, who might well soon become the general manager again, in a phase in which the national government alternated between Crispi and Rudinì and Giolitti. Giolitti intended to reduce the disproportionate power of the shipowners' trust.

"Anfossi," Biagini declared, "who is nothing more than an exchange middleman, and not a member of the association of businessmen of the Chamber of Commerce, is of little value himself, leaves much to be desired in terms of personal ethics."[123] It would therefore be unthinkable for the Banco di Sicilia to risk large sums of money based on the word of such an individual. Here, perhaps, the ministerial inspector remained at a superficial level, at least in comparison with the investigation of Antonino Cutrera, the *delegato di PS*–criminologist whom the *questura* sent to dig into Anfossi's story. Cutrera discovered that the banks accepted the exchange agent's guarantee even for large sums of money, even though he was widely known to be an individual "who was involved in all the shadiest operations of the business world." He had no assets of his own, and yet he was a fiduciary for a number of British import-export companies involved in financing middlemen prior to the beginning of the citrus season. At the same time, Anfossi stocked up on the checks of other businessmen, which he then exchanged, taking a commission on each one.[124] Anfossi's work as a middleman must indeed have been strategic if he was capable of turning into exporters individuals such as Antonio Rizzuto, aka Perez, and Pietro La Mantia, *manutengoli,* or abettors, and ex-convicts, well known to be deeply involved with the Mafia, both of whom had been rescued from "entanglements" with the law through Palizzolo's intervention.[125] They had been involved in the citrus trade in partnership with Fontana precisely during the winter of the Notarbartolo murder. That had been in Tunisia, so as to provide the killer with a lavish, almost perfect alibi.

Anfossi played in the world of mafioso profiteering the same liaison role with Palizzolo that Filippello played in the world of Mafia banditry. The power of the

Palermo *cosche* remained tied to the territorial control of the *borgate*, but the networks of relations and the business of the mafiosi rose to a far different scale. This range was linked first and foremost to their roles as trustees of the major merchants or landowners. Salvatore Di Paola, one of those sentenced to death in the Amoroso trial, moved from Palermo to the sulphur mines of the Agrigento district in the service of Signore Reys. In order to track down Fontana, the police were obliged to put the "squeeze" on a certain Santomauro and a certain Perricone, respectively, the administrator and the business agent of the prince of Mirto in Villafrati and in Agrigento.[126]

In other cases, it was the charitable organizations concentrated in Palermo, but with large landholdings throughout the island, that constituted a vehicle for expanding the Mafia network, and it was within one of these structures that we find one of the Badalamentis (Bartolomeo) as far off as in the province of Catania, in Palagonia, the administrator and later the occult *gabellotto* of the large landholdings belonging to the Fidecommissaria "Principe di Palagonia":

> In that case, Badalamenti exchanged . . . his usual farm clothing for elegant and costly cloth suits; the heavy staff of the *campieri*, or private guards of farmland for the slender cane with a silver and gold handle; and on his waistcoat he wore an ostentatious gold chain with a bunch of trinkets and on his fingers those large rings with diamonds that in Sicily are usually considered a distinctive emblem of the capos of the Camorra. Thus, the former prisoner under house arrest, newly attired and decked out, from field worker to rural supervisor, was easily given a new identity and summoned to assume the delicate office of procurator for a charitable organization. The power of the Mafia![127]

The Badalamenti family left a trail of corpses and engaged in profitable business ventures over an increasingly vast territory extending from Palermo to New York, in accordance with a tradition of converting custodians or watchmen into profiteers. That tradition took Gaetano Badalamenti, *già giardiniere* ("formerly keeper of a citrus grove"), and turned him into an exporter of citrus fruit.[128] The former middlemen, lacking sizable capital of their own, established relations with shipowners such as the Florios or else with easygoing bankers like the Muratoris, the financiers of the *Camera di commercio italo-americana* (Italian American Chamber of Commerce), and the Jews who controlled the citrus auctions in New York City. This was the worst of the agricultural crisis that swept away the entire old generation of large-scale exporters, often of foreign birth, who established residence and set up business in Sicily before Italian unification. In Palermo, the growing fragmentation of the commercial structures was very evident: in 1892 there were eighty-one exporters in comparison with the thirty-nine exporters operating in the most important citrus marketplace in Sicily, Messina; there were a great many "speculators, who show absolutely no restraint . . . in their illegal trafficking." Many demanded a closer examination of the criminal records of those speculators. One solution that might help to reduce the role they played could have been the establishment of bonded customs warehouses, but one attempt to do so in 1898 ended in failure because (as the Chamber of Commerce pointed out) the success of such a venture "would offend the powerful interests of loan-sharking organizations."[129]

Economics and politics, but especially the relationship between the two sectors, the profiteering at the end of the century, shattered the class-based configuration of the power structures of Palermo, but also of the Mafia, which for the first time, with Palizzolo and his intimate ties at both the top and the bottom of society, glimpsed a huge stake and reached out to grab it. "Whoever was interested in arranging for a report to vanish from the office of a cabinet-level minister, spending thousands of lire to do so, this time must have spent twice as much money to kill Notarbartolo," a Mafia member stated without particular concern, speaking with Cervis in the aftermath of the murder.[130] In fact, someone capable of reaching the minister's desk could also eliminate a troublesome scion of an age-old aristocracy. We therefore have a motive that ties together exceedingly diverse settings: the inland countryside of Sicily, the stamping ground of brigands, the gardens of Villabate, the beaches of Tunis, the branch offices of the Banco di Sicilia (Bank of Sicily), the office of Anfossi, and the far more luxurious offices of the Navigazione Generale Italiana, the stock exchange, or Borsa, of Milan, and the halls of the Italian parliament in Montecitorio. All of this takes on a logic all its own in relation to Sicily, to this new Italy at the end of the century, in which profiteering, the Mafia, and politics provoked a chain reaction in connection with the issue of banking, a crucial topic for a modernizing nation.

MORAL REVOLT

On 31 July 1902, the court of assizes of Bologna sentenced Palizzolo and Fontana to sentences of thirty years in prison, but on the basis of a technical shortcoming, the court of cassation overturned the verdict and ordered a retrial, which was held in Florence.

By this point, many years had passed since the murder, as well as since the scandal that had exploded in Milan. The intense involvement of public opinion in the first two trials was nothing more than a faded memory. The elements of evidence "were falling to the ground one after the other like the tiles of a decaying mosaic, and the tragic core that had endowed them with life was missing by now."[131] A single new important witness, Filippello, was summoned to testify by the civil plaintiffs, whose suspicions were aroused by the fact that he had not been called by the defense during the trial at Bologna. In fact, Palizzolo's *castaldo,* or agricultural administrator, did represent the sole potential weak point in the front of *omertà.* In 1896, the *castaldo* had been wounded in an attack, according to numerous rumors, in the wake of a dispute with his partners over sharing the payment for the murder.[132] A few days prior to his scheduled deposition, he was found in a Florentine *pensione,* hanging by the neck. The inquiry ruled it suicide. There followed a general acquittal for lack of evidence, and the Notarbartolo case was finally closed (23 July 1904).

Palizzolo returned aboard a steamer of the Navigazione Generale Italiana shipping line to Palermo, where he was given a hero's welcome:

> The martyrdom of the victim, beginning with the first calumny of the cowardly informers, would culminate, step by step, in the triumph of Justice. And thus triumphed Raffaele Palizzolo, after fifty-six months of excruciating martyrdom: a triumph circumfused by the glittering halo of his Suffering and his Virtue. And this Suffering and this Virtue, consecrated with sublime abnegation, through the unprecedented torments of the previous five years, in a tribute to this mistreated and outraged Sicily, were the tear-stained laurels with which, in the sad hours of his durance vile, Raffaele Palizzolo was enabled to compose the garlands of his harsh torment; those Memories that made us quiver in horror, that make us recoil in infinite pity.[133]

The paradox of this spreading rhetoric of martyrdom and persecution shocked, among others, Mosca, who responded that the supposed apotheosis "offended his sense of morality." He went on: "Certainly, it was impossible or almost impossible to bring solid evidence against the man accused of the murders of Miceli and Notarbartolo, but the man was shown in the worst possible light, if not as a criminal at the very least a protector of criminals and even suspected of having relations with brigands."[134] A pro-innocence movement had taken form well before the verdict in the Florence trial, put into operation by Palizzolo's clientelistic network, and given the name of "Pro-Sicilia." What was going on, in fact, was an attempt to assemble a broad consensus on the basis of the most low-minded regionalistic ideology. This movement pointed to Palizzolo, the member of parliament and mafioso, as yet another victim of the wrongs and oppressions visited upon the long-suffering island of Sicily. The "Pro-Sicilia" movement grew in strength and support, expanding well beyond the Palermo area, but over the course of its geographic expansion all references to the specific details of the Palizzolo case began to fade, while themes modeled on Nitti's arguments concerning northern and southern Italy gradually prevailed, as did the free-market polemics concerning the "colonial market" and the other dynamics of the southern protest movement.[135] It was exactly the same as what had happened with "Nasism," another, even larger Sicilianist movement that formed in relation to the cause of Nunzio Nasi, a Trapani-born cabinet minister who was accused of corruption. In these early years around the turn of the twentieth century, the Sicilian governing class increasingly relied on the regionalist theme because it could no longer drape itself in the great national function it boasted in the preceding phase, with Crispi and Rudinì, concerned as it was over the states of equilibrium that threatened to marginalize and penalize that class, in economic terms as well.

The rallying point of the alignment favoring Palizzolo was represented by *L'Ora*, the daily newspaper owned by the Florio family,[136] in a clear demonstration of an enduring political relationship that lasted throughout the array of hearings and trials. Presiding over the committee that presented Palizzolo as a candidate for parliament, though in 1900 he was still imprisoned, for his traditional district of Palazzo Reale, was none other than Signora Florio. Marchesano, who had planned to run in the same district, was apparently persuaded to desist by the promise of an electoral financing by the shipowning company. A singular transaction between the two opposing alignments may perhaps be explained with the subsequent hiring of the socialist leader to a position on the legal staff of the NGI. He later even took on the role of head mediator in the negotiations with Giolitti and the Bank of Italy.[137]

Florio was interrogated in Bologna (through a rogatory letter) as a defense witness. Here is the account offered by the Palermo socialist newspaper *La Battaglia*:

WITNESS: The maffia? I've never heard of such a thing.

PROSECUTING MAGISTRATE: Yes, the maffia, an association to commit crimes against persons and property, and occasionally used in elections as well.

WITNESS (ANGRILY): It's incredible how people insult Sicily! The maffia used in elections! Never! Never!

PROSECUTING MAGISTRATE: And so you exclude the possibility that elections are run in Sicily with the maffia and with money.

WITNESS: Well, to tell the truth, I must say that, on one recent occasion, in September of last year, the socialists did spend one hundred thousand francs in an attempt to beat the monarchist platform, but they were unsuccessful.[138]

This news item does not appear in any other source, and we can consider it an exercise in satire, justified, however, by the political stances taken by the great shipowner, who managed to remain miraculously exempt from the brawl. He was not involved, for instance, in the episode of the killing of the two coach drivers, evoked by the popular press as evidence of the power of "certain mafiosi in kid gloves" but attributed to a certain "gentleman of Palermo," not otherwise identified.[139] It was only one of the prudent omissions made every time the well-known name of Ignazio Florio appeared: in the minutes of the trials, in the summation of Marchesano, or in the *Memoirs* of Notarbartolo, Jr., we find no reference to the NGI as part of the bloc of forces hostile to the murder victim, or at least as a political cohort of Palizzolo; while we have seen in what ways and how frequently the shipowning trust surfaces in the story, the pride and major industry of the cities of Genoa and Palermo.

Florio maintained active relations in every sector of the political landscape, including the socialists. Just a few years afterward, the popular bloc and Casa Florio would be described as the true trust of Palermo's political life.[140] In this specific case, however, the operation being carried out was distinctly conservative in nature, aiming to restore to power the conservative forces that had been soundly defeated by the socialists and radicals in the administrative elections of July 1900. In the new elections in September, a result of the dissolution of the city council, that outcome was overturned by the success of a list of candidates with a strong monarchist focus, led by the prince of Camporeale. This turn of events was portrayed as a mending of divisions among the ruling class, triggered by the Notarbartolo-Palizzolo case, "to prevent the triumph of those who hope to turn Palermo city hall into a pulpit for anti-institutional propaganda, propaganda that would rail against the sacred patrimony of the ideas of family, homeland, and liberty."[141] The supporters of the "Pro-Sicilia" movement were also limited to the moderate forces in Sicily, almost entirely excluding the left wing. In contrast, the left wing proved to be a useful interclass component in the subsequent case of Nunzio Nasi and the larger mobilization on the issues of sulphur mining and the citrus industry. The "persecution" that Palizzolo suffered was, moreover, laid to a plot put together against a Sicilian member of parliament by northern Italians and by that "motley crew of police spies, highwaymen and extortionists, barroom slanderers and bordello libelers who usurp in Italy the honorable name of the Socialist Party."[142] It would not be the topic of the Mafia that would lend itself to a straightforward and untroubled communication between the conservative wing and the progressive wing of the Sicilian political landscape.

It is clear here how much time had passed since 1875. Concerning these themes, the regionalist stance, once the exclusive property of the Italian left, was inherited by the moderate forces, while the struggle against the Mafia, once a warhorse of the *Destra storica* (historic right wing), became an integral part of the Italian left's polemical arsenal. These political forces defined themselves in a radically different manner from the past: it was the extreme left, radical or socialist, that played in ideological terms the decisive role in managing the Notarbartolo affair. All the same, five years of discussion did not pass in vain, and by now the public, the common people who got their news from the daily press, could rightly think that behind the shadowy mysteries of Sicily could be found one of the interpretative codes for deciphering the history of Italy, shaken to its foundations by the explosion of the political and banking scandals.

As a tool for renewal, the moral question proved quite effective. On the other hand, in radically different situations involving radically different players, the major political transitions in the postunification history of Palermo were inevitably linked to anti-Mafia mobilizations. The offensive launched by Malusardi had marked the advent of the left wing in power; the Mori operation was the Fascists' attempt to induce a significant shift in the mechanisms of political representation and the relationship between state and society. In a comparable intertwining, the Notarbartolo case demonstrated that the Mafia flourishes in an atmosphere of "normality" and began to be the subject of discussion in a climate of mobilization. Indeed, this very phenomenon has occurred in very recent years. "The moment of moral rebellion has arrived," declared De Felice.[143] The moral issue alone at the turn of the century was capable of restoring energy and momentum to the urban socialist movement in the south, both the Palermo group and the Neapolitan group of "La Propaganda,"[144] and to the battle being waged against the various "mafias" and camorras. Eventually, that battle led to investigations into the "urban government corruption," or "malgovernment," in the major cities of southern Italy, an essential foundation for the Giolitti government's operation of renewing the local political staff. In Sicily, in particular, there was an increasing trend toward the period of "popular blocs," the new "open" system of alliances with which the far left offered to play a leading role in the political and administrative role of the early twentieth century. In this way, the "democratic and socialist elements on the island" attempted to complete the project of "reclamation of social terrain" that the leaders of the Italian Socialist Party (PSI) had assigned to them in the aftermath of the verdict of Bologna.[145]

In reality, during the course of their populist experience, the former subversives who had converted to reform socialism did not display a moral profile much superior to that of their adversaries, just as the administrations under Giolitti did not stand out for their ethics, at least in the south, although they were more ethical (despite what is widely believed) than their predecessors had been.

Northern radicals and socialists wavered between acknowledging the complexity of relations between state and society and a demonization of southern Italian society, concerned first and foremost, based on their experience of the Crispi-led reaction, that their civil Italy might be exposed to the contagion of a barbarous Italy, both corrupted and corrupting, an obstacle to the development of the country as a whole.

> In the south, where there was no industry, no extensive agriculture, no initiative, no inborn vigor to found industries and undertake agriculture, there sprang up, out of an emulation for quick money, out of envy for the wealth of northern Italy, a breed of adventurers and conmen, who . . . sank their claws into the political life suddenly laid bare to their vanity and greed, and they invaded the administrations, began to connive with the banks, and they had as their minimalist and maximalist platform the program of selling themselves to the highest bidder. This sort of improvised barons, of whom De' Zerbi was the brightest and most refined example, and Crispi the most ruthless and energetic (hence the king of the tribe, as in savage hordes, by divine right), attired in ceremonial cutaway coats, but beneath them, the bandolier of the old-style brigand, living on filth and in filth, they are the true political saprophytes of the nation.[146]

It is only in appearance that these anthropologic observations concerning the southern political class were shared by the socialists of the north and those of the south, Turati and Salvemini, that is, on the interior of the same radical-positivist culture, shared with Lombroso and Colajanni. Here we encounter a crucial question: should the moral disease of southern Italy be laid simply to a "lower" level of civilization or to a national intertwining with the large system of power? And in any case, could the corruption of the ruling classes entail a negative judgment of an entire society? "To me—wrote Arturo Labriola, in [a] polemic with the *Critica sociale*—it appears a glaring defection from every criterion of historical materialism to believe that regions or nations taken as a whole can be considered corrupt or perfect [as] the chosen people and the damned people, elevated or rejected by the Lord."[147]

The Notarbartolo case offered a new opportunity to develop this theme. Faced with the balanced opinion of such moderate newspapers as *Il Corriere della Sera,* the radical press often gave signals of intemperance. Thus Alfredo Oriani, the republican and imperialist who was destined to be elevated to the empyrean as one of the forerunners of Italian Fascism, in an article headlined *Le voci della fogna* ("Voices from the Sewer") called Sicily "a paradise inhabited by demons," "a cancer on Italy's foot, . . . a province in which neither customs nor laws can be civil."[148] The answer that came from an individual above all suspicion like Colajanni still focused more on the responsibilities of the state than on those of society: "The Sicilians are tired of being civilized by people like Govone, Serpi, Pinna, Medici, and Bardesono. Among those who have happily swilled and rolled about in that sewer are Ballabio, Venturini, Codronchi, . . . and Mirri . . . all born and raised north of the river Tronto."[149]

The question of the Mafia represents only one of the possible occasions for regionalist quarrels. For the Neapolitan area, devoid though it might be of the Sicilian separatist traditions, we should consider, for instance, the excessive reactions of someone like Scarfoglio in the face of Rosano's suicide, caused by accusations of profiteering and corruption with the Camorra, charges leveled by the extreme left. This is still in the context of the polemic of southern *moderatismo* (moderation) against socialists and northerners:

Nothing links us any longer to this state, nourished as it was on our finest blood. The link of national solidarity has been shattered within us; we are the ones slated to perish. And in order to hasten our death throes, our Italian brothers have unleashed against us the socialist horde, which has lunged at us, its mouth filled with mud, its heart boiling over with murderous rage. . . . This is a full-fledged state of war being waged against us; waged against a flock of sheep that does not react to protect itself, that exposes its neck to the fraternal knife, placidly allowing itself to be slaughtered.[150]

The intertwining of the controversy between left and right with a regionalist quarrel makes it all the more difficult to analyze and evaluate the complex relationships that were established in these same years among politics, finance, corruption, common criminality, and Mafia-driven criminality. The fundamental problem was that of the by-products of the modernization and democratization of the country, bringing new social actors into the inner circles of power, with new mechanisms. The risk involved in a debate of this sort is the demonization, in the eyes of the public, of the trial itself, and not that of its less attractive ramifications.

This again opened the way to a position comparable to that of the old *Destra storica* (historic right wing), which progressively imposed itself in the face of the impossibility of eliminating the obstacles blocking the political system save through the slow adjustments of "Giolittism." In Leopoldo Notarbartolo's *Memorie* (Memoirs), written during the years of the "regenerative" Great War, the respective figures of a father with a rigid code of Kantian ethics and a son on a desperate quest for justice, would stand out in stark isolation, and necessarily in defeat, within a historical context marked by the perverse effects of a "parliamentarianism," identified less in the person of the mafioso Palizzolo and more in the persons of the dishonest Cosenza, the malevolent Crispi, the slimy Rudinì, and the cowardly Giolitti. There was no reference, save for a few merely personal considerations, to the forces that worked to fight against the Mafia: Marchesano and the other socialists, Sangiorgi, the public opinion of Milan, Bologna, and (in some cases) Palermo, the radical papers and the moderate papers, including the leading daily on the island, *Il Giornale di Sicilia*. Italy at the turn of the century, torn between a conservative camp and a progressive camp capable of providing, for the first time, an acute and critical analysis of the concealed workings of power, in part through the news media and other instruments of information and the mass political debate, all freely employed for the first time, would eventually degenerate into a cluster of the corrupted and the corruptors. It would become a land in which "it was raining mud, and everyone played with balls of mud," in which "every public square became a pillory of shame; and the role of torturer fell to every muddy newspaperman who brandished as a weapon the filthy rag pumped out from the sewers of the workshops of extortion."[151]

This is the interpretation, perhaps, of someone who has already set out in search of a Duce to whom they could entrust their destiny.

CULTURES: INSIDE AND OUTSIDE OF THE ORGANIZATION

In comparison with the trials of the *stoppagghieri* and the Amorosos, the Palizzolo-Notarbartolo trial marked a giant step forward in terms of the logical concatenation of events and the absence of the more evident contradictions in the construction of a prosecution position in Mafia cases. Amazed that the Bologna trial had not ended in acquittal for absence of evidence, the correspondent of *The Times* wrote that "the jurors seem to have based their verdict on general impressions . . . rather than on one specific fact or another."[152] And the "general impressions" were those created by the only solid piece of factual evidence in Milan and Bologna (but already less burning in its significance at Florence): the role played by the public institutions in the maneuvers to cover and protect Palizzolo and, more in general, in the genesis and continuation of the phenomenon of the Mafia. That role had been indicated by the prosecution, and it had been abandoned, for reasons of interest, by the defense, managed by the Marinuzzis and the Gestivos. This major murder cast a beam of light, as had the political developments of 1875–1876. Colajanni with his successful pamphlet, *Nel regno della mafia*, reconstructed a piece of history in which, beginning from the Risorgimento, the governments on both the right and the left had adhered to a line of appalling continuity with more recent ones. This emerged as well from the trial. For instance, consider the public's scandalized reaction in Bologna to the revelation of the negotiations between Palizzolo and Malusardi-Nicotera in 1877: "These elections held with the Damocles' sword of the special security regimen of *ammonizione* held over the heads of the candidates cast a tawdry light, on the one hand, on the candidates but also, on the other hand, on the activity of the government."[153] The responsibility of the public institutions was present even in the works of the two functionaries Cutrera and Alongi, printed or reprinted in this period, and rich with other observations of considerable interest. In the daily press, numerous articles were published, one of which, in the *Giornale di Sicilia*, deserves to be cited among the finest writing on the topic. This article contains a denunciation of the factional nature of the relationship between *cosche* (Mafia families) and police, the Albaneses, the Bardesonos, and the Lucchesis, who made use "of a part of the Mafia to uncover the mischief of the other part." It concludes that in the countryside around Palermo, the "secret relations" between *"guardiani, curatoli,* and all such people" point to "a vast organization."[154] This is the topic, as we know, of the Sangiorgi Report. However, considerable linguistic confusion remains:

> During the Palizzolo trial, both in court and in the press, and even in the Italian parliament, the definitions of Mafia swarmed, proliferating in an astonishing manner, ranging from the most complete negation of all antijuridical content to the clustering together of everything and everyone, so that for some commentators there is no such thing as Mafia or of mafiosi, while for others Sicily and every Sicilian are nothing more than a den and a conspiracy of mafiosi.[155]

In fact, all knowledge and understanding seem to have been overwhelmed and concealed within a political and journalistic debate that was as chaotic as it was unrestrained, on the one hand incapable of restricting the subject within reasoned bounds, and on the other hand excessively greedy for explanations concerning the nature of the Mafia.

This is the sort of question that, during the three separate phases of the trial, the "continental" judges asked of a great many witnesses, just as witnesses had heard those questions in the preceding years when they were interviewed by the parliamentary commissions. It is the sort of question that might be asked of a demo-psychologist, that is, an ethnologist, an expert by definition of the peculiarities, "beliefs," and "prejudices" of the Sicilian people. In Bologna, Giuseppe Pitrè, summoned as a defense witness, reiterated that the word "Mafia" was originally used to indicate the concept of "beauty, gracefulness, and excellence in a certain context." In the modern era, it came to indicate "the awareness, in some cases exaggerated, of one's own personality, superiority, and dignity, which does not willingly accept abuses of any sort" and can "lead to criminality."[156] Pitrè tended to identify a custom of the Sicilians, originally positive and, in this sense, attributable as had been done at an earlier point by Member of Parliament Morana: "If by Mafia [we] are describing those individuals who are unwilling to submit to abuse, violence, and offenses . . . then everyone in Sicily is a *maffioso*."[157] With Franchetti (*mutatis mutandis*), Oriani instead believed that all the inhabitants of the island were lost to civilization, and therefore, mafiosi. The third, intermediate, position remains that of Rudinì expressed by Mosca, with his distinction between criminality and the "Mafia spirit," in this case, amiable or even benign, but always widely diffused throughout the island.[158] The three theories, and in particular the two extreme ones, are singularly convergent inasmuch as they presuppose that the Mafia is nothing other than a regional culture and represents a phenomenon that is not limitable, in and of itself not recognizable, and practically invincible, in part because the identification makes all Sicilians, at least in terms of a logical reaction, the defenders of the Mafia itself: it is the scheme describing movements such as the "Pro-Sicilia."

During his summation in the trial of Bologna, Marchesano called Pitrè an "outstanding scholar of folklore, but a very poor witness. When questioned about the Mafia, instead of telling us what it is, he told us the origin of the word."[159] In fact, this reference to a Mafia that was originally benign and always a presupposition, never glimpsed in operation, this continual research of the definition as an *ecceitas,* or fundamental uniqueness, of the phenomenon to be studied in the profound (and unplumbable) recesses of social psychology, represents an extremely slippery field of endeavor. A compilation of the countless references to the few pages that Pitrè actually devoted to the Mafia would offer us an accurate and reliable map of the naïve and the corrupt from the end of the nineteenth century to the present day, all of them failing to realize (or pretending to overlook) the openly apologetic and misleading nature of those observations; all of them believing (or pretending to believe) that they were in the presence of the objective source of the culture of the Sicilians. There are highly concrete elements that will allow us to judge the ethnologist's position: his close collaboration in the town council and in the management of charitable works and agencies with Palizzolo, "a true gentleman, . . . a scrupulous and honest administrator"; his rejection of the government's invitation to run for office in the Palizzolo-run district of the Palazzo Reale; his active involvement, as an ideologue as well, in "Pro-Sicilia."[160]

Between an old and a positive meaning and a new meaning—vernacular and imprecise, which could also indicate something negative—Pitrè refers to an inscrutable essence ("it is almost impossible to define [it]"),[161] and therefore not greatly differentiated from the defendants and the defense lawyers in the Mafia trials, who all claimed that they had no idea what the word means. This was the answer given by Carmelo Mendola, a member of the Amoroso *cosca*, to the magistrate who asked him if he belonged to the Mafia: "I don't know what that means."[162] The exchange of question and answer appeared revealing to Hess, who used it as an epigraph at the beginning of his book, as well as to Sciascia, who cited it repeatedly.[163] A mafioso actually does not know what the Mafia is, since legality is a fairly abstract concept for the Sicilians, a legality embodied by an alien state, and what we would describe as mafioso behavior is the only behavior possible in this society. For that matter, this is not the only case in which the witnesses heard in the Amoroso trial appeared as somewhat extremist supporters of various social and anthropological theories, for instance, the theory of southern familism. When he was asked whether the members of the *cosca* were friends of his, Caravello answered: "I am a friend only to my wife and my children . . . outside of that, I know no one." When asked about his "party" hatreds, Emanuele Amoroso answered: "My party is my wife and my children." Adhering to this line, the defendants wound up exaggerating, emphasizing their "true" family (the core group of fellow criminals) in opposition to their blood relatives. For instance, one of the Amorosos claimed a total absence of interactions with his own brothers to keep anyone from supposing that he could serve as an intermediary in the vendetta against the Badalamentis, who had murdered another brother of his.[164]

Hess has interpreted a tremendously intentional source, that is, a judicial source, as if it somehow reflected the "culture of the Sicilians." It evidently did not occur to him that the Sicilians can say things, or fail to say things, as it serves them best: that may be a matter of political and ideological utility (or utility of other sorts?) in Pitrè's case, a last-ditch attempt to save their lives in the case of the targets of a trial destined to conclude with a round of death sentences. When Giuseppe Amoroso, uncle of the defendants, revealed circumstances that implicated them in the murder of his own son (their cousin), the defendant Emanuele Amoroso dared him to swear an oath on the soul of his father, a shared ancestor of both the victim and the alleged murderers. The chief magistrate, with some consternation, observed: "Here, we have only one kind of oath, the oath called for by the law," but the lawyer Marinuzzi insisted: "That is not appropriate to this case . . . because the populace does not believe in that," and finally the witness was sworn as requested by the defense.[165] For Hess, this would be a demonstration of the social and cultural distance separating the Italian state from the Sicilians, of the "gap between the social sensibility and the morality of state government," which engendered the behavior of mafiosi.[166] To my eye, however, it looks more like a skillfully maneuvered piece of stagecraft put on by Marinuzzi, tending to construct before the eyes of the jurors (and perhaps even in the view of the witness himself) an image of his clients as individuals who had been wrongfully accused, who believed in the same family values as the ordinary people around them, and who could therefore absolutely not be the cold-blooded savage murderers of one of their own close relatives. But it is clear that such instrumentalizing use of a traditional culture can create a certain amount of confusion in the mind of a German sociologist, if only through a complex and learned mediation, in which Pitrè himself played a central role, and which the lawyerly culture of the island helped to diffuse.

This culture set out primarily to conceal beneath the folk tradition the reality of conspiracy, calling it a "chimera, a dream sprung from the overheated imagination of a *delegato di PS*," the "mysterious something," the "pasted-on tail" denounced by the defending lawyers of the *stoppagghieri* and the Amorosos.[167] The war among Mafia families was reduced to family hatreds, in a world artfully depicted as primitive, in which wealthy smugglers and businessmen like the Amorosos were passed off as "commonfolk," and someone like Fontana who dealt in citrus fruit on an intercontinental basis was described as illiterate.[168] Gone was the effect of the great scandal. The perception of the Mafia was adjusted to this folkloristic and traditional level, thus losing, among other things, its link with the larger topic of banking scandals, which for a moment had endowed the phenomenon with a far different, a "modern," and a particularly dangerous dimension.

Sensing the advantage that a disagreement concerning the essential nature of the Mafia offered to the defense, Marchesano began his summation for the defense by stating that he wanted to speak only about specific criminal actions and behaviors, a promise that he did not keep in full:

> What is the Mafia today? An organization, as some believe, with capos and under-capos? No. Such a thing does not exist, save in the wildest dreams of some *questore*. No, this is not the Mafia, the Mafia is a natural sentiment, a spontaneous form of cooperation, a solidarity that joins all the rebels under the laws of civil society.... The *cosche* are bound together by an ideal link, a common interest, and share their common protectors.[169]

Here the information provided by the *questura*, who was an invaluable ally for the civil plaintiffs, is almost rendered ridiculous. The interrelations among the Mafia families are reduced to the mere commonality of protectors; concepts of no particular heuristic value are employed, such as "natural sentiment." Clinging to the old and superficial definition supplied by Bonfadini, Marchesano undercuts the massive job of documentation on the connections among events and individuals done by himself and by Sangiorgi, from which a much different story is derived, certainly not one of working "spontaneously in concert." Once again, the trial strategy leads the prosecution to simplify without obtaining the desired goal in the end. Pitrè and Palizzolo lost the battle, but they were preparing to win the war: the Mafia was thus neither "sect nor association," it had no "regulations nor statutes,"[170] it was identifiable as a certain behavior and culture. Instead, I believe that there exists a Mafia ideology that reflects its cultural codes, but primarily to deform them, reappropriate them, and make out of them a mass of rules designed to ensure the survival of the organization, its cohesiveness, its ability to create consensus and to strike terror into hearts both within and without.

The *canti carcerari* (prison songs) express great contempt for "l'omu chi parra assai," who "cu la sò stissa vucca si disterra."[171] Rosario La Mantia was rejected even by his own family. The accusation of spy, *'nfami,* or *cascittuni,* constituted a weighty burden for all those who were targeted as informers, as well as a useful justification for those who killed them. Therefore, it lent itself to use as a weapon in the factional wars. After murdering Damiano Sedita, the Amorosos exclaimed: "he will no longer have a carte-blanche weapons permit from the police"; Cusumano was described as an "infamous spy." The organization called for a boycott of the people of the *borgata* against Di Sano, a woman who ran a dive and who was thought to be an informant, and after that attempted to murder her. In the context of accusing Filippo Siino of being "in league with the *questura,*" Giuseppe Biondo did nothing other than "what he needed to obtain power for himself,"[172] which is to say, that he worked to slander his adversary in the face of a larger public opinion made up of *cagnolazzi* (literally "wild dogs," or young thugs) and confederates. *Omertà,* understood as a sense of "moral" repulsion with respect to the idea of availing oneself of the legal system, may perhaps represent a general value, an ideal model of behavior of the Sicilian populace and, in particular, of the larger criminal universe. Certainly, it is no guide to the actual behavior of mafiosi, who—as we have seen over and over—collaborate with the law whenever and however it furthers their own interests. We should not forget that the organization must mediate between state and criminals, and must therefore be credible in the eyes of all sides. The authorities frequently know who is responsible for committing crimes and murders because the mafiosi are willing to speak, without any ideological preclusions, although they are unwilling to expose themselves by testifying in court. It is from here, not from a more generic society at large, that the police obtain their frequently cited *voce pubblica* or "public opinion." Then there is the case of the mafioso on the losing side of a gang war who turns to the police in search of help and protection, perhaps obtaining a passport to escape to America, as was the case with the *castaldo,* or agricultural administrator, Santo Vassallo, sentenced to death for betraying his fellow mafiosi from the same *cosca.* In this specific case, however, the unfortunate informer was tracked down and followed all the way to New Orleans, where he was murdered.[173] The Vassallos, or even worse, the La Mantias and the D'Amicos, threatened to leave the *cosca* to the mercy of the collaborationist impulses of its members and enemies. The response to a *propalazione* (the information provided by an informant) that endangers the organization's very existence had to be one involving terror, since individuals necessarily made their own calculations of the likelihood of reprisals, even many years later and thousands of miles away. As Sangiorgi put it, "everyone, from the most prosperous landowners to the poorest peasants, from the most renowned notables to the most obscure individualists, says nothing, because they are afraid,"[174] but the previously emphasized factor, that not all of them were equally afraid, because they did not all fear the same penalty—death—gave the precept imparted to the world of criminals a varying degree of efficacy.

Unless the mafiosi were willing to be reduced to the role of confidential informers, if they intended to maintain or accentuate their independence of the authorities, they would need to safeguard the coherence of the association with methods other than exclusively terroristic ones, ensuring loyalty, like the method that led Filippello, despite the fact that he had been abandoned and threatened by his confederates, to kill himself rather than testify against Palizzolo.

Clearly, blood ties are not sufficient to guarantee all the alliances, although they (in this and any other society) do represent a solid core. Mazzara might take on Giammona, boasting of the "active solidarity of the members of his family."[175] The Siino party had a distinctively family-oriented physiognomy. In a context of nuclear families like that of the island, it was the setting that determined whether the potential for compact coherence intrinsic to the institute of the family would be utilized. The Schneiders, for instance, demonstrated with a careful analysis how relations among brothers, fragile at best in the laboring families of the Agrigento village of Sambuca, were instead exalted in the sheepherding enterprises that spawned the middle classes of the *gabellotti* because that type of activity entails an especially trust-based relationship among its various adherents.[176] That requirement is of course particularly important in a criminal organization, though the context of family and relatives would not always be sufficient to supply the *cosche*: the *comparaggio,* an artificially created family tie, represents a bridge toward more complex relationships, in which, as we know, diverse links and bonds are at play, based on the models of *Carbonari* or Freemasons from the period of the Risorgimento.

In many cases, for instance, in that of the *fratellanza* of Favara, the inductee promises to abandon such common crimes as theft, readying himself to take on the role of the *uomo d'ordine*, literally, the man of order, the notable, or at least the business intermediary. This is how the Mafia likes to present itself, even though the reality is more prosaic, and, as Alongi already noted, matters are more complicated: those who guarantee generally act in close coordination with those who violate it, a scheme that tends to expand from its original setting of rural custodianship to a diverse array of criminal manifestations. The *santoni* (literally, "big holy men," roughly equivalent to "high muckamucks"), who promise the Palermitan coach drivers to get back their coaches in exchange for sums of money that they "claim has been claimed by the *picciotti* (lower-level mafiosi)," had already made a prior deal with them to split the ransom.[177] The *Mafia d'ordine* represents more than anything else an ideal model, to be dangled before the ruling classes, but also attractive to the ordinary, "common" criminals. The chief of the band of safecrackers and muggers of Albergheria broken up in 1904, when questioned by the police, did his best to elevate himself high above the level of small-time criminals: "Skilled and experienced mafioso that he was, he took on the pose of an offended gentleman. . . . He said in fact that he could have been involved in murders and assaults, and that he had been convicted of assault and battery, but that he displayed a lofty scorn for thieves and burglars."[178]

Therefore, the codes of the Mafia are linked to the necessity of preserving an internally compact structure and a public acknowledgment of a capacity to strike terror into potential rivals and spies. The most efficient of the *guardiani* would be the one who, with his reputation alone, not so much by his physical presence, would discourage thieves, in accordance with the popular saying, "Fear guards a vineyard." The archival documents, as well as the pages of Alongi and Cutrera, take us into a world where a theft of lemons might constitute an offense to be washed away with blood, where even the slightest damage to crops represents a *sgarro*, a grave insult to one's authority, a ritual provocation to which one must respond in an unfailingly and overwhelmingly disproportionate manner. As in any and all kinds of feud, "the gravity of the crime lies not so much in the intrinsic characteristics as in the challenge to the victim's prestige."[179] That is the symbolism present in so many episodes already familiar to us, in which the son of the landowner who has been forced to sell his citrus grove to a mafioso continues to make a point of stealing lemons every evening from that same grove until the final, inevitable, bloody settling of accounts.[180]

But, without being either an ethnologist or a man of letters, Sangiorgi already utilized the twofold concept of economic damage and an offense to the *cosca* to explain why the refusal to provide water to the Vitale cousins (the ones from the Miceli murder) led to the killing of the *fontaniere* La Mantia. Sangiorgi urges us not to be surprised if, "for this reason, in appearance and in any other context, not particularly serious, the Vitales and their partners decided, as they did, to kill him."[181] The inability to respond to an offense is an element of dishonor, which adversaries will harp on in a ritual manner. The *curatolo* Ajello, fired from a farm that he had run for many years, was persecuted on a nightly basis by a "serenade" entitled "Senti l'acqua e di siti mori"—literally, "You hear water and you die of thirst," which means: you are close to the source of authority, power, and wealth, but you can't touch it. This took him to the brink of exasperation and to the crucial error that led to his death. His corpse was taken below the windows of the Ucciardone prison and displayed to his convict sons in a final act of disrespect.[182]

For that matter, the honor that mafiosi attribute to themselves diverges in significant ways from the general understanding of honor, in southern Italian society and elsewhere. It would not be necessary to recall how many murders have masqueraded behind alleged but nonexistent questions of sexual honor, if behind one of those murders there were not the presence of the "Alta Maffia dei Ciaculli," in the persons of Salvatore and Giuseppe Greco. In December 1916 they ordered the murder of the priest Giorgio Gennaro, who, during his Sunday sermon, denounced the Mafia's interference in the administration of ecclesiastical revenues. Of course, rumors were circulated that it was the vendetta of a cuckolded husband.[183] The *gabellotto* Gaetano Cinà was, instead, eliminated by a plot crafted by his brother Luigi, who had fallen in love with his sister-in-law, and by the Mafia capo Giuseppe Biondo, determined to punish someone who deprived him of control over a citrus grove:[184] brothers who murder brothers, establishing alliances with "outsiders," passions and interests ferociously pursued with no regard for family ties. There are murders of women, as in the case of the serving girl seduced by one of the Amorosos or in the murder of the Di Sano girl. There was the torpedo of Monreale, who having failed to find the enemies of his *cosca* capo, killed their young son so that he would not have to return empty-handed.[185] On the other hand, in an extreme situation, the mafiosi themselves would remark on the difference between "true" honor and the honor the *cosche* attributed to themselves. While Antonio Badalamenti was running to find a midwife for his wife who was going into labor, he was killed by Amoroso killers, cursing at his enemies who "murdered treacherously"; Scalici referred sarcastically to the "loyal gentlemen of Piazza Montalto" in a novel published in installments, which was inspired by those tragic events.[186]

The model of fair competition, or a fair fight, solidly rooted in popular culture, and still identifiable in the dagger duels between Camorrists or *ricottari*, or pimps, in the duels of the *spataioli* (criminals) of Palermo, Catania, or Messina, is absolutely distinct from the ambushes laid by killers armed with rifles, concealed behind the enclosure walls around the *giardini*, who carried out Mafia murders without offering the victim the slightest possibility of self-defense. The term *usticano*, used by *ricottari* to describe someone who attacks treacherously,[187] might well be a reference to behaviors and associations that developed out of confinement on the island of Ustica or other such islands. Arlacchi's view that the hierarchies among mafiosi were determined by a "free competition for honor" involving "challenges and fights"[188] may perhaps reflect a difference between the "traditional" *'ndrangheta* and the Mafia but especially in a literary documentation very far removed from reality. In the real Mafia, the elimination of one's enemies was generally accompanied by *ragionamenti* (reasonings), false claims, and alleged agreements that served primarily to make the condemned victims lower their guard. Thus, the murder of Filippo Siino, preceded by a solemn reconciliation in church between the two sides, was made possible by the betrayal of a friend of the intended victim, who led him to the site of the ambush, and thus by *spergiuro* (falsehood) and *tradimento* (betrayal).[189] The honor-saving provocation to a duel was only utilized in a utilitarian context. Antonino D'Alba, whom the *cosca* of Falde had decided to eliminate, was a man who had been warned, and he took great care never to be caught outside of his home. Only when an enemy provoked him, and dared him to fight face-to-face, did he leave the house armed with a revolver, but on the proposed site of the duel he found a dozen people, who shot him down like a dog.[190] Opposing the rite of individual competition based on courage and prowess was that of the collective execution, an emphasis on the fact that it was the organization that had ordered the death penalty and its members were taking on the responsibility for that action together, much like the state firing squad; it was on the state that the Mafia tended to model itself.

The defendant Mendola and the others knew perfectly well what the Mafia was; but it was not in their interest to say so.

CHAPTER IV

DEMOCRATIZATION, TOTALITARIANISM, DEMOCRACY

FROM SICILY TO AMERICA

In 1890, Captain David Hennessy of the local police in New Orleans died in an ambush for which eighteen Sicilians were charged. They were tried and acquitted.[1] Control of the docks and the fruit trade was the classic Mafia-related motive for conflict between two groups, the Provenzanos and the Matrangas, and that conflict constitutes the background of the murder. We are also very familiar with the general outline of the alliance between one of the factions (the Provenzanos) and the police. Apparently, that alliance led to Hennessy's murder, as a reprisal. The conclusion of the affair, on the other hand, is as American as apple pie: the lynching of eleven of the acquitted men by an enraged mob. It appears that the mob had been incited by those who wished to prevent an alliance of interests between the Irish and the Italians, which might have led to their taking control of the city government.

The "Mafia" makes its first appearance in Louisiana, and from there we see the development of the theory of the "foreign plot" that was subsequently destined to reemerge in various forms and circumstances. Nothing can provide a more gripping confirmation of that theory than a mysterious and "subversive" organization. We may suppose that it dates back to the Sicilian Vespers, that its mastermind and control center was in Sicily, and that it had adherents everywhere. A variant on that theory provides some information about the situation in Sicily by stating that the Mafia was commanded by a brigand named Leoni.[2]

White Anglo-Saxon Protestant America, moreover, refused to tolerate the voluntary "segregation" from "other races" or from the "natives . . . wherever there is a concentration of Italian manpower,"[3] a situation that was blamed for the persistence of a number of deplorable habits, including the existence of the Mafia. It is an unpersuasive argument. In the United States, the Mafia lost its regional characteristics and crossbreeds with other forms of criminality. It began to connect with a phenomenon rife with problems of its own: the new and multiethnic universe of immigrant America, which was much more significant than the residual world of the society from which it originated. The very same Anglo-Saxons who were so scandalized by the reluctance to accept the cultural standardization that is a requisite feature of the melting pot were the same ones who reinforced the internal forces binding the world of Little Italys. These were the same Anglo-Saxons who made use of prominent Italian Americans as mediators, who directed the immigrants, via the so-called padrone system (a term used by Italian immigrants, referring to a system revolving around the *padrone,* the intermediary who procured work and other benefits for the immigrants), toward various markets—the labor market, the housing market, and the credit market—and who made substantial profits off their compatriots.[4] In this case, organized crime represents a variant on the political, business, or trade union tradition of "bossism." Ever since the 1920s, using a straightforward functionalist approach, numerous American scholars, often of Italian descent, have worked on these topics, identifying the link between crime and the clientelistic and political "machines" that have run major cities, one of the few vehicles offering social integration and promotion to new emigrants. This function of the political machines was acknowledged as early as the turn of the twentieth century with amiable shamelessness by one of the top leaders of Tammany Hall, New York's Democratic electoral organization.[5] These political "machines," depending on the phases of the migratory cycle, were made up of Germans, Irish, Jews, and Italians, and unfailingly they took their place as the leaders of "organized crime." And the organized crime they operated took its place as the link between public institutions (the local police, city hall) and the demimonde of gambling, prostitution, and smuggling. As Joseph Albini has pointed out, Anglo-Saxon xenophobia presupposes that the "innocent, defenseless American public is the victim of foreign evil-doers who secretly rob it of its moral virginity."[6] In reality, by offering a demand for these more-or-less illegal goods and services, American society expresses for itself sufficient pathogenic germs to offer a venue for any and all "immigrant" criminal traditions. One such tradition is the Sicilian criminal tradition, which here, just as back in Italy, finds a triangular system made up of political class, police, and criminality.

Nonetheless, the theory of transplantation, alongside various accompanying paranoid extremisms, expresses fragments of realism that, perhaps out of piety toward their homeland (or ethnic group), Italian American scholars have failed to appreciate adequately. Viewed from the Sicilian perspective, the Hennessy case does little more than to indicate the considerable expanse of the business network of Palermitan intermediaries with greater or lesser degrees of Mafia ties. For them, New Orleans represents nothing more than a terminal, as does Tunisia with its immigration from the Italian Mezzogiorno, its teeming traffic of fugitives from the law and merchandise of all sorts (the citrus fruit Fontana was selling, but also stolen livestock) crossing from one bank to the other of the Strait of Sicily (Canale di Sicilia). At the turn of the twentieth century, New Orleans was the second-ranked port for the Sicilian citrus fruit trade in the United States. Smaller importers and businesses turned to New Orleans if they wished to break free of the giant Palermo–New York mercantile organization.[7] It was in New Orleans that Salvatore Marino[8] died twelve years before the Hennessy murder. It had been from New Orleans that one thread of the complex skein had run, resulting back in Sicily in a series of trials for criminal conspiracy. Here, Vassallo, who fell under suspicion as a spy for the Palermo *cosca* (Mafia family) had been found and killed. Marino was a trader in fruit. The Provenzanos and the Matrangas were traders and importers. The surname Matranga would surface frequently during the Badalamenti-Amoroso wars of the 1870s and 1880s, and it is not clear whether those are people who just happened to share the same surname. There is no question, however, that the two groups warring in Louisiana took on the well-known denominations of *stoppagghieri* and *giardinieri* (keepers of a citrus grove).

Between 1901 and 1914 alone, more than 800,000 Sicilians landed in the United States. While Sicily was arriving in America through its people, in every tiny village throughout Sicily, America presented itself in the person of the "emigration agent," a broker who readily paid for trans-Atlantic passages and who would find work on the far side of the ocean. At first, going to America was tantamount to disappearing. In fact, according to the authoritative testimony of the brigand Bufalino (1901), the expression "send [someone] to America, buy someone a ticket to America" was an ironic way of saying "to kill someone."[9] Over time, however, the two opposite shores of the Atlantic Ocean seemed to draw much closer together as temporary emigration between them became exceedingly common. All sorts of people left Italy, returned, and left again—the poor, the adventuresome, fugitives from political persecution, and other fugitives for less noble reasons. Obviously, convicts, people who had been subjected to the special security regimen of *ammonizione*, and fugitives from Sicily all met again in the New World, just as back in Sicily we find newly repatriated mafiosi attempting to reinsert themselves into the local balances of power, "bringing with them sizable amounts of cash of suspicious origin"; in some cases those attempts led to their deaths.[10] Mafia families, like natural families, split up and reassembled in the complex and intertwining welter of relations extending across the Atlantic Ocean in both directions.

It has been pointed out that the Black Hand (*mano nera*), which took its name from the symbol inscribed on a great many extortion letters, represented not an actual organization but a criminal phenomenology, a form of crime practiced by groups operating independently, and not specifically Sicilian, but generally Italian; I would further venture to say that these groups operated on the model of the Camorra more than that of the Mafia. In fact, like the Camorra, the Black Hand focused on skimming from the economic transactions of the poor, which in this concrete case involved a community located at the lowest level of the social hierarchy, a community to which both the extorters and their victims belonged. Nonetheless, we cannot rule out the possibility that in a major immigration center such as New York, the Sicilian mafiosi might have played an important role in the underworld even before the formation of a native crime network.

This was, in fact, the working hypothesis on which the New York City government set to work in 1908, in the person of Commissioner Theodore Bingham, and based on a report provided by an "expert" who was absolutely convinced that "the ordinary Italian immigrant, as a rule, never becomes a criminal once he has reached America." This report stated that the Black Hand was composed of criminals "who had already been criminals in Italy and that, once they arrived in America, they tended to gather into groups with others of their same kind."[11] The American legal system—the report went on—was not equipped to fight these people because it lacked the sort of law enforcement tools (the special security regimen of *ammonizione*, *domicilio coatto*, or obligatory residence) that alone had proved effective in Italy. It was necessary to expel undesirables, proving that they had concealed their criminal records and that they had therefore entered the United States illegally.

Bingham therefore set up a "secret" operation, but the press immediately reported on it. The New York police lieutenant Joe Petrosino, originally from Padula, was sent to Italy to investigate criminal records of immigrants. Petrosino was a much feared persecutor of members of the Black Hand. In particular, he had been responsible for the repatriation of numerous immigrants whose papers were not in order.[12] He assumed that Italian authorities were in league with the criminals, or at the very best, were simply incompetent.[13] And in fact, leaving aside a few informal contacts, Petrosino refused all offers of institutional collaboration and even the discreet police bodyguard offered to him when he landed in Palermo. As the *questore* (administrative director of the district police) Baldassarre Ceola later commented, Petrosino "completely accepted the prejudices held by those Sicilians who believe that they are better protected by turning to some notorious and greatly feared criminal who commands great respect and influence, rather than relying on the authorities and on the system of justice."[14] Above all, Petrosino adhered to the tradition of the Palermo police, though he did not realize it, and most importantly, despite the fact that he lacked any of the negotiating power enjoyed by the police, except for the power of the dollars that he paid to his informers and the feeble shadow of a legal authority from across the Atlantic Ocean. Thus, Petrosino was virtually defenseless, and with a "recklessness that appears almost inconceivable in such a renowned detective,"[15] he ventured into the most classic triangle of police–Mafia–criminality. On 12 March 1909, he fell under a hail of bullets in the center of Palermo, in the Piazza Marina.

There followed a series of bitter accusations in the American press, once again leveling charges against the Italians of complicity, while the Italians in turn emphasized how amateurish Petrosino's operation had been. The investigations, of course, focused on the route linking Palermo and New York. The usual confidential informers, together with anonymous letters mailed from New York, pointed an accusing finger at the Corleonese Giuseppe Morello, head of a group of New York counterfeiters who had resolved a business dispute with a fellow Italian in 1903 by killing him. This had brought them to Petrosino's attention. Among the members of the group was an individual whom we know quite well, Giuseppe Fontana. After his acquittal at the Florence trial, Fontana had moved to the New World where he took up an old occupation, the fabrication and passing of counterfeit banknotes. Two other members of the group, Carlo Costantino and Antonino Passananti, had suddenly reappeared in their hometown of Partinico in perfect synchronization with Petrosino's arrival. Using enigmatic coded telegrams, they had stayed in contact with Morello, who was back in America. Perhaps they were afraid that Petrosino might discover that Morello had a criminal record sufficient to provide grounds for his expulsion from the United States.[16] Many reasons, linked both to the past and the present, might have prompted Costantino and Passananti to take concrete action. In addition to these two, the police arrested about fifteen other individuals, almost all of whom had returned from America, the entire network of the detective's informers; and last of all, a Mafia capo, Don Vito Cascio-Ferro.

The criminal record of this interesting individual, prior to 1914, was marked by a number, not overwhelmingly large, of indictments (extortion, arson, kidnapping), all of which were resolved in acquittals. Cascio-Ferro certainly could not have been considered a provincial notable. In fact, his power was based on a network of relations extending over two continents, as well as an event of such international resonance—the Petrosino murder—that his reputation allowed him "to take sure-handed control of the Mafia throughout the entire territory of the province of Palermo."[17] Cascio-Ferro, together with Morello and Fontana, belonged to the group of counterfeiters that Petrosino arrested in 1903. Cascio-Ferro's stay in New York, which began in 1901, ended suddenly on that occasion, though not without the customary trip to New Orleans. Following the murder, a photograph of Petrosino was found among Cascio-Ferro's papers. Among Petrosino's papers, moreover, a note was found that referred to Cascio-Ferro as a "highly dangerous criminal." The New York policeman planned, among other things, to take a trip to Bisacquino, the feudal stronghold of the Mafia capo. Could it have been that Petrosino was hoping to obtain the invaluable information from none other than Don Vito Cascio-Ferro? This hypothesis has not previously been proposed, but it seems to be in keeping with the aims of Petrosino's journey, as well as with the observation by the *questore* concerning criminals who command "great respect and influence." As well as we can reconstruct, Petrosino was investigating an organization that falsified passports, under the control of the notorious aristocrat Francesco di Villarosa, that is, a network with footholds in both Sicily and America. It is worth noting that, at least until the 1920s, one of the leading activities of an eminent Sicilian American mafioso like Salvatore Maranzano was the clandestine importation of laborers.[18] It would appear that Don Vito was also involved in clandestine expatriations, which he organized aboard fishing boats from Mazara del Vallo that sailed to Tunis, and from there, by ocean liners on the Marseilles–New York route.[19] The Mafia capo was officially employed as the "representative of the Caruso postal shipping company."[20] Could that have been another way of saying emigration agent? Perhaps Cascio-Ferro, after delving into the double game of the informer, decided to help out both himself and his American friends. Those American friends had made the voyage to Bisacquino that had proved unattainable to Petrosino—in the persons of Costantino and Passananti. In any case, many years later, Don Vito Cascio-Ferro boasted that he had killed Petrosino "in a disinterested manner," with his own hands.[21]

The preliminary investigation (*istruttoria*) resulted in the decision not to proceed against any of the defendants. Cascio-Ferro brought in his own defense the testimony of the Honorable Domenico De Michele Ferrantelli, who claimed to have had Cascio-Ferro as his guest the evening of the murder. The alibi is not particularly credible, considering the close ties between the two. De Michele was a major trader in oil and grains, and Cascio-Ferro was his "business agent." De Michele was the much discussed and controversial mayor of Burgio, rock-solid in that office, as well as the member of parliament for the district of Bivona, whereas Cascio-Ferro was his *capo-elettore* (this Italian term was used, especially by the press, to describe a political activist who worked to gather votes, roughly equivalent to the American "ward heeler"—*translator's note*). It would be interesting to know whether De Michele had taken part in the expansion of Sicilian American trade that went hand in hand with the growth in migration.[22] If so, Don Vito, with his trips to New York and New Orleans, would mirror on a larger scale the smaller figure, already familiar to us, of the mafioso who creates a network along the lines marked out by the business interests of important individuals. Let us not forget, in any case, the protective functions that inevitably accompany the business interests. Born in Palermo, Don Vito Cascio-Ferro moved to Bisacquino to follow his father, who was a *campiere,* or private guard of farmland, of Baron Antonino Inglese, a notorious usurper of state-owned lands. This was one of the effects of the growing centralization to Palermo of the market for leases and custodianships. Let us think back to Don Peppino il Lombardo who, through Giammona's help, succeeded in obtaining a job as a *sovrastante* (local superintendent) in Alia. Or let us remember Don Bartolomeo Badalamenti traveling to Caltagirone with his entourage "of servants, roustabouts, and outlaws such as had never been seen before, who came and went and vanished without the slightest trace."[23] And last of all, let us remember the operation undertaken by the prince of Mirto, who moved Fontana into the areas plundered by the brigand Varsalona,[24] that is, the Corleone–Sambuca–Burgio area, on the boundaries of the province of Palermo and the province of Agrigento. Here Cascio-Ferro lived, though with frequent stays in Palermo, which clearly remained a strategic location for the function of Mafia capo: *gabellotto* (renter and sublessor of parcels of farmland) or administrator of the Honorable De Michele and Baron Inglese in the Corleonese district, and an elegant gentleman in Palermo.

If we work our way backward into the earlier years of Cascio-Ferro's life, we encounter an extraordinary political situation, that of the *Fasci Siciliani* of 1892–1893. To our surprise, we find Don Vito as the vice president of the Fascio of Bisacquino, while, in the role of lecturer on behalf of socialism, he succeeded in obtaining "something that would appear difficult to believe, . . . that the women no longer followed the processions of the Last Sacraments and that they say confession to him and to the president of the Fascio." It is difficult to imagine the content of those confessions. When the Fasci Siciliani were suppressed, Cascio-Ferro fled to Tunis (December 1893), and from there a short while later he "returned, voluntarily, to the homeland, offering assurances to His Honor the *questore* of Palermo and the subprefect of Corleone that he would never again be involved in politics."[25] From that time forward, his "political behavior was impeccable," and through "his friendship with Baron Inglese and with the

Honorable De Michele Ferrantelli" he won a position as a local notable; he enrolled in the town circle, winning "the respect of his fellow townspeople" and of the authorities.[26] This was in December 1908, less than a year before the murder of Petrosino.

A subversive thus becomes a *uomo d'ordine*, literally, man of order, a description that is not at odds with the description of a mafioso. What remains to be puzzled out is the underlying logic of his adherence to a left-wing movement opposed with a hint of hysteria by the ruling class and by the Crispi government, which undertook the suppression of that movement with military force. By examining that logic more carefully, we will be able to understand how, not only with the clientelistic machinery of New York and Chicago, but also with the same machinery in Corleone and Monreale, the phenomenon of the Mafia is linked to processes, however distorted and perverted, of democratization; how in both America, land of opportunity, and in postfeudal Sicily the success and growth of the Mafia fit into a larger context of social mobility and profound historical transformations.

LANDS AND VILLAGES

In the immediate wake of the proclamation of the state of siege (December 1893), many militants in the Fasci were ordered to appear before military tribunals as a result of accusations "by convicts and people with prior convictions for common crimes."[27] Among these people were the *guardie comunali*, the *guardie campestri*, or the *guardie daziarie* (respectively, town, rural, and financial gendarmeries), whom we recognize as manifestations of Mafia power. In many cases, these people shot into crowds, provoking insurrections in order to justify the repression of those same insurrections.[28] In the provinces of Palermo and Agrigento, when the Fasci campaigned concerning issues of municipal politics, taxes, use of state-owned lands, or even agricultural contracts, they might well have found that they were going up against oppressive and corrupt ruling classes, capable of all sorts of violent reactions. There was, however, no absolute ideological incompatibility between the left wing and the Mafia: "If the government abandons [the Mafia], it will place itself in the service of the clergy; if everyone abandons it, it will pose as a revolutionary movement,"[29] noted the socialist Drago, confirming something we already know about the post-Risorgimento period.

This problem can only be defined within a local context. Although it is impossible to hypothesize a shared and common political position of the Mafia, it is equally cumbersome to imagine complete homogeneity among a number of municipal Fasci that formed in just a few convulsive months, devoid of any significant coordination from above, with the exception of a self-proclaimed central committee in Palermo. It is possible, however, to identify a line of continuity into which the sudden flare-up of activity inserted itself. At Misilmeri, the Fascio organization was founded by Girolamo Sparti, a young university student related to both of the families that had been battling for years to take control of the town administration. In Monreale, no fewer than three Fasci were founded; one of them was under the leadership of the mayor, Rocco Balsano, a follower of Crispi, who suddenly decided to convert to socialism in order to safeguard the future of the farming association that served as the hub for his clientelistic network. In Lercara the Fascio was powerful, but it was impossible to say who led it. The bloody uprising of Christmas 1893 was to some degree incited by the Nicolosi party. The Nicolosis were well-known long-term abettors and accomplices of bandits; the uprising was directed against the party of the Sartorios, which had had control of town hall ever since 1876. In Marineo, the Fascio enjoyed the support of the Calderone party, which had recently lost power after wielding it in an absolute and dictatorial manner for more than ten years.[30]

In some cases, this was nothing more than camouflage. In other cases we are looking at contrasts between progressives and conservatives, and in any event factional and family struggles, groups that split apart and then join together again using an ideological idiom for their ulterior motives. In a great many cases in the 1890s, an equilibrium was established among the local parties that would remain in place until the Great War. "In small villages, the families of moderate prosperity are nearly all relations of one kind or another . . . and not merely in a single party, even the members of opposition parties are related even though they are in opposing camps."[31] It is unlikely that new men would emerge, while new instruments linking the ruling class and society at large (agricultural associations, mutual aid societies, clubs) developed, in part to adapt the clientelistic machines to the expansion of suffrage as ordered by the electoral reforms of 1882 (political elections) and 1889 (administrative elections), a process that culminated in 1913 with universal male suffrage. Moreover, even in small cities and large villages in Sicily, between the end of the nineteenth century and the turn of the twentieth century, state legislation and the very processes of modernization began to call for the implementation of a system of public lighting, either gas or, later, electric, a road system and a sewer system, a health system, and public education. These were new opportunities to make money and control jobs, alongside the more traditional systems of controlling state resources and local taxes (What needs to be taxed? Who has to pay? Who has to collect the taxes, and how?), establishing a strong interest in controlling municipal administrations on the part of country political groups, with their entourage of contractors, landlords, leaseholders, long-term leaseholders, and uprooted lawyers, schoolteachers, pharmacists, clients, electors, cousins, aspirants, and plotters.[32]

This was the tumultuous world of southern clientelism as depicted by the ferocious and brilliant observer Gaetano Salvemini; this was the world to which journalists and police sources refer when they use the term *Mafia*. Anyone attempting to distinguish between this concept and the concept of clientelism, however, would encounter serious difficulties. Quite frequently *delegati di PS* (or police inspectors) and *questori* describe as "mafiosi" those who are simply opponents of the government, such as, for instance, in Misilmeri the Sparti, Scozzari, and Di Pisa families.[33] However, the group favored by the government itself was the one headed on a provincial basis by Salvatore Avellone, one of the most controversial members of the Italian parliament owing to his ties with the Mafia. The frequent *commissariamenti* (establishment of government control) to which the prefect subjected this township should be put in the context of that disagreement, rather than any real effort to subdue the "Mafia." In Monreale the municipal party led by Balsano, the future member of parliament, was accused of favoring its clients in the administration of public finance and contracts. Here, too, at the behest of Member of Parliament Masi (an opponent of Balsano) there intervened prefectorial commissioners (*commissari prefettizi*) who ascertained irregularities and, after a certain period of time, called for elections that, much as was the case in Misilmeri, only reinforced the existing balance of power. Note how the prefect, a follower of Giolitti, described by historians as omnipotent, acted not on behalf of a central and centralizing program, but simply to benefit a member of parliament eager to subdue an unruly municipal administration. Note, too, how municipal "mafias" successfully withstood all comers. In Monreale, people ironically wondered why *commissari prefettizi* were appointed for life as in a "Turkish city." Alongside the municipalist debates over the "proud Athens of Sicily" that refused to bow, there were other regionalist debates, previously rehearsed many times, on the "liberties conquered at the cost of blood" by an "unfortunate Sicily" and not respected by the government.[34]

All of this, however, belongs largely to the realm of political history. In the specific terms of the present topic, we can record a generic but significant array of links between the governing groups and the criminal world. Of the Balsano party, "there were friends and supporters among people who had been arrested and tried."[35] Di Pisa was a bloody-minded individual who frequently resolved his arguments with the sword cane that he always carried around with him, until he was wounded by pistol shots. A more clearly defined figure was Salvatore Sparti, who took office as mayor shortly after being released from jail; his murder trial ended in acquittal (though he was convicted for assault and battery, making threats, and other charges). He was a "natural protector of Mafia and scum." He testified in favor of those who had been proposed as subjects for the special security regimen of *ammonizione,* with the inevitable refrain that he had been forced to do so in order to stave off the attempts of his adversaries.[36]

Two towns such as Misilmeri and Monreale—towns that were certainly *paesi di Mafia*—failed to reflect the presence of the Mafia itself within their municipal institutions as clearly as we would have expected.

Let us attempt to broaden the picture. Both situations share a single element: the presence of large quantities of state-owned properties that are repeatedly parceled out, while the town administrations are unwilling or unable to exact the corresponding fees. In particular, only the *commissari prefettizi,* who are periodically appointed in the wake of the dissolution of those administrations, take any actions against those responsible for those usurpations "of many hundreds of hectares" of these lands, "since none of the peasants, out of fear of retaliation, is willing to take the initiative in starting legal action."[37] Then there is geographic location: Misilmeri and especially Monreale are located on the boundary between the zone of large landholdings and the area of intensive agriculture; they have vast areas of farmland that gravitate economically around Palermo. The city's governing class apparently has no particular interest in this countryside. This is one key to interpreting the factional struggle provided by the protagonists of that struggle. The majority groups in the two towns thus represent a bourgeoisie that does not own any *beni rusticani*—rural land—against whom the healthy public opinion of the "authorities" would turn as one, the *uomini d'ordine* (men of order) and the *latifondisti* (large landholders).[38] Part of the ruling class had in fact greater interest in municipal finance, the assignment of contracts, and the convergence of business interests around those contracts. And that portion of the ruling class won support by allowing the leaseholders to not pay the required fees for the use of township-owned lands and to purchase those lands at rock-bottom prices and resell them at a profit. These groups were interested in the countryside because it was a source of revenue for the municipal administration (surtaxes on the land, fees for emphyteusis) and because they were called on to ensure order in that countryside. We see the old problem of the *guardie campestri,* or rural and agricultural police, resurfacing, a problem along which we slide directly from the milieu of violent clientelism to the issue of Mafia violence. The service appears to be inefficient "because of the lack of discipline and the disagreements that exist in the Corps,"[39] but probably it is more accurate to talk of corruption. In Misilmeri, in 1903–1906, five *guardie campestri* were murdered; in 1907, eight of the twenty-five members of the Corps were put on trial for criminal conspiracy, two were imprisoned on charges of murder, and one was fired for stealing. Every so often the system of private and public *guardianìa* (the business of providing custodianship) imploded. In Monreale around 1911, Vittorio Calò, Mafia capo of the small agricultural town of Borgo Molara, developed a strong disagreement with the farming family of the Sciortinos, who apparently formed part of the tradition of the *stoppagghieri*; the Sciortinos were massacred. In November 1912, while Giuseppe Cavallaro, town treasurer, was returning from one of his *giardini,* or citrus groves, he was shot and killed by an unidentified assassin hidden behind a hedge. This murder took place thirty years after that of Father Simone and employed the exact same technique.[40] In the meanwhile, Calò perfected "the system of *locuplamento,* the *guardianìe* or custodianships, and the systems of ransom or collecting tributes," until he reached the point of demanding a percentage on "any and all signs of human life."[41]

As one landowner in Misilmeri wrote, the municipal *consorteria* (political association of aristocratic families) was responsible for "vandalous crimes, such as cutting down trees and grapevines, burning haystacks and barnyards," the "social cancer" known as the *mafia.* In a more moderate description, the police declared that "commissioners and councilors, many of whom have also suffered property damage, avoid meddling in police matters, for fear of more serious reprisals."[42] Perhaps what we are seeing here is a division of labor between the small-town politicians and the rural rackets, two distinct spheres that were nonetheless reciprocally functional. This situation corresponds to what Giovanna Fiume describes in connection with the Calderones of Marineo in the immediately preceding period.[43]

If from the partially transformed area that rotates around Palermo we turn inland, toward the provincial hinterland with its large landholders, or further down, as far as the so-called Vallone, where it meets the boundaries of the Agrigento area and the Caltanissetta area, we encounter different conditions, and a much closer relationship between town and countryside. Here too, the episode of the *fasci* forms part of the continuity of the local parties. In Burgio in 1891, there existed three organizations that mirrored the division into town parishes (Parish of the Madonna del Carmine, Parish of Maria, and Parish of S. Nicola) and which, "because of the ferocious competition among the parties . . . exerted an influence on the masses." In 1893, the first two organizations were transformed into *fasci* and then returned to their previous form in the wake of the repression.[44] In Casteltermini, the *fascio,* which was considered to be extremist, defended itself from police attempts to infiltrate it by holding its meetings in the palazzo of the major landowner, Francesco Lo Bue Perez, nephew of a senator, to the cry of "Viva il cavalier Lo Bue, viva il socialismo, viva i fasci!" ("Long live Cavalier Lo Bue, long live socialism, and long live the *fasci!*")[45] At Contessa Entellina it was the Lo Jacono family who established the *fascio;* with various ups and downs, that family had controlled all local power and the market of the *gabelle,* or subcontracting of farmland leases, as far back as the late eighteenth century. The Lo Jacono family had also allowed its lands to be worked on a sharecropper basis, rather than with the traditional rental and sublease system.[46] With this outlook of potential reforms of the agricultural contracts, the townships offered a view of the large landholders and their grip on the countryside. "In the *fasci* of Girgenti (the old name for Agrigento—*translator's note*), there is a praiseworthy example in S. Maria Belice, where the leaders are landowners. They have taught the peasants to believe . . . that he who works hard, saves his money, and cooperates will also become a landowner." In S. Stefano Quisquina, the *fascio* was founded to the cry "Viva il Re e Margherita, evviva la legge!" ("Long live the King and Queen Margherita, long live the law!") by the town councilor, Lorenzo Panepinto, who, however, like the founders of the *fasci* of Prizzi and Bisacquino (which included Cascio-Ferro), took part in the strikes over the division of products proclaimed by Nicola Barbato and Bernardino Verro, the prestigious socialist leaders of Piana degli Albanesi and Corleone, respectively. For moderates and radicals the objective was still the introduction of sharecropping.

The depression of the 1880s and 1890s reduced revenues, but, more than anything else, the profits of farming concerns. The result was the collapse of the market of the *gabelle.* This made the absentee landowners, who lived in Palermo, Rome, or even Madrid, even more the objects of hostility on the part of a municipal ruling class that was suddenly won over to the alternative of sharecropping, eager to establish new relations with the bourgeoisie—that is, middle-level peasants who were beginning to despair of ever rising to the rank of *gabellotto.* These peasants constituted the fundamental structure of the *fasci,* as they rode from one estate to another on horseback to persuade the laborers to boycott the landowners who were unwilling to accept the conditions established, those who even after the repression under Crispi kept alive "internal" socialism, at least in a number of agricultural situations where the leadership of the Verros, the Barbatos, and the Panepintos was emerging.[47] It is possible to state that here socialism and Mafia were founded on the same social groups while still setting forth two different models of mobility and relations with the country bourgeoisie and the large landholders. The simultaneous presence in a single area of a high level of both political mobilization and Mafia mobilization cannot be resolved in the oppositional logic of action and reaction. The report that in his youth Verro underwent a sort of Mafia initiation,[48] whether true or false, shows the roots in this common soil, ideally exemplified in the two figures of Verro himself and Cascio-Ferro, neighbors in their origins, though distant in their final destinies.

Many of the *fasci* charters called for the denial of membership to individuals responsible for public scandal, convicts, or mafiosi. All the same, the door was left open for those that *L'Avanti!* naïvely described as "a Mafia faithful to its generous origins, rooted in a legitimate rebellion against all forms of arrogance."[49] *La Plebe,* a socialist newspaper published in S. Stefano Quisquina, describes the chance encounter between two groups—the group of those enrolled in the peasant league and the group of the "mafiosi." The encounter ended with an exchange of witticisms and a common recognition of the moral superiority of the league supporters and adherents.[50] In a speech delivered in Prizzi in 1902, Verro stated that "as long as socialism has been preached, the lower forms of criminality have declined, and we hope that over time there will be a similar decline in the murders ordered by the *alta Mafia.*"[51] This is a hypothesis of linear civilization of the social conflict in the course of which socialism would take the place of the Mafia, at least the "low Mafia," eliminating its reasons for existence. When Cavalier Emanuele Arezzo accused his striking peasants of maintaining an "attitude that was in no wise civil and absolutely mafioso," Panepinto replied that the Mafia represented only the "spontaneous product" of the large landholding.[52]

Even Panepinto himself, confident—earnest elementary schoolteacher that he was—that socialism represented a form of collective pedagogy, was still obliged to convince himself of the empty inanity of all progressive automatism when he paid a visit to the community of his compatriots who had emigrated to Florida: "We had placed our trust in illusions concerning our townsfolk who had gone to work in Tampa but unfortunately, even the distance and the change in milieu seem to have done nothing to moderate their age-old propensities for reckless and criminal behavior. Dollars and good pay seem to have been of no help, unless someone can step in to help shape the political and moral consciousness of these proletarians."[53]

Panepinto's trip also constituted an attempt to escape the difficulties inherent in the socialism of S. Stefano Quisquina, which was unable to carve out any space for itself in the wake of the excitement and enthusiasm of the great agrarian strikes of 1902, at least at the district or provincial level because of the age-old and unresolved conflict with De Michele Ferrantelli. Verro, too, the target of persecution by the authorities, left Corleone and sought refuge outside of Italy, or else decided to take party offices in Messina and Reggio Calabria. It is difficult to identify a "class-based" line in the towns of the large landholdings in

Sicily. However, it was even less likely that men of this sort would be able to find new opportunities for themselves outside of the municipal stage.

The peasant movement emerged from its impasse around the end of the first decade of the twentieth century with the explosive growth of the collective tenancies, which took the place of the leagues as chief instrument of the organization. Thanks to the Sonnino Law of 1906, the cooperatives were now able to operate as terminals of the Banco di Sicilia for the issuance of agricultural credits, and thus take large landholdings in rental and then make them available to members in small lots. Among other things, in this phase, the more extensive use of crops that improved the soil (broadbean, clover) and the first introduction of chemical fertilizers allowed an intensification of crop rotations. This development finally broke the iron chain between cultivating wheat and letting the land lay fallow, which underlay the great nineteenth-century subleases, making peasant agriculture relatively prosperous. After an initial phase of hostility, the landowners began to consider "the collective intervention of the peasants in the rents as a natural effect of social evolution,"[54] especially appreciating the support offered in terms of revenue, which had first been threatened by the general crisis and subsequently by the dwindling of labor due to growing emigration. The demand generated by cooperatives primed the rental market, which now also involved both the *gabellotto singolo* (individual renter and sublessor of parcels of farmland) and the *gabellotto collettivo* (collective renter and sublessor of parcels of farmland), to use the terminology of the period, which significantly underscored the common role of the economic and politico-social intermediary with respect to the major (indeed, sole) resource that existed for peasant society. By transforming proximity into rivalry, the cooperatives found themselves in competition for the monopoly that, as we know, can trigger the greatest possible punishment.

The story begins with Bernardino Verro, forced by an attack in 1910 to leave Corleone. Clearly aware of the situation, he sketched out the levels of the Mafia network: in the town, the *gabellotto* and Mafia capo, Michelangelo Gennaro; on a provincial scale, the *cricca* protected by the subprefect Spata, married to a woman from the Torina family of Caccamo, and therefore a descendant of a venerable Mafia dynasty, and by Vincenzo Cascio of the provincial administrative coalition. Clientelism and family tied both of them to Member of Parliament Avellone, who had testified on Palizzolo's behalf. Avellone, like Palizzolo, was a member of Rudinì's entourage and had come out of the "moralizing" operation of Codronchi. There was of course also a connection with Palermo:

> Avellone did not suggest or order [the attack], but he is a member of parliament for the district and must maintain ties with relatives and *grandi*

elettori, or major ward heelers. I saw him with my own eyes in the Teatro Massimo café in Palermo, talking animatedly with Gaspare Tedeschi, a native of Palermo who lives in Villafrati, where he acts as Mafia capo and conceals Giovanni Mancuso, one of the pair, the one who shot me and then was in turn shot, and was then taken to the Palermo clinic run by Doctor Giuffrè, brother of the Mafia capo of Caltavuturo and well aware of the tenancy that was the reason I was shot. What a network! What a tangled ball of string! Tedeschi is well known to the Palermo magistrature, and one evening he even came to pay a call on me in the Piazza Bologni, offering to serve as a peace negotiator between me and the Mafia.[55]

The story continues with Lorenzo Panepinto, leader of the socialists of S. Stefano Quisquina, then fully on the rebound after obtaining financing from the Banco di Sicilia to rent the former Mailla *feudo,* or estate. "Unquestionably the 'subversive' of 1911 was much more worrisome to their lordships than had been the subversive of 1893,"[56] and therefore the punishment had to be much harsher. On 16 May 1911, outside his front door, Panepinto was assassinated. His well-attended and massive funeral brought to public attention a profound and ancient Sicily, which appeared to the correspondent of *L'Ora* to be a "savage tribe" where the expression of grief was entirely focused on female figures. Surrounding the daughter of the capo, "the women of S. Stefano, wrapped tightly in their black shawls, seemed possessed by some unknown passion as they emitted frightful shrieks. . . . Vendetta was the word on everyone's lips." "Avenge him, avenge him," the widow repeated as if it were a nursery rhyme.[57] But of course socialism could not face off with its enemies using their weapons: "It hardly seems as if this is 1911," wrote a disconsolate Verro, accused of being a *cascittuni* (spy), incapable of finding an intermediate path between "becoming a criminal, inciting to criminal acts, or being assassinated."[58]

When, in the spring of 1914, the Corleonese left wing triumphed in the administrative elections, Verro was obliged to return home and serve as mayor, though he was fully aware of the dangers he faced. "Either drink or drown. . . . What would have become of this socialist movement if the workers, once they had power in their hands, decided not to take it?"[59] Less than a year later, he was shot down in the middle of the town. Another year passed and Nicolò Alongi, formerly a member of the *fasci,* leader of the peasant movement in Prizzi, himself a peasant, was attacked. A truce was called, and then, in September 1919, the secretary of the league, Giuseppe Rumore, was killed. From that day forth, Alongi described himself as a "dead man on vacation," and he bid his friends farewell. "I don't know if tomorrow I can embrace you again, but I am sure that others will rise to wave the banner that they want to tear from my hand."[60] Not even a month went by, and the socialism of the large landholdings wept over a new victim.

The progress of the battles over the rental of the large landholdings around Prizzi, before the war but especially after, clearly indicates the motive for the murder. While the landowners were "willing to give in," "the negative power" came entirely from the local *gabellotti* and their "relations of reciprocality, mutuality, interests, and even Mafia."[61] The most authoritative among them was Silvestre Cristina, closely tied to Cascio-Ferro, who would later wind up murdered, though in Palermo, just a few years later.[62] The second-rank leader was Giorgio D'Angelo, the son of Luciano D'Angelo whom we saw as a Mafia capo in the 1880s and earlier, in the 1860s, as an accomplice and abettor of the gang of Don Peppino il Lombardo. On the other hand, the suspected murderer of Panepinto was a certain Giuseppe Anzalone, a young *gabellotto* from Lercara, with the same place of birth and the same name (a grandson then?) of another of the most notorious abettors and accomplices of the gang. A well-known figure, Anzalone, Jr., was especially respected for his family ties, as is shown by his title as "godson" of Camillo Finocchiaro-Aprile, the member of parliament from Lercara and the Italian minister of justice.[63] Thus, fifty or sixty years later, the foundational role of the experience as a brigand of Don Peppino proved its significance.

The picture of the Mafia in large landholdings in the first two decades of the twentieth century, however, is more complex and more intimately linked to the new structure that was emerging. The death of Panepinto does indeed fit into the context of the "uprising of the *Mafia gabellotta*,"[64] but it also forms part of the conflict with the Catholic rural savings and loans, with which apparently the mafiosi were especially close. A substantial element of Verro's problem in Corleone had to do with the difficulty of preventing the socialist cooperative from falling prey to the appetites of profiteers. The police believed that the Mafia had succeeded in finding a position within that cooperative in the person of Angelo Palazzo, the administrator whom Verro had denounced for misappropriation of funds.[65] In short, an attempt was made to block the progress of the cooperatives, on the one hand, but also to take them over in other areas. The collective *gabellotto* may represent an instrument of the restructuring of Mafia power— just as in a more general sense around 1910 the peasant political machine was taking on a new articulation in western Sicily, with the spread of the instruments of tenancies and rural savings and loans. This led to the creation of such powerful entities as the Federazione Siciliana delle Cooperative (Sicilian Federation of Cooperatives), which in 1911 gathered 313 organizations of the Agrigento area under the leadership of the radical-socialist Enrico La Loggia. Similarly, the priests Michele Sclafani and Luigi Sturzo, the first a moderate clericalist and the other a Christian Democrat, brought renewal to the Catholic movement.

Let us consider the case of Villalba, a village in the Vallone that was traditionally the theater of brigandage as well as conflict between large landholders, who did not live in the village, and the *borgesi,* who staged major strikes as early as 1875, and again in 1893, 1901, and 1907, alternately allied "with the *gabellotti* against the large landowner or with the large landowner against the *gabellotti.*"[66] The quarrel focused on the two Miccichè and Belici *feudi,* or estates. The first estate was owned by the princely Palermo family of the Trabias, while the second estate was also administered from Palermo but belonged to Duke Francesco Thomas de Barberin, who lived in Paris. The Trabia family's firm control over the first estate contrasted with the power of the intermediaries over the second one. Those intermediaries were none other than the Gucciones, who turned the estate into a refuge for brigands, including, at one period, Antonino Leone. It was the Belici estate that the people of Villalba, organized into the Cassa Rurale Cattolica (Catholic Rural Fund), asked for the tenancy and succeeded in 1908:

"The ideal had been attained," the priest Sgarlata, chairman of the company, would later write. "Usury had practically been eliminated; the oppressors and the gouging middlemen had been eliminated. The peasant has once again attained with his liberation a love for the fields and for hard work; now that the peasants have become *gabellotto* and are working on their own behalf . . . they know that the sweat of their brow will come back to them in the form of prosperity and nourishment."[67]

But in the townsfolk's eyes, all credit for the success of the operation was due to the priest's young nephew, the very same Calogero Vizzini, who had been arrested just a few years earlier as an accomplice and abettor of the bandit Varsalona. Now, however, as guarantor of the transaction between the Paris-based landowner, the Palermo-based administrator, the cooperative, the peasants (and the Gucciones), Calogero Vizzini won for himself the title of "Don," a title that would accompany his name throughout the course of a long and emblematic career. The *gabella* was assigned personally to Vizzini in accordance with a practice that was not uncommon in transactions between large landholders and peasant organizations, an indication of the central role played by that individual's personal, financial, or political credibility. In this specific case, Don Calogero, or more familiarly Don Calò, kept for himself a substantial portion of the estate (290 hectares, or 717 acres), and graciously handed over the rest to the Cassa Rurale, or rural savings and loan.[68] The collective mobilization offered new areas of endeavor for the mediation services of Mafia notables.

OLD/NEW MAFIA

Cammarata, 1891. Luigi Varsalona, son of a former member of the gang of Don Peppino who had died in prison, quarreled with his accomplices over the shares of the loot from a theft from the prince of Mirto and was killed. The trial of the killers ended with a mild sentence, in part owing to a witness for the defendants. Less than a year later, that witness was in turn killed in an ambush set for him by the brother of the dead man, Francesco Paolo Varsalona; immediately afterward, Francesco Paolo Varsalona fled and went into hiding.[69]
S. Mauro Castelverde, 1894. The peasant Mariano Farinella was killed by several members of the Glorioso clan whom he had accused of stealing a cow. The young son of the victim, Vincenzo, witnessed the crime and after a lengthy hesitation, "broke the customary silence" and turned to the authorities. The trial, however, ended in acquittal, followed by the ineluctable elimination of the "spy" (1899). A few months later, during a nighttime attack on a farm, three of the alleged killers of the Farinellas were murdered, according to the investigators, by Antonio Farinella, son and brother, respectively, of the two dead men. Two other Gloriosos then escaped to America, but when they returned to their village fourteen years later, they found the vendetta of Farinella and his four brothers awaiting them.[70]

Both of these cases involve a classic sequence out of the saga of brigandage: the murdered relative, justice denied, feud, and vendetta. The correspondence between legend and reality ends there, however. Farinella turned into a typical figure of the *Alta Maffia*, leaseholder, mayor, but also accomplice and abettor of Melchiorre Candino, a leading figure in local banditry.[71] Varsalona remained a fugitive from the law for more than ten years, personifying what Detective Alongi called the turning point of brigandage: the abandonment of the old technique of kidnapping and the institution in the hinterland of a racket strategy borrowed from the coastal Mafia, with the creation of a network composed of bandits, *campieri,* or private guards of farmland, peasants, and landowners, with the levying of "a new type of land-based surtax that allowed landowners and *gabellotti* to move freely through the countryside . . . confident that they could buy back whatever was stolen from them by criminals not affiliated with the gang, who were inexorably suppressed."[72]

In the Varsalona and Farinella cases, then, there emerges a close similarity between the roles of mafioso and brigand, with the prime difference to be found in the warrant for the arrest of each. Candino lived in hiding for well over three decades, and according to public opinion his presence was tolerated "for services rendered to the police,"[73] feeding himself "with checks from the feudal landowners." His time on the run would come to an end in 1922 with the surreal touch of a public manifestation of approval from the notables of Gangi, concerned about preserving order in the countryside after the "brigand" retired to a private existence.[74] We are quite distant, in this Sicilian setting, from the figure of the primitive rebel, the vindicator of the wrongs suffered by the poor at the hands of the wealthy and the powerful. This was made excruciatingly clear as well to two members of the Varsalona gang when they suggested, "in a moment of giddiness," the kidnapping of a certain G. G. (Guccione) who had ordered the expropriation of the property of the father of one of the two gang members. Here was the problem: this Guccione, however, was (as usual) "the most generous and substantial contributor to the association," and the very idea of such an act was so abhorrent to the brigand chief that he decided to inflict a death sentence, executed immediately and on the spot, on the imprudent foot soldiers.[75] There are those who, in the face of the "astonishing growth of cattle theft," will be forced to give up "working the fields and the large landholdings," the mayor of Contessa Entellina, Nicolò Lo Jacono, complained, and his family was exposed to the pressures of the brigand Grisafi. On the other hand, there were others who made use of their positive relations with the bandit to venture into the rental and lease market. As a result, Emanuele Coco, Mafia capo in Chiusa Sclafani, was able to take the place of the Lo Jacono family.[76] Orbiting around brigands in hiding, we always find the same basic characters: the notable who serves as an intermediary with the peasant society, the Palermo mafioso, the middlemen, the peasants, and the outcasts and misfits.[77] On the lower end of the social ladder, too, are the victims and the usufructuaries (roughly speaking, something like long-term sharecroppers) of the farmlands, grazing lands, businesses, and even manufactories,[78] which the brigand in hiding manages within the context of relations and clientele.

Many police officials continued to "say that criminality has grown to such excessive proportions that all measures against it are ineffective."[79] One Catanian construction company working on a new railroad line was unable to prevent its (Siracusan) laborers from fleeing, "terrified" as they were at the murder of a technician in charge of construction, and more in general at the twelve murders that had taken place in a single year in the territory of Prizzi-Palazzo Adriano. The authorities unconcernedly observed that "in all this, taking into account the location and the setting, there is nothing abnormal."[80] In any case, anyone who ventured to investigate highly placed protection complicity was walking out onto a minefield. Cutrera incurred the disapproval of his superiors on two occasions: the first time when during an investigation he attempted to "nail" as an accomplice and abettor of Varsalona the *baronello* (baronet) Peppino Coffari di Cammarata, and the second time when as a scholar he underscored the impotence of the authorities.[81] The middleman who was robbed of a large sum of cash during an assault on the Palermo-Camporeale "postal automobile" feared that the situation would continue ad infinitum "with the wiles and those protected and guaranteed by the Honorables of Sicily which [are] in cahoots with the Mafia and when the case finally comes to trial, they impose their will on the judges and jurors with threats and are let loose in complete liberty."[82]

Of course, the system was neither so all-encompassing nor so stable: protection, as always, has a clientelistic character, and there are those who truckle under and pay, and others who resist. Every so often, in the form of open denunciations or anonymous letters, protests came to the ears of the authorities, who mobilized their forces in the hot zones. When that happened, there was a general exodus of abettors and accomplices from the towns in the center of the network, Cammarata and Castronovo in the case of Varsalona, "even before the squads and officials could reach the places they were assigned to cover—spontaneous and unnecessary evidence of the broad base of support of the criminal society."[83] The *squadriglie,* or squadrons, were mobile groups made up of Carabinieri and police officers, who over time came to replace the army in garrisoning the territory, under the supervision of such skilled functionaries as Commissioner Cesare Mori and Commissioner Augusto Battioni.

Many bandits were in fact captured in this way, but the Great War arrived and only worsened the situation with the return of ex-convicts from Tunisia and America, and especially given the reactivation of the circuit of draft evasion, living undercover, and banditry.

> More than half of the farmland is left uncultivated and barren, and here poverty and unrest and revolution are synonymous. Add to that equation the fact that there is an enormous resurgence in cattle theft and murders in the fields. The countryside is riddled with many thousands of deserters, anywhere from twenty to thirty thousand, who are now demanding bread and will soon be organized in armed gangs: the classical brigandage of the worst periods.[84]

Cattle theft, in fact, is the chief pursuit of old and new fugitives, while the *campieri* allow the passage of herds through the large landholdings, and the mafiosi falsify the necessary documentation to make it through the checkpoints. The limited availability of manpower and capital leads to the decline of the cultivation of grains in favor of grazing livestock, in part because of the high price of meat, given the demand of the army, inflation, and the abolition of the tariff on wheat, which would not be restored until 1924. This is just a typical oscillation of an economy based on large landholdings, which—depending on cyclical variations—focuses either on grazing livestock or cultivating crops. The wartime and postwar legislation, with freezes on rents, also makes *gabella* increasingly attractive to those who are concerned about falling victim to cattle rustlers, or rather who succeed in ensuring that these and other misfortunes befall their rivals. "A former large estate leased for eleven thousand lire would yield almost one hundred fifty. And so it was necessary to bend the landowners to one's will, to ensure that they would rent us, at negligible, ridiculously low rates, their lands; and thus were made ready fortunes, quickly, reliably, a barony."[85]

The state's response took into account the numerical inferiority of force and left unguarded such strategic areas as the Palermo countryside. In the interior, "squads for the prevention and punishment of cattle theft" were in operation and completed the turnaround that was begun during the earlier period. The squads, groups of seven or eight men on horseback, moved from one province to the other, rarely returning to their base, never relying on reinforcements in case of conflict. This was a risky tactic, as became evident in October 1916, when two policemen were killed near Contessa while chasing Grisafi. There was no thought of a return to the postunification period, with the besieging of small towns and blind repression. The squads remained a police tool; they moved according to a refined system of information, which allowed Mori, between Caltanissetta, Agrigento, and Palermo, to destroy the Carlino and Grillo gangs and at last to capture Grisafi. Grisafi worked with a network of no fewer than 375 abettors and accomplices, of whom 90 were in Caltabellotta, the village where he was born.[86]

At the end of the war, the situation was quite serious. To the east, in the Madonie, the dissolution of the domain of Candino left room for his adversaries, such as the other aged fugitive from the law, Gaetano Ferrarello, who was joined by his nephew Salvatore Ferrarello, Nicolò Andaloro, the Dino brothers, and Onofrio Lisuzzo. The objective, here as well, was the creation of a network of *campieri* and leaseholders, skimming money from the properties through "begging letters," the theft of livestock, and various forms of harassment and damage. The high mediator, Baron Sgadari of Gangi, guaranteed the agreements: "To put the matter to an end, I have persuaded them to settle for eight thousand lire," he wrote to his brother-in-law, Leonardo Signorino, who was being plagued by extortion letters, "while on their part the undertakings that they made in my presence remain solid." Signorino (Baron Pottino), on the other hand, was obliged to yield to the demands of his *campiere*, who even admitted that he was well aware that the previous payment "ought to have exempted him from paying any further tributes." "I ask you for no more than an additional ten thousand lire," Andaloro wrote to Signorino. "And I warn you, take care not to believe in the flatteries of some false friend, who will certainly enjoy the party between you and me, because I assure you that I will let you feel my most ferocious disdain."[87]

This is a reference to internal conflicts among the would-be protectors. In fact, the system of banditry in Gangi, which in some phases of its history operated in an organized manner, also went through periods of internal conflict like the feud that in 1922 led to the arrest of Andaloro himself by Battioni, guided by a tip from his sometime friend/sometime enemy Ferrarello. The settling of accounts became more complicated than in the times when Candino and Varsalona came to a ready agreement over how to split up the province, one taking the east and the other the west; criminal supply and appetites multiplied significantly. In this period, feuds began between the Barbaccias and the Lorellos for control of the forest of Ficuzza, a storage point for the herds stolen between Corleone and Palermo.[88] In the small town of Godrano, in the years between the end of the First World War and the period following the Second World War, fifty-eight men were killed over that property. There were bloodcurdling raids on farms, with massacres of entire families, including women and children. For instance, at Burgio and Sclafani in 1922 there were, respectively, seven and eight dead. The cause? "The predominance of the Mafia in the fields."[89]

The first massacre took place in the context of an endless feud that began at the turn of the century between Lucca Sicula, Bivona, and of course Burgio. During that feud, one faction swore it would "even kill the cats" of the opposing faction.[90] The second massacre occurred during the war between the Dino gang, expanding southwest from Gangi (Petralie, Polizzi, Alimena) and the "old Mafia" commanded by the Mogaveros of Polizzi and the Sorces of Mussomeli, with whom the other Gangi gang commanded by Lisuzzo made an alliance. Among the ferocious reprisals of the respective abettors and accomplices, the feigned peace treaties, betrayals, and schisms between brothers, it would be idle speculation to speak of a tension between banditry and a *Mafia d'ordine* (order-keeping Mafia) prompted by a simple "impulse of self-defense," because on both sides we find a "greedy yearning for wealth, . . . robberies, extortions, and murders."[91] On both sides, there was ambition to establish one's own form of order.

Less harsh was the battle going on to the east, toward the Mistretta area. For local *gabellotti* and *campieri,* chasing after the cattle rustlers meant venturing into "Ferrarello territory." It was advisable to make use of a mediator and ask him to "say a few words to Gangi" in order to negotiate a price for the ransom and the recovery of the livestock.[92] A great number of letters of this sort were found during the course of two searches (1925 and 1926) in the office of the lawyer Antonio Ortoleva of Mistretta, a member of the town council, a landowner, and a criminal lawyer who, in the years 1901–1913, successfully defended various men charged with cattle theft (including one of the Farinellas). The letters reveal Ortoleva's role in the mechanism of cattle theft and extortion, in jury tampering, and in the racket of the *gabelle*. Through Ortoleva the landowners frequently paid the protection money intended for fugitives from the law. Instructions and reports appeared concerning the murders, in a code that is still relatively unclear. A former adept of the lawyer confessed that he chaired a Mafia tribunal active since 1913, which made not only business decisions, but also decisions of life and death. And in fact the adept-turned-informer was killed, as ordered.[93]

It is noteworthy that letters were sent to Ortoleva from the Mistretta area and, more in general, from the province of Messina, from both the eastern and the western sectors of the province of Palermo, from the Caltanissetta area and the area around Enna, and even from the province of Catania. This outward expansion of the Mafia networks to take in eastern Sicily took place in accordance with an overriding logic of territorial proximity that was somewhat different from the approach that is familiar to us from the story of Bartolomeo Badalamenti in the neighboring Palagonia. Let us take the case of two of the lawyer-correspondents, the Tusa brothers from Mistretta who made agreements with Bartolomeo Badalamenti on the people to be hired on an estate after learning the "wishes of the well-known friends," in a mediation between a priest and landowner and the brigand Salvatore Rapisarda of Adrano who wished to "protect him."[94] The Tusas and their cousins, the Seminaras, moved progressively southeast along the trails of the transhumance, or seasonal movement of livestock, that brought the herds from the mountain above Messina to spend the winter in the Calatino area (an area corresponding to the Diocese of Caltagirone). In 1906 they were in Leonforte as administrators of the estates of the prince of Gangi, and following the First World War they had pushed almost all the way to Catania.[95] For that matter, in the interior zone of the Etna province, the *gabellotti* usually arrived from the east and brought with them a standard entourage of "tough" *campieri* and good relationships with fugitives from the law.[96] "It is a tradition in my family," stated the Honorable Gesualdo Libertini, "to employ excellent individuals from Mistretta as *campieri*."[97] That tradition was still in effect in 1926 when Libertini himself summoned the Tusas and the Seminaras to manage the large estate of Mandrerosse in the territory of Ramacca, formerly owned by the township of Caltagirone; it was subsequently sold to a local notable through the mediation of Luigi Sturzo and confirmed as such in the 1930s and 1940s when Sebastano Tusa, the sole brother not involved in the investigation,[98] continued to administer the property, also serving as *delegato podestà* or Fascist governor in the newly founded *borgo* (village) of Libertinia.

Once the trail had been blazed, a flow in the opposite direction took fugitives from the law from eastern Sicily under Mafia protection into the Madonie, or Madonia Mountains. That was, for instance, the story of the Catanian smuggler Luigi Saitta, a story that had important repercussions.[99] Less peaceful was the expansion of *gabellotti* and *campieri* from Mistretta into zones of the old Mafia. The Catanian baron Giuseppe Camilleri, who had entrusted his lands in the Agrigento area to the Tusas since 1913, was forced to change his policies in the face of the harsh reaction from Canicattì.[100]

The vastness of Ortoleva's network of relations as well as his social qualities finally seems to have risen to the level of *Alta Mafia*. The protagonists of the trial of 1928–1929 were convinced that they had finally reached Sicily's "interprovincial high command." The following is from the summation of Member of Parliament Angelo Abisso, a native of Agrigento, who represented the civil plaintiffs:

> Since the Mafia is a state within the state, it requires a decorative individual who, practically in the role of a minister plenipotentiary, is able to represent its interests in the diplomatic negotiations with the other, larger state. The lawyer Ortoleva . . . is capable of taking part in political battles and can influence their outcomes, enter into contact with the authorities of the state and bring them into line, stealthily insinuate himself into the administration of justice and subvert it. The robe of a lawyer for the defense provides excellent cover for shady connivances and murky relationships.[101]

In truth, the role of ambassador is not the same as that of chief or capo, and that is the difference crucial to any understanding of why we are suddenly asked to believe that Mistretta is the capital of the Mafia. This is a town that in the past had showed little if any Mafia presence, a place where traditionally "the arrogance of power . . . had no need of any specific instruments other than its well-oiled mechanisms of self-reproduction and corruption."[102]

A distinction can be made between two levels. The first level was that of the network of relations in which Ortoleva served as a mediator for the recovery of stolen livestock, a level as wide-ranging as the cattle herds themselves, as well as the *campieri* and *gabellotti*. There was also a second level, in the narrow space of the Mistretta area, an aggregate of interests whose postwar mutation, from the sphere of clientelism to that of crime, should not be interpreted on the basis of an entirely internal evolutionary logic, but rather in light of pressure from the Madonie. That pressure provoked reorderings of the territorial systems in adjoining areas in order to allow landowners and intermediaries to fight or negotiate.[103] On the other hand, the history of Contessa Entellina as reconstructed by Blok based on the minutes of the 1929 trial indicates an analogous process, the violent marginalization of the local *cosca* commanded by the Gassisi family by the Cascio-Ferro group, operating along the Burgio–Bisacquino–Corleone axis. Despite what clearly emerges from his own work, the Dutch anthropologist Blok emphasized that it was necessary to take into account exclusively the municipal dimension: "There is no local term to describe an array of mafiosi in areas larger than a single community. Each village or township had its own *cosca*. The members of that body operated within a distinct and limited territory that generally coincided with the township. . . . The local *cosca* was a small and relatively autonomous unit."[104]

In fact, it was precisely in this historic phase that the concept of *cosca* as a closed system of town or village, already fairly unrealistic within the context of the nineteenth century, became false.

A FIRST POSTWAR PERIOD

The years following the First World War witnessed the extraordinary transformation of the proportional electoral system (1919), a culmination of the various effects of universal male suffrage (1913), the return home of hundreds of thousands of veterans determined to win a better life for themselves, and the struggle for land. This was the penultimate act of the centuries-old crisis/transformation of the economy based on the latifundium, or large landed estate. That crisis coincided with other factors related to the business cycle, such as the conversion of grain fields into pastureland, prompting the anger and protests of peasant movements. The resulting wave of protests involved occupations, country and small-town insurrections, demands for the intervention of the Opera Nazionale Combattenti (ONC, or National Veterans' Association), and plans for agrarian reform. The process culminated in a mobilization of the market for farmland that would extend until the deflationary downturn of the second half of the 1920s. A total of 341 large estates were sold and broken up, for a total area of 139,802 hectares (345,458 acres), of which 51,971 hectares (128,423 acres) was sold through direct negotiations between parties, 45,346 hectares (112,052 acres) between private seller and buyer, and 41,482 hectares (102,504 acres) through the cooperatives.[105] The last two categories show how in many cases the peasant movement, in order to attain the desired result, required the help of intermediaries, both individual and collective: cooperatives, agricultural banks, and "workers' associations," all of which were emanations of the peasant or village parties. This context brought about a certain Mafia component. There were significant, though isolated, examples in eastern Sicily. To name a few, we have Palagonia, where Bartolomeo Badalamenti controlled the division of the large landholding; and Adrano, where an ex-convict who had returned from America took the office of mayor and gained access to the *Cassa Rurale Cattolica* (Catholic agricultural bank) and thus the operations of parceling out land.[106] Ortoleva took part in the distributions of state-owned land in 1921–1922,[107] but it would be difficult to describe him as a mafioso for that fact alone, were we not already familiar with his activities in the areas of cattle theft, racketeering, and close relations with fugitives from the law.

In Ribera there were two factions. One faction was led by the pharmacist Liborio Friscia, uncle of the *combattentista* (or pro-veteran) member of parliament, Abisso; the other faction was headed by the Honorable Antonino Parlapiano-Vella, a moderate and clericalist, as well as by his brother, Gaetano, mayor of the town. In the summer of 1919, the "Cesare Battisti" cooperative headed by Friscia turned to the ONC and, on behalf of its eight hundred members, asked for the lease of the large landholding that extended over half of the township's territory. That large landholding belonged to Don Eristano Alvarez de Toledo, duke of Bivona, senator, and Spanish grandee. Somewhat concerned, Don Eristano traveled to the town, his very first visit, with the plan of selling everything to the Parlapianos. But the *combattenti* (or veterans) kidnapped the duke and held him for three days (26–28 January 1920) in his ancestral palazzo, subjecting him to intense pressure. They forced him to rent the land to the "Cesare Battisti" cooperative. As soon as he was liberated, however, His Grace created an international incident over the violence he had suffered at the hands of the "Bolsheviks" of Ribera.[108] And so the Parlapianos purchased the large landholding and rented it to three cooperatives established for that purpose by *campieri* "belonging to the local Mafia." They, in turn, subleased the land, "at very high prices," to other members of the same cooperatives. In the meantime, they prepared to sell the land to members of their clientelistic network.[109]

In the matter at hand, it was the large landholders who wanted to sell, and they had come to an agreement with the political and financial middlemen. It was a different matter with the Polizzello estate in Mussomeli, the property of the princely family of the Trabias. Here the "Combattenti" and "Pastorizia" cooperatives at first requested the intervention of the ONC to expropriate the land, but in the face of the Trabias' strong reaction, they decided to agree to preserve the status quo in a way that would preserve a role for the intermediating agencies. The stakeholders in those intermediaries frequently represented an elite that then managed the issuance of subleases. This was the field in which Giuseppe Genco Russo developed his career. Genco Russo was widely considered to be operating on behalf of Calogero Vizzini, to whom he was in fact linked by ties of *comparaggio* (although not quite the same as the "godfa-ther" of the movies, this is a relationship of godfather/godmother and godson/goddaughter—*translator's note*). Members of the Genco family worked as *campieri* on Don Calò's estates. The personality of Genco Russo, however, dis-played a clearer criminal identity. He was frequently at odds with the law, espe-cially because of the violent fighting with the various groups (which in turn also fought among themselves) in the Sorce family, fighting fiercely to stem the ad-vance of the Dino gang from Gangi.[110]

Now let us examine the case of Villalba. Here the *combattentistica*, or pro-veteran, cooperative had occupied the Belici estate and asked to rent it, for now. Since 1909, ownership of that estate had passed into the hands of Matteo Guc-cione in person. Guccione was a new large landholder, who was no more in favor of the cooperatives than the old landholders had been. He held an equally dim view of the provincial commissions for untilled land and the "expropriating" agencies such as the ONC. Once again, through the mediation of Calogero Vizzini, the *combattenti* were cut out of the negotiations, and a contract for the purchase of the estate was signed by the Catholic cooperative. However, when the coop-erative was unable to close the transaction before the expiration of the legal terms, it was again Don Calò who persuaded Guccione not to give up.[111] Was this an agreement between men of honor determined not to lose out on a major deal? Or was this a showdown between two different generations? Considering the fact that in the same period Guccione was forced, "with fraudulent meth-ods," to accept Giuseppe Sorce as a partner in another piece of property that he owned,[112] we can safely consider the changing of the guard of the Belici estate to be an emblematic event. To Vizzini it brought excellent land, authority, and re-nown among his fellow townsfolk, aside from the numerous questionable as-pects of the complicated transaction.

A comparison between Mussomeli, Villalba, and Ribera is enlightening. Genco Russo remained for the moment the intermediary between the prince and the community. In contrast, Vizzini already had, to the same degree as the Parlapianos, the political and financial capacity to mastermind and control the entire operation of the land transactions. Vizzini was "a wealthy, powerful, feared man," a "*cavaliere*, or knight, a multimillionaire," who owned "large estates, some even outside of the province,"[113] deeply involved in the operation (*gabella*) and the purchase of sulphur mines. However, like other "industrialists" in the sul-phur sector of the Caltanissetta area, he too would be devastated by the crisis. In this context as well, he gave proof of his stature: he received sizable loans from the Banco di Sicilia, he was involved in the discussions of the fate of the *Consorzio zolfifero* (Sulphur-Mining Consortium), and he took part in London in the negotiations for the establishment of an international sulphur cartel (1922), alongside individuals with the status of Donegani, founder of Montecatini, or Jung, future minister of finance.[114]

In this context, Vizzini no longer corresponded to the stereotype of the country uncle who has never ventured out of his hometown, the notable interested in status and not profit, which is the source of the traditional and protective model of the Mafia. While the first depiction is false inasmuch as here we are dealing with evident historical discontinuities, the issue of community "protection" does in fact seem to play a role. Vizzini, Ortoleva, and Genco Russo show that in this historic phase the figure of the mafioso is comparable to that of the notable who, with the phraseology of a progressive, but with the intentions of a profiteer and clientelist, trampled on and instrumentalized the processes of democratization.

Moreover, the groups that won the greatest blocs of votes in the elections of 1919 and 1921 were progressive. They were the *combattentistica* (or pro-veteran) array that expanded on the Sicilian stage: radicals, social reformers, and social democrats. The popular—or Catholic—party, fit just as easily as the others (if not more easily?) into this political and criminal array, as we have already seen in the cases of Parlapiano and Vizzini and as we shall see as well in other cases. The Gassisis of Contessa Entellina supported Giovanni Lo Monte, owner of Mezzojuso and "political chief of the Mafia," opposing the local large landholder Antonio Pecoraro, who was in turn supported by the Cascio-Ferro group and by the previously mentioned Coco, who had age-old clientelistic relations with him. This panorama would seem to offer the traditional model of relations between the ruling classes and the criminal classes, if it were not for the fact that Pecoraro himself was the proponent of one of the projects for agrarian reform as well as a leading figure in a new party. The bloody feud that resulted in the deaths of a number of members of the Gassisi–Lo Voi family stemmed from the introduction of the new proportional vote and the expansion of the electoral districts to cover the provincial scale, which therefore, in accordance with the more general line of development of the postwar years, only increased the territories of influence (and therefore offered greater terrain for combat) among the various Mafia groups. There was a corresponding decline in plebiscites and the serene intermediation on the part of notables among the array of interests present in the electoral district, according to the model of the older electoral system. Many years later the period's leading Sicilian politician, Vittorio Emanuele Orlando, evoked this atmosphere with a strong element of nostalgia: "Now if this unanimity of sentiments and votes included elements that are qualified as Mafia, that would not undercut the solidarity that links me to these people, even if that were to mean that I would be perceived as a mafioso."[115]

It was Orlando who, once again, made the distinction between a "bad" Mafia involved in criminal behavior and a "good" Mafia, an expression of honor and loyalty: "I declare that I am a mafioso and proud of the fact!" he stated in a renowned speech from 1925,[116] echoing the words uttered by Morana in 1875. In both cases, the paradoxical declaration of Sicilian pride came from a ruling class in a state of difficulty, in the first case struggling against police laws, in the second case with Fascism. The steady and progressive clarification, however, of the concept of the Mafia over the fifty years that had passed between the two cases, and in particular the burst of violence in the postwar years, rendered far more evident the degree of connivance with the criminal milieu that formed part of the "unanimous consensus" observed in Partinico in the election of a member of parliament. The ruling class was so intimately involved in the mechanism that it seemed incapable of perceiving the danger of the phenomenon: the young Catholic member of parliament from Gela, Salvatore Aldisio, a future Christian Democratic leader, defended a claimed freedom by launching an attack on the government decision to revoke weapons permits, which he considered a "clear offense" to the "Sicilian people" and would cause "an economic hardship" with the sole rationale of giving credence to "musty legends."[117] And yet the nature of events in this same period in his own electoral district should have given Aldisio at least some degree of pause. There were the 109 murders in the city of Canicattì in 1919 alone; there were daily pitched battles in Sommatino, where rival groups of sulphur miners faced off with hand grenades and pistol fights in the center of town, with the rival groups rearming each evening at the town's gun shop.[118]

In the Fascist context, the situation appeared equally grim. As the prefect of Palermo telegraphed in 1925: "Here Fascism consists of existing common individual groups. . . . Each section takes on, within its own township, specific attitudes in accordance with the prevalence in municipal administration or according to ties [with] elements of the Mafia or personal relations [with] situations in the past."[119]

In 1924, Ortoleva was a Fascist; in Gangi Baron Sgadari and Baron Li Destri led a municipal administration that the police called "Fascist-Mafioso."[120] Tending toward Fascism were the Cascio-Ferro group in Bisacquino and the group of Santo Termini, including the notorious mayor of S. Giuseppe Jato. In many cases, the mafiosi reserved their support for the notable "supporters" of the Mussolini government. Thus, the Farinellas founded the *fascio* in S. Mauro but supported Lo Monte, as well as Ciccio Cuccia, mayor of Piana degli Albanesi, with prior indictments for a long series of crimes, including a number of murders.[121] In an unprecedented orgy of transformism, the large- or small-scale notables attempted to jump on the Fascist bandwagon in search of votes with which to run against Finocchiaro Aprile and Orlando, who did not go over to the opposition until 1925. The Lo Monte case shows how certain profoundly unqualified individuals got their start. Among the few new men was Alfredo Cucco, the *ducino* (or Little Duce) of Palermo, who in any case boasted of relations with the surgeon of Bagheria, Giuseppe Cirincione, who someone described as "a feared and horrifying capo, for the previous thirty years, of the Palermo Mafia."[122]

As we can see, the "political" chief of the Mafia is too often identified for that identification to be considered credible. However, the overstatement in this case highlights the link between political system and criminality, and the reciprocal pervasiveness between one sphere and the other. Listen to the tones of the despairing appeal to the royal prosecutor from a man destined to be murdered: "If it is true what Pietro Palazzolo says, and that is that he is the master not only of Gangi but even of Italy because everyone is one of his subjects, from the ministers on down to the lowliest copper, if this catastrophe really existed in Italy, as I almost feel it does, then forgive me for having disturbed you."[123]

The arrogant statement of Palazzolo, lieutenant to Ferrarello, corresponds to the general belief of both mafiosi and proper citizens, and therefore blazes the path to the reintroduction of the Fascist antidemocratic polemic. This allows a movement that is amply contaminated by the presence of notables to recover its own physiognomy: if the Mafia established a tie to "parliamentarianism," then it would be necessary to move against the Mafia in order to overcome Sicilian Fascism's weakness and lack of appeal. "If we want to save Sicily"—wrote the secretary of the *fascio* of Alcamo—"then we must crush this strange sort of organization that is the Mafia; if Fascism wants to do something meritorious for Sicily it must solve this problem, and then it may be sure to pitch tents on this island that are even more solid than the ones it pitched in the north by undermining Bolshevism."[124]

The pendulum of the anti-Mafia fight swung back to the right, as it had in the period following the Risorgimento. During his trip to Sicily in May 1924, Mussolini identified the struggle as a proving ground for a "regenerated" Italian state, avoiding, with skillful political instincts, the dangerous identification of the Mafia with Sicily: "It should no longer be tolerated that a few hundred criminals abuse, impoverish, and harm a population as magnificent as the people of Sicily."[125] On 23 October 1925, Cesare Mori was appointed, with expansive powers, as prefect of Palermo.[126]

This was a crucial turning point. Mori was certainly no Fascist. In fact, he was the Nitti loyalist and prefect who in Bologna in 1921 faced off against the Fascist *squadracce,* or violent "evil squads," earning himself the undying enmity of the extremists. To appoint him to the position meant resuming the effort that the state had been carrying out during the war years, focusing again on a unified command and the mobility of forces moving over the entire western sector of Sicily. A man who was capable of personally killing a brigand as well as writing a book (however badly written)[127] constituted a safe investment for a government in search of effective propaganda. Mori's experience, moreover, was not limited to those points. In 1920, in Trapani, he had succeeded in creating a position of equilibrium by supporting the peasant movement while at the same time keeping order in a way that was highly praised by the landowners.[128] Prior to that, he had fought against the anti-Giolitti faction led by Nunzio Nasi with such vigor and determination that the witticism was coined: "vedi Trapani e poi Mori" (a variant on the old saying "See Naples and Die," which in Italian is "Vedi Napoli e poi mori"—*translator's note*).[129] He was thus both a crime-fighter and someone who had vigorously opposed the adversaries of the government, a figure similar to the model that Mussolini projected, though the Duce did so on a far vaster scale. There was a personal dimension. In 1925 Mori portrayed— and saw—himself as "the little man who for many months with scanty resources nearly mastered the Mafia, until a member of parliament managed to secure his transfer."[130] No differently from other technicians who had served under Nitti, such as Serpieri or Beneduce, he saw totalitarianism as offering a chance to obtain results that had been hindered by the red tape of democracy.

In this context, the work of a prefect was to be "not a police campaign on a more or less grand scale, but instead an insurrection of consciences, a revolt of spirits, the action of a people."[131] In the face of the risks of such repression becoming unpopular, and the threat of potential "Sicilianist" reactions, Mori was exceedingly careful to seek out points of contact, a code of communication with the culture, real or presumed, of the masses. In his view, as for Pitrè before him, there existed a good *omertà* that corresponded more or less to the concept of virility, with honorable corollaries that could be classed as national and Fascist values. The only task that remained was to eliminate the unfortunate criminal by-products of that "good *omertà*." "*Omertà* contains within it the specific means to combat its own degenerations. Hence we must turn—and it is this that I mean to say—to pride as an instrument with which to react to arrogance and bullying; courage to react to violence; strength to react to strength; and rifles to react to rifles."[132]

The reader may note the crescendo of qualities, until the final pairing whereby strength and force were clearly representative of a value, whatever the means being pursued. The elements of the Sicilian cultural codes that Mori believed he had understood resembled, all too closely, the strength codes of Fascism. "The strength that defends production" was written on the badge that the prefect pinned on the chests of *campieri* in individual ceremonies because he wanted a personal relationship with the Sicilians. An interesting exchange of views occurred on one of those occasions. Mori: "If others happened to call you a *sbirro* (cop) when they see you wearing this badge?" and the *campiere* replied: "Your Excellency would have to forgive me, but in that case I would shoot them." The prefect was pleased with that answer ("bravo," he said),[133] since he was clearly not interested in the concept of legality, but only in establishing loyalty and strength. All of this took place in the context of vast assemblies during which there was inevitably a ringing appeal to the idea of individual and social self-defense, the exaltation of the courage of those, both landowners and peasants, who refused to give in and took up arms, just as in an earlier period, they had "dared to face Austrian machine guns."[134] Mori praised the exemplary behavior in war of even mafiosi, who were still patriots, however corrupt. That thesis was laughable, if we remember the direct tie between banditry and draft-dodging, but it was useful in promoting the notion of an Italic community that was stronger than any secondary consideration. It is reasonable to wonder to what degree the prefect's rhetoric created genuine consensus in bourgeois public opinion, but I would feel safe in ruling out that the para-mafioso *campieri* were greatly moved by it. *Mutatis mutandis,* the Lombard Mori is reminiscent of the Tuscan Fanfani as, during the campaign against divorce in the mid-1970s, he pointed (without success) to the danger that the citizens of Caltanissetta might be cuckolded, in an attempt to instrumentalize their fears of women's sexual freedom.

The year 1926 was a succession of vast roundups, each of which resulted in hundreds of arrests, with a grand total by 1928 of eleven thousand people in prison: five thousand in the province of Palermo alone.[135] The sweep began in Gangi, continued on toward Mistretta, Bagheria, Misilmeri, the *borgate* of Palermo, Monreale, Corleone, and Partinico; then continued south toward the Agrigento area and the Caltanissetta area, next eastward, pushing through the area around Enna until it lapped at the edges of the zone around Caltagirone and the western Enean province. In this phase, a major central force was employed, moving from one town to the next. For instance, eight hundred agents descended on Bagheria, a mix of Carabinieri, militia detachments, and police officers, and arrested three hundred people.[136] The operation in the Conca d'Oro was somewhat complex. It targeted the two groups of the Sparacinos and the Gentiles, whose civil war in 1923–1924 had resulted in forty-six murders and attempted murders. But the complications ensued because many of those targeted for arrest took shelter in sophisticated underground hiding places. The same thing happened in Gangi, which in January 1926 was placed under military occupation as an example to international, national, and local public opinion. It was the prefect who wanted this crushing victory, in place of the prearranged surrender that had previously been set up in December 1925 in a negotiation between Inspector Spanò and the Ferrarello–Andaloro gangs, with the decisive mediation of Baron Sgadari.[137]

In order to win on the terrain of folk values, the state had to gain itself a degree of "respect" by behaving in a more mafioso fashion than the mafiosi themselves, culminating in the harsh speech that Mori delivered on the town piazza of Gangi before an audience stunned by the arrest of 450 individuals, including 300 "accomplices and abettors."[138] This led to the pointless deployment of public forces, the fake negotiations that led to betrayals that were proudly vaunted, and ferocious threats of reprisals against fugitives from the law that took the form of public slaughtering of their livestock, the auctioning off of their possessions, the deportation of their families, and, in a veiled threat, the raping of their women. A strange type of propaganda emerged, which would still be remembered many years later: when his mother and sister were arrested, Salvatore Giuliano responded that he would not behave like "those pathetic mafiosi of 1926" who surrendered without striking a blow in the face of such tactics.[139] The arrest of 213 women and children led to the surrender of thirty-five fugitives from the law in the Palermo countryside. This was no "stroll in the park"; rather, it was a terrorist operation; to Mori (a latter-day Javert), for that matter, relatives could only be innocent "in a manner of speaking."[140] An American anthropologist working in Sicily in those years describes the inhabitants of Milocca being forced by the Italian Carabinieri to march toward Mussomeli, along with their livestock and (again) the families of those who had managed to escape. More than 100 of the 2,500 inhabitants would be sent to prison.[141] One of them, a peasant who was acquitted after four years of imprisonment, told the story of the terrible episode in verse:

A lu milli novicentu lu ventottu
a li setti di innaru fu lu fattu.
Dormivanu tutti comu gigli all'ortu
'ntri 'na nuttata l'arrestu fu fattu.
L'arrestu principià di Mussumeli
fu tirminatu 'ntra du uri.
Cu dici figghiu, cu dici mugghieri,
Cu dici sà cu fu 'stu tradituri.[142]
(On the seventh of January of
1928 this is what happened.
Everyone was sleeping like lilies of the field
When in one night the arrests were made.
The arrests began in Mussomeli

And were completed within two hours.
Some cried "son," some cried "wife,"
Some cried "who betrayed us?")

FIGHTING THE MAFIA AT CLOSE QUARTERS

At the end of 1926, Mori sent back to Rome a voluminous dossier on crimes committed by Cucco, the head of Palermo's Fascist Party. In January 1927, the party federation was dissolved, and the *ducino* was put on trial after a blindingly rapid parliamentary authorization. In 1928, another scandal hit the Honorable Antonino Di Giorgio, formerly a cabinet-level minister in a Mussolini government and a brilliant military commander in the Great War. It seemed as if the attack had been carried all the way up to the *Alta Mafia:* hadn't the Duce ordered his men to attack "at the top and at the bottom"? Di Giorgio was pulled into Spanò's investigations among his electorate in the Caronie,[143] and, though there was not the slightest proof or even evidence of any guilt, he was forced to retire from political life. Cucco, too, had close and compromising electoral ties, but the charges against him did not rise to the level of Mafia crimes; rather, they were administrative and professional irregularities, abuses of power. He was in any case absolved of wrongdoing after eleven separate trials. One verdict used the term *conspiracy,* reflecting a widespread impression.[144]

This episode unfolded far more in the political aspect than the police-enforcement dimension of the Mori campaign. In the middle of the 1920s, Fascism liquidated the liberal outriders that had made its victory possible. Then it went on the attack against the positions of the notables within the party, destined to be ultimately transformed into a gray propagandistic apparatus of a hypercentralized regime in which decisions played out within the inner circles and in conflict with the "strong" powers: the church, the monarchy, the bureaucracies, both state and nonstate, and the manufacturers' association, Confindustria. In the outlying areas, the prefects were encouraged to protect the PNF (Partito Nazionale Fascista, or National Fascist Party) and were supported in their frequent clashes with federal officials; in all of Sicily, and perhaps in all of Italy, the elimination of individuals considered troublesome solely because they were independent was justified by issues of alleged immorality or profiteering.[145] In Palermo, the accusation was linked to the Mafia. "The designation of Mafioso . . . is often used in perfectly bad faith and in every field, including the field of politics, as a way of performing vendettas, venting resentments, and defeating adversaries."[146]

It was Mori who said these words, and it was Mori himself who cynically applied the concept. The prefect knew perfectly well who would provide him with evidence to construct a dossier against Cucco: Roberto Paternostro, a lawyer defending numerous mafiosi, and now disgraced director of the *fascio*, who a few years before had expressed the concerns of the people of Palermo over the hypothesis of the arrival of someone like Mori, as well as a "Movimento italiano impero e lavoro" (Italian Empire and Labor Movement) composed for the most part of ex-convicts, which distinguished itself by its clearly sympathetic stance toward the Mafia as a supposed form of "syndicalism" through which the peasants "seized by force . . . the means of survival from the local seigneurs and large estate owners." One last member was the highly compromised Honorable Lo Monte.[147] Paternostro, however, was the only one who would even momentarily return to power. The others would soon vanish, along with the *ludi cartacei* (paper playthings) of political liberty. There were other winners. The liquidation of the political personnel encouraged by Fascism led to a full-fledged current of agrarian revanchism, of which the Mori operation was only one of various components. "He aimed too high, and was cut down to size,"[148] Tina Whitaker wrote of Cucco. She was the mouthpiece of the dominant classes who did not believe the charges but who still desired to see strong state control over the party, and who were concerned over the refusal of Cucco's followers to make Fascism nothing more than an updated version of moderateness, and the threats of new revolutionary "Vespers" against the large landholders. In Cucco's description, in 1927 Mori was a man "in a genuine aristocratic frenzy," moving "from one elegant drawing room to another, and from this reception to that soiree," "intoxicated" with high society[149] and willing to elevate that society by placing at the head of the PNF (the Partito Nazionale Fascista, or National Fascist Party) the Marchese Paternò di Spedalotto and the duke of Belsito. This was the terrain, far more than the propagandistic field of the reconquest of folk values, where the relationship was constructed between Fascism and Sicily, a relationship that was meant to be a direct tie, without intermediaries, between the state and the various social classes. The intermediaries par excellence were the parasitic *gabellotti*, while Mori absolved the producers, meaning the landowners, inasmuch as they were victims of a state of necessity.[150]

It is fair to wonder to what degree these sharp distinctions of role corresponded to the minutes of the major trials for criminal conspiracy, which succeeded one another beginning in 1927. These trials involved hundreds and hundreds of defendants, rising to a peak of 450 for the association of Casteltermini. In the judicial accounts, the parties oscillate ambiguously between the figure of the victim and the figure of the accomplice: extortion winds up being transformed into protection and even into partnership for taxes or sheepherd-ing; there are cases in which cattle thieves, in exchange for the return of the stolen animals, demand and receive not money, but the thefts of other ani-mals. In general, in war those who want to defend their positions are obliged to employ the same means as the enemy. That would constitute the state of ne-cessity, which, however, could be applied to many individuals in different walks of life, both involved, found guilty, and acquitted.

Let us take as an example Giuseppe Ortoleva, brother of Antonio Ortoleva, indicted on charges of extortion against the priest-*gabellotto* Filadelfio Versaci, the former mayor of San Fratello.[151] According to Ortoleva, it had been Versaci himself, after receiving threats from the bandit Russo, who had begged him "to order one of [his] *campieri* to settle the matter" until the *campieri* reported the demand for 8,000 lire, which on his own authority the middleman had reduced to 4,000 lire and had paid the sum out of his own pocket. However, Russo was not happy and began to target Versaci with thefts of livestock. The *campieri* themselves investigated those thefts, and thus another 3,000 lire was paid out, but the livestock was not returned because in the meanwhile the bandit had killed himself. As the reader can clearly see, defendant and accuser were as alike as two peas in a pod. By his own admission, this other Ortoleva was the commander of a military organization that negotiated with fugitives from the law of one zone and, it would appear, also in other areas. He played the role of mediator for which he was either paid in cash or else given the power to control an area that he could then convert into money by administering the *gabella*. The discourse became more complicated with the introduction, as realities de-manded, of the varying independence of the *campieri* and the rake-off that they might choose to take for themselves. Similarly, there was the consideration of the advantage over his competitors that Versaci might enjoy from a potential link to the Ortoleva-*campieri*. Even the ritual of the begging letters (*lettere di scrocco*) was meant to create complicity among the various opposing parties, focus on the informality of the relationship with the middleman, and conceal from both judicial and ideological observers the reality of well-organized "in-dustries." The extorter urged his victim to turn to "trusted individuals" for the negotiation, and that victim was obliged to dig furiously among his various con-tacts. This is what the Messinese businessman threatened by brigands was forced to do, and after searching among his clients in Gangi he found one who told him that "these people exist, and it is not just, in fact, by no means prudent, to fail to satisfy their demands, it is necessary to act immediately, and you can rely implicitly upon me to help."[152]

This was the "society of the mafiosi, active and operational" that, according to the attorney general of Palermo, Luigi Giampietro, represented "in and of itself a criminal conspiracy,"[153] which did not require any evidence in the form of criminal actions by each of its members. In the two trials in which Calogero Vizzini faced charges as a capo and for a Mafia association, it is difficult to understand not only the defendant's degree of guilt but even the reason for the charges themselves, which boiled down to the fact that the crimes were committed by his *cottimisti* (or pieceworkers) in the mines and by his *campieri* on the large landholdings, and therefore in relation to a profiteering network, without even a legal theory that this network served a criminal purpose.[154] The charges of association with the Mafia, which were so easily leveled against major *gabellotti* and poverty-stricken peasants, were instead avoided when dealing with large landholders, even in cases where they were linked to murders. One typical example concerned Pecoraro, whom numerous witnesses named in the Burgio trial against Cascio-Ferro and company. Still, Pecoraro was not indicted in that trial. *Il Giornale di Sicilia* even went so far as to eliminate, in its version of the letter written by the murder victim Gioachino Lo Voi before his death, one of the pillars of the prosecution's case, a passage concerning the large landholder, "who is catholic in his views and thus protects all criminals. His supporters kill whoever they choose, steal constantly, and that scoundrel wishes to be elected to parliament and therefore protects them. Damned thieving rogue!"[155] Even more astonishing were the cases of Gangi. During the course of the negotiations with Spanò, Salvatore Ferrarello asked naïvely (or perhaps mischievously): "If we were to turn ourselves in, who would guarantee peace in the countryside?"[156] Order was kept on behalf of individuals such as Baron Sgadari, who for many years had protected fugitives from the law, carrying out financial transactions on their behalf and acting as intermediary with social and political authorities. Finally, he even negotiated their surrender on (false) promises of impunity, the reason for the chilling promises of reprisal in the courtroom during the trial at Termini. And yet, the same bandit, when he escaped from the prison where he was serving a life sentence during the subsequent world war, renounced any attempts at vendetta. "Have you ever heard of a certain Ferrarello?" Vizzini asked Montanelli, explaining to him the benefits of Mafia mediation. "He started his career like Giuliano and he wound up like a priest. He even decided, after he escaped from prison, not to kill Baron Sgadari, who was responsible for sending him to prison. Someone must have settled the matter through negotiation."[157] Therefore, we can understand the astonishment of the English ambassador, Sir Ronald Graham, when he spotted Sgadari, whom he considered a *capo dei capi* of the *capintesta* (or top boss) Mafia, among the prominent supporters of Mori, elevated to the position of *podestà*.[158] And it was in fact at Gangi that we find one of the most noteworthy instances of a continuity of local power during Fascism around the families of the *ricconi* (roughly, tycoons) (Li Destri, Sgadari, and Mocciato), who commit "infamies," as denounced in 1937 by the mounted Carabiniere, Francesco Cardenti:

> The baron Li Destri in the time of the Mafia was strongly supported by the brigands now imprisoned in Portolongone (Elba); if anyone crossed his property, of which he was very protective, he would say: Don't cross over my land again or I will have you eliminated, but now that times have changed and he is a friend of the authorities . . . he says: Don't cross over my land again or I will have you sent into internal exile.[159]

Here, reasonably enough, brigands and internal exile appear to be interchangeable instruments; it is impossible to separate class power from its intimate connection with Mafia power.

Let us take, for instance, an episode that took place in the Conca d'Oro after the major roundup of April–May 1926. In June 1927, Giuseppe Carella was killed at Villa Adriana, the residence of Baron Luigi Bordonaro di Gebbiarossa.[160] The confessed murderer was Salvatore Sciacca, Jr., who claimed that he had killed Carella during a quarrel. In contrast, the investigation revealed that Sciacca had carefully prepared an ambush, and it also uncovered a longstanding series of disagreements between Carella and the Sciacca family. Salvatore Sciacca, Sr., also known as Cola Innusa, was indicted for ordering the killing. For nearly thirty years, the father had been *curatolo* of the villa, which was considered a family possession. In fact, the same position had previously been held by the father-in-law of Salvatore Sciacca, Sr., a certain Giuseppe Biondo who is familiar as the *alto papavero* (literally, top poppy, meaning powerful figure) of the cupola in the late nineteenth century. Carella was hired to improve the efficiency of the estate's management, after the Sciaccas were relieved of command, and this put the family in a bad light in the baron's eyes. As a result, Carella was punished. This was a classic Mafia situation. The prosecution asked for serious punishment, and the jury and magistrates complied. It was scandalous that Don Cola described as a "colleague" someone who was an "officer and a gentleman."[161] The people of Palermo were accustomed to seeing the spilling of blood of criminals, but not the blood of other members of society. Further evidence that the planners had misjudged the situation was the way that the crime was carried out. The victim was hacked to death with a billhook as in any other country murder. This may have been because reports that would have made it possible to stage the more customary ambush on the way home were absent. Sciacca, Sr., had an alibi, the best kind: when the murder was taking place, he was in the countryside with his *padrone* (or boss). However, as soon as the baron learned of the (unexpected) discovery of the corpse, he vanished, leaving his bodyguard alone on the road back to Palermo.

On behalf of the defense, Sciacca, Sr., identified the figure of the *Homo sicilianus*, uneducated and rough, but loyal to his superiors. In the parable that lay at the heart of his summation, the lawyer Ferdinando Li Donni[162] imagined an argument among the jurors: a Neapolitan, a Lombard, and a Palermitan, the only one capable of understanding matters, who explained to the others that Cola was a mafioso "if what we mean by mafioso is a man who shares the beliefs of the countryside, *omertà*, minding one's own business, obtaining testimonials. This, yes, colleagues. A man of the *giardino*, or citrus grove, he was." However, "the court has asked us to determine not whether he was a mafioso, but whether he was a criminal. And I will prove to your satisfaction that he was forced to fight against criminals." In Villa Adriana, there had been no theft or robbery in thirty years. "The criminals of the area knew perfectly well that they were not permitted to do any harm to any member of it [the baronial family]; otherwise the *uomo del giardino* (citrus grove custodian) would surely have them killed, to protect and defend those family members." Having thus explained the mysteries to the outsiders, everything was now in place and the central point emerged, the saving link between the mafioso and the baron and the tie with other mafiosi and other barons: Cola would survive only if it was evident that he was in all ways a creature of his master, capable of killing at his orders but not on his own behalf. "Men of the countryside," according to the lawyer Berna, "still remain primitive." Instead, Cola

traveled with Baron Gebbiarossa, came to know cities, lived in them for long periods, performed banking operations, was always at his master's side, lived with him in the same hotels, traveled in the same railroad compartment, smoked the same cigars, was invited to lunch with the baron, and even ate in the home dining room in the Casa Gangitano. That is why Cola Innusa is no longer, can no longer be "u zu Cola," but as a result of the efforts of his master, because his master wished it so, is now Don Cola.[163]

The prosecution described a pre-Fascist world of anti–property-owner abuses and arrogance, which ended with the blood of the "heroic" Carella. The defense noted that already, just a year ago, with the roundups, that world had collapsed, that the landowner had confirmed his faith beyond all restrictions, and that therefore the mafioso could not be a criminal.

Had the Sciaccas managed to keep from being overwhelmed by panic, they might well have succeeded in preserving some power in Villa Adriana. That power would certainly have been undermined and would have required some degree of caution, but it would have endured. This tells us a great deal about the space that remained within the context of the system of social relations while the Mafia as an association was swept away. In the *giardini,* as well as in the large landholdings, the perpetuation of the traditional systems throughout the Fascist period, even in untroubled "environmental" situations, represented a radical refutation of all supposed states of necessity. Mori showed off with great pride the thanks which the large landholders who had been enabled to raise the legal rents expressed to him;[164] in some cases, it was from 10 lire annually to 110,000 lire per year. A special commission decided which were the "infected towns" and dissolved the leases in those towns and villages, claiming that the result would be a return of the no-longer absentee farmers to the duties and delights of the fields. According to the chairman of that commission, the system of the *gabella* "sinks its roots in violence and blood and finds, when necessary, the perfection of its two contractual extremes in the rifle and the murder."[165] But that was not how matters stood. The union agreements that called for the elimination of subleasing were evaded with various subterfuges.[166] The landowners were unable, or unwilling, to eliminate the intermediary and were satisfied with having put that intermediary (for the moment) in his place.

The special and favorable treatment accorded the large landholders constitutes the common element in all these trials, which otherwise show considerable differences one from another. Some of the trials rested on a fairly solid evidentiary foundation: the letters of Ortoleva and the letter from Lo Voi (Mistretta and Bisacquino), the testimony of the injured parties, and the accusations of complicity from various defendants. In order to obtain these results, the police employed methods that the British ambassador described as "energetic and ruthless," beatings and genuine torture that in certain cases, such as during the trial for a Mafia association in Sommatino, came to light, destroying the prosecution's case.[167] This, however, was only one of the components that shattered the *omertà* with which the grandfathers urged their grandsons to take revenge. "In any case, there is no justice, and the jurors are willing to acquit even in cases where they themselves were witnesses to the crime."[168] There was a general and decisive change of course. For the most part, the "losers" were the ones who talked. Giuseppe Gassisi, "after someone murdered his son, put the law of emotion ahead of the law of *omertà.*"[169] Giovanni Latino, who survived the massacre of his entire family, identified the murderers after remaining silent for ten years. The clash between factions continued in the halls of justice; and in this process, there were further risks of instrumentalism, with a political configuration underlying the criminal road map. We should not be surprised to learn that behind the accusations leveled against the archpriest of Burgio, Vincenzo Baiamonte, in the trial of Sciacca, was the son of De Michele Ferrantelli, his political adversary and a longtime accomplice and abettor of Cascio-Ferro.[170] The accusations of the canon Giuseppe Di Prima of Campofranco against the former *popolare* (People's Party) mayor Gaetano Bongiorno and various other religious were rooted in a bitter atmosphere of personal resentments and reciprocal extortions.[171] Spanò held in reserve the indictment of the mayor of Casteldilucio, Domenico Di Giorgio, in case his brother, a general and former cabinet-level minister, might appear "as a witness on behalf of his friends" in politics.[172] The testimony of a notable could prove decisive. At the trial of the association of Burgio, one faction attempted to block the revelations offered by the wife of a defendant belonging to the enemy group. "We have a powerful piece to move, the notary Musso, and through him we will do all imaginable harm to your husband."[173] The reputation of being a mafioso, as we know, is based on the *vox populi*. Given the system of defamation and anonymous letters that would characterize the Fascist regime in other areas as well, "anyone who had resentments to air, or positions to achieve, found, with secret accusations made to the police and false testimony, a field of unhoped-for opportunities."[174]

This transfer of the political struggle to the judicial front threatened to create a new Cucco case in each of the villages and towns in central and western Sicily. In any case, the magistrature was prudent, handing down acquittals or lenient sentences in cases of alleged bid-fixing, alleged fraudulent bankruptcies of cooperatives, and alleged plundering of municipal treasuries (S. Giuseppe Jato, Partinico, and Sancipirrello). The game turned intricate. As the attack moved inland, it became secondary to the dynamic of local parties alternatively co-opted, fought over, or brought under the wing of the Fascist regime.[175] The Fascists' ambition in any case was to chase down the local notables to the very inner and formative mechanism of their power, with the dissolution of cooperatives and associations. That was the case in Mistretta with the Cerere, formerly headed by Ortoleva; in Sommatino with the Circolo Nuovo linked to Lo Monte; in Corleone where the authorities dubbed the Circolo Agricolo (farmers' association) the *casino della mafia*, alleging that it had always been called by that name. In Ribera the adherents of Abisso turned against the Parlapianos, but the Fascist regime wound up dissolving their organizations when Abisso fell into disfavor and disgrace. In Piana dei Greci, the three cooperatives were shut down in 1927 inasmuch as they were party vehicles. Among them was the socialist cooperative founded by Barbato, which had supported Mori and which had been allocated the leases of the *feudi*, confiscated from the notorious Mayor Cuccia. To the officials who were dissolving the cooperative, even though they acknowledged that it had been run and managed well and honestly, a peasant bitterly replied: "If the prefect Mori had listened to anything that we, the people directly interested, had to say, and had paid no attention to your idle chatter, we would never have come to this mess."[176] Like the king and the Duce, the prefect had no idea of how many bad things had been done in his name.

In this case, the antidemocratic operation and the operation on behalf of the large landowners coincided in the general equation—so dear to the Fascists—of Democracy = Mafia. The suspicion arises that in a number of roundups the true link among the hundreds of individuals who were later found guilty of nothing more than association with the others was political. It is not difficult to imagine that in a town individuals linked by common interests or family ties should be associated one with another with vague aims, so as to give a judicial appearance to the "Nights of St. Bartholomew in which, in order to arrest fifty criminals, fifty more honest men were dragged into the abyss."[177] Is it reasonable to think that the eleven thousand people imprisoned (and how many might have been arrested?) were all mafiosi? As a preliminary investigator noted, "It was considered a sect when there were a number of individuals working in collusion, or at least when there existed an associative relationship that I don't believe can be identified but which, in conclusion, was something like a federation, at least the way I saw it."[178]

This statement from one of the magistrates involved in the campaign implies a certain lack of conceptual rigor. Mori, no lover of juridical technicalities, openly considered the charge of "criminal conspiracy" as little more than a technical expedient[179] and, with Orlando, was late in arriving at a formulation of the phenomenon of the Mafia as being due to a deviant regional culture that had a central aspect of individualism. We have seen that a lawyerly culture offers a proliferation of such new and old anthropological figures as the "man of the countryside" or the "man of the gardens." The defense lawyers admitted the designation of mafioso for men such as Cascio-Ferro, while associating it with attitudes of "brash individualism, certainly not criminal acts."[180] If the Mafia is a traditional phenomenon, the traditional Sicilian, always an individualist, would never dream of associating with anyone else in order to commit a crime, or indeed for any other reason. The lawyer Puglia responded with a letter-perfect syllogism, calling upon the "true and irreplaceable expert on the Sicilian soul" as his authority, as usual, Pitrè.[181] With a somewhat greater degree of realism, Giampietro, on the other hand, described the arc that brought the Mafia to configure itself as a pseudo-state ordering, as well as a form of "insurance" underwritten by "landowners" and "businesspeople" in order to ensure the protection of their "property and persons." The blood "vendetta" derived from internal competition and rivalry, and in keeping with the collective nature of the phenomenon, the vendetta could be "transverse," that is, targeted "against others in the family or the association." It always took the form of "an ambush, a betrayal," and was executed with spectacular ferocity, "with an additional defilement of the corpse, pouring gasoline on it, or decapitating it, or else mutilating it or ravaging it in a horrifying manner, indicative of the terrible power of the Mafia."

> One must have read the pages of the minutes of the trials concerning the small-scale and large-scale combinations, the murders, the depredations, the arson, the violence, the rapes, the savage and atrocious vendettas . . . carried out in broad daylight, in public piazzas, in this city as well as others, the dead bodies lying on the ground, the murderers safe and sound . . . to have even the most pallid idea of Mafia criminality.[182]

Aside from the various exaggerations and falsehoods, the collective dimension that was documented, however crudely, in the *maxiprocessi* (maxitrials) of the Fascist era remained the foundation of the phenomenon of the Mafia, and therefore, of the struggle against the Mafia. In our eyes as scholars, not judges, the verisimilitude of the prosecution case lies in the personal and family biographies of the various characters, in the historical continuity of the criminal powers, and in the logic of the action/reaction dynamic that characterized the nature of the association, such a difficult thing to prove in a court of law. In many of the legal proceedings, one fundamental detail was the delegation of trust to the (extrajudicial) information provided by the police. Giampietro attributed full evidentiary value to that information. This was also true of the Palermo Mafia trials, in which there was practically none of the variously honest, extorted, instrumental, or false testimony that the political and factional struggle tended to produce in small towns. See, for instance, the verdict against the 213 defendants of Piana dei Colli. Even the admittedly domesticated newspaper accounts describe a trial that took place in a surreal atmosphere, with the presiding magistrate "from time to time . . . barking out a name," examinations that lasted a few moments, witnesses that denied everything, the prosecuting attorney urging the jurors, in the absence of factual evidence, to issue a guilty verdict on the basis of their "free beliefs."[183] Finally, the trial made continual reliance on the police records of interviews and interrogations; at the same time, those accounts constituted the preliminary judicial investigation, the evidence, and the verdict and sentence themselves. It is unlikely that this sort of trial could offer any genuine safeguards against police power, which was, if anything, strengthened by a law passed in 1926, specifically for the "Sicilian provinces," which called for internal exile for those whom the usual *vox populi* identified as the "leaders, participants, accomplices, and abettors" of criminal organizations. "Internal exile," reiterated the public prosecutor, "is a deadly weapon"[184] to be used against those acquitted or sentenced to "moderate" punishments. One such case involved the Farinella brothers. One of them, Mauro Farinella, was sentenced to eight years in prison but was then obliged to serve first a four-year term of internal exile and then (without a break), a second four-year term of internal exile, and wound up dying on a small island (1940).

That aside, we will not pretend to believe that the preventive administrative policies were measures introduced by Fascism; they were the instrument that allowed the liberal state to bring the Mafia under control. Trials had always been based on police reports and transcripts. Indeed, if we think back to the *stoppagghieri* and Amoroso cases, we can consider defensive of civil rights the prohibition imposed on Spanò "against relying upon rumors and commonly accepted versions of events," as well as the obligation to supply the source "where it is based on confidential reports."[185] We cannot be certain that some of the verdicts might not have been "prepackaged" (though in any case there were a fair number of acquittals, especially in the "smaller" or "minor" trials). We cannot vouch for the veracity of accusations contained in far too many posthumous letters, and in testimony and confessions that may have been retracted in court. This, however, is true as well of regimes both previous and subsequent to Fascism.

What then should we say about the effects of the operation taken as a whole? We cannot ignore the operation's intentional damage to civil rights, nor can we limit our observations to that aspect. The Mafia was not invented by Fascism, as Christopher Duggan seems to theorize; Duggan, in his very noteworthy study, failed to make the (difficult) distinction between the actions of the prefect and those of the police, which for a great many years to come (the last documented instance was the memories of Calderone)[186] the mafiosi remembered as a nightmarish ordeal. All observers agreed that there was a sharp decline in the number of murders after 1925. Statistics, however, provide only a partial picture of the actual phenomenon.[187] There are two opposing theses. According to some observers, Mori annihilated the Mafia, which then sprang back into existence in 1943, fully armed, like Pallas Athena bursting from Zeus's forehead. Others believe that the prefect Mori was ordered to halt just as he was about to reach the "highest ranks,"[188] that is, that the campaign was directed primarily against small-time criminals, in accordance with a class-denominated approach. Discrimination by class was certainly present, but that separated the large landholders from everyone else. The repression struck at professionals, mayors, primarily large-scale *gabellotti* like the Ortolevas, the Tusas, the Gucciones, and the Farinellas. A few of them reemerged in the postwar years: Vizzini, Genco Russo, and Volpe.[189] Others left no heirs: Cascio-Ferro and Candino, Ferrarello and Andaloro, the two Palermo factions of the Gentiles and the Sparacinos. There are important names of the past and the future. Among the names of the past were a certain Giuseppe Fontana from Villabate and Salvatore Licata, a fourth-generation member, I believe, of the Mafia family of the Conca d'Oro; among the names of the future were a certain Giuseppe Di Cristina from Riesi, a Santo Fleres from Partinico, Giuseppe Panzeca from Caccamo, Calogero Lo Bue from Prizzi, Antonino Cottone from Villabate, and even a certain Stefano Bontà.[190] Among the five hundred mafiosi who escaped to the United States, "fleeing the same intolerable political climate,"[191] we find many of the future bosses of Cosa Nostra: Joe Bonanno, Joe Masseria, Carlo Gambino, Joe Profaci, Stefano Magaddino; as well as a top-ranking narcotics smuggler like Frank Coppola.

Amidst terroristic excesses, the conviction of innocent defendants, and political persecutions, the policeman Mori and the inquisitor Giampietro met and soundly beat the Mafia.

ANOTHER POSTWAR ERA

The Mafia showed signs of life even before the Allied landings in July 1943. In 1932, in the center of Canicattì, three murders took place "whose method of execution and the profound mystery in which they remain shrouded" point to "murders typical of Mafia organizations." In the area outside of Partinico, in the mid-1930s, there were "fires, destruction, and murders . . . with a clear organized crime background." We could cite a great many other episodes not mentioned in the press, to which the regime responded with a "few sentences of execution by firing squad" and a new wave of orders of internal exile.[192]

But all linear historical continuity ended with the foreign occupation of Italy and the dissolution of the state, the adversary, model, and accomplice of the Mafia. The formidable shock was enough to get everything going again, without any need for the deus ex machina of a conspiracy with the Americans, and such elements as airplanes and tanks that arrived in Villalba with scarves with embroidered L's (for Lucky Luciano), with the improbable consequence of a Mafia mobilization led by Don Calò to neutralize the Italian-German armies.[193] In any case, it seems quite unlikely that in 1942 there existed a Mafia with which the high command of the Allied intelligence services could come to any agreements at all. Instead, there is documentation that the U.S. Navy entrusted Luciano with defending the New York docks against German saboteurs, which, however, had never existed, because it was the boss himself who simulated the attacks to obtain release from prison.[194] Truly here was the classic Mafia style: threat and protection from the same source! On the Sicilian side, Luciano denies having played any role at all: "Back home, I didn't have a single contact."[195]

Salvatore Lucania, also known as Lucky Luciano, left Lercara at the age of nine. The last wave of mafiosi who moved to America was the surge of refugees fleeing Mori. Then, with the collapse of migration, the channels were blocked.[196] In this phase, in part owing to Luciano's efforts, an American organization was created that utilized the Sicilian model of affiliation but emerged from the previous restrictions, owing primarily to the enormous opportunity offered by Prohibition. In the meanwhile, in the wake of the Mori cyclone, the island component retreated, so that when the Mafia finally revived, there was a very evident gap.

The Mafia had some credits to redeem after combat on Sicily ended. The Anglo-American forces had a territory to administrate. The only institutions that survived from the wreckage of the collapsed government structure were the Carabinieri and the interprovincial police service (Servizio Interprovinciale di PS) created by Mori. Therefore, the occupying Allied forces looked around for anyone who held any informal power (priests, aristocrats); in so doing, they had in mind the model of the Italian American boss or that of the native chief who collaborated with British colonialists. For the municipal role of mayor, they entrusted themselves to pre-Fascist notables, and among them were a fair number of men "of respect." The immediate problem was to restore or ensure order and to safeguard the food supplies that were threatened by the burgeoning black market. A number of officers called for a compromise that might perhaps entail "the acceptance to a certain degree on the part of the Allies of the principle of *omertà*, a code which the Mafia really understands and respects."[197] But for that approach to work, what was required was a centralized Mafia, capable of controlling the teeming welter of swindlers, connivers, and bandits.

In the meanwhile, the other side was busily reorganizing. Sicily was in point of fact separate from Italy; the anti-Fascist parties were weak there and lacked national connections. (This was around the major historical turning point of 8 September 1943, when Dwight Eisenhower announced Italy's unconditional surrender.) Some of the notables made early moves, demanding the formation of a separate Sicilian republic and founding the Movimento per l'Indipendenza Siciliana (MIS, Movement for Sicilian Independence). The leader of this organization was Andrea Finocchiaro Aprile, the leading exponent of the Nitti movement in Sicily in 1919–1924. He was the son of Camillo Finocchiaro Aprile, a cabinet minister during the Giolitti government. There were others as well, such as Lucio Tasca Bordonaro, who was active with Vizzini in the agrarian party in the years following the First World War, and formerly a representative of the landowners in the Consiglio Provinciale dell'Economia Corporativa (Provincial Council of Corporative Economics), and now mayor of Palermo.

Orlando, on the other hand, remained behind the scenes, the leading figure of a past that was returning to power.

Here, as elsewhere throughout this book, I will refrain from narrating the general history of Sicily *sub specie mafiosa* up to and including the return to Italian administration, the defeat of Sicilian separatism, the creation of the Italian region of Sicily, and the fight for agrarian reform.[198] I only wish to emphasize that a great many mafiosi spent time in the ranks of the MIS: Vizzini, Navarra, Genco Russo; Paolino Bontate, and Gaetano Filippone; Pippo Calò and the young Tommaso Buscetta. According to Calderone, Concetto Gallo, a Catanian landowner and the commander of the Esercito Volontario per l'Indipendenza Siciliana (EVIS, Volunteer Army for Sicilian Independence), was also a mafioso.[199] In September 1945, on a Tasca estate, the leading figures of the movement decided to make use of some of the gangs that were marauding through the countryside to bring young blood to the EVIS. "That evening," commented our old acquaintance, Francesco Spanò, "the ancient society of the Mafia in which all the *cosche* of Sicily were represented was duly reorganized."[200] And in fact the network of relations that Mori had lacerated and demolished found this opportunity to return to life, winding itself around the MIS. For the first and last time, the Mafia, instead of inserting itself into an existing power structure, seemed bent on contributing directly to a political hypothesis. It is hard to say how important Sicilianism, long cited and evoked by mafiosi and their lawyers, really was. Certainly, if they possessed any political ideology at all, this would be it. In more concrete terms, a focus on the movements of the liberal political class had emerged from Fascism but could not necessarily be recycled in a new Italy.

Like others, the Mafia claimed it was a victim of Fascism; but with a greater degree of credibility than the same claim advanced by the notables, and especially the large landholders to whom the Fascist regime had restored social power, if not political power.[201] Many preserved a vivid memory of the roundups and the *maxiprocessi*, which offered the spectacle of *campieri* and *gabellotti* tossed out on their ears, denounced, and persecuted by their protectors/protégés. Was what followed an automatic reconstitution of a conservative front that grouped these intermediate elements alongside the large landholders? Or might the *gabellotti* find a place for themselves in the antifeudal (and anti-Fascist) struggle that was being readied in the Sicilian countryside?[202] These were the problems facing the Sicilian left as it searched for a progressive bourgeoisie, or at least a "low" Mafia to set against the *mafia "alt"* or "high" Mafia.

On 16 September 1944, a truck arrived in Villalba, loaded with militants accompanying the Sicilian regional Communist leader Girolamo Li Causi, formerly a major figure in the area of political emigration and in the Resistance. Vizzini and his nephew, Benedetto Farina, who took turns being mayor of the town, controlled a local Christian Democratic Party that was affiliated with the MIS. Nonetheless, they were willing to welcome the outsiders to Villalba. They asked only that they avoid making references to local issues "out of respect for the hospitality that was being accorded them."[203] The small-town society was not accustomed to outside interventions, which were reminiscent of Fascism. Indeed, it was the *prepotenze* or arrogant bullying of the Fascists that gave Don Calò, who was found innocent in court and who avoided internal exile twice thanks to the recommendations of a myriad of relatives in the priesthood, a certain element of his personal and political prestige. Internally, the community was lacerated by the conflict between the Catholic separatist faction led by the Vizzini-Farinas and the venerable local Pantaleone family whose scion, Michele, had founded a socialist group. Li Causi presented himself for the rally standing next to Michele Pantaleone: a signal that he did not wish to "remain at the surface level of ideological propaganda," but instead meant to delve into questions that might not concern him directly, in particular the issue of the lease on the Miccichè estate. The Trabias had warded off the mediators for decades, and then, in the end (*sic transit gloria mundi*), the estate had fallen into the hands of the Catholic cooperative that was opposed to the left-wing cooperative. Note how the "high-level" political and ideological language is overlaid on the small-town political and factional idiom. When the Communist leader began to criticize the clientelistic management of the subleases implemented by the Catholics through the actions of a *gabellotto*, Don Calò shouted: "That's a lie!" and mayhem (*babbilonia*) broke loose, with dozens of pistol shots and the tossing and explosion of five hand grenades. Fourteen people were wounded, including Li Causi, who, according to popular legend, "pointing his finger straight at his attacker," continued to shout: "Why are you shooting, who are you shooting at? Can't you see that you're shooting at yourself?"

Evidently, the Communist leader, heir to Verro and Panepinto, could not refrain from a civilizing pedagogy concerning class conflict, bringing the Sicilian anomaly into the normative scheme whereby "the members of the old-style Mafia, in the battle over ownership of the land, would no longer need to operate outside the framework of the law." For that reason, he condemned Vizzini as "unworthy of belonging even to the Mafia." This is not all that far from the position of the Christian Democrat Bernardo Mattarella, who emphasized that "those elements in Villalba who looked sympathetically toward the Christian Democratic movement, which they were considering joining, were in no wise reactionaries. They were by and large peasants and small landowners" who only by chance happened to be in alliance with the "feudal landowners" of the MIS (the Sicilian Independentist Movement or Movimento Indipendentista Siciliano). To the contrary, that alliance was anything but accidental. The massacre of Villalba was in no way similar to the classic Mafia ambush; instead it represented an act of terrorism "justified and hailed by the separatist press."[204] The mastermind behind that massacre meant to take sides openly.

The same political outlook understood as a subversive operation, and not as mere political management of power (which would have remained firmly within the context of tradition), emerges from the most spectacular and distressing episodes of the postwar years in Sicily, the story of Salvatore Giuliano.[205] And yet the future prince of Sicilian bandits began his career as a penniless black-market operator who happened to be taken by surprise by the Carabinieri and instinctively shot at them. This was a latter-day variant on a bandit tradition that generally begins on the highest notes of a vendetta carried out against an arrogant abuser or an infamous traitor, and therefore a case of defending one's honor. The Sicily of the postwar years was a setting of poverty and desperation, a place that refused to contribute the wheat it produced to the government pool, thereby making it available to the other poor wretches in areas that failed to produce sufficient wheat. Sicily was increasingly closed behind the small-town barrier that the Communists were attempting to shatter by dubbing the government wheat pools "people's granaries" and calling for a mobilization against the greedy large-scale farmers. In many towns, however, resistance was general, extending to all social layers, including many of the more left-leaning peasants. According to a rumor that was spreading in Villalba, Li Causi had been sent "by the government to force the peasants to take their crops to the government pool."[206] Emerging from this context, the Giuliano case would move in unexpected directions. The lord of Montelepre would wind up fighting on behalf of the more general (and generic) concept of "Sicily" and would ultimately become a protagonist in the first "strategy of tension" in the history of the Italian republic, the massacre of the peasants assembling with their red banners at Portella della Ginestra to commemorate May Day of 1947.

Such an outcome would have been inconceivable had it not been for Giuliano's enrollment in EVIS as a colonel. The supply of violence bubbling up from below met with a significant demand. We are exploring the case of the first political bandit in the history of Sicily, a bandit who attacked the barracks of the forces of law and order as well as local Communist headquarters, a bandit who robbed eminent individuals, who killed high-ranking mafiosi such as Santo Fleres, and who personally assaulted columns of the Italian army. He did his best to give overall meaning to his actions, but with a series of zigzagging operations that betrayed no detectable strategic drive. In some cases, he attacked the police because they were a republican institution, while respecting the monarchist institution of the Carabinieri. At times he was in touch with the right-wing and monarchist MIS run by the Tascas and the Carcacis, while at other times he contacted the left-wing movement led by his lawyer, Antonino Varvaro, who won a considerable victory in Montelepre in the 1947 elections at the head of a separatist republican movement. Among those suspected of ordering the massacre of Portella we find not only the separatists of the various factions, but also the highest ranking leaders of the Christian Democratic Party and monarchist leaders in Palermo. It is likely that Giuliano was at some point in contact with all of these figures during his many peregrinations within and around the MIS, that he was entrusted (or believed that he had been) with major roles, while on a regional scale the Italian left wing won the elections of 1947, at the same time that the monarchy fell on a national scale and the north became increasingly powerful. It would seem that the decisive point was this transition from monarchy to republic, the moment of a plot involving the separatist right with Savoy politicians and generals. That separatist right, in order to take part in a reactionary front, appeared to be willing to discard its supposed vocation as an anti-unification and anti-Risorgimento movement.[207] The point is that overlying this (possible) plot was another plot to take Giuliano dead or alive, with a corresponding emulation among the Carabinieri and police, with disconcerting results. For instance, the high police official Ciro Verdiani, who regularly paid friendly visits to Giuliano (as did the public attorney Emanuele Pili), informed the bandit: "Beware of your cousin." The cousin in question was none other than Gaspare Pisciotta, with whom, through Nitto Minasola and the Mafia of Monreale, the Carabinieri of the Comando forze repressione banditismo (CFRB, or Command of the Forces for the Suppression of Banditry) under the leadership of Colonel Ugo Luca were then establishing contacts. Clearly, it was of some importance exactly who wound up capturing the bandit, or at least persuaded him to surrender with the complex baggage of his (supposed) secrets.

And so it was logical that Giuliano should be captured dead—murdered (it seems) by Pisciotta, according to a prior agreement with the CFRB. It was 4 July 1950, and the postwar years were winding down. The staging of a firefight with the Carabinieri was miserably flimsy, adding more doubts to those already existing; but more than anything else it was the murder of Pisciotta with the notorious strychnine-laced cup of coffee served to him in the prison of the Ucciardone that made it inevitable for a theory of a plot to emerge. Nor should the reader expect the mystery to be solved here. I will do no more than to emphasize that the story of the Mafia was strengthened on this occasion, legitimized in its order-keeping functions by the police officers who served in the Mori operation: Messana, Verdiani, and Spanò, as well as Luca himself: "Unless Giuliano soon falls into the hands of the law," Messana wrote, "he will have to become a victim of the Mafia. . . . In these days, and it is no strange coincidence, not a few criminals, several of them notorious gang leaders, have been found murdered."[208]

The period in question was the beginning of 1946, and Giuliano would be active for four more years. The murdered bandits represented the victims, not so much of the orders of some superorganization, but rather of the struggle over the redefinition of the criminal hierarchies in the chaos of the postwar years, which constituted the "humiliation" of the idea of a *Mafia d'ordine*, "the daily demonstration of the nonexistence of any mediating or regulating function for it."[209] It was the state institutions that, by insisting on evoking it, wound up finally bringing it into existence. One example only is in order here. Messana had a contact in the gang: Salvatore Ferreri, also known as Fra' Diavolo, a man "in the hands" of the *cosca* of Alcamo, who promised to hand over Giuliano (but failed to deliver him). Fra' Diavolo was mysteriously killed while he was under arrest in a Carabinieri barracks. According to Spanò, the Mafia capo of Alcamo, Vincenzo Rimi, was the "trustee for the murder of Ferreri by the Carabinieri, because he was afraid that Ferreri—if arrested—would talk."[210] This is the opinion of a *questore*, not of a subversive. If we consider that Rimi would later become one of the most important and most "protected" figures of the Mafia in the 1950s and 1960s, we can make a few guesses about the corrupting effects of these ties. What effects did the victorious plot, the one linking Luca, Minasola, and Pisciotta, have? "We are a single body, bandits, police, and Mafia, like the Father, the Son, and the Holy Ghost," Pisciotta shouted during his trial in Viterbo.[211]

There was, however, a difference in accentuation between the "orphans of Mori," who reactivated the channels of communications with the mafiosi of the Madonie or of Alcamo, and Colonel Ugo Luca, a specialist in antiguerrilla warfare who had served in the Balkans. Luca also aimed at a political distinction between the category of the government forces and the subversive forces. He further claimed that Giuliano and the Communists were allied with the subversive forces.[212] What was needed was a sacrificial victim, a scapegoat for a *fronte d'ordine* (order-keeping front) founded on the contrast between a supposedly good Mafia and the bad bandits. This resulted in an even worse version of what had happened in 1877, overturning the direction of the events of 1926. This was the basis of Giuliano's bitter jest about the collaborationist vocation of the Mafia.[213] It also led to the legend (otherwise entirely baseless) of Giuliano as the Robin Hood of Montelepre. In any event, the case of Giuliano, however spectacular, was only part of a larger and more complex operation to bring the Sicilian separatists into the Christian Democratic Party: Mattarella's prediction that the Villalbese would return to the Christian Democratic Party proved far more accurate than the corresponding Communist prediction of a breakup from within of the Mafia-associated political alignment. Let us listen to the version offered by another Christian Democratic leader, Giuseppe Alessi, from the province of Caltanissetta. Alessi described how the separatists of the Vallone, under the leadership of Calogero Volpe, and with the support of Genco Russo, entered the party en bloc. Alessi opposed the move, knowing full well (in part from his experience as a lawyer in a number of the trials held under the Fascist regime) that this was "the world of the three M's: . . . Mills, Money, and Mafia, that is, the united forces that control life in the *Vallone*." His friends, however, objected: "We need the protection of powerful individuals to halt the violence of the Communists."[214] A longer road lay ahead for Vanni Sacco, the Mafia capo of Camporeale who went over to the liberal side and waited until the end of the 1950s to join forces with the Christian Democrats, over the objections of the mayor of Camporeale, Pasquale Almerico. Fanfani's lieutenant Giovanni Gioia, later a cabinet-level minister, replied to Almerico: "The party needs people with whom we can build coalitions, it needs new blood, we cannot stand in the way of certain attempts to create a compromise." Almerico was thus isolated and was killed in an attack in March 1957.

Beginning at the end of the war, with the agreement of the large landholders, control of the Mafia *campieri* over the large estates of western Sicily was restored.[215] This was done in a bid not only to control the bandits but also the peasant movement. The list of union organizers murdered in the postwar years grew horrifyingly long, with the killings of Accursio Miraglia, Placido Rizzotto, Salvatore Carnevale, and many others. Moreover, the defense of the existing situation was transformed, as usual, into an ambitious effort to take over new terrain. The Mafia path to social mobility and the redistribution of assets was an approach that competed with, and was therefore antagonistic to, all those paths proposed by the left beginning in the early twentieth century. This conflict was all the sharper now that the latifundium, or large landholding, was about to enter the last of its numerous crises, one that would prove ultimately to be fatal. Both before and after the great land reform of 1950, the large landholders began to sell, partly in order to forestall potential legal expropriation. When all was said and done, 500,000 hectares (1.25 million acres) of land changed hands. These transactions were often quite murky, and they frequently involved preemptive purchases by the usual buyers, who often managed to purchase the land at "affectionate" prices.[216] The large estates of Polizzello, Miccichè, Mandrebianche, and Mandrerosse were purchased and sold through the intermediation of Genco Russo,[217] Vizzini, and Tusa. Giuseppe Bua and Mariano Licari in Marsala, Vincenzo Di Carlo in Raffadali, and more or less all the former *campieri* with greater or lesser ties to the Mafia controlled this gigantic divestiture of the property of their former masters, and the resulting transactions resulted in new fortunes and new clientelism. One essential relationship was that with the Christian Democratic Party and the Coldiretti, or farmers' association, which in turn offered access to the ERAS (Ente di Riforma Agraria Siciliana, or Sicilian

Agency for Agricultural Reform) and to regional financing for the development of small-scale peasant land ownership.

Beginning from an affiliation with the separatists, then progressing through the liberal party, and winding up with the Christian Democratic Party and the Coldiretti, Michele Navarra (known as *u patri nostru,* or our father), a doctor and profiteer who created a shipping company by purchasing trucks from the Anglo-American administration, joined forces with Vanni Sacco in an attempt to seize control of the Consorzio di Bonifica dell'Alto e Medio Belice (Consortium for the Reclamation of Upper and Middle Belice). Navarra led the Corleonese Mafia in its revival "following the roundups of the prefect Mori." During those roundups, wrote Sergeant Vignali, "local organized crime ceased all activity because . . . even the relatives of the *cosca* members were uprooted." Navarra was a relative of the Lo Bues from Prizzi, the Gaglianos, and the Gennaros, who were involved in the Verro murder and were prosecuted by the Fascists. Filippo Gennaro, son of Michelangelo Gennaro, then identified as the Mafia capo, was again active in the years after the Second World War in the market for rental leases and intimidations.[218] Navarra, on the other hand, reacted badly to the return from America of Vincent Collura, an individual with ties to Frank Coppola and Joe Profaci. He saw Collura as overambitious, and soon afterward Collura died in a hail of lead (1957). Another annoying individual was the union organizer Placido Rizzotto whom one member of the *cosca,* Luciano Leggio, waylaid in the middle of town, inviting him to come along for a "heart to heart." "As we were leaving town, Placido kept saying 'Where are you taking me? Let me go!' He was being taken to his death."[219] Another individual who was taken to his death was a teenager who had the misfortune of witnessing something awful. He was admitted to the hospital for a nervous breakdown and was personally treated by Navarra with an injection.

At the end of the war, Leggio "was a young peasant, without possessions or resources."[220] He was a *scassapagghiara* in the literal meaning of the term, that is, a thief stealing sheaves of straw, caught in 1944 by the *guardia campestre* (rural watchman) Calogero Comajanni and transported by him from one end of town to the other, "practically kicking him all the way,"[221] to the Carabinieri barracks. Six months later, the young man took his revenge for this humiliation, with the classic ambush outside the victim's house. It is not entirely true to say that Leggio had no resources, because he had a natural skill in handling weapons, evident from his youth. Thanks to this skill, he became a *campiere* for a certain Doctor Caruso, taking the place of a predecessor who had mysteriously been murdered (1945). At the age of twenty, Leggio was already a *gabellotto,* the youngest one in Sicily, and he became involved in the networks of cattle theft and clandestine slaughtering, while remaining a fugitive from the law, with a few intervals, from 1948 on. This Dottore Navarra was the channel through which Leggio avoided the fate of a "new Giuliano," despite predictions to that effect in the headlines of Palermo newspapers in 1958. Still, the "bandit" was not content to act as a simple triggerman. His spirit of independence aroused Navarra's suspicions, and so the big boss organized a murder plot against Leggio. The ambush failed because of the great fear that Leggio inspired in the professional killers. Leggio's reaction was murderous. Navarra, *u patri nostru,* dismissive of precautions, was killed, his body riddled with bullets along with that of an unfortunate medical colleague (1958). The war culminated in a furious shootout that involved "forty or so criminals on both sides," in the middle of the day, in the center of Corleone, prompting no reaction from the law enforcement authorities.[222] The Navarrians emerged in complete defeat.

And yet everyone expected Navarra to win; he controlled the social power, and he had the political contacts. If the Mafia really was nothing more than a club of notables, profiteers, and obedient thugs, the episode would have been incomprehensible. If the Mafia's hierarchies reflected nothing more than the natural (that is, social) hierarchies, then Leggio would have remained the nonentity that he was. Instead, one essential piece of capital was the capacity to deal out violence. And it is important to see where that capital was placed. Giuliano played in the field of major-power politics, and that is where he died; Leggio invested in the circuits of the Mafia.

Let us consider the clash between the two sections of the Greco family, based, respectively, in the Palermo *borgate* of Croceverde Giardini and Ciaculli. The first section was led by Giuseppe Greco, known as *Piddu u tinenti* (Piddu is a nickname for Giuseppe, and *tinenti* is dialect for lieutenant); the second originated with a certain Salvatore Greco, already dead by the time of the events in question, thought to be the same Salvatore Greco whom we first encountered as the capo, or chief, of the *Alta maffia* (or "high Mafia") in the years spanning the late nineteenth century and the early twentieth century.[223] The history begins in 1939 with a clash over "issues of honor": the right to sit on a bench in front of a church during the religious festival of the *borgata*. It continued with a nighttime ambush on the return home, and the first victim was a son of the "lieutenant." Beginning in 1946, war broke out, consisting of raids, executions, and "mysterious disappearances," culminating in an attack with the involvement of the Greco women of Ciaculli in a knife assault and wounding of a member of the opposing group. One of the women (Antonina) was in turn attacked and killed (1947). These developments were so stunning in their methods as to justify the hypothesis of the Giuliano gang's involvement on the "lieutenant's side": but in all likelihood, that was an attempt to assign this ferocious and illegal violence to unidentified brigands, so distant from the regulations based on the code of honor

and chivalry, traditionally attributed to infra-Mafia competition. I would venture to express my doubts concerning the history of the bench and the festival,
considering the issues at stake: the lease on one of the largest citrus plantations
in Sicily, belonging to the Tagliavias, shipowners and exporters as early as the
middle of the nineteenth century; the management of companies dealing in
citrus derivatives and shipping companies; the battle to control eastern Palermo (cattle theft, supplies for the city markets, and smuggling), which in 1956
led to the murder of the Mafia capo of Villabate Nino Cottone, related to the
Grecos of Croceverde.[224] By this date, the two Greco cousins of Ciaculli, Salvatore *"chicchiteddu"* and Totò *"il lungo,"* also known as *"l'ingegnere,"* were rising
to the summit of power and dealings of the Palermo Mafia, and there were no
further conflicts among relatives.[225] As far as can be determined, an agreement
was achieved through the mediation of Joe Profaci, who was originally from
Villabate and had temporarily returned to Sicily.

And yet there were many, many victims, including the father of *"chicchiteddu,"* and the father and mother of *"l'ingegnere."* "The old mafiosi of the *giardini* could worship two idols: wealth and the vendetta."[226] Here, evidently, prevailing over the vendetta was the demand for management of family business,
which during this phase was undergoing a major expansion. We are not in the
presence of a feud, blindly pursued or culturally determined, but rather a clear-
eyed choice that, depending on circumstances, called for peace or war: the war
of the Grecos, the "ferocity" of Leggio, the many bloody conflicts, involving the
Mafia or bandits, in the years following the Second World War.

CHAPTER V

LA COSA LORO—THEIR THING

THE ANTI-MAFIA

If a shapely young woman walks by, a Sicilian will say that she is a *ragazza mafiosa* (mafiosa girl), and if a young man is alert and intelligent, he will say that the boy is quite *mafioso*. People talk of the Mafia in every context and condition, but, honorable colleagues, it strikes me that there is a great deal of exaggeration.[1]

The year is 1949. The dismissive and minimalizing interpretation printed above feigns to be based on "field" observations. In fact, it is solidly based on a literary tradition and specifically on the usual Pitrè. The person who put it forth was Mario Scelba, the Italian minister of the interior (a cabinet-level post that oversees the national police), renowned for his harsh stance toward demonstrators of all kinds, both peasants and blue-collar workers. Scelba, moreover, was named by Gasparre Pisciotta, the lieutenant of bandit Salvatore Giuliano, as the man who ordered the massacre of demonstrators in favor of land reform at Portella di Ginestra in 1947. Thus, the Mafia does not exist, or else it can be reduced to nothing more than a pallid cultural category. In the 1950s, a substantial portion of Sicilian and indeed Italian society subscribed to this theory, as mafiosi gradually became an integral part of the majority Christian Democratic political party. The mafiosi entered that party even more easily than did the traditional governing groups who swallowed the bitter pill of land reform and maneuvered their way through a gilded age of decadence amidst regional financing and regional employment. The right-wing Anti-Mafia vanished, and with it went the Anti-Mafia tension in state structures. These were the years in which Lo Schiavo sang the praises of Vizzini, Genco Russo, and the *Mafia d'ordine* (order-keeping Mafia).[2]

The Mafia won itself a certain number of rewards by choosing to take on the same adversaries as the government and the bourgeoisie. We may assign a certain symbolic value to the fact that, in the town of Sciara, the men who killed Salvatore Carnevale met in the same building that housed the barracks of the Carabinieri, though they entered by a different set of stairs. Both the Mafia and the Carabinieri had long applied pressure on the labor organizer to "stay clear of political parties" and to get out of politics: "Picca nn'hai di 'sta maladrineria" ("You'll gain nothing from this villainy"),[3] a *campiere*, or private guard of farmland, warned him. Another emblematic figure was that of the suspected mastermind behind the Miraglia killing, Gaetano Parlapiano-Vella, who had returned to the heights of power after his internal exile under the Fascists.[4] The investigations of these murders remain masterpieces of mediocrity; they stumble and come to a halt at either the level of the police or the courts. They display defects more serious than idle ignorance but fall somewhat short of outright complicity. One official who became the target of furious attacks was Carlo Alberto Dalla Chiesa, a junior officer of the Comando forze repressione banditismo (CFRB), commander of the *squadriglia*, or squadron, of Corleone, who made some efforts to break out of the bureaucratic box.

And so the left was relegated to a solitary position of shouting and protesting against the Mafia, crying out for justice for its dead, denouncing the unholy alliances. The likelihood that those protests and denunciations would have any effect was all the more diminished by the fact that they came from a political party that was entirely isolated after 1948. The authorities in the United States seemed to have a radically different attitude. Moreover, impulses seemed to be coming from the United States for reopening the debate in Italy as well. In 1953, the publisher Einaudi brought out an Italian edition of the Kefauver Investigation,[5] which can be considered the first book of the postwar years on this topic in Italy. That book was followed in 1956 by Ed Reid's *Mafia*, providing the (somewhat confused) story of the Sicilian plot against virtuous America. This book was given the undeserved honor of an introduction by the great Italian jurist Piero Calamandrei, who specifically approved the idea that Sicily should be considered "the central incubator of American criminality,"[6] and supported the idea that some pressure, perhaps an international investigation, might help to raise the lid to show what was simmering in the Christian Democratic cauldron. The Communist Francesco Renda opined that this was "a courageous book . . . that offers a bitter reminder of the extended silence that has characterized Italian literature over all these years."[7] The reasons for these expressions of approval are quite evident. Any acknowledgment of the existence of the Mafia from the United States came from the great protector, on the far shore of the Atlantic Ocean, of precisely the political forces in Italy that claimed the opposite: that the Mafia did not exist. American congressional committees and commissions served as models for the Italian left, which had been excluded from the governing coalition and harbored lingering suspicions of the repressive approaches entrusted to Scelba's police. These developments pointed to the mobilization of a type of "frontline" press and publishing that the mainstream, central parties of Italy regarded with misgivings.

> Kefauver . . . in fact points out that credit for the very idea of starting the investigation was due to sixteen "aggressive" daily newspapers in America that fought tooth and nail. . . . We should be aware from the very beginning of the considerably different conditions in which the Italian press has been working, in comparison with the American press. . . . American newspapers or journalists of the Fifties may have been forced to take on not only the gangsters, but also a corrupt governor, complicit policemen, cowardly and corrupt judges; still it must be said that the entire machinery of the federal government was not arrayed against them.[8]

These words were written by Vittorio Nisticò, the editor-in-chief of the left-wing Palermo newspaper *L'Ora*, which, on two separate occasions, in the late 1950s and early 1960s, launched major investigative series that denounced the relations between the Christian Democratic Party and the Mafia. (There was also an astonishing dynamite attack on the offices of *L'Ora*.) The newspaper carried on a form of journalism that made extensive use of spectacular and sensationalistic headlines, but also ongoing efforts to dig deeper into the cases of Corleone and the architectural and structural ravaging of Palermo, and to establish the historical background of those stories by exhuming the old stories of Cascio-Ferro or accounts of trials from the 1920s. But there was an entire milieu of engaged journalists and intellectuals at the end of the period of *centrismo*, who examined or returned to the issue. One unusual individual was the Trieste-born sociologist Danilo Dolci, who introduced the hunger strike as part of the Italian repertoire of protest methods, built social centers in the Partinico area, and undertook research projects and wrote dossiers on banditry, poverty, and clientelism.[9] Other notable individuals came from the depths of an ancient Sicily: a surveyor from Villalba, Michele Pantaleone; a doctor from Montemaggiore, Simone Gatto;[10] and a schoolteacher from Racalmuto, Leonardo Sciascia. Pantaleone traced the Mafia back to the concrete context of a rural history and the figure of a local notable, Don Calò. Gatto established a context built on the theme of the classic *meridionalismo* (focusing on the Meridione, or southern Italy) that followed in the tradition of Franchetti. In a mixture of fiction and nonfiction, Sciascia explored the idea that the Mafia was an indicator of a more general corruption, and it was not clear whether it was generally Italian or specifically Sicilian.

> We ought to do here what they do in America: grab them for tax evasion. But not only people like Mariano Arena; and not only in Sicily. There should be a swoop made . . . on the luxury villas, custom-built cars, the wives and mistresses of certain civil servants; and their tenor of life compared to their salaries. Then the proper conclusions should be drawn. That's the only way men like Don Mariano can feel the ground begin to give way under their feet.[11]

In the view of these intellectuals, the Mafia was a phenomenon of power: an archaic power that issued from the alliance between the Christian Democratic Party and various right-wing forces, both the bourgeoisie and an older feudalism; and that therefore reproduced all of the worst defects of Italian and Sicilian political *trasformismo* (transformism). In 1959, *Il gattopardo* (*The Leopard*, by Tomasi di Lampedusa) was published, with its ideology of "everything must change so that nothing will change," an ideology toward which the Italian left had a love-hate relationship. The left detested that ideology as reactionary, and yet, at the same time, it considered it a realistic portrayal of Sicilian conditions, and perhaps also a consolation for the left wing's inability to do anything to alter those conditions.

Sicilian Communists and socialists managed to emerge from their ghetto in 1959–1960 with what they called Operation Milazzo. The operation took its name from the Caltagirone notable, Silvio Milazzo, a former separatist, and a leading figure in the schism within the Christian Democratic Party thanks to which an anomalous regional government was established, with the support of both the extreme right and the extreme left. In this government, the old political class of agrarian extraction made its last stand, winning votes on a platform of fervent Sicilianism. The belief is that a number of the mafioso groups, transitioning from right-wing groups to the Christian Democratic Party, supported this attempt to preserve some element of the old aristocratic autonomies in opposition to the new party machine created by Amintore Fanfani. That was certainly the case with Francesco Paolo Bontate, also known as Don Paolino Bontà, landowner and leaseholder of vast citrus groves, one of Palermo's leading Mafia capos, and formerly a separatist and a monarchist. This political alliance also witnessed the debut of two entrepreneurial groups that would in later years be the targets of harsh attacks and polemics over their ties to Mafia milieux: the financiers Salvo of Salemi and the Catanian builders Costanzo. It would appear that the Salvo-Bontate group was among the groups that masterminded

Milazzo's fall, with a shift in orientation that would eventually provide the Salvos with a "sort of benevolence" from the entire Christian Democratic Party. That "benevolence" was expressed in an enduring monopoly on the municipal offices of rates and taxes with an *aggio* (that is, a percentage or bonus) amounting to 10 percent, as compared with a national average of 3.3 percent.[12] According to the *pentito* Calderone, the Mafia had supported Milazzo "with great effort and determination," in part because of the laws aiding entrepreneurs in this early experiment in the politics of compromise.[13] The idea that "Sicilian" finance and capital should in any case be protected, a typical feature of the perverse approach of the regionalist pursuit of unanimity at all costs, ensured that the past would lay the worst kind of dead hand onto the island's future.

With the fall of Milazzo, the next coalition to take power was the center-left, and the regional assembly asked the Italian parliament to establish the parliamentary commission of inquest on the Mafia (Commissione d'inchiesta sulla Mafia) that had long been demanded by the left and that was finally created in 1963. It appeared that with a centrist Italy and a Sicily of large landholdings, the Mafia was heading for ultimate defeat. The commission began a very substantial project of gathering documentation, the results of which, however, remained hidden from most people. The chair of the commission, the Christian Democrat Pafundi, first of all openly announced that the archives of the commission contained a slowly growing "powder keg," but then he continually put off lighting its fuse, until at last, at the end of the legislature (1968), the mountain gave birth to the ridiculous little mouse of a few, anodyne pages of a watered-down report. Those who had hoped for a public trial of the ruling class began to judge the Anti-Mafia as a "missed opportunity."[14] The majority party, the Christian Democratic Party, that is, was unwilling to subject itself to judgment. At the worst, it was willing to admit that in the Christian Democratic barrel there might be a few, isolated rotten apples, such as the loyal follower of Fanfani, Vito Ciancimino. In contrast, the opposition party energetically insisted that a figure of this stature (mayor of Palermo, commissioner for urban planning, city secretary of the Christian Democratic Party) could only represent the personification of a larger system of power made up of clientelism and business interests, which was intricately intertwined with the city administration of Palermo. For that matter, for years the press had been making ironic comments on the so-called VaLiGio business consortium (Vassallo–Lima–Gioia, one builder and two Christian Democratic politicians), which held the monopoly over the ruthless ravaging of a city that was frantically expanding and swelling with new inhabitants. Previously, the investigation of a ministerial commission under the guidance of the prefect Bevivino (1964) had clearly identified a process that the documentation assembled by the parliamentary commission of inquest fully confirmed:

the rampant destruction of both old buildings and vast expanses of public or private green space, the manipulation of regulatory plans, rigged contract competitions, licenses and permits in exchange for bribes, and false-front shell companies.

> Five shadowy individuals, for instance, monopolized 80 percent of the permits. . . . Four of those five were in different lines of work: one was a former bricklayer, another was a coal dealer, a third was an engineer who had received a restraining order in 1957 for having put his name to projects that he had neither drawn up himself nor supervised, and the fourth was a manual laborer and construction yard watchman, hoping to obtain a job as a concierge in one of the 1,465 buildings for which he had been issued permits.[15]

A typical successful builder, Francesco Vassallo, came from the Sicilian interior, the Tommaso Natale *borgata*. He served an apprenticeship as a *scassapagghiara* in the 1930s. Then he married into a local Mafia family that suffered two murder victims (both brothers of Francesco Vassallo's wife) in 1961–1962. In the postwar years, Vassallo's rapid climb in the business world took place through the vehicle of the cooperative, which in this and numerous other cases, mafiosi utilized, in preference to corporations with shares, "in order to create entrepreneurial microstructures in which they were not only partners, but could also extend partnerships to include individuals that were 'collateral' to the organization."[16] In short, at first Vassallo was short on capital but had plenty of connections. For instance, he had ties to a major shipping company and to the Montecatini plant in the Tommaso Natale neighborhood. Those connections allowed him to take part in competitions for public works contracts, as they offered reassurances as to his reliability. The road became smoother with the passage of time, thanks to low-interest, easily issued loans, useful variations in the zoning code, and exchanges of favors and services with the Limas, the Gioias, and such other local notables as Di Fresco and Giovanni Matta. Matta came into the spotlight when the Christian Democratic Party attempted to slip him in as a member of the Anti-Mafia Commission, prompting the vigorous and successful opposition of the Communists under the leadership of Pio La Torre, who was later murdered by the Mafia.

A conflict was therefore brewing between the Christian Democratic Party and the Italian Communist Party, culminating in the opposition between the majority report (Carraro)[17] and the left-wing minority report (La Torre) and the right-wing minority report (Pisanò), which marked the end of the first phase of the existence of the parliamentary commission of inquest on the Mafia (Commission) (1976). This, however, should not conceal the agreement that had come about between the second chairman of the commission, Cattanei, and his deputy, Li Causi. And from 1972 on, their cooperation led to the publication of a great volume of documentation. Generally, that cooperation served in the evaluation of the underlying foundations and the history of the phenomenon of the Mafia.[18] With a retrospective view, the issue of political responsibility and involvement became less of a divisive issue. This meant that in part it was possible to discard the centralism with which the politician and premier (1954–1955) Mario Scelba was identified; this also meant that centralism was no longer as popular as it had been. More importantly, with it went the liberal state, which was blamed for all the problems afflicting the country, to the shared advantage of the two chief "anti-Risorgimental" forces, the Catholics and the Communists. The Communists in particular benefited from the fallout from the case of Salvatore Giuliano, and more in general from an analysis of the Mafia as a tool used by the large landholders against the peasants. The schematic opposition between bad guys and good guys became the overriding theme in an interpretation of Sicilian history that extended from the abolition of the feudal system (1812). That analysis of history was carried out by a varied array of writers with a shortage of analytical tools but with a great deal of Sicilianist ideology and in a left-wing version, based on a theoretical ongoing plot to prevent the Sicilian "people" from attaining its long-term (supposed) objectives: ownership of the land and regional autonomy. According to this interpretation, there was already a well-defined Mafia in the period of the Risorgimento. That Mafia allied itself with the forces supporting Victor Emmanuel II, and opposed Garibaldi, who wished to give land to the peasants. In 1867, this same Mafia supported the landed agrarian bourgeoisie against (invented) government projects for social reform. And of course, this Mafia was opposed to the Fasci.[19] Significantly, the Communist report overturned the very tradition of Grieco and Sereni, onetime leaders of the party, denying any independent role that might have been played by the intermediate classes (the *gabellotti*, or renters and sublessors of parcels of farmland), with the none-too-persuasive argument that the mere existence of a class-denominated power (that of the large landholders) necessarily made the Mafia "a phenomenon of the ruling classes."[20] Thus, the Mafia itself was not only depicted as the mastermind controlling everything that had happened in Sicilian history, it was also recategorized as nothing more than a mirroring of politics and society at large. This went directly against the warning offered by Rosario Romeo that it was necessary to establish proper conceptual boundaries to the topic, and not to "give in to the temptation" to make the history of the Mafia somehow coincide "with the history of Sicily,"[21] or perhaps more accurately, the temptation to make the history of the Mafia coincide with the depiction that would best match the version that is useful in political terms. This applied to the general reports of the Anti-Mafia, not to the enormous mass of documentation assembled and then (in part) published in dozens and dozens of volumes, in which we can glimpse other tattered fragments of the truth and other interpretative approaches.

Meanwhile, the Mafia gave unmistakable and tragic signs of vigor. In 1960, the police *commissario* (detective sergeant) Cataldo Tandoj was murdered in Agrigento. The usual rumors started by people with ulterior motives attempted to lead the investigators and public opinion astray by striving to whip up a sordid provincial sexual scandal with the involvement of Christian Democratic notables, while in fact this was the far more prosaic story of a functionary who established excessively close ties to the *cosca* (Mafia family) of Raffadali, a *cosca* that was involved in the purchase and sale of large landholdings in the region. He paid for his indiscretions with his life. The big headlines, however, always had to do with Palermo. Between 1955 and 1963, the city was shaken by the battle for control of the Mercati Generali, or city markets. That struggle produced dozens of deaths. In 1962, the so-called first Mafia war broke out between the two opposing groups of the Grecos (from Ciaculli) and the La Barbera brothers. The La Barberas lost the war. One of them (Salvatore) vanished, a victim of the *lupara bianca* (literally, "white shotgun," slang for a murder in which the body is simply made to vanish). The other (Angelo) fled to Milan, where the killers of the opposing family caught up with him, but amazingly he survived. This shooting attracted attention because it marked the first appearance of the Mafia in the very capital of industrialized Italy. Even more astonishing was the explosion of an Alfa Romeo Giulietta packed with dynamite in Ciaculli, on 30 June 1963. It had been intended as an attack on the Grecos, but instead it killed seven policemen. Cars filled with mafiosi roared through the streets, chasing one another. Bombs went off, and machine guns rattled as if it were Chicago in the 1930s. Milan, the Alfa Romeo Giulietta, and the dynamite all constituted unmistakable symbols of modernity. The *latifondo,* or large landholding, was dying, and with it was dying the traditional Sicilian society. Still, in defiance of all predictions, the Palermo Mafia prospered in the field of construction, as well as in smuggling and selling both cigarettes and drugs. How to draw a link between the past and this present? The parliamentary commission presumed a "transplant" of both Mafia and mafiosi from the countryside to the city, mechanically corresponding to the macrosocial phenomenon of the transition from a fundamentally rural society to an urban one. This watershed transition from one era to another entails the substitution of a "new Mafia" in place of an "old Mafia." There seems to have been no awareness of the fact that this type of conceptual opposition had already been employed repeatedly in the past, in relation to other watersheds and turning points, both real and supposed. In any case, the thesis was universally accepted by a diverse array of observers, and so it was established as an unquestionable foundation for the formulation of questionnaires and interviews.

Villalba and Mussomeli, considered exemplary sites of the Mafia phenomenon, are difficult to compare not only with Palermo but also with Corleone, for numerous reasons, not least of which was the absence of a significant level of violence in these two towns in the Caltanissetta area. The way in which Leggio took power bears no resemblance to the mechanism of untroubled succession with which, according to Pantaleone, Genco Russo took over the role of king of the Sicilian Mafia, a role that had previously belonged to Vizzini.[22] In the books written by Pantaleone himself, in the reports of the Anti-Mafia, and in the journalism on the subject, we are clearly in the presence of an obvious overvaluing of the role played by these two characters in the Mafia organizational chart. That chart has recently been drastically revised through the revelations of various *pentiti*. Meanwhile, an improper generalization of the model of the Caltanissetta area has been propagated, even though the specific nature of that model was already pointed out by *L'Ora* journalist Felice Chilanti:

> The capos of the *cosca* of Palermo, of the Trapani and Agrigentino areas, tend to keep to the shadows, avoiding attention. In some cases they actually go into hiding. . . . In Palermo it happens that, when the police provide the biographical details of [a] Mafia capo that has been killed, they may describe him as a "shepherd" or a "manual laborer," even in cases where the capo was a businessman. . . . In Caltanissetta and its province, a mafioso who has become a businessman will put his name on the sign outside the store.

This "prefectorial" Mafia, which grew "under the eyes of the Honorable Aldisio and the Honorable Volpe,"[23] is not the real Mafia. It is a group that, since it had more obvious political characteristics, succeeded in attracting the attention of journalists at the same time as the debates over the struggles for land reform, separatism, and the confluence into the Christian Democratic Party. For that matter, in the long run the overvaluation of the importance of this case tended to deform the perception of the phenomenon as a whole. Suffice it to consider the difficulties in imagining an urban Mafia, or the impossibility of fitting into the conception of the Mafia an individual like Leggio, who was so bound up with a rough and ready violence. As a result, Leggio was for many years described as a "bandit" (or a "gangster") in preference to the other term "mafioso." The Don Calò model, on the other hand, focused on mediation more than violence, ultimately culminating in the paradox of a mafioso who had never ordered a murder, whose power represented a straightforward translation into a local idiom of a larger social power: the *gabellotto*-qua-notable thus corresponding *ipso facto* to the Mafia capo.

In the 1960s, a number of non-Italian sociologists who had come to Sicily to do field research on the Mafia encountered this phenomenon. We already know that the problem in question was American, not Sicilian.[24] The American investigations during the postwar years revived the view of the Mafia as a centralized entity bound up with the issue of ethnic identity and the idea of a foreign conspiracy, with an implicit accusation of the Roosevelt-led Democratic alliance, typically multiethnic, that supposedly was unable or unwilling to oppose the Mafia. Here lies the first misunderstanding in the broad Italian grasp of this issue. At least until Robert Kennedy, the American Anti-Mafia was quintessentially a right-wing phenomenon, while American liberal culture attempted to distill everything to a congeries of clientelistic relations, bossism, small-scale criminality, and, in any case, disorganized crime, devoid of any particular ethnic connotations.

I am no expert on this topic, and so I will not explore the issue of the centralized and monopolistic nature of the various activities of the American Mafia, upon which the majority of the issues are focused.[25] What interests me is the feedback effect in Italy. Jeremy Boissevain, Henner Hess, Anton Blok, and Jane and Peter Schneider came to Sicily in the 1960s in search of a Mafia that mirrored the "traditional" society, with its hierarchies and its culture. The Americans would come to the conclusion that, as they suspected, in its original home as well, the Mafia was nothing more than "a system of godfathers and clients exchanging favors, services, and other advantages."[26] This was a Mafia reduced to the general category of clientelism, which would inevitably wane as the country modernized. "Before there was the Mafia; now there is politics," was the not-very-realistic epitaph that Blok placed on the turning point of the postwar years' "great transformation," at the conclusion of his book.[27] That thesis in various ways corresponded to those prevailing in Italy, ranging from Pantaleone to the general reports of the Anti-Mafia. This was the state of matters when the scholarly debate turned in a new direction with Pino Arlacchi's *La mafia imprenditrice* (1983; English translation, *Mafia Business: The Mafia Ethic and the Spirit of Capitalism* [London: Verso, 1987]), which begins with an observation that is as unambiguous as it is a contrast with the empirical data. In the "two decades following the Second World War," Arlacchi wrote, the Mafia experienced a phase of decline, a "profound crisis"[28] owing to the disintegration of the macrosocial factors (the "traditional" universe) of which it was said to be an emanation. And so, the old Mafia, he claimed, was on the path to extinction, making way for the new Mafia. Thus, *La mafia imprenditrice* adopted the interpretation of the

Anti-Mafia and carried out the politically important operation of focusing on the dynamic, and therefore dangerous, nature of the phenomenon. At the same time, it relegated the past to the chronicles, ignoring the significant and valuable connection with the present. Most importantly, Arlacchi either entirely overlooked the theme of the Mafia as an organization or explored it in a wholly misleading fashion.

I don't know how frequently or extensively the *questore* (administrative director of the district police) of Palermo in 1974, Migliorini, read the social sciences, but it appears that a Mediterranean anthropologist must have been in part responsible for his description of a Mafia sinking into crisis for the collapse of the "sense of respect," a Mafia made up of "individual associations" with order or hierarchies, associations that endure until they have "attained their individual objectives" and then are dissolved. The operative conclusion, then, is triumphally nihilistic: "The repression of the general phenomenon is impossible! Repression of what? Of an idea, of a mentality?"[29]

TERRITORIAL POWER

Leonardo Vitale, son of the late Francesco Paolo, belonged to a venerable Mafia family—family in the sense of both the *cosca* and blood relations. In all likelihood, Vitale was a descendant of one of the two Vitale cousins, Filippo and Francesco Paolo, who were the suspected murderers of Francesco Miceli (1892) as well as clients of Palizzolo and Mafia capos in Altarello di Baida. Altarello di Baida is a *borgata,* or outlying suburb, in which, more than seventy years later, a senior position was still held by a certain Giovan Battista Vitale, Leonardo's uncle, "and a construction contractor [who] in that field committed abuses and acts of violence both in order to purchase land on which to build and in order to sell apartments."[30] Leonardo, therefore, was predestined to become a mafioso, however little there was in his personality to suggest the "hypertrophic ego," the macho behavior, and other cultural traits that we have come to expect in our collective imagination of the mafioso, as consolidated, for the umpteenth time, in the 1970s. He was an emotionally fragile young man, orphaned from an early age, fascinated by the powerful figure of his uncle, to whom he felt a need to prove that he was a "real man," in part to ward off his own doubts about the possibility that he was a homosexual. That was the root of the extreme conformity that he showed with respect to the Mafia environment and the group of mafiosi who surrounded him, as well as his inability to perceive himself as an independent individual. Later, he would reflect on this issue: "I cared nothing about myself, or my life . . . that is to say, I attributed importance only to others,"

"I admired all the others." He became a mafioso because he wanted to feel that he was a member of the gang (*gregario*). In order to prove his toughness, first he killed a horse and then a human being, with no other reason for his actions than that someone else wanted him to do so. It was 1960, and Leonardo was twenty years old. A short time earlier, his uncle may have made an attempt to pull him back from the brink of the abyss. "You see my hands?" he had asked him. "They're stained with blood, and your father's hands were even bloodier."[31] Then, however, it was his uncle who ordered him to commit his first murder and who then took him hunting afterward as a reward.

Immediately thereafter, Leonardo Vitale was inducted with the same ritual described long ago by nineteenth-century sources; a ritual whose existence Hess refused even to admit as a remote "possibility."[32] Hess's skepticism was based on the evident reference to models that were impossible to reconcile with the family- and friendship-based models that social scientists seemed to fixate on. Meanwhile, other information had become available, in addition to that provided by nineteenth-century sources. Years ago Valachi revealed the systems for induction into the American Cosa Nostra. In Sicily, a certain Giuseppe Luppino stated in 1958 that he had refused to carry out a murder after swearing the oath of induction into the *cosca* of Campobello di Mazzara; that information proved sound after Luppino was murdered.[33] The Mafia clearly had handed down its rituals, keeping them intact in a variety of highly diverse contexts, unvaried from one continent to another, and almost never revealing them to outsiders. This offers an explanation of the persistence even of those who are obliged to acknowledge these gaps revealing aspects of the underworld: the affiliations, the organization by "families" and by zones existed in America, too, but only as artificial replacements for the natural "Mafia humus" that existed in Sicily; "rituals and secret languages" can also "emerge here and there ... but they belong to archaic customs and 'philosophies' that have been rendered entirely obsolete."[34] The mind recoils before the things that the ritual unveils: an organization rooted in a specific territory for generations, and therefore relatively impersonal and bound up with a profound self-awareness, which in the Mafia *dei giardini*, or citrus groves, of Altarello was expressed with the detail of puncturing the index finger, not with the usual needle, but rather with a bitter-orange thorn.

The judge for preliminary investigations, Aldo Rizzo, who heard Vitale's confession in 1974, did his best to establish a juridical context for the phenomenon as a criminal conspiracy, which had an "indeterminate program" and was therefore distinct from other conspiracies that had specific limitations in terms of time and scope.[35] In effect, even in a very unfavorable cultural climate, those legal minds that intended to fight the Mafia still insisted on placing it in an associative context. Likewise, already as early as 1965, Cesare Terranova, whose verdicts never lacked some historical and theoretical aspect, emphasized: "[L]et us set aside the fantasies of the past, because the Mafia is not an abstract concept, it is not a state of mind, it is an organized crime structure, efficient and dangerous, articulated into clusters or groups or 'families,' or even more significant, '*cosche.*' . . . There is only one Mafia, neither old nor young, neither good nor bad, there is only the Mafia that is a criminal association."[36]

Let us stop for a moment to explore the targets of this debate. They include conservative opinion that attributes to the old Mafia "a role, even, of preserving equilibrium, or in any case, a positive role in society, replacing or integrating powers that are lacking in the state." They also include liberal or Christian Democratic notables, whose "indulgent and sentimental attitudes, in some cases accepted as authoritative, in other cases steeped in an unmistakable sympathy toward the Mafia or the old Mafia, have on the whole proved to be nothing more than an obstacle to the efforts made to rid our society of this disease." They include lawyers such as Giuseppe Mario Puglia and (more prudently) the fundamental Giuseppe Pitrè. A basis for refuting the myth of the honorable and unbending mafioso is available in the records of the trials conducted under the Fascists, with the "cowardly behavior . . . of the defendants, who rivaled one another in their profusion of confessions, accusations of others, attempts at recriminations and vendettas, and pleading for clemency and pardons."[37] The reference to "His Excellency Giampietro" should come as no surprise in the work of a leftist like Terranova. It serves to reiterate the point, made emphatically under Fascism, that the Mafia is per se a criminal conspiracy. That point is less obvious than it might appear nowadays. In the two major trials put together based on Terranova's preliminary investigations, one against the Corleonese and the other against the top ranks of the Palermo organization, the fundamental juridical tool employed was the same one that had been employed over the past century by both the liberal state and the Fascist state: the relationship between the police and confidential sources who still do not want to be, and cannot be, "named" during the trial.[38] In order for the magistrature that presides over the trial to have full confidence in the basis and reliability of descriptions that are often unsupported by any factual evidence, it is necessary that the reputation (on the basis of which the mafioso is involved in the testimony and the trial) should be sufficient to demonstrate that he is truly capable of bloodcurdling murders. This requirement tends to clash with the concepts expressed in a verdict handed down in 1964: "Even mafiosi have loved ones, even they live a life of human relations that may involve principles of social interaction and rectitude, if not that of honesty. It is not the man who characterizes the action; it is the action that characterizes the man."[39]

Quite to the contrary, it is precisely the fact of being a mafioso that characterizes an action—as long as that status is not confused with a harmless *mafiosità*, but actually represents the explicatory context in which actions and reactions are set, along with agreements, *sgarri* (or breaches of the criminal's code), and reprisals, such as those that took place in the clash between Leggio and Navarra or in the first Mafia war, and as long as the array of interrelations among the various mafiosi serve to identify and explain the alliances in play. Certainly, there are those who might ask: "How can we speak of a criminal conspiracy, of an *'associazione a delinquere,'* when the conspirators, instead of acting in concert, kill one another in turn?" This, however, is mere "nitpicking," as was pointed out as early as 1929 by Natale Costa, prosecuting attorney in the trial of the *cosca* of Piana dei Colli,[40] and even earlier, by the investigators in the trials of the Amorosos and the *stoppagghieri*. In Mafia wars, there is always a "one" that splits into "two," something unified that is then divided. Indeed, conflict is the most powerful evidence, deductive and circumstantial though it may be, of the existence of the organization that the *pentiti* of the 1980s always described with the esoteric name that was already familiar in the United States: La Cosa Nostra.

Buscetta conveys the impression that the term has always been used in Sicily to indicate the Mafia ("We exported it to America").[41] It seems plausible, however, that the oral tradition on which the *pentito* draws for his information has overemphasized the elements of continuity, and perhaps this is one of those feedback effects of the American model, considering the fact that in 1943 in Sicily there was no organization and it would take a new "Gospel of the Mafia" to found it. That new word might well have been brought back by the numerous undesirables, such as Luciano, Coppola, and Genovese, who had been expelled from the United States by the American authorities and sent back to Italy. Another American borrowing might be the use of the term *famiglia* (family) to indicate the *cosca,* or Mafia clan or basic organization. That term is used, among others, by Vitale and Buscetta. Buscetta, however, also emphasized the entirely Palermitan tradition of a Mafia organized wholly on the basis of the territorial unit of the *borgata*. In fact, the reality that emerged from those revelations was entirely "Palermocentric." The same was true of the findings of the ambitious preliminary investigation put together by Terranova in 1965, which in 1968 led to the trial of Catanzaro. That preliminary investigation was based on Carabinieri and police reports, which, in the context of the establishment of the Anti-Mafia, but especially in the wake of the massacre of Ciaculli, had stopped relying on the false comfort of the old bromide, "after all, they're just killing one another off." This bromide had been used to assuage the consciences of the bourgeoisie in the nineteenth century and, still, in the 1950s.

Here the facts speak a different language from that spoken by the Anti-Mafia. There is no evidence of the hypothetical transplantation of the large landhold-ing into the city. If anything, there is evidence of a massive continuity in the settlement of mafiosi in the center of town and especially in the *borgate,* or out-lying suburbs, of Palermo, confirming the facts we have already heard from the stories of the Grecos of Ciaculli-Croceverde and the Vitales of Altarello. This continuity would persist right up to the most recent period and would prove a source of astonishment even to a mafioso from a radically different background, such as the Catania-born Antonino Calderone:

> The mafiosi of Palermo ... are born, live their lives, and die in the same place. Their quarter is everything to them, their families have lived there for generations, and they are all related by blood. There are four or five main surnames; anyone else is an *aggregato* (hireling). At the very most, they might buy a nicer, more impressive-looking house. Stefano Bontade demol-ished his father's house, in Santa Maria di Gesù, and he built a palace on the site; that's what his brother Giovanni did, and Salvatore Inzerillo did the same thing at Bellolampo. They didn't move out of their domain, not even a yard's length away, and they have been the absolute masters there for decades and decades.[42]

This is the sort of background that distinguished the twenty-four capos of Palermo cited in the 1963 report by Carabinieri Lieutenant Mario Malausa, who was killed in the massacre of Ciaculli. They were all natives of the city or the surrounding area; they had all been the targets of prosecution (age permitting) during the trials in the Fascist period that took on the same Palermo *cosche* in which they were still soldiers; and they had been through the same political labyrinths as their colleagues from the interior of the island, right up to their universal affiliation with the Christian Democratic Party.

"He was a fervent supporter of separatism," wrote Malausa about Bene-detto Targia, "but when that movement began to lose power, he followed in the wake of other mafiosi, hopping from one party to another (liberal–monarchic–Christian Democrat). The distaste that he felt for legality clearly demonstrates that it was not a political belief that pushed him toward the Christian Demo-cratic Party, but only personal self-interest."[43]

In effect, even this instrumentalization of the political sphere, in the wake of the separatist binge, represents a constant. Baldassarre Motisi, landowner of *giardini,* wholesale dealer in citrus fruit, Christian Democratic member of the city council who, according to Malausa, "had numerous affiliations with im-portant individuals and who took advantage of them ... in order to consolidate both his position as a mafioso and as a politician," had the same surname and answered to the same description as Francesco Motisi, member of the city council in 1899, and a representative of the Mafia of Mezzomorreale. The twenty-four capos in the report were "criminals of the middle classes" as described by Franchetti: *gabellotti,* landowners and renters of citrus groves, middlemen, importers and exporters, the "industrious" and the "industrialists." This does not rule out social mobility. The clash between the La Barberas and the Grecos involved a new Mafia and an old Mafia, both generated within the Palermo area, in accordance with a dialectic dating back all the way to the times of Palizzolo and the conflict and distinction between the western area and the eastern zone. As Terranova explains it, "The Grecos, we might say, had the necessary four quarters of nobility."

> [T]hey represented the traditional Mafia, the Mafia in trappings of respectability . . . and they are linked by a dense network of friendships, interests, and protections with the leading mafiosi of the Palermo area. They occupy a position of preeminence in the sector of cigarette and drug smugglers. The La Barberas, in contrast, come out of obscurity and their power consists especially in their enterprising ways and their following—a determined band of professional killers.[44]

Among the allies of the La Barberas there was a young Tommaso Buscetta, the son of a glassmaker who also came up "from obscurity." There was also Pietro Torretta, a former confederate of the Giuliano gang and now capo of the Uditore *cosca,* of even greater mafioso nobility. Administrator of the possessions of the Marchesi Di Gregorio, a well-to-do man of the "greatest respect,"[45] Pietro Torretta is thought to have been the son of another Francesco Torretta, whom we find mentioned in the Sangiorgi Report as a member, and not a particularly high-ranking one, of the *cosca* in 1895. Among the other accusations leveled against the younger Torretta was that of the murder of a certain Salvatore Gambino, who was finished off with rifle shots, following a ferocious beating (1963). Just a few hours earlier, Gambino had murdered Filippo and Michele Bonura for frivolous reasons and had then gone to seek refuge with Torretta. Confidential sources attribute his death to the Mafia capo's determination to exercise his role as a regulator and visitor of punishment upon someone responsible for an "unjustified" murder. Nonetheless, the court found that the motive was insufficient, given the minimal nature of relations between the Bonuras and Torretta, in contrast with Torretta's role as godfather to Gambino. The matter might have been clearer if it had been known that sixty years earlier, in this same *borgata,* which represents the cradle of the Palermo Mafia, other members of the Bonura family had been the *cosca* capos of the elder Torretta; and that twenty years later another Bonura would serve in the same position in the same location.

Judicial investigations into various kinds of crimes provide occasional glimpses of this dizzying historical depth. Let us consider the 1970s for a moment. The engineer Giuseppe Di Benedetto, a construction contractor who was short on cash, was pursued for repayment by Baron Sebastiano Provenzano, who had made a loan to him of 30 million lire and who now wanted it back, with interest. Di Benedetto therefore reached out for the mediation of the old Mafia capo of Passo di Rigano, Rosario Di Maggio, who immediately offered to "fix" the situation; to the engineer, who was pleasantly surprised, he explained that he had been a "friend" of his father and *grande elettore* (major electoral lieutenant—*translator's note*) of his grandfather, the Honorable Lo Monte, protector of the Mafia in the years following the First World War. There would be no interest to pay, and the payments would be spread out over an extended period: Rosario Spatola would take over the debt. He was the nephew of Di Maggio, a builder, banker, and money launderer in the group headed by Salvatore Inzerillo, successor to Di Maggio as the head of the *cosca* and chief of the largest gang of drug dealers on the Palermo–New York route.[46] Was this old Mafia or new Mafia? Classical Mafia of the *borgate,* an expression of the continuity of control over a territory that constituted the setting of speculation on land and the ruinous reconstruction, or "Sack," of Palermo? The veto that Michele Greco had exercised on the sale of land that formed part of the hereditary Tagliavia property is explained in light of the traditional role that the Grecos played as leaseholders of that land, and therefore as a sort of Mafia "usucapion" (a mode of acquiring title to property by uninterrupted possession of it for a definite period—such as one year for movables or two for immovables—under a title acquired in good faith) supported by the Honorable Luigi Gioia, liquidator of the Tagliavia estate and a relative of the family. As such, he was in all likelihood at the center of an old network of relations involving the Grecos themselves. "It was unthinkable," commented the preliminary investigators of the *maxiprocesso,* or maxitrial, "that Michele Greco would allow others to purchase, even in part, lands that he already considered to be his property."[47] As beneficiaries of the parceling out of building sites on the Scalea estate, we are not surprised to see the names of the children of the mafioso Gaetano Cinà,[48] formerly *curatolo* of those *giardini* and probably a descendant of another Gaetano Cinà, who already, at the end of the nineteenth century, was a member of the organization.

Let us add another consideration. This is the Palermo of aristocratic decline, the Palermo that still (until the mid-1950s) was governed by a liberal-moderate coalition, and therefore a city that allowed itself to be won over by the (Christian Democratic) political class, originally from the Sicilian interior, which assumed control of the region.[49] We might say that the mafioso class was the only urban "political" class that was able to defend and expand its own power.

The case of the Corleonesi would appear to be an exception, considering the central role that they took on in this story. It remains to be seen whether they were truly interior Mafia. Navarra was the Mafia capo of Corleone. Leggio almost always remained in hiding and spent most of his time in Palermo, where his cattle-rustling interests focused on the meat market. He maintained a permanent garrison in the very heart of the old *Mafia dei giardini* in Piana dei Colli, with a shipping company run by Giacomo Riina and his young nephew Salvatore, who would in fact assume the leadership of the group. What happened in the Corleone area, however, had immediate effects in Palermo. Following the elimination of Navarra, Leggio was summoned to an interview with Salvatore Greco, who demanded he explain his actions, prompting a furious reaction from the new boss.[50] Apparently, the *Mafia dei giardini* was in agreement with Navarra on blocking the construction of a dam to take water from the Corleone area to the Conca d'Oro. By so doing, it would have broken the monopoly on water distribution. Instead, however, Leggio intended to exploit the business opportunities offered in the construction of the dam.[51] The problems of Corleone, then, were not limited to the town itself; instead, they extended along "the chain that, via state route 118, leads to the capital of Sicily."[52] Along that chain there was created a subprovincial space in which the mafiosi of Cinisi (Cesare Manzella and Gaetano Badalamenti), Corleone (Leggio), and Caccamo (Giuseppe Panzeca) played a considerable role. The center, in any case, remained Palermo, the *capoluogo*, which, with the establishment of the Italian region of Sicily, became a capital once again.

What activities safeguard and promote the network of Mafia affiliations? In what way is the Mafia useful?

Let us return to Leonardo Vitale, who—like Henry Hill in *Goodfellas,* who became a gangster because he wanted to "park in front of a fire hydrant and not worry about getting a ticket"—set fire to the car of a Calabrian movie house owner who made the mistake of not offering him free tickets. That was the sole occasion on which Leonardo Vitale acted on his own personal initiative. On every other occasion, his crimes and murders formed part of the daily routine of a collective entity, the *cosca*, or family of Altarello–Porta Nuova, under the leadership of Pippo Calò. His job was to obtain positions guarding *giardini* and construction sites, collect protection fees, make threatening phone calls and write threatening letters, poison watchdogs, set fire to machinery now and again, and, when necessary, murder someone with the old-style shotgun from concealment behind a wall or, in a more modern version, standing up in a Fiat "Topolino," with the top open. Like their fathers and their grandfathers had done, Vitale and his fellow mafiosi generally killed other criminals, such as lemon thieves [*sic!*], rivals in the Mafia hierarchy. Once a businessman died in the course of an attempted kidnapping: if he hadn't made an unexpected move, one of the associates involved in the attempt commented bitterly, "he'd still be alive and we'd have the money."[53]

This mechanism of territorial control made no distinction among the sectors agriculture, construction, and business. The important consideration was that a monopoly over certain sectors of activity, first and foremost protection and guarding, should be the province of the *cosca* and that all other activities should be carried on only with its permission, along with a kickback from the profits from those activities. This was also true for what little manufacturing and industrial activity was carried on in Palermo. The shipyard owned by the Genoan Piaggio Company hired out the Acquasanta *cosca* to perform a number of internal services, including responsibility for maintaining order among the employees, using various methods of bland clientelism or harsh repression. The latter was the case in 1947, when Zu Cola D'Alessandro and his *picciotti* (lower-level mafiosi) drew their guns. Another Genoan company, which founded a branch company called Elettronica Sicula, began with the very purchase of the land on which it planned to build its plants. In that context, the company relied on the mediation of the Mafia capo of S. Maria di Gesù, Don Paolino Bontate. Don Paolino exerted his authority, among other things, to overcome local resistance to the drilling done to gain access to the water table, a topic that was always contentious in the Palermo area. When the time came to inaugurate the plant and put it into operation, a "truly depressing . . . spectacle" unfolded. The new plant director, Aldo Profumo, had only just begun his speech when he suddenly realized he had lost his audience. The "numerous group of representatives and functionaries from the regional government and the city administration" that had been seated listening to his speech suddenly leapt to their feet and, as one man, ran toward the door. It was a race to see who could be the first to greet and bow to Don Paolino, who had just walked into the hall. We have to assume that the Mafia capo, in a bid to acquire "productive" investment, must have called in chits on many of his relationships as a former monarchist, now a Christian Democrat, perhaps even relying on his blood ties to the member of parliament (also a Christian Democrat), Margherita Bontate. In exchange, he was given say over the hiring of the factory workers and the contracts for supplying the factory cafeteria, as well as some substantial cash payments. In 1959, he personally demanded, and his request was granted, that the CGIL (Italian labor union) should be prevented from running its list of candidates for the internal commission. As Profumo declared, "Paolo Bontà is useful to me, because he makes sure that I have water, he gives me the land to expand the factory, and I rely upon him to find workers for the factory."[54]

The relationship between the engineer and plant director Profumo and Don Paolino is useful in understanding the continuum linking protection, mediation, and partnership, and how that continuum should be considered in the familiar phenomenon of the conversion of *guardiani* (rural watchmen) into profiteers, *gabellotti*, and businessmen of all sorts. The mediocrity of the crimes of someone like Leonardo Vitale represents nothing more than the ground-floor level of Mafia activities. The same tools, when placed in the hands of more skilled individuals, led to quite different outcomes. Let us take the case of the La Barbera brothers, whose point of departure was much lower down the social scale. They were a pair of punk *borgata* muggers. In fact, the Anti-Mafia described them as "common criminals who have infiltrated their way into the meshes of the Mafia nework."[55] As in Leggio's case, there was a continuing tendency to place excessive emphasis on the old stereotype of the mafioso-qua-notable, with a corresponding underestimation of the role of violence in establishing the Mafia hierarchies and propelling quick and ambitious rises through the ranks. The two former thieves were soon transformed into extortionate protection-providing guardians of villas, then construction sites. In this context, they served an ancillary role that was a customary one to Salvatore La Barbera, who from his youth had served in the position of *garzone carrettiere* (apprentice teamster), in the Partanna *borgata*. Finally, the two brothers founded a company working in construction, serving contractors and entrepreneurs who enjoyed— and paid for—Mafia protection. The Mafia capo Bartolo Porcelli put them in touch with Eugenio Ricciardi, the right-hand man of the builder and developer Salvatore Moncada. Of course, the career of the protector and profiteer needed to proceed within the context of a Mafia group. In this specific case, that group was the "central Palermo" family. It was in that context that relations with other aspiring rivals had to be moderated. Here, in fact, Angelo La Barbera brought his rivalry with Ricciardi to a head by luring him into an ambush with Gaetano Galatolo, also known as Tanu Alatu (1952). This murder marked the beginning of the two brothers' climb into the heart of the Mafia power, at the leadership of the group of families that included the family of Altarello-Porta Nuova.

The La Barberas replaced Ricciardi not only in terms of status but also in his various businesses. When Giuseppe Ricciardi, son of the victim, found the trucks of his father's small shipping company stripped of wheels and theatrically jacked up on hoists, he understood that it was time to sell everything to the victors, and he found a job in a store selling household appliances. But the environment remained the same. The young man's new employers, Giulio Pisciotta and Vincenzo Maniscalco, were scheming against the *cosca*'s leadership. They pooled forces with other questionable individuals and wound up putting forward an extortion scheme targeting none other than Moncada (1960). Maniscalco was killed in an ambush. Then the La Barberas presented themselves, along with Tommaso Buscetta and Salvatore Gnoffo, in front of the Brancaccio train station, where Pisciotta and his partner Natale Carollo, accompanied by Ricciardi, had come to take delivery of merchandise for their store. It had been Ricciardi himself who had provided (involuntarily?) accurate information to the men who had murdered his father. At gunpoint, Pisciotta and Carollo were invited to come along to a "meeting of the minds" from which they were never to return. Ricciardi was told to go home and forget everything he had seen. At least, that was the first version that Ricciardi provided. He later changed his account of events, saying that he had been subjected to torture. Finally, he denied even that detail in a desperate round of contradictions, claiming "that he knew no one, that he was a sick man, that he had lost a well-paid job because he was his father's son, that he was afraid of everything and everyone," and that all he wanted was to "be allowed to live in peace."[56] Clearly, the life of the son of a Mafia capo is not an easy one.

MILITARY ROLES AND TRAFFICKERS

The primitivist and ruralist lenses through which most observers filtered their views were the main factor responsible for the astonishment that greeted the presence, immediately after the Second World War and thereafter, of mafiosi along the international smuggling routes, both for cigarettes and for drugs heading for the United States. The trans-Atlantic trade represented one of the initial characteristics of the history that is narrated here, first of all with the citrus exports, without which there never would have been the Mafia of the *giardini* and the *giardini* themselves. Hidden, in fact, in the crates of citrus fruit were opium and morphine, which were traveling from Palermo to New York in the 1920s, in sufficient quantities to trigger a series of trade restrictions from the American authorities in reprisal.[57] Alongside the traffic in merchandise of various sorts was a trade in people, with the flow of emigration beginning at the turn of the century and subsequently, even though these flows steadily declined in volume. Among others, individuals like Calogero Orlando continued to cross the ocean. Calogero Orlando was born in Terrasini in 1906. He left for Detroit in 1922 with $400, and he returned home in 1928 with $800. Over time he became wealthy in the course of a steady series of voyages between America, Sicily, and Spain, with an oil and cheese import-export business and with the processing, packaging, and sale of sardines and salted anchovies. At least, that is what he claimed. According to the police, the merchandise he was trafficking in was drugs.[58] Let us keep in mind that in the 1930s, Lucky Luciano was already importing drugs from Europe, perhaps through individuals such as Pietro Davì, also known as Jimmy l'Americano, who returned from the United States in 1934 and had already been arrested in Milan in 1935 for this unsavory traffic. In 1950 he resurfaced as an importer of morphine from Germany. But this was already after the Second World War, when it was America that came to Italy, with the Marshall Plan and a flow of "undesirables."

Foremost among these undesirables was none other than Luciano, released early from prison and sent back to his birthplace following an obscure negotiation with his former nemesis, Governor Thomas Dewey. It was unquestionably Luciano who got the operation started again, beginning with the identification of the "gold-bearing vein" that was available for profitable mining in the pharmaceutical industries in northern Italy, for a steady supply of raw materials.[59] Luciano then proceeded to establish relationships with drug refiners in Marseilles. Once they had freed him, the Americans seemed obsessed with Luciano; they considered him the "king, or at least a member of the royal family,"[60] guiding a traffic that was pouring into their country. Hence protests arose aimed at Italian authorities, whom they accused of overlooking these illegal activities. In effect, the Italians were reluctant to construct an investigative mechanism capable of tracing the complex meanders of the drug trade. Luciano was a respectable foreign businessman; perhaps his business was illegal, but it was harmless to Italy, where no one produced or (more importantly) consumed drugs. The social alarm triggered by smuggling was inevitably mild: here it was inaudible.

The "lieutenant of Lucky Luciano in Palermo" was Antonio Sorci, also known as *"Ninu u riccu"* ("Nino the Wealthy") because he had made good use of the profits from drug dealing to purchase land from the breakup of the old Villa d'Orléans.[61] He was joined by Rosario Mancino, a former longshoreman who had become the owner of a company exporting citrus fruit, at least apparently, though in reality the main export was heroin. That heroin might well have come through Lebanese channels procured by Mancino, who was quite at home in Beirut. One of those mixed citrus-heroin shipments was received in America by Gaetano Badalamenti (1951). Badalamenti was a mafioso from Cinisi who often enjoyed the hospitality in Detroit of his brother Emanuele and the local Mafia. Apparently, there was a Luciano–Sorci–Mancino–La Barbera network, corresponding perhaps to the Palermo organization for drug and cigarette smuggling. The sources of the Guardia di finanza (Italian treasury police) stated that

that organization was under the command of Pietro Davì, whom we have already encountered. Whether this could be a "monopolistic structure governed by Luciano" cannot be stated.[62] Also according to the same source, aside from Davì's organization, there was another (competing?) organization of international drug traffickers operating in Palermo under the command of Gaspare Ponente. Ponente was killed in 1958 and was replaced by Salvatore Greco "*l'ingegnere*" ("the engineer"). Independent of Luciano, another Sicilian American, Frank Coppola from Partinico, went into the drug business. He was later caught red-handed, thanks, apparently, to a tip from none other than Luciano. Although the exact links were unclear, there were others in the same line of business, such as the Caneba brothers or Serafino Mancuso, from Alcamo, who went back and forth between the United States and Italy, negotiated with the Marseilles drug traffickers on the quality and price of the product, and arranged shipments.

At this point, it would be reasonable to explore the question of why the heroin trade passed through the hands of the Sicilians; it was produced in the form of opium in the Near and Far East, transformed into heroin in France, and consumed in the United States. The fact that the drugs were hidden in the trunks of Sicilian emigrants offers a first clue to the way in which the networks linking Sicily and America were reutilized. The Nice-born Pascal Molinelli, for instance, worked with mafiosi (Buscetta) because they arranged "to find customers and negotiate with them."[63] The Sicilian drug traffickers possessed a strategic resource: trust-based relationships that linked them to the buyers for the product. In fact, they were trustees of the purchasers—hence the role of groups that, even in comparison with the "grand" Palermo organization, seem to have specialized in working both shores of the Atlantic Ocean. Especially to the west of Palermo, an area with age-old ties to Tunisia and therefore with clandestine emigration, there were *cosche* that were notoriously linked to drug trafficking and were distinctly Sicilian American, such as the *cosche* of Cinisi, Alcamo, and Partinico, and especially the *cosche* of Castellammare del Golfo, the hometown of the Bonannos of New York and the Magaddinos of Buffalo. Castellammare del Golfo produced an outsized share of the mafiosi of the United States, even though it claimed no such role in the Mafia of Sicily. Here Gaspare Magaddino and Diego Plaja, relatives and friends of the American bosses, still reigned. As at the turn of the century, the circuit of migration triggered a network of commercial Mafia "colonies" that were in some sense comparable to the close-knit Jewish or Greek colonies that managed the long-distance trade of the modern age; or else the British and the Americans at the beginning of the nineteenth century, who sent their sons to Sicily to organize the citrus imports, transfer financial resources to ensure the citrus crops were produced reliably, and ship these perishable goods across the ocean aboard fragile sailing ships. In all these cases, the fiduciary bond, whether it was based on family ties or ethnic ties, served to reduce the great risks that were intrinsic to the transaction. In the drug trade, the risks were confiscation by the police, but also the *bidone* (or rip-off), the fraud that always lay in ambush.

These organizations do not correspond to the "families" of Palermo's Cosa Nostra, inasmuch as they work in terms not of territorial control but of long-distance trading. Two distinct organizational models are at play here, and in order to analyze them we can begin with the dialectic, suggested for the New York case by Alan Block, between power syndicate and enterprise syndicate. A power syndicate essentially tends toward "extortion, not business," while enterprise syndicates "tend to operate in the arena of such illicit undertakings as prostitution, gambling, smuggling, and drugs."[64] In Palermo, we describe as a power syndicate the territorial structure of the families, with their rigid affiliations, their formidable stability over time, their military force, and therefore their ability to perform, beginning with the mechanism of the *guardianìa,* the function of substituting the institutions responsible for law enforcement throughout the circuit of the administration of extortion and protection. An enterprise syndicate, on the other hand, represented the far more mobile business network that already existed in the nineteenth century for cattle rustling and smuggling, and that now managed the trade in cigarettes and drugs. The fact that the soldiers of the *cosche* themselves should be involved in those networks does nothing to invalidate the distinction, either conceptually or empirically. Buscetta explained that the families did no more than to issue to their adherents "permission" to participate in various illicit businesses. For that matter, the network could not be entirely mafioso in nature. Among those involved in the network were natives of Tangiers (Tangerines), Americans, Neapolitans, Marseillais, and Chinese, adventurers, women, the honorable and the dishonorable, thugs or *scassapagghiara,* and bankers. That is what happened with the smuggling of cigarettes, a line of commerce that developed out of the initiative of "groups of international adventurers, mostly Americans" who took up residence in the free ports of Tangiers and, later, Gibraltar. They extended their reach from there toward Genoa and Sicily, respectively, through contacts with Marseillais and mafiosi; relying upon "certain import-export companies in Tangiers and in Switzerland, and on Jewish-controlled banks in Tangiers for the financing."[65] The traffic required

> the availability of immense capital and considerable resources to purchase or lease ships . . . ; purchase or deploy in France and Italy clandestine radio transmitting equipment; arrange to pay for the tobacco embarked in

Tangiers and Gibraltar (the cargo of a single ship generally cost the organizers of the traffic an average of forty thousand dollars); hire, pay, and deploy in Italy and in other countries the officers and crews of the ships, and the radio operators; accept and absorb the eventual losses of men and vehicles; transfer sizable financial resources to Switzerland, Italy, France, and Malta.[66]

We find mafiosi such as Badalamenti, Buscetta, Angelo La Barbera, Calcedonio Di Pisa, and Vincenzo Spadaro waiting for deliveries on the beach, moving from country to country, negotiating with such notables of the Corsican and Marseillais underworld as Paul Paoli or with Milanese gangsters like Romano Scarabelli. We find them establishing contacts with the Neapolitans to create another terminus in the distribution network when the police began to monitor the Sicilian coasts a little too closely. A fundamental role was played on a trans-European scale by Salvatore Greco *"l'ingegnere,"* "the financier who was also in charge of contacts with foreign organizations,"[67] working in close coordination with the other Marseillais boss, Elio Forni. But there were also lower levels at which the mafiosi came into contact with individuals who had nothing in common with their myths and their rituals or with their ethnic and cultural extraction. The pregnant wife of a Tangerine smuggler who was arrested in 1960 claimed for herself and her child-to-be the money owed by the "friends of Palermo" to her jailed husband: "You over there are numerous, and with all your numbers you'll never notice a little contribution to one person. . . . I feel certain that if you were [in my position] you would already have drawn your pistols." Then she threatened vendetta, adding, "I'm not afraid of your Mafia."[68] Here we should note not only the recklessness of a "foreign" woman using the word "Mafia" in writing (which could represent a threat that she would reveal secrets to the authorities), but also the absence of internal solidarity in the group of smugglers, in clear contrast with the care customarily devoted to the families of members within a Mafia group who had been arrested.

This diversity led to negative consequences in terms of security. In contrast, the security of the power syndicate had been well protected by the organization's compact structure. This was a root cause of the great power of Sicilian American families (both Mafia families and blood families). The drug traffickers were in greater danger from betrayals and tips, and in any case were involved in activities that inevitably left evidence (ships, merchandise, telephone calls, letters, bank accounts and transfers), and they were occasionally caught red-handed. Their level was always on the surface and visible, and subject to forensic proof of crime, while the level of the territorial organization remained mysterious and subterranean. There was also a potential conflict between the two organizational spheres. Buscetta described being temporarily *posato* (expelled) from his family in 1958 for having established too many outside contacts. "Smuggling cigarettes involved people that did not share the Mafia mind-set."[69] Let us recall the concerned notes from the American families in relation to the drug trade. Moreover, in the management of large-scale traffic, the mafiosi necessarily had to work side-by-side not only with "outsiders," but also with members of different *cosche*, with the risk that family solidarity might be outweighed by business loyalties. Shared affiliation entailed a simple, generic right to enter into the business of fellow-affiliated members. In practical terms, however, in order to exercise that right, managerial skills and more importantly, financial resources, were needed. "In the drug trade, everyone worked on their own. If you had more economic resources, you got more work."[70] This explains the vast economic and social differences among the individuals operating in the Mafia universe and within the individual *cosche*. And among them (as in any other universe), there were both rich and poor.

The territorial structures could provide limiting or moderating influences, through more-or-less instrumental internal polemics, or they could rebalance access to resources among the affiliates, but they could never hinder the development of profitable activities: the conversion of *guardiani* into profiteers is a phenomenon that is repeated continuously throughout the entire history of the Mafia, a phenomenon that should be considered an essential part of that history. Broken down, then, into vast networks of relationships, the affiliation with the Mafia continued to encourage the identification of Sicilian groups and Sicilian American groups, with their "similar customs, similar criminal philosophy, and a shared heritage."[71] This represented a privileged space for communication comparable to that of Masonic membership for politicians, officials, and businessmen. There existed, however, a more specific level of reciprocal functionality between the enterprise syndicate and the power syndicate. Illegal undertakings need protection as much as and more than legal ones do, since they cannot turn to the public authorities to safeguard their interests.

> The economic consequences of this unusual situation are numerous and varied: illegal assets are subject both to legal confiscation and to theft; property rights cannot be based on written documents, and they are in general defined in an unclear and uncertain manner. . . . Theft, fraud, bankruptcy, and insolvency, mistrust and disagreements . . . are much more common in illegal markets than in legal ones. As a result, there is not only a greater demand for protection, but protection is also all the more difficult to supply. And needless to say, those markets are invariably attractive to the Mafia.[72]

In the smuggling of cigarettes, the Italian Guardia di Finanza, or financial police, does not rule out "that certain Mafia *cosche* do no more than take a percentage of the earnings of the smuggling organizations (the so-called *pizzu*)."[73] The Mafia, Gambetta would further say, enjoys a commercial "brand" that is particularly respected as a result of the venerable age of the "company," which means continuity in business and (presumably) honesty in business. But, I would add, there are other features, such as its (presumed) capacity to act as a "state," to establish rules, to monitor, and to punish. This relation between common criminality and Mafia criminality also emerges in Reuter's study of the New York case.[74] "The nature of my office is to determine if there has been abuse," wrote Calogero Di Carlo, a member of the Gambino family, in the language of a ministerial inspector, to the drug courier from Marsala, Vincenzo Martinez.[75] In a broad array of circumstances, during the course of frenetic negotiations to resolve disputes, ascertain frauds, regulate payments, and attribute the ownership of goods and capital, the role of both American and Sicilian hierarchies appears to be that of guarantor.

Using these tools, let us attempt to reexplore the history of the Mafia in the 1950s. When Lucky Luciano first arrived in Italy, he took great care to refrain from any interference in restructuring territorial powers in Sicily: he had neither the interest nor the strength to enter into that issue. Instead he took up residence in Naples,[76] an ideal location from which to carry on relations with America, France, northern Italy, and Sicily. The man who was slapped in the face, without consequences, by a small-time local gangster at the Agnano[77] racetrack was not the head of the Mafia but a businessman and mediator. The famous Palermo meeting at the Hotel des Palmes (October 1957) represented an effort to shift the course of events into a new direction. In view of the imminent shutdown of the Cuban base of operations, the result of the burgeoning Castro revolution, Joe Bonanno and other American Cosa Nostra capos did their best to persuade the locals to agree to an amicable division of resources. That effort was not especially successful, at least according to the observation that is attributed to Genco Russo. Speaking to his American compatriot Santo Sorge in the luxurious hallways of the hotel, Genco Russo said: "Quannu ci sunu troppi cani supra un ossu, beato chiddu chi pò stari arrassu ["When there are too many dogs fighting for a bone, you're lucky if you can stay far away from it," a comment overheard by an undercover policeman]."[78] Aside from this colorful but anomalous individual, the other attendees represented the more typically Sicilian American Mafias: the Badalamentis of Cinisi-Detroit, perhaps a few people from Alcamo, certainly the Magaddinos and the Plajas, and the Castellamarese Frank Garofalo, who had just returned that year to Sicily from America.[79] Seen from the point of view of the Bonanno and Magaddino families of

New York City and Buffalo, that is to say, from the terminus of the migratory chain, Sicily might have seemed like a minor appendage of Castellammare del Golfo where everything is subordinate to the American connection; that, however, would be an optical illusion.

According to Buscetta,[80] it was the Americans who suggested creating a commission in Sicily based on the New York model. However, we should explore to what degree the results matched the intentions. A decision-making body for the Palermo provincial area was established, from which the Trapanese were necessarily excluded. Initially, second-rank figures (simple "soldiers") were seated on the commission, not family capos, an element that was symbolically meant to emphasize the fact that the territorial leadership of the *cosche* remained sovereign. Despite the fact that thereafter the powers of the commission rapidly expanded, within it the commanding groups, the Grecos, the La Barberas, Torretta, and Leggio, were independent of the Americans. Indeed, to the best of our knowledge, they had no trans-Atlantic blood relations of any importance. Certainly, the traffickers had their points of contact in Palermo. Luciano was most frequently in touch with the La Barberas, while within the Greco group, there was an especially close interaction between the two cousins: the great smuggler ("*l'ingegnere*") and the *cosca* capo that everyone described as the true leader ("*chicchiteddu*"). The fact that Luciano (and therefore, the Americans?) should have supported the La Barberas[81] was not enough to save them from defeat. This is a useful demonstration of the fact that the enterprise syndicate cannot settle power struggles within the power syndicate. Following the initial period of control by the Caccamese Giuseppe Panzeca, *chicchiteddu* took over as head of the Mafia Commission. According to the Carabinieri and the police, that commission was founded in response to the formation of the Anti-Mafia Commission: the official state continued to constitute a good model for the anti-state. Even Terranova described as "vague and unconfirmed"[82] these police reports, which instead displayed an admittedly relative capacity to penetrate secretly into secret matters. I do not believe that the commission was founded merely as an imitation of the American model, nor do I find decisive what Bonanno wrote: "The commission was not a part of my Tradition; there was no body of this kind in Sicily."[83] In Palermo there existed a supervisory body at the end of the nineteenth century, and probably there was such a body in other periods as well. As early as 1951, the Palermo Centro families expressed a common decision-making structure, and there were a series of meetings with other city groups.[84]

Indeed, the principle of the territorial monopoly is easy to set forth but difficult to maintain, except through the reciprocal recognition among the various groups, with negotiations to obtain permission to act in territories controlled by others or to establish the degree of advantage (a percentage, an exchange of favors) that can be obtained by allowing others to operate in one's own territory. A portion of Leonardo Vitale's daily life was devoted to precisely this sort of negotiation, and in order to simplify them it was necessary to establish a permanent venue for those negotiations. In order to resolve a dispute between the Altarello–Porta Nuova *cosca* and the Noce *cosca* over the right to impose bribes over a certain zone, Salvatore Riina, Leggio's former hired killer, who had now risen to the rank of person of authority, was appointed to manage, mediate, and coordinate the negotiations. From the little island where he was confined, Giovan Battista Vitale accepted the decision that had gone against him, while still insisting that in any case Altarello needed to be given a "taste."[85] In some cases, the victim of extortion reached out to mafiosi from other areas. That was what the businessman Silvio Faldetta did. When he was faced with the demand for 50 million lire (an especially daunting sum in 1983), he set out to find his "usual interlocutor." This time, however, he was unable to track him down. The zone was in fact controlled by Pippo Calò, capo of the Porta Nuova *cosca*, and it was to Calò that Faldetta was obliged to turn for the negotiations.[86] In some cases, however, this intersection produced clashes. A nephew of Buscetta who owned a construction firm that operated in Termini Imerese, for instance, received a series of threats and attacks from the local Mafia capo Pino Gaeta. Here the territorial jurisdiction clearly clashed with the eminent authority of a Cosa Nostra notable of the stature of Don Masino Buscetta. When Don Masino attempted to reason with Gaeta, Gaeta responded with a defamatory accusation. Buscetta's nephew, he said, spent too much time hanging out with policemen. In the end, a compromise was reached through Calò's mediation. In other cases, however, the differences of opinion would have bloodier consequences.

Evidently, relations span territorial boundaries, and influences intersect and overlap. Not only the vast networks of international traffic, but also the more restricted network of city business follows power axes that cannot be limited within the perimeter of the territorial sovereignty of individual families. The boundaries are not so clearly definable, and here we are not talking only about the topographic meaning of the term. A mafioso can control the political relations necessary for activities to be performed in various areas. A company may need protection in all the geographic contexts in which it operates, and it may turn to a single *cosca* for that protection; a company providing construction-related services such as the one run by the La Barberas might have clients in various locations around the city (or even in other cities). I don't believe that Recredit—*Società di riscossione crediti per conto di aziende private*, or Company for Collecting Debt on Behalf of Private Companies—can be restricted to the territories controlled by a single family; Salvatore Inzerillo was a partner in the company. Likewise, the two mafiosi hired by a northern company involved in the construction of the Palermo–Mazzara *autostrada* necessarily worked over broad geographic areas, as they had been assigned to oversee "the issuance of permits by the landowners involved in the execution of the work, in order to ensure that construction itself should immediately get under way."[87]

A single group, the Acquasanta group, controlled the *guardianìa* of the Hotel delle Palme and of Villa Igea, both of which were managed by the same company but located in two different sections of the city. The Acquasanta group demanded that the management make use of its own suppliers for the meat purchased—this is indicative of a move toward a monopoly over a given sector rather than over a certain territory. A new development such as the move of the general markets from the Zisa quarter to the Acquasanta quarter (January 1955) provoked a ferocious fight. In that fight, the groups that controlled the system of advances to producers and commercial intermediation were on one side, along with the more traditional Mafia of the *giardini,* where the Grecos were consolidating their power, especially following the death of Antonino Cottone. On the other side was the *cosca* that claimed to have the right to control the market owing to territorial jurisdiction.[88] There were dozens of killings. In the Ciaculli group, a Francesco Greco, a "wholesaler dealing in fruit and vegetables," was killed. The Acquasanta *cosca* paid a much heavier price in blood. Two of its chiefs were killed in rapid succession—the previously mentioned Tanu Alatu and Cola D'Alessandro; a third capo, Salvatore Licandro, was pursued all the way to Como and murdered there.[89]

The Mafia war proved that the rules of territorial jurisdiction were not automatically applied when major overriding interests were in play. We could certainly seek the reasons for the disagreement in the very nature of the market, in the system of relationships among producers, middlemen, promoters, and wholesalers. We could accuse the authorities of having failed (or declined) to find a way to encourage free competition, instead of conniving in the perpetuation of the monopoly over which these groups were battling. Here, however, we are focusing on the external, surface nature of the phenomenon, as if the Mafia were continually regenerated from given economic or social conditions. In reality, however, there already exists a power that considers certain sectors of the economy as a strategic objective. That power is capable of imposing its will with the application of a form and degree of terror such that it renders moot any internal modifications of that sector. The triggering factor of the war consists of an interference, a short circuit between the network of potential interests and territorial powers. The claim has been made that the elimination of Mafia violence from the sector in the most recent period is a result of the antimonopoly policy adopted by municipal authorities, and that the market was thus responsible for defeating the Mafia.[90] It is my view that the real factor at play was a shift in the equilibrium among the *cosche*; for instance, the weakening (and subsequent destruction) of the Acquasanta *cosca*. These developments made possible the reestablishment of a market dialectic, while at the same time, among other things, facilitating certain "courageous" decisions made in the municipal bureaucracies. The determining factor lay in the power syndicate's decision of whether to occupy or abandon a given sector. Among other considerations, let us point out that green markets, fishing facilities, slaughterhouses, and construction sites are the setting, not necessarily the cause, of conflicts. Drug dealers may shoot one another, but drugs may not be the triggering cause, or the sole cause, of these wars.

Let us attempt to analyze the reasons for the first Mafia war (1962). It all began, we are told, with a large drug deal organized by Cesare Manzella, an Italian American in Cinisi, with the involvement of the Grecos and a group that financed it; the La Barberas also formed part of that group. The person who directly and physically managed the transaction as a trustee for Manzella and his partners was Calcedonio Di Pisa. Unfortunately, Di Pisa delivered to the investors a sum that was lower than the expected yield, by "many millions of lire," claiming that one of the American buyers had defrauded him. The La Barberas made inquiries in America and concluded that, quite to the contrary, it was Di Pisa who had pocketed the money. But the commission responsible for the investigation decided otherwise, and Di Pisa was allowed to go unpunished. The decision did not settle the matter for the La Barberas, who decided to take measures on their own against Di Pisa and against Manzella. Both men were killed, triggering a murderous reaction from the Grecos, a series of actions and reprisals. The final outcome was the ruin of the La Barberas and the dissolution of the family of central Palermo (Palermo Centro).

It is quite evident even in this reconstruction that the failure to find a solution to the conflict that developed out of the drug traffic was attributable to other questions. The Grecos and the La Barberas who financed the business in partnership were, however, split by rivalries inasmuch as they represented two potentates that were expanding, respectively, in eastern Palermo and in western Palermo. As the battle grew, groups split along existing lines of division and, in all likelihood, were unable to reconcile their differences because of preexisting rivalries. Another factor was the independent attitude of the La Barberas, which called into question the commission's capacity to govern, judge, and punish (or acquit). I should, however, point out another interpretation that was offered by the Mafia itself, that is, by the two *pentiti* Buscetta and Calderone.[91] According to them, the person responsible for the death of Di Pisa was Michele Cavataio, successor to Tanu Alatu as the capo of the Acquasanta Mafia; they claimed that Cavataio intended to put the blame for the killing on the La Barberas in order to provoke a split in the commission. The problems were only made worse by the refusal of certain senior Mafia figures to implement the rule that called for each of them to choose between the position of family capo and that of representatives seated on the commission. Clearly, such a rule was intended to reduce individual power in favor of a more collegial style of supervision, and perhaps also to accelerate the pace at which young blood would be introduced into the leadership. The two interpretations are not mutually exclusive, but the second version focuses more on the internal problems of the power syndicate in creating and applying a common law through the commission, while military power was left in the hands of the individual families. Even if all the groups accepted a rule, they could always arrange to sabotage that rule through self-serving moves, misinformation, and the cunning ploys of the members. In the ongoing battle between the eastern sector, controlled by the Grecos, and the central and western zone of Porta Nuova–Altarello–Acquasanta–Piana dei Colli, that is, La Barbera–Cavataio–Torretta, the Grecos continually emerged victorious but never could manage to bring the fighting to a halt. The bomb at Ciaculli brought a thundering collapse to the commission's attempts to ensure peace, that is, an equilibrium among the groups.

METASTASIS

After the massacre of Ciaculli, the generation of the Grecos, the La Barberas, the Buscettas, and the Leggios (all born between 1923 and 1928) encountered for the first time an antagonist that had been largely absent throughout the course of the 1950s. That antagonist was state repression, guided not by the ordinary administrative considerations, but by a more specific political will. At first, the impact was substantial. A new law relegating mafiosi to internal exile and the preliminary investigations being carried out by Terranova unhinged and dismantled the Mafia's organizational structures, triggering the dissolution of the commission, and a general and complete paralysis of the families. "Cosa Nostra no longer existed in the Palermo area after 1963. It was out of operation."[92] A number of the leaders went into hiding. The Grecos did not emerge from hiding again, while Leggio seemed to be in intermittent clandestinity. Leggio was arrested and then released, managed mysteriously to elude the restrictive measures imposed by the police, and then vanished, only to be caught, arrested, and finally brought to justice in 1974. By this time, however, we are firmly in the midst of a phase of revival for the Mafia groups. That revival was encouraged by the outcome of the trials of Catanzaro (1968) and Bari (1969): most of the bosses emerged undamaged and unpunished. Those were the years in which the Mafia networks extended to cover northern Italy, in part through an unintended consequence of the measures of internal exile, based on the usual prejudice that saw the Mafia as a simple by-product of a "primitive" environment, and not something that could take root and flourish in the "developed" world. The "developed" world, quite to the contrary, proved to be a market that was perhaps more fruitful even than Sicily. Among the new business opportunities were kidnapping and drug dealing. For varying periods of time, and in some cases, permanently, Pippo Calò and Luciano Leggio (among others) moved to the Italian mainland.

Meanwhile, the problem of the man who was by now identified as the common enemy of the *cosche* of Palermo, Cavataio, had come to the forefront. After a series of inconclusive negotiations, Salvatore Greco decided to cut the Gordian knot of that situation. He sent a team of killers disguised as policemen to the offices of the building company in Viale Lazio where Cavataio had his lair. Cavataio was one of several who were killed in the furious shootout that followed (December 1969). The membership of the squad of killers offers a clear X-ray of the alliances at work. There were two Corleonese killers, including the group's chief torpedo, Bernardo Provenzano. There were two men from the Bontate family, and a certain Damiano Caruso, who lived in Villabate but was a member of the Riesi family.[93] For the first time, we see the capo of a Caltanissetta *cosca*, Giuseppe Di Cristina, drawn into the resolution of an internal matter of the Palermo power syndicate, at the request of the Palermitans themselves, precisely in the role of an outsider. He was appointed to negotiate with Cavataio and, ultimately, to betray him, along with the Pippo Calderone of the Catanian family of Cosa Nostra.

There thus emerged especially close ties between Palermo and the rest of the island. Certainly, two particular cases, the Caltanissetta area and the Catania area, were different. On the Sicilian interior, there are numerous noteworthy cases of historical continuity: in Riesi, Favara, Raffadali, and Siculiana, the network of Mafia affiliations must never have been interrupted. Di Cristina was the son of a Mafia capo; Leonardo Messina, the young *pentito* from San Cataldo in the 1980s, could boast a genuine Mafia pedigree: "My family is one that has belonged by tradition to Cosa Nostra, and I am a seventh-generation member. . . . I was not *affiliato,* or made a member, because I was a robber or because I was capable of killing people; it's because by family tradition I was destined to be a member."[94]

In these areas, the Mafia—which seemed on the verge of extinction, destined to go the way of the large landholdings and the sulphur mines—was revitalized by a new contact with Cosa Nostra; Messina says "regenerated."[95] The regional government represented an important element of centralization around the focal point of public spending. One emblematic case concerns the dam of Solarino, built by the Rendo group of Catania. The construction of the dam was subcontracted to satisfy the appetites of the mafiosi of Caltanissetta, such as Giuseppe Madonia, leaving a trail of murders.[96] Di Cristina took a position with the Ente Minerario Siciliano (Sicilian Mining Agency), a big, inefficient regional pork barrel that managed the decline of the sulphur mines of the Sicilian interior.[97] From there, he cast his eyes toward Palermo and worked his way into the heroin market. The Mafia of the town of Siculiana was likewise regenerated, but by the emigration to Canada of the members of the Cuntrera-Caruana family, formerly *campieri* for the Baron Agnello, who later moved to Venezuela to supervise a gigantic drug-trafficking business.

In contrast, the Mafia of Catania was new Mafia, even though the local *cosca* was founded in 1925, imported by Nino Saitta, uncle of the Calderones, the veteran of a period in hiding in the Madonie (with the Farinellas?).[98] For the 1950s, there are reports of another *cosca* in Ramacca, founded by mafiosi who had come up from Agrigentino along a line that, as we have seen, is typical of communications between the western and eastern sections of the island of Sicily. As the ties of friendship and *comparaggio* between Pippo Calderone and Di Cristina seem to indicate, the other path was the one linking Mazzarino and Riesi, the ancient road along which sulphur was transported to the refineries and the seaport of Catania. It appears that the Santapaola family was composed of sulphur transporters; this family produced another of the *cosca*'s notables, Benedetto Santapaola, also known as Nitto Santapaola. Last of all, there is solid proof of the Catanians' involvement in cigarette smuggling, alongside the Grecos and the Badalamentis.[99] On the whole, this group influenced the reputation of Catania very little, up until the 1960s and even beyond. In Catania, everyone attributed the Mafia (with a certain hint of gratification) to the rival city Palermo and the western part of the island, which was viewed as less developed and dynamic. Catania was fond of depicting itself as the Milan of the south. It was a city of traders, builders, businessmen, and speculators, governed by the political machine assembled by Nino Drago, yet another member of Fanfani's political court.[100] The city's criminals, of various extractions, may have constituted small cogs of that machine, though the more attentive sector of Catania's public opinion had perceived various unsettling signals for some time. For instance, one such signal came at the beginning of the 1960s, when Giovanni Leone, a leading criminal lawyer, a leader of the Christian Democratic Party, and a future president of the Italian Republic, came down from Rome to Catania to defend an unknown member of the unknown *cosca* (Franco Ferrera). Catania preferred to identify itself with the Cavalieri del Lavoro (an honorary appellation translating roughly as "knights of labor"—*translator's note*), Costanzo, Graci,

Finocchiaro, and Rendo, major builders with interests in private and public construction on a regional scale. The city overlooked or tried to overlook the fact that these builders, in the course of their business dealings all over Sicily, regularly came into contact with Mafia groups and that, in accordance with the usual model, they assigned subcontracts to the mafiosi in exchange for protection. Many northern companies adopted this same attitude, but the effects tended to be much more deleterious because of the closer nature of the connections. According to the confessions of Antonino Calderone (Pippo's younger brother), Carmelo Costanzo was connected to Luigi Saitta, from his very beginnings as a *capo-mastro,* or supervisor, and then passed under the protection of the elder Calderone during the course of his climb up through the ranks of the grand bourgeoisie in the period of Silvio Milazzo. Again, according to the *pentito,* the mafiosi of both Catania and Trapani (the Minore family) won subcontracts, facilitations, and cash payments from Costanzo. Santapaola appeared at the entrepreneur's side whenever he went out to mingle with his workers. He purchased a Renault dealership, frequented the drawing rooms of respectable Catanian society, and in short became part of the city's establishment. What remains in the documentation is a portrait of the city, a photograph taken at Giuseppe Costanzo's wedding. The photograph shows, all in a row, the mayor of Catania, the president of the province, the provincial secretary of the Christian Democratic Party, the honorable Social-Democratic member of parliament, Costanzo's nephews, and Nitto Santapaola.

In a certain sense, Catania in the 1970s resembled Palermo in the 1870s, with a Mafia group that found its link to a ruling class that was willing to close one eye, or perhaps both, if needed. The hundred years of history that the mafiosi of Palermo have at their backs, however, makes a substantial difference. The mafiosi of Catania lacked a sense of deep roots in their territory, and as soon as they could, they fled the ghetto quarters in which they were born and went to live in the residential areas. It was impossible for them to extend claims of territorial control: the only local *cosca* managed a vague and ill-defined space (the space of the Costanzo companies?) with its thirty-five members, and it requires a considerable stretch of the imagination even to attempt to compare it to the fifty-four families of Palermo, with their roughly three thousand affiliated members. Those families covered the entire territory, and as they grew they fished among the bright young men to staff their growing ranks.[101] Traditionally, in Catania, the territorial grid served the purpose of easily identifying the *'ntisu* (well-known) individual to whom one could turn, in each quarter, in order to recover a stolen car or other purloined objects. This regulatory mechanism, however, broke down in the 1970s along with many others, while from the belly of the city there began to spread an aggressive and anarchic criminality that first devoted itself to purse snatchings, then local armed robbery, and (with rapid air travel) even armed robbery in northern Italy. These criminals began to shake down shops and companies. The Mafia group, whose network of relations aimed both upward (the local establishment) and outward (Cosa Nostra), viewed "common" criminals with aristocratic disdain. The younger Calderone and Santapaola condescended on one occasion to take part in a country festivity held by the group of the *carcagnusi,* but, accustomed as they were to the hospitality of the Costanzos or the Salvos, they could hardly help but feel ill at ease among the grilled chickens, with Vespas zipping in every direction, and rough backslapping:

> It truly was a thieves' feast. Nothing that surrounded, none of what we were using, belonged to the *carcagnusi.* The Vespas were stolen, the chickens were stolen, the wine was stolen, the radio had just been stolen, and the pistols and rifles were stolen. Not even the country land on which we were celebrating belonged to the *carcagnusi.* We were there on the sly, because the *guardiano* was a friend of theirs.[102]

Relations were not always so friendly. Indeed, Santapaola decided to take the role of protector of public order and began killing off blackmailers without pity. With that objective, the family found itself obliged to expand its ranks, admitting to membership a great number of efficient killers, who would be capable of sustaining the level of combat. In any case, the idea of bringing order to the city proved to be fairly illusory. Catania remained a battlefield for warring groups. As the *cosca* expanded, it, too, split into groups. The Mafia model spread, but it proved impossible to attain a comparable degree of compact solidarity with the zones where the Mafia had the deepest and oldest roots.

When asked his view of the proportional influence and presence of the provincial groups inside Cosa Nostra, Buscetta responded: "From 1 to 10: Palermo, 10, Agrigento, 8, Trapani, 8, Caltanissetta, 6, and Catania, 4."[103] This ranking, though it refers to the present-day situation, also reflects to a certain degree the historical dimension as well. The reader should note the absence of Siracusa, Ragusa, and Messina, zones that were traditionally immune to the Mafia.[104] There was, however, a family in Mistretta, obviously affiliated with Palermo along with Gangi and S. Mauro Castelverde, under the command of a certain Giuseppe Farinella[105]—a surname that is quite familiar. Even from inside the organization, matters can be viewed from a number of different standpoints, depending on the observer's personal experience. Leonardo Messina emphasized the importance of the Caltanissetta area, even with reference to his own position: "In general, people think that unless the *pentito* is from Palermo, he has nothing of interest to say."[106] Vincenzo Marsala, who was from Vicari (a village in the Palermo hinterland), offered a piece of advice: "Judge Your Honor, . . . unless you start with the villages, this evil plant will never be uprooted. The hinterland is the reservoir of the Mafia."[107] Gaspare Mutolo, a certified native of Palermo, declared: "The Mafia, sadly, is native to Palermo," and recounted a line of Rosario Di Maggio's concerning Riina: "What does he expect to accomplish here in Palermo, if we are all in agreement? We'll give him a kick in the ass and send him back to Corleone to grow wheat."[108] It was in fact a wisecrack, since the only farming Riina ever did was cultivating the urban Mafia.

With the clarity of vision that came from being in a peripheral vantage point, to wit, Catania, the younger Calderone noted that the equality among families and provinces "was honored only in form," while in reality there existed "a hegemonic power held by the Palermitans." "In particular, the Grecos have held effective power over all of Sicily forever."[109] It would be interesting to know what the *pentito* meant by "forever" (in the Italian, *sempre*). In the 1970s, Salvatore Greco "*chicchiteddu*," and his cousin, also Salvatore, "*l'ingegnere*," moved to Venezuela, and after returning once or twice to Sicily, disappear from this history. Unverified reports tell us that *chicchiteddu* died of natural causes, and there is silence on the fate of *l'ingegnere*. Buscetta describes *chicchiteddu* as disgusted, determined to pull out of the situation; this is in line with Buscetta's thesis of a formerly noble Mafia, which was now in the process of degeneration and which would have found its last prestigious leader in the person of none other than Salvatore Greco, or "*chicchiteddu*." It is reasonable, however, to question whether the two cousins actually meant to retire entirely. It was precisely in this period, with the Cuntrera-Caruana families, that Venezuela became an important base of operations for the drug business. We might hypothesize that, following the bloody Mafia war and the collapse of the overarching coordinating structures, the Grecos decided that the structure of the power syndicate of Palermo was no longer governable. Moreover, they might have chosen to invest their skills, relations, and capital in the area of the enterprise syndicate. In the network of trafficking and business, the South American territory began to constitute a significant terminus.[110]

In Ciaculli, the heritage of the two cousins was adopted by Michele Greco, the son of Don Piddu *u tinenti*, and therefore a member of the Croceverde Giardini faction. *Chicchiteddu*, a blood relation of both sides (his mother was from Croceverde, his father was from Ciaculli), had represented an ideal point of equilibrium and reconciliation. It was he, according to Buscetta, who had made the magnanimous gesture of taking the Croceverde cousins back into the family, even though Mafia circles recognized that "he would have been entirely right not to"[111] (that is: that Ciaculli had emerged victorious from the war). The resentments of the long-ago Greco-versus-Greco war could still be felt even in recent years. *"L'ingegnere,"* whose parents had both been killed in that war, attempted to disqualify Michele Greco by reminding his peers that Don Piddu had once broken every rule by appearing in court demanding justice for his son. Once again we see evidence of the sense of historical continuity with the *Mafia dei giardini;* more than thirty-five years had passed, if the reference is to the killing of Giuseppe Greco (1939). In his turn, when Michele Greco was arrested, he complained publicly that he had been the victim of mistaken identity, given the fact that the two Mafia capos, with whom he had nothing in common, shared his name.[112] This marks an unmistakable distancing. Therefore, the victors of the 1960s had abandoned not only the provincial organization, but even the family, and left them in the hands of a different and, in a certain sense, opposing group.

A triumvirate composed of Riina, Badalamenti, and Stefano Bontate (the son of Don Paolino) was appointed around 1970 to reorganize the Mafia of Palermo, reconstitute its families, and ensure its supervision and coordination. The Palermo Centro *cosca* (the former La Barbera family) was dissolved and then reformed; the Acquasanta *cosca* that had caused so many problems, from Tanu Alatu to Cavataio, was eliminated.[113] Around 1973, the provincial commission was reconstituted under the chairmanship of Badalamenti; in 1975, the regional commission led by Pippo Calderone was formed. And that was not all. Several Neapolitan bosses were affiliated members who had been doing business for years with the Sicilians in cigarette smuggling; the Sicilians hoped that this move would help to keep the Neapolitans under control. The solution was basically formal; it would not prevent disagreements and reciprocal cheating and fraud. The already poorly functioning system of regulation in western Sicily was unlikely to bring into line even more distant and more diverse groups. In any case, it seems impossible to compare the Mafia, in the strictest sense, to similar phenomena springing up in the Mezzogiorno. In fact, as the younger Calderone repeatedly emphasized, the authority of the regional commission would never rise to the same level as that of the commission of Palermo. What was under way was an attempt to internalize (an unlovely but effective term used by social scientists), that is, to bring all the transactions under the umbrella of the territorial structure of Cosa Nostra, in order to eliminate the disputes of the past and establish a geometric and hierarchical order.

The Badalamenti administration began with the elimination of the small-time Camorrist who, many years before, had dared to slap Lucky Luciano in the face. The new leader took care to inform the Americans "that the insult had been washed away with blood, however belatedly."[114] Perhaps it was not belatedly, but very timely indeed. Badalamenti wanted to pay a compliment to his friends across the Atlantic, who had always been his own chief interlocutors as well as for the entire Mafia of Cinisi, at the very moment that he took power. The message did not please Leggio, who criticized Badalamenti "because he had informed the American Cosa Nostra that it was to his credit that the entire province of Palermo was now under control, and that he had become the '*capo dei capi.*' "[115] The leadership of this major Sicilian American drug trafficker came to a sudden end in 1977, but not with a dramatic settling of accounts from his adversaries, nor with a negotiated succession. Instead, quite simply, Badalamenti was expelled from Cosa Nostra, in a painless but total manner. This suggests that his power had more to do with external relationships than with any force he himself wielded within the power syndicate. Buscetta, who described what happened, firmly refused to offer even the slightest attempt to interpret this episode. Calderone, on the other hand, recalled that Badalamenti, originally quite close to the Corleonese and to Michele Greco, was later accused by them of "having enriched himself by dealing drugs at the same time that many families were in financial trouble and many men of honor were practically going hungry."[116]

The new capo, who was none other than Michele Greco, did not follow the same line as his more prestigious cousin, Salvatore *chicchiteddu*; instead he carried out a general reversal of alliances, with a close adherence to the Corleonese. In direct opposition, Stefano Bontate, capo of the Santa Maria di Gesù family, emerged as a powerful figure and made an alliance with the young Mafia capo of Passo di Rigano, Salvatore Inzerillo. The alliances were thus in place for new business and new and bloodier wars.

POWER AND MONEY AT WAR

When a mafioso extends his protection to a businessman, he will brook no interference of any kind, even from other members of the organization. Let us examine the case of Pasquale Costanzo, for instance. The Calderones apparently considered the hypothesis of affiliating him. The final decision, however, was against it because it would have allowed Costanzo to have too much inside say in the interplay of pressure "on the part of all men of honor, who would have then felt that they had every right to contact him directly."[117] The decision, therefore, was made in order to protect not only Costanzo's autonomy, but also the exclusive nature of communications with the Catanian family or with Calderone. Members affiliated with the Salemi *cosca* and mafiosi extending back numerous generations were the cousins Nino and Ignazio Salvo. Their status—according to

Buscetta's emphatic and convincing declaration—did not, however, derive so much from the positions they held within Cosa Nostra, as from their wealth and from their assiduously cultivated political relations within and outside of the Christian Democratic Party, with cash payments made strategically to ensure that no one would question their monopoly on the contract for tax collections. As the Christian Democrat Giuseppe Alessi stated in 1964, "this topic is red hot, because there are billions of lire at stake, and control can ensure life and prosperity to parties, to political currents, and to groups of people. I would not want us to chase away the sparrows, and then leave the predatory eagles undisturbed."[118]

The fact that Badalamenti should have been "particularly proud" of the friendship of the Salvos, as well as fiercely determined to preserve it from the incursions of other affiliated members, shows a contact among peers between the hierarchy of Mafia power and the hierarchy of money. Even more long-lived and well established was Badalamenti's relation with the Bontates, father and son. It is in this logical context that we can also place the kidnapping and murder of Luigi Corleo (1975), father-in-law of Nino Salvo. That killing made it clear to Nino Salvo that his connections and sources of protection would not be sufficient to keep him safe. When he was faced with accusations from the magistrature, Salvo claimed that he was not a mafioso, but a victim no different from all the other entrepreneurs in Sicily, and that he had turned to Bontate only to obtain his protection. He added an interesting note: "Until the kidnapping of my father-in-law Luigi Corleo, I believed that I had established a peaceful if somewhat uneasy coexistence with those organizations, wrongly thinking that it was sufficient to behave well in order to avoid having problems with anyone."[119]

Here we can perceive the bewilderment of a Mafia that is attempting to join the grand bourgeoisie and that believes it has adequate protection from its network of prior relations in Cosa Nostra, only to discover that, even though it has "behaved impeccably," it is still sucked back into the criminal universe by the competition between its protectors. On the other hand, a kidnapping industry proved to be unacceptable in Sicily, on the Sardinian or Calabrian model, because it would have violated the understanding between protectors and the protection that was first established in long-ago 1877, whose effects waned only in the chaos of the two postwar periods. Let me mention one case from 1976, which could, however, just as easily have taken place a century before. An independent gang from Trapani kidnapped a certain Campisi, to the displeasure of the "men of honor," who expressed their disapproval by furnishing the usual tip to the Carabinieri via the Mafia capo of Partanna, Stefano Accardo. In reaction to that tip, the Trapani gang responded with an attempted assassination, which the mafioso miraculously survived. Then came the slaughter of all five gang

members responsible for the twofold code violation.[120] Thus, the Mafia continued to insist on showing respect for forces outside of itself. This was the reason
for the commission vote to ban kidnapping from Sicilian territory (outside of
Sicily was a different matter, as can be seen from Leggio's activities). The rule
was, by and large, respected, though occasionally violated during especially
hot periods of infra-Mafia competition.

In the case of the Salvos, the protection contract reveals something more
than the usual ambiguity. Referring to the businessman Moncada, a close associate of the La Barberas, Terranova commented: "It is not clear whether he was a
victim or an abettor of the Mafiosi, or perhaps both, depending on the various
phases and the varying degrees of self-interest."[121] What was referred to in the
nineteenth- and twentieth-century discussions as *manutengolismo*, or abetting
of the Mafia, is today termed *contiguità* (contiguity), with the same indeterminate nature of the term's actual significance. In the preliminary investigation of
the *maxiprocesso*, or maxitrial, Falcone and the others noted that some of the
businessmen described by Vitale as victims of extortion had, in the ten or fifteen years that had since passed, become partners, beneficiaries, and accomplices of their extorters.[122] And in fact, the price demanded, even from shopkeepers, was quite often this: to facilitate, by becoming business partners, the
transformation of the protectors into "entrepreneurs." What needs to be analyzed differently are the cases of those who enjoy the benefits of the network of
Mafia relationships and then suffer corresponding damage from that same network. Salvo denounced the state as being "practically absent from the struggle against the Mafia,"[123] with polemical tones that are age-old but, in this specific case, also purely self-serving. These are people who, like the Gucciones of
the past, owe their positions of power precisely to their contacts with the Mafia
network in a market from which all other competitors are excluded because of
their lack of Mafia support. Is it possible to speak of a state of necessity when
someone prospers from a more general state of necessity, a state in which others
are obliged to live without enjoying the same benefits? This, for instance, is the
case of the Costanzos, who did construction work and enjoyed profitable business, free of any intimidation thanks to the violent actions ordered independently by their Mafia protectors. In this context, we should mention the 1991
verdict of a Catanian judge with the illustrious name of Luigi Russo, in comparison with which the lifelines thrown to the large landowners in the trials
during the Fascist regime are mere trifles. The magistrate ascertained the validity of most of the revelations offered by the younger Calderone concerning the
Costanzos, but also determined that their actions were not subject to legal
sanction because those actions were prompted by a state of necessity entirely
comparable to that of a shopowner who was the victim of a protection racket.

We are not interested in examining the matter here in judicial terms, but let's just view it from the sociological point of view, which Judge Russo expands on with disconcerting emotional pathos. Judge Russo expresses sympathy for the plight of the multimillionaire businessmen who are forced to host Mafia meetings in their offices; he shares the distress of the Costanzos over the marriage of one of their nieces to a leader of the *cosca*, Salvatore Marchese (a Calderone cousin); and he subscribes to the thesis of the social utility of collusion with the Mafia. "The rejection of any dialogue designed to attain a certain point of equilibrium [with the mafiosi] would lead the entrepreneur to renounce the idea of doing business; and paradoxically this would happen precisely in those areas of the country in which maintaining and increasing employment should serve to encourage the population to break free of the presence of the Mafia."[124]

We are still engaged with the fallacious equation of underdevelopment and Mafia; from that fallacious correspondence one obtains the even more fallacious corollary according to which development counters the Mafia. This corollary has led broad sectors of Italian public opinion, both among entrepreneurs and labor organizers in Catania and elsewhere, to express worries about the "criminalization" of entrepreneurs. More original was Russo's theory, which stated that even the possible affiliation with Cosa Nostra of the recipient of the threat would represent a defensive ploy, which could therefore no longer be classed as association with the Mafia, which is juridically a crime.[125] Historically and conceptually, such a defensive theory represents the very essence of the Mafia phenomenon.

The possession of one's own capital of ties to the political and economic establishment seemed to constitute, within Cosa Nostra, a mechanism for power and advancement. In fact, we can describe as a notable anyone who, within an organization, is able to bring about a legitimization that is independent of the organization itself. First and foremost among the other factors at work in that direction is the prestige that is an essential factor in the role of the mafioso. For instance, according to Buscetta, Vincenzo Rimi had never held executive positions of any sort: "he was nothing more than a man of honor of the Alcamo family, whose capo I do not even know, but he was a person who enjoyed a very great reputation and influence within Cosa Nostra" on account of his qualities "of equilibrium and wisdom."[126] It strikes me as excessive to claim, as does Buscetta with the pride of a self-made man, that Mafia power could in no way be handed down to one's offspring or inherited. Otherwise, what sense can we make of the continuity of family dynasties like that of the Grecos? How can we explain the rapid rise of a young man such as Stefano Bontate to the leadership of the S. Maria di Gesù *cosca* in which his father had held the same position? Moreover, according to Calderone and Buscetta, Michele

Greco was an "insipid" individual, who therefore rose to the head of the commission for no reason other than his illustrious surname. Since they had been wealthy and powerful for generations, the Grecos and the Bontates were also *signori* ("gentlemen"), which was not a bad credential in a traditionalist environment like that of Cosa Nostra. Mere wealth, on the other hand, did not establish "rank," as we can see from the fairly modest prestige and reputation enjoyed by Tommaso Spadaro, even though he was a prominent boss in the sectors of cigarette smuggling and drug trafficking.

It is difficult to identify the rank of Tommaso Buscetta, who at various points was called the "boss of two worlds" because of his incessant travels through Europe and South and North America. Buscetta was pursued by the police forces of half the planet as a top-level drug trafficker, but then, in his renowned confessions, he claimed that he had never dealt drugs, that he had never held high Mafia office, that he was never anything more than a simple "soldier" of the Porta Nuova family commanded by Pippo Calò, and that he had always allied himself with the losing side, ranging from the La Barberas to Stefano Bontate. Buscetta probably did not wish to reveal his activities in the enterprise syndicate. And yet it remains difficult to understand the source of his great prestige among the mafiosi in prison or confined in the courtroom cages during the *maxiprocesso*. Those mafiosi listened to his accusations in respectful silence. We could, perhaps, accept the *pentito*'s psychological interpretation of his own reputation. "Mother Nature gave me a certain charisma, I have an extra something."[127] But in reality there is a sharp discrepancy between the objectively modest role that Buscetta attributed to himself in his confessions to Falcone and the tones of the autobiography that he dictated to Enzo Biagi, as well as the revelations of the U.S. Drug Enforcement Agency (DEA). The director of the DEA, Frank Monastero, declared: "Buscetta should be considered to occupy the highest level of the Mafia, with contacts on three continents. . . . Valachi never had the same power, charisma, and rank in the organization that Buscetta enjoys."[128]

The divergence might be explicable in terms of the two different points of view, Sicilian and American, and the way in which a Sicilian American drug trafficker can act as a leader even though he holds no high offices in the Cosa Nostra hierarchy. The end of the 1970s was an unprecedented boom time in the narcotics business. That business inevitably spanned the two worlds, Old World and New World, in which Buscetta was a leading boss. From the New World came a surging river of cash, through banking channels that represented the trail that the new investigative bloodhound of the Palermo prosecutor's office, Judge Giovanni Falcone, began to follow, thanks to his experience with financial crimes. And from the Old World there flowed a river of heroin, which in 1982 managed to supply 80 percent of the market in the northeastern United States.

At either end of the two rivers were two cousins, Carlo Gambino and Salvatore Inzerillo; thus, the most powerful *cosca* of New York served as the purchaser, while the capo of one of Palermo's oldest *cosche* was the seller. In the middle were recent Sicilian immigrants, living on the east coast of the United States, in part to escape the repression of the early 1960s. They ran another link in the chain, the import link. The investigators came to the conclusion that there was a third Mafia, after the Italian American Mafia and the Sicilian Mafia, a Sicilian narcotics-trafficking Mafia commanded by Badalamenti.[129] The fundamental role played by this individual, who had just been expelled from the Cosa Nostra of Palermo, makes it clear that this Sicilian American group did not represent a branch of the main organization; it was not a terminus of the Sicilian territorial organization.[130] (Nor was it a subsidiary of the American organization.) Instead, it was a relatively independent enterprise syndicate, autonomous of both Sicily and America. It marked the reversal of the trend of the 1950s, when the purchasers came to Europe. Now it was the sellers who were going to America. We are still looking at an alternating flow of merchandise, money, and people who mixed with trade in the context of emigration. Now the trade was in drugs, just as it once had been in oil and citrus fruit, but it was still being moved by the "friends" and "family" of "tested loyalty" that for the past century had been moving in both directions, from one continent to the other. In the Inzerillo group "the incredible labyrinth of family ties," Falcone observed, "is such that one struggles to keep it all clear, and it is interesting to note that, with each successive generation, the connections become increasingly close, with marriages between cousins." This endogamy was methodically pursued in the context of an "apparent restoration of traditional values . . . , used in an instrumental bid to increase the cohesion and homogeneity of the group."[131] This was the old model of the narcotics-dealing Mafias of Cinisi and Alcamo, but now it was managed on a much broader scale from Palermo, where family ties replaced the structures of the territorial Mafia, unsuited to a transcontinental network.

Once the French Connection had become obsolete, at the end of the 1970s the former cigarette smugglers, now rich in cash and contacts they had developed in recent years, began to supply themselves directly from the Far East. Tommaso Spadaro, Nunzio La Mattina, and Pino Savoca were just three of these. Now, the Sicilians began to refine the heroin for themselves, by importing Marseillais technicians, and they also began to ship directly to America. They now controlled numerous links in the chain. In certain aspects, this management was unified, since all the mafiosi were able to take advantage of this "industrial" structure as well as the commercial channels, by financing a partial share of the merchandise. Nonetheless, there was an evident fragmentation and growing suspicion and mistrust among the various power centers. Giovanni Bontate, for instance, applied a system that was reminiscent of mechanisms employed in the protocapitalism of the modern era, the "putting out" system common in the Flemish economy. He did not merely hire refiners to process his morphine for a certain fee. First, he would sell the morphine to the refiners, then he would buy it back once it had been refined into heroin.[132] Furthermore, there were two choke points in the free access to resources: the first lay with the importation of the morphine, which was firmly controlled by the three individuals named above. As a result, anyone else (for instance, the Corleonese) had to "make do with the share that was assigned to them."[133] The second choke point lay in the export of the heroin to America, where Inzerillo exerted a certain degree of control—we cannot say to what extent it was exclusive. Falcone's preliminary investigation, and prior to that investigation, the investigations of a police official who worked in close coordination with the DEA, Boris Giuliano, allow us to form some notion of the structure of that group. Around the group there flourished a vast system of entrepreneurs, bankers, and money launderers, with an internal division of roles between the drug-dealing sector and the larger business section. In the latter area, the most important individual was a cousin of the Inzerillos, Rosario Spatola, who was also notorious as the host of the Gambino family's friend, the powerful banker Michele Sindona, at the time in serious straits, during his mysterious trip to Sicily (1979). The difference between Spadaro and his partners, on the one hand, and Inzerillo on the other, lies in the fact that Spadaro and partners had status purely in the area of the enterprise syndicate, while Inzerillo combined the role of large-scale drug trafficker with the rank of family capo of Cosa Nostra, and had ties, respectively, with the traditional Sicilian American controlling figure "of the international trade in narcotics," Badalamenti, and on the other hand with Di Cristina and, ultimately, Bontate,[134] leader of the "minority" group in the commission. On both sides of the investigation, both American and Italian, the name of Buscetta appeared frequently.

In this crucial period, the annual profits from the Sicilian American drug trade were on the order of hundreds of millions (perhaps as much as a billion?) of dollars. In this context we can see the early roots of the so-called second Mafia war, already impending in the wings with the murders of Di Cristina and Pippo Calderone, and then fully in progress with the deaths of Stefano Bontate, Salvatore Inzerillo, and a substantial number of members of his (blood) family. That war came to an end over the course of two years (1981–1982) with the horrifying mass slaughter of around five hundred to a thousand individuals. Many of the businessmen in Inzerillo's entourage were killed: among them were an early figure in the heroin trade, Antonino Sorci, former partner of Luciano; and Leonardo Caruana, from the famous Agrigento-Venezuelan family of heroin traffickers. There is a significant fact: even after the killing of Bontate, Inzerillo declared that he felt certain that Riina would never touch him, since Riina still expected to be paid many hundreds of millions as his share of a drug deal. His opinion was soon proved wrong by the burst of bullets from an AK-47 that penetrated the bulletproof armor of his automobile. The corpse of Salvatore's brother, Pietro Inzerillo, was found in New York "with a wad of dollar bills stuffed in his mouth and wedged under his genitalia. Message: 'You tried to swallow too much money.'"[135] This was the same message as the one sent by the *carta d'oro* (gold certificate) tossed on the dead body of Don Giuseppe Lumia, 120 years earlier. The power syndicate, and with it, the alliance of the "winners," clearly intended to cut the Sicilian American component out of the deal and to take for itself not so much the profits from the narcotics traffic (which, as we have seen, was open to everyone, though to what degree we cannot say), but rather the fundamental levers of control over that trade. Here we should make a distinction between the commission, in which Greco and Riina controlled the majority, and the families, first and foremost the family of S. Maria di Gesù, the most numerous and powerful of all, which watched its prestigious capo murdered without the slightest reaction. Indeed, the "losers" did not even make an attempt to defend themselves. That is a disconcerting fact, if we compare it to the continuous and reciprocal reprisals in the first Greco–La Barbera war.

"When people talk about a Mafia war, I am not clear on the meaning of these words," Mutolo declared. "There is a Mafia war when two or more Mafia families take up weapons and they know that they are fighting against another group of people. In Palermo, in contrast, in my opinion, according to the way I see things, there has been no such Mafia war; there was a betrayal."[136]

There had indeed been a "betrayal," in the sense that the commission offensive carved straight into and through the families, highlighting the fragility of their internal cohesion. The *cosca* no longer represented the cell or base structure of the Mafia as an organization, subject as it was to the opposing and conflicting pressure of two forces: the centralization of military power in the commission and the centrifugal forces produced by the development of profiteering networks. Already Cavataio had created an occult and transverse alignment, that of the Corleonese: "When I say Corleonese," explained Buscetta in the courtroom during the *maxiprocesso,* "I am not referring to a Corleonese as someone born in Corleone. I mean to refer to the Corleonese alignment." "You mean the family?" asked the presiding magistrate. "No, the alignment," reiterated the *pentito.*[137] Buscetta himself, aligned with Bontate and Inzerillo even though he belonged to the *cosca* of Calò allied with Riina, was an example of this redeployment of forces arrayed along the lines of the major trafficking routes. The two Bontate brothers, Stefano and Giovanni, were both narcotics traffickers, each keeping his activity concealed from the other. Certainly, that situation had some bearing on Giovanni's decision to ally himself with the winning side, accepting (or encouraging?) his brother's murder, in defiance of all codes of family loyalty. The rule that the family, as such, never manages business directly can lead only to the enrichment of some of the affiliated members, resulting in a sort of class war on the interior of the *cosche*. In this case, the Corleonese alignment could include most of the territorial and military structure of Palermo, rebelling against certain of its capos. That would explain the absence of a battle and the ease with which the leadership was changed.

The fact that not only were family capos killed without repercussions, but above all that members of the same families took the place of the capos means, without the possibility of the slightest doubt on the matter, that the replacements had come to a prior agreement on the elimination of the capos.[138]

Here we can make the same argument made concerning the Leggio-Navarra war: money, external relations, both economic and political, Gambino, Sindona, the Salvos, and Lima were all on one side, and yet that side lost the war the minute the fighting entered a military phase. The Mafia is an expression of profiteering and notables, but it is not transformed into a club of notables and profiteers. In fact, when faced with a challenge, it reacts by accentuating its military nature, of which a man like Riina is the finest (worst) representative.

It should be stated at this point that this interpretation of events corresponds only in part with the version provided by Buscetta. The *pentito,* in fact, claimed that underlying everything that happened "there was no major motive. It was the Corleonese taking a strong position,"[139] a sort of power grab on the part of Riina and his partners. This analysis points to three types of contradiction: a clash between the business network and military organization; a clash between the individual families and the commission; and a clash between the "alignments," which correspond neither to the blood nor Mafia families. This was the case of the two Bontate brothers or the two Badalamenti cousins, fighting on opposing sides.[140] The war was gradually transformed into a centralized operation that ultimately overwhelmed and swept away the independence of the families, concluding (though on this point Buscetta would differ) a process that Salvatore Greco "*chicchiteddu*" had already set into motion, though in a far more cautious manner. Clearly, however, the drug trade was the triggering factor, an obvious point that Buscetta admitted only generically as a decline in the "moral" tone of Cosa Nostra, "confusion" in its governing bodies. Not only did he deny, in the face of obvious evidence to the contrary, his own personal involvement in the narcotics traffic, but he also did his best to clear his friends of that involvement—not Inzerillo (that would have been impossible) but Stefano Bontate. Despite Buscetta's protestations, of course, Stefano Bontate was an active narcotics trafficker, as was widely known and as other *pentiti* have confirmed. Buscetta even went so far as to claim that in the 1960s, the Sicilian Cosa Nostra had nothing to do with the narcotics business, and as we have seen, he provided alternative explanations (in reality, complementary explanations) for the outbreak of the first Mafia war. He was momentarily disconcerted only when Falcone replied that Di Pisa certainly sold heroin, since he had even tried to sell some to an agent of the Narcotics Bureau.[141] Buscetta made the distinction between the Sicilian Cosa Nostra in America, which dealt heroin, and the American Cosa Nostra, which refused to engage in these activities. Buscetta was clearly contradicted by the involvement of the Gambinos in the Sicilians' import-export business, but clearly he was interested in covering the North and South American areas,[142] which were his territory at least as much as the Sicilian territory. Concerning that territory, he instead provided a harvest of clear and largely truthful information. It is significant that one of the few holes in his version involved the expulsion of Badalamenti in 1977, a crucial point in the Sicilian-American connection.

And yet, let us consider how matters concluded. Badalamenti on the run showed up in Brazil and went to see Buscetta. He asked Buscetta to come back to Palermo "to direct," Buscetta explained, "in consideration of my recognized prestige, the fight against the Corleonese."[143] Here, too, there is corroborating evidence: a number of tapped phone calls show that the Salvos were trying to contact him with this same objective.[144] Understandably, Buscetta considered the idea "crazy." What could his personal "charisma" (and we still don't understand the source of that charisma) do against the overwhelming military force of the commission, at a time when every day dozens of dead bodies were turning up in Palermo? The strange thing is that the "crazy" idea was proposed by extremely authoritative individuals and was taken so seriously by Buscetta's enemies (who had mysteriously been informed of Badalamenti's plan, but not of Buscetta's firm refusal to cooperate) that they implemented a merciless preemptive reaction, killing two of his sons, his brother, and a number of other relatives. One is tempted to think that the "boss of two worlds" had been summoned to negotiate on behalf of someone else, located in one of these other worlds, and that the commission had decided to communicate with ferocious symbolism its refusal to accept any outside interference. We have the ambiguous testimony of Mutolo, according to whom, following the deaths of Bontate and Inzerillo, John Gambino came to Italy from the United States to begin a dialogue, "since the channels that had existed for communication had been recently interrupted," and Inzerillo had been one of the links in the chain that "brought the largest volume of drugs to America." On the other hand, in February 1984, Badalamenti phoned the United States from Rio de Janeiro reiterating (perhaps driven by desperation): "we have the license to import it [heroin]; no one else has the license." Michele Greco on the other hand declared that he was ready to resume the trade on a different basis, but he asked that the Americans "strike a few 'blows' to fuck up Buscetta," that they make an effort "to kill all those who had escaped to America."[145] In Brazil, Buscetta was arrested, and, after being questioned by Falcone, he made up his mind to talk.

TERRORISTS AND *PENTITI*

Corresponding to the years of the Mafia war was the beginning of a series of massacres of very prominent figures in Sicily. The string of murders began in September 1979 with Terranova, who had been elected to parliament on the Italian Communist Party ticket and had taken part in the Anti-Mafia and had then gone back to being a magistrate. Next, among the magistrates, came Gaetano Costa (1980) and Rocco Chinnici (1983), to name only those killed in Palermo. There was no shortage of politicians among the victims, such as Piersanti Mattarella, the president of the Sicilian Region; Mattarella was not helped by the great number of good relations in Mafia circles that his father, Bernardo Mattarella, had built up. Another was Pio La Torre, the Communist regional secretary who was killed in 1982. There were also various policemen among the victims: the deputy *questore* Boris Giuliano, the Carabinieri officers Russo and Basile, and finally, Carlo Alberto Dalla Chiesa, the Carabinieri general appointed prefect of Palermo in 1982. We are faced with a substantial dilemma in terms of interpretation here. With the exception of Notarbartolo, the Palermo Mafia had never produced *cadaveri eccellenti* ("excellent cadavers," meaning "prominent victims"). At least, that was the case until 1971, when people of the time generally viewed the murder of the district attorney Pietro Scaglione as evidence that this magistrate had Mafia ties, in accordance with the interpretation that "they only kill one another." Viewed from the context of the post–Dalla Chiesa years, however, the Scaglione murder instead appears to be the first of the many subsequent episodes of intimidation of the public institutions and the political system.

In a number of cases, the direction of the shots seems a good basis for the ensuing interpretation. Russo and Boris Giuliano were leading investigators, and in particular, Giuliano had close ties to the DEA. The same logical connections lead to Costa for the investigation against the Inzerillos and to Rocco Chinnici, who was killed in the brutal explosion of a car bomb while he was supervising the pool of magistrates working on the preliminary investigation against the "winning side" in the Mafia war. Here, an aspect emerges that is no less grounded in reality for having been the subject of great rhetorical emphasis and perhaps even exaggeration: the isolation that results in death. In the milieux of the police and the judiciary, the majority remain on the safe terrain of routine administration out of, variously, incompetence, laziness, fear, or complicity. If one reads through the interviews conducted by the parliamentary commission in the mid-1970s among the various professionals in the field, it is immediately clear which ones are fated to be killed: the few who give committed and intelligent replies. Among them was General Dalla Chiesa, a man of great prestige and great and widely acknowledged experience in the field, who was dispatched to Palermo to serve as a symbol[146] and who was immediately, and symbolically, assassinated. The old expedient, employed in other historical periods, of holding in reserve a high official who is well informed and is sent to Sicily when the situation demands it (let us name, for example, Sangiorgi or Mori), clearly no longer worked. It was easy to hit such a visible target, just as it was easy to hit Terranova, who even in the judicial circles of Bari was considered a "persecutor" of the unfortunate Leggio.[147] The same can be said of Costa, who had been obliged to sign, alone, in violation of standard procedure, the warrant for the arrests of the members of the Spatola-Inzerillo group, in order to overcome the hesitation and reluctance of his colleagues.

The repercussions were substantial. "For the policemen and the Carabinieri . . . the attack on Costa represented an unmistakable message. They now knew that the more seriously someone investigated the Mafia, the greater the danger to that person's life."[148] In order to have a full and convincing reaction, something quite different from the state that existed would have been required. The Italian state was profoundly tainted by the corruption of its political class, shackled by the lockstep of a committee- and assembly-driven governance, identifiable in the practice and theory of "weak government." And that state was incapable, as was evident in the Dalla Chiesa case, of sending a clear and unmistakable signal to its component parts. Nonetheless, it was in the wake of the tragic assassination of Dalla Chiesa that a remarkable period of significant results ensued, a product of the work done by the Anti-Mafia pool made up of the magistrates Falcone, Borsellino, Di Lello, and Guarnotta, under the leadership of Antonino Caponnetto. The team obtained the confessions of Buscetta and, in time, of other *pentiti,* and it completed the preliminary judicial investigation that led to the indictment of an astonishing 707 alleged affiliated members of Cosa Nostra. A manhunt ensued, designed to ensure that the cages designed to hold the defendants of what would be known as the Palermo *maxiprocesso* would not be empty during the trial.

Here police sources continue the story. The police had brilliantly dismantled the network of heroin refineries. And the police had provided the pool of magistrates with its report on "the 162" (that is, the 162 targets of the investigation), a map of the winning side. Already at the end of 1983, the Palermo mobile squad lost a man, the agent Calogero Zucchetto, who had identified in the citrus groves and the bars of Ciaculli the fugitive from justice Salvatore Montalto, in the territory of the Grecos and their allies the Prestifilippos. Apparently, the fact that the policeman had managed to infiltrate their ranks and that he had in some sense used them to lay the trap sealed his fate. In the Mafia circles, word spread that the dead officer's superiors, Beppe Montana and Ninni Cassarà, had declared that Mario Prestifilippo and Pino Greco *scarpazzedda* ("little shoe"), the feared "superkiller" of the winning side, should be killed, not taken alive. It is conceivable that in the heat of the moment, out of rage and grief, they said such a thing. But the real question is through what mysterious channels could such a rumor have reached the enemy?[149] Meanwhile, Montana devoted himself to hunting the fugitives. He even made use of his vacation time to spy on the luxurious villas along the Sicilian coast from his powerboat. That is where he was killed, dressed in shorts and wooden clogs, in the summer of 1985. The entire mobile squad set out to catch the killers and arrested a certain Salvatore Marino. Marino died after being beaten in the *questura* (police administration). At Marino's funeral, now that the *cosca* had suddenly discovered a profound attachment to civil rights, the head of the Italian Radical Party, Marco Pannella, led a protest. The Italian minister of the interior, Scalfaro, hurried down to Palermo, and with a celerity that had never been seen in other similar cases (first and foremost among them, the "accidental" death of the anarchist Pinelli), he dissolved the finest investigative team that had ever existed in Palermo, transferring the officers to the furthest corners of the Italian peninsula. The death of Marino proved to be a genuine boon for the Mafia. Cassarà only returned to his home at unpredictable intervals. He traveled everywhere in an armored car, with a bodyguard of two police officers. One of them, Roberto Antiochia, had cut short his vacation and hurried back to guard his superior's back. It has never been determined how an army made up of at least fifteen killers succeeded in obtaining a tip that allowed them to attack the three, in the street outside the Cassarà residence, and finish them off in a hurricane of bullets. This was just twenty-four hours after Scalfaro's decision. At this crucial moment, the men of the mobile squad were as isolated and alone as if they were the criminals, the subversives on whom the enormous power of a modern state was brought crashing down.

· In this tragic story, the state rhetorically declared a great portion of the problems of a struggle, which was actually waged by only a few of its officials. These are people who work on their vacations, risk their lives to defend their friends, enter into polemics with their inept colleagues, encounter constant betrayal, but continue to do what they believe in, even though they know that "all investigators who are really doing their job wind up getting killed."[150] It is precisely for this reason that they enter into a personal conflict with the mafiosi, which only facilitates the murderous reaction. Since all institutional involvement is unpredictable and contradictory, there would be no struggle if it were not for the esprit de corps, the cult of fallen victims, the point of honor of those who refuse to surrender. Then what happens is the sort of thing that happened at the funeral of Cassarà, with policemen and Carabinieri facing off, practically drawing their guns, with the coffin of the young Antiochia "removed by police officers from the official venue of the *questura*" and taken to the offices of the mobile squad, wrapped in the Italian flag.[151] The second officer in the bodyguard escort (Natale Mondio) miraculously survived the attack, only to be killed in his turn in 1989. Scalfaro, Pannella, and the other easygoing exponents of the Italian political routine were incapable of understanding that there is an Italy "on the front line," an Italy that fights and dies, I would venture to say, unremarked by one and all, even though the funeral was shown on live national television. This provoked a further sense of isolation, as well as conflicts that inevitably took on the appearance of factional splits. Let us remember the furious debates provoked by the activities of the pool, or the now proverbial *veleni* (toxins) of the hall of justice of Palermo and the Consiglio Superiore della Magistratura (Superior Council of the Magistrature).[152]

The same contradictions, but at a far higher level, appear in the debate that pitted against one another two alignments, which we identify as Giampaolo Pansa and Nando Dalla Chiesa on the one hand, and Leonardo Sciascia on the other. This was the period of the *maxiprocesso*, which began in February 1986. Pansa frequently described a Palermo that was insufficiently understood on the great occasion, where in fact there existed a "swamp" that stood ready to bog down and "swallow up the giant trial."[153] Distinct from this Palermo was another Palermo, which was adopting the struggle against the Mafia as a lever for a general renewal. Corresponding to this shift was a movement within the political class that brought to the forefront of the Christian Democratic Party individuals such as Elda Pucci and Leoluca Orlando, an "Anti-Mafia" mayor supported by an atypical majority that wound up even including Communists. In opposition to them was the stance of Sciascia, suspicious, libertarian that he was, of a "culture of handcuffs."[154] What could emerge from a political movement that claimed to have a say in a judicial matter? The danger is that the Anti-Mafia front might represent a footstool that a few ambitious individuals, such as Orlando, intended to use in building their own careers. There would be an even greater danger if the ambitious ones were Falcone & Co. As these magistrates proceeded by deductive logic through the tools of *pentiti* and *pentitismo* (turncoats and state's witnesses), they ran the risk of forgetting to ascertain carefully questions of individual guilt.

It is important to recall that the context for this polemic on the "professionals of the Anti-Mafia" was provided by a review that Sciascia wrote of Duggan's book on the Mori operation,[155] a book that, as we have said, lays out so exceedingly well the political instrumentalization that lay at the foundation of the fight against the Mafia in the Fascist period that along the way it lost any perception of what the Mafia was or could become. It is especially disconcerting that the author of *Il giorno della civetta* (English edition: *The Day of the Owl*) should have clearly failed to realize this. Sciascia may also have overlooked the fact that, leaving aside the case of the Fascists, ever since the time of the *Destra storica* (historic right wing) and the time of the socialist, pro-Rudinì bloc on the Notarbartolo case, the Anti-Mafia front had always fought against the opposing front as one power against another, or even one faction against another, attempting to outflank its adversaries and take their place. (In each case, there were better factions and worse factions: the Palizzolos, the Lo Montes, the Cianciminos). Strangely and entirely unexpectedly, the review concluded with an attack against Paolo Borsellino and the pool of magistrates, who had nothing to do with political factions and ambitions. Here the general disputes came into play with which Italian socialists and radicals attacked the magistrature.[156] However, it is my impression that Sciascia foresaw that the *maxiprocesso*, or maxitrial, was going to transform itself into a liberty-suppressing operation for a reason that was much more specifically related to the problem under discussion here. He did not believe that Cosa Nostra was a subject that could be put on trial or even identified. This is no different from what he believed in 1973, when he claimed that a mafioso does not even know that he is one, because the Mafia is a behavior and not an organization.[157]

The *maxiprocesso* aimed specifically at the power syndicate, in contrast with the focus of Falcone's preliminary investigation against the Spatola-Inzerillo group. That investigation attacked the enterprise syndicate using, primarily, the tool of banking investigations to unveil the gigantic network of the drug-trafficking business. For the first time, Cosa Nostra as such became the target of a trial. Already in Catanzaro and Bari, at the end of the 1960s, it had been evident that the *vox populi* gathered in the transcripts of police interviews was no longer sufficient to win convictions of individuals. In 1974, Major Russo (yet another name from the long, sad list of men destined to die) expressed in a hearing of the Anti-Mafia his frustration at "yet another demonstration of the power and intelligence of the Mafia," demonstrated by the unsuccessful outcome of the trials: "When there are fiduciary reports that we have gathered, those fiduciary reports are given no weight; [telephone] tapping, by law, cannot be used in court; confessions are not believed. What are we then to do? Wait for a mafioso to declare that he is guilty of certain crimes? He will never do that."[158]

The existence of confessions, if Russo was referring to Leonardo Vitale, could have proven the opposite. Vitale, however, did not represent the stereotypical cliché of a big-time mafioso. In fact, he was dismissed as the quintessential "Valachi from the *borgata*," as if the *borgate* that were treated so ironically weren't the *borgate* of Palermo, and therefore the heart and breeding ground of the phenomenon of the Mafia. Nonetheless, paradoxically, Vitale was by and large believed, since the crimes he was reporting could be corroborated by objective evidence. The lack of interest, as usual, had to do with the topic of Mafia association, in part because of the juridical obstacles to bringing cases on that basis. Is it a crime to stick a needle in your finger or to burn a paper image of a saint? What is the importance of the fact that certain hierarchies issue permissions for certain other generic territorial influences?[159]

By introducing the concept of *associazione mafiosa* (Mafia association), the La Torre law of 1982 marked a substantial step forward. It was subsequent events that showed the way. If in fact a clash inevitably indicates the existence of warring organizations, a series of crimes like those that took place in 1981–1982, no longer based on the logical sequence of an action followed by a reprisal as is typical of gang wars, points to the existence of a super-organization that judges and punishes. Here the contribution of the *pentiti* was crucial, no matter how much the members of the pool might insist, in an attempt to dampen public outcry, that "the *pentiti*, all things considered, play a fairly marginal role."[160]

The oversimplifications of the mass media and the limited understanding of the history of the Mafia did little to help anyone understand the phenomenon of *pentitismo* (turncoats and state's witnesses). Buscetta and his ilk were not—as the media tended to claim—the first mafiosi to speak, the first to break the "ironbound" wall of *omertà*. Mafiosi have always talked to the police. They put the police on the trail of their enemies with anonymous letters, with confidential conversations, with back-scratching arrangements. In Terranova's preliminary investigations the "informers" always knew everything, even of the existence of the commission. The ultimate case was that of Di Cristina, who, face-to-face with a Carabinieri officer, said everything that he could to damage the Corleonese.[161] Indeed, while from the exterior the organization may seem perfectly compact, in part owing to the rule of *omertà,* on the interior there is the constant and perfectly opposite sensation of a normally impending betrayal. In fact, the mafiosi regularly accused one another of being spies, *'nfami* or "infamous" (with a subtle assonance to the word "informer"—*translator's note*) and *tragediatore* (or truth-teller). Thus, Giuseppe Luppino, speaking to the Carabinieri, emphasized that his enemies were the real spies; Vitale killed another affiliated member who was going around saying that his uncle was a police informer. The new development of the *maxiprocesso* was that the mafiosi were actually speaking in court. And so, we are not looking at a progressive barbarization of the law, as some claimed, but rather at the introduction into the mechanism of trial law a phenomenon that had previously been relegated to the domain of the personal, and necessarily ambiguous, relationship between mafioso and policeman. Therefore, the innovation was not absolute, and it could be found as early as trials from the Fascist era, in contrast with what Sciascia claimed. It was true, for instance, of Giuseppe Gassisi who accused Cascio-Ferro and associates.[162]

In a *maxiprocesso*, identifying individual guilt is a daunting task. This was true both for the hundreds of foot soldiers of Cosa Nostra and for the members of the commission. They were accused of a great number of crimes both because of the avowed centralized nature of the organization itself and, in particular, on the basis of a rule stated by Buscetta. An "excellent" murder can only be committed with the authorization of the commission; a "normal" murder requires the permission of the family on whose territory the operation takes place. It is especially improbable that the obligation to tell the truth at all times among all members of Cosa Nostra actually exists and is regularly respected. If it were so, we would have to place the same reliance on events witnessed by a *pentito* in person and on information that he obtained in conversations with other affiliated members. In any case, Buscetta demonstrates that on a considerable series of occasions these laws are freely violated, prompting the unsurprising objection of one defense lawyer: "The rule that brooks no objections on page 14 of the deposition is subject to a vast number of exceptions in the other 400 pages."[163] Sciascia drew the conclusion that the *pentiti* provided "a cross section that is reliable in its details, but unreliable taken as a whole. In the revelations, in short, there is an intrinsic and essential contradiction: it offers the statement that the Mafia is a unified whole, that like a cathedral culminates in a 'cupola,' and at the same time provides a depiction of great disorder, murderous internal disagreements, internal abuses of power and bullying."[164]

I will not explore the evidentiary importance of the issue.[165] For any overall interpretation of the phenomenon, Sciascia's observation is misleading, however. The commission is not the cupola of a cathedral, nor is it the intelligent head of an octopus (in Italian, *piovra*, synonymous with Mafia—*translator's note*). It is a coordinating organism endowed with concrete powers with which its members intend to endow it. The fact that the first group to violate the rules was the Riina-Greco "majority" only proves something that was already clear to everyone: Mafiosi are no better than other men who establish institutions and then attempt to turn them to their own advantage. The description of Contorno, the second *pentito*, and Bontate's man of action, is simplistic and therefore absolutely perceptive: "The oath is like the Ten Commandments . . . don't look at the women of others, always tell the truth,"[166] all precepts that no good Catholic actually respects. Calderone tells about the oath-taking of the thief who, when he heard the prohibition against theft, refused to go along. It was necessary to explain to him that it was only forbidden to steal from his Mafia brothers.[167] Buscetta's description has the defect of "juridical" formalism for two reasons. First, explaining a system of rules to someone who does not know them means, by definition, rendering them absolute; the same problem occurs with any manual of law, because when a system of regulation no longer functions and tragically implodes, the most obvious solution is to attribute responsibility for the degeneration to the "ferocity" of one's adversaries, by depicting the Mafia "of the old days" as a good organization that followed the rules. On the other hand, Buscetta knew perfectly well that might makes right and that the representative institutions in Cosa Nostra were a reflection of power relationships. Calderone emphasized the same thing in reference to the weakness of the regional commission in the face of the overwhelming power of the Palermo Mafia.

Why do people become *pentiti*? First, because they lose, and this is another way of carrying on the battle and pursuing vendetta. Buscetta denounced the crimes of his enemies and concealed the crimes of his friends as well as his own. In this sense, it is true that he preserved not only the *sentire mafioso* (Mafia mindset) but also the *agire mafioso* (Mafia actions).[168] He held up a model of the old-school Mafia, abandoned by the Corleonese, and worked hard to convince others, and himself as well, that the true *pentito* was not really him but his enemies. In much the same manner, Valachi, according to the FBI agent who interrogated him, "did not consider himself at all a traitor to Cosa Nostra: in his view the true traitor was Vito Genovese."[169] From the very beginning of his confession to Falcone, Buscetta intended to prove that he was credible by elevating his discourse to a higher plane: "I would like to point out, first of all, that I am not a spy, in the sense that what I am going to say is not dictated by the intention of winning for myself the favors of Justice. And I am not a '*pentito*,' either, in the sense that my revelations are not dictated by tawdry considerations of self-interest."[170]

In this context, a dialogue, even a relationship of respect and trust, was established between the investigators and their superwitness. In the book/interview that was published a few months before his murder,[171] Falcone spoke of Sicilianity as a shared symbolic and cultural code that allowed a judge and a mafioso to understand one another. If he was referring to anything more than an understanding of dialect or gestures, allow this author to express some doubt. The ability to create a personal contact is the product of a judge's skill and commitment and his clear pursuit of an objective. The manifestation of a degree of empathy with the condition of a mafioso was meant as a way of offering a way out of Cosa Nostra to the increasingly numerous affiliated members living in fear of being crushed by that organization. On the very direct level of the relationship between judge and *pentito,* Falcone pursued the same reappropriation and reversal of the codes of folk culture that Mori attempted. It is necessary to demonstrate that the antivalues of the Mafia conceal, deep down, values that can be reutilized for purposes of civilization. On Buscetta's part, this common ground could only be identified in the old concept of a *Mafia d'ordine* (order-keeping Mafia), in opposition to a Mafia that is unrecognizable because it is terroristic, disfigured by greed and drug trafficking. Drugs in particular represent in and of themselves a factor that tends to subvert the social order. Because of this ideological objective, as well as other more practical considerations, the title of drug trafficker was attributed to the winning side and spared the losing side. However, if it were possible to make these distinctions, matters would actually stand the other way around.

The ideology of the *Mafia d'ordine* constitutes the terrain of communication between underworld and overworld. By this we mean not only the public institutions, but the vast array of clientele and sympathizers of the Mafia. Calogero Vizzini presented himself as someone who could "arrange" matters and forestall serious clashes. With these aims in mind, the word "Mafia" could still be applied, though it allowed for the technique of a rhetorical and polemical reversal that highlighted the inability of northerners truly to understand, as previously employed in the declarations by Pitrè, Morana, and Orlando, as well as in the previously cited epitaph of Ciccio Di Cristina, Giuseppe's father, with its invocation of the "law of honor, defense of all rights." This is not a holdover from the agrarian Mafia with its supposed patriarchal and protective characteristics. Leggio cites Pitrè in a learned fashion, conveying quite clearly the idea that his dimension, if not Mafia, could certainly be *mafiosità* (a coinage meaning, literally, "mafiosoness, mafiosity, mafianess"). Spatola, after working as an energetic entrepreneur in the field of money laundering, found time during his stay in prison to lay out in a few pages of notes his personal credo concerning the Mafia, and to wit—as he put it—on the kind of *omertà* that "helps the weak, and does not exploit them," and that "always does good." [172]

The Mafia preserves an ideology of order-keeping because it continues to serve a function of order-keeping (as in the *Mafia d'ordine*). Every so often, the

Mafia kills some purse snatcher or mugger. Indeed, Michele Greco, during one of the sessions of the *maxiprocesso*, expressed his own and his colleagues' disavowal of the mysterious murder of the eleven-year-old son of the man who held the contract for the cleaning service of the courthouse. Apparently, this disavowal was followed by the exemplary punishment of the killers.[173] And so it is logical that the ideological breaking point turned on issues of this type. Certainly, Buscetta is one of the least likely figures in terms of identifying the old-school mafioso. He was divorced repeatedly and was therefore liable to change his women and his alliances too often. He was "vainglorious," according to the unanimous opinion of the Anti-Mafia and his former colleagues at the *maxiprocesso*, a new man, with no family tradition. Moreover, if the Mafia is not a form of behavior, then, despite what people seem to think, there is no such thing as a common human type that can be identified as a mafioso. There is a model, the model of the mafioso, who speaks only in maxims and parables, in the style of Michele Greco. If, however, we turn our attention away from the ideological depictions provided by both mafiosi and mafiologists and take a look at reality, we find all sorts of individuals: Buscetta, a great man and a *disonorato* ("dishonored one"), the various cunning or sadistic mafiosi, those who find flimsy excuses to get out of participating in a murder, like Antonino Calderone, and others who are miserable unless they are given a chance to kill someone. Giuseppe Sirchia discovered literature during his internal exile on the island of Linosa and carried on a correspondence with Leonardo Sciascia, claiming in his letters that he wanted only to live a peaceful life. Upon his return from exile, however, Sirchia was murdered, the victim of Bontate's vendetta. And Bontate himself, the alleged gentleman described by Buscetta, was a man who could show up late for an appointment, apologizing and offering as a reason for the delay the fact that he had had to change a flat tire and stop to *inchiaccare* (strangle) a human being.[174] The only category that seems to stand out is that of the soldiers, extremely loyal to their capi—for instance, Caruso, the inept killer of Di Cristina, or the ferocious and nimble Contorno, who spoke at a rapid pace, the same pace at which he skillfully avoided ambushes. During one of those ambushes, on at least one occasion, Contorno found himself fighting a friend. "He was my long-time friend, when he came up to me, he had the face of a dead man, I understood completely: *Finivu!* [I'm done for] I thought."[175]

Another mafioso who acted out of a spirit of belonging was Leonardo Vitale. He could explain what the old Mafia was and justifiably employ its ideology, but he was insane, and perhaps in his insanity he was able to see more clearly: he smeared himself with excrement to purge himself of sin, he burned the clothing that he had purchased with the fee earned for committing murder, and he showed leniency toward and understanding of his uncle, but not for their shared heritage, which he considered the source of all his problems:

> Partial mental infirmity = psychic disease; Mafia = social disease; Mafia politica = social disease; corrupt authorities = social disease; prostitution = social disease; syphilis, condylomas, etc. = a physical disease that has echoed in the diseased psyche since childhood; religious crises = psychic disease caused by these diseases. These are the diseases of which I, Leonardo Vitale, was a victim, and am now risen again in my faith in a true God.[176]

And in the end, when Vitale left the insane asylum, he emerged from the logic of the Mafia, and it was in this peaceful condition that the killers found him and mercilessly shot him down.

Evidently, while all mafiosi are not the same, neither are all the *pentiti;* nor does a break with the Mafia need to be based on insanity in order to be complete. Women, for instance, achieve that break with the Mafia early and more completely. Not all of them, of course. And it may be that some of them play the alleged role of vestal virgins of vendetta; however, at the time when it becomes necessary to change sides, they have displayed a mental flexibility that is greater than that shown by their men. The Mafia trials are filled with female characters, such as the wife of the *campiere* Comaianni, killed by Leggio, who found the courage to accuse him after lengthy hesitation. She encountered a prosecuting attorney, according to whom "we should not pay attention to a little woman who first said one thing and later said another."[177] Serafina Battaglia lost her man, a mafioso, and was attempting to spare her son the same fate by turning to the boss Torretta who promised her protection and instead allowed the Rimi from Alcamo to kill him. At that point, the woman denounced her son's killers and in the courtroom of the Catanzaro trial faced Torretta and openly showed him her defiance and contempt: "And you like to call yourself men of honor. . . . You are a man worth half a lira."[178] Then there is the story of Felicia Bartolotto, the wife of Luigi Impastato of Cinisi, a mafioso dating back many generations, whose son, Peppino, was a militant in Democrazia proletaria (Proletarian Democracy), who openly railed in public meetings and over local radio broadcasts against such "excellent" individuals as Don Gaetano Badalamenti. Here the Mafia and the Anti-Mafia came face to face in the same family, in a crescendo of hatred, threats, and ambiguous promises of protection. The father was killed, and the son too was killed. The Mafia had a prank in store for the son, Peppino: he was killed in the context of a frame-up, a staged dynamite attack, to be blamed on the young subversive. In honor of Peppino's memory, Felicia learned to fight as best she was able, giving unfiltered interviews to journalists from the mainland:

> Because I like to speak to them, so that the story of my son can be dissemi-
> nated, and they can understand what the Mafia means. . . . They imagine to
> themselves: "She is Sicilian and she keeps her mouth closed." But that's not
> how it is. I have to defend my son, politically, I have to defend him. My son
> was not a terrorist. He was fighting for certain specific and just things.[179]

POLITICS AS SEEN BY THE MAFIA . . .

Over the course of the horrifying year of 1992, the Mafia managed to land four murderous blows, assassinating two of its most estimable enemies, Giovanni Falcone and Paolo Borsellino, but also two of its most authoritative links to official power, Salvo Lima and Ignazio Salvo. Following these attacks, there was a state reaction that resulted in the deployment of the Italian army in Sicily and the arrest of numerous Mafia bosses, who had been in hiding as long as anyone could remember. Among them was Totò Riina himself—a pupil of Leggio, the leader of the Corleonese, the successor to Michele Greco as the head of the commission. Immediately thereafter, Giulio Andreotti was indicted. Andreotti could safely be called the most eminent politician in republican Italy (three times prime minister, and cabinet-level minister about a dozen times), and he was charged with collaboration with the Mafia, and specifically with a continual and frequent exchange of favors that originated with the adherence to the Andreotti current (a political group loyal to Andreotti within the now defunct Christian Democratic Party)—dating back to the end of the 1960s—of the most significant group in the Sicilian Christian Democratic Party. That group had once been followers of Fanfani but had broken away from Fanfani and from Gioia, under the leadership of none other than Salvo Lima. Andreotti, a former Italian prime minister, was also alleged to have ordered Cosa Nostra to murder the Roman journalist Mino Pecorelli. Even more clamorously, Andreotti was alleged to have been involved in the Dalla Chiesa murder. According to the Palermo investigating magistrates, the motives for the Dalla Chiesa murder lay not in the hostility of the Mafia but rather in a political plot originating out of the kidnapping and assassination of Aldo Moro. This outcome, astonishing and unpredictable, went hand in hand with the debacle of the parties in the governing coalition in the face of the raging cyclone of Tangentopoli (the Bribesville investigation). This state of affairs led many Italians to wonder just what relations existed between the Mafia and other powers that either openly or clandestinely governed Italy over the past thirty years. And in the mid-1990s for the first time an answer to that question emerged from the interior of Cosa Nostra, a harvest of information that seemed to confirm all the worst hypotheses that Italian public opinion had formulated concerning the relationship between the Mafia and politics.

In this case, the sources are numerous—in contrast with the situation in the 1980s. The sources were a substantial group of mid- and high-ranking mafiosi willing to collaborate with the law. It was an avalanche, a landslide, a general crisis that undermined the organization, triggered by an increasingly determined repression from the forces of order and by the simultaneous centralizing vise grip implemented by the Corleonese. Lacking, however, was the testimony of the leaders who interacted directly with major politicians; we hear nothing from Riina, nor from Badalamenti, much less from Bontate, of course. Then Buscetta finally admitted his age-old relationship with Lima, as well as his participation in the alleged attempt to free Moro; however, he too based his testimony on information from Badalamenti or Bontate.

It was therefore the Cosa Nostra grapevine, at all levels, that identified Lima's and Andreotti's ties with Bontate, first, and Riina later. The *communis opinio,* or common opinion, among mafiosi in and of itself represents a significant element, considering that in the interior of that secret organization, but extending over numerous continents and involved in diverse yet linked activities, there must necessarily be an instrument of communication that is acceptable and commonly accepted. That must be true even in contexts where it is not believed that the obligation always to tell the truth among affiliated members is actually respected in practice. In that context, the Mafia capo will explain to his colleagues and soldiers political events and their relations with politicians in accordance with codes that are prevalent among the mafiosi themselves, and he will give an interpretation that is suitable and accessible to himself and his fellow mafiosi of everything that happens in the "overworld," in contrast with the "underworld" of the Mafia. Among the things that he will think and say are that Judge Corrado Carnevale is willing and will therefore always succeed in "fixing" trials, for money or for friendship; that Salvo Lima is willing to, and can therefore be relied upon to intervene in issues of judicial policy, out of loyalty and gratitude to those who procure votes for him; and that if Lima were to be out of the picture, then "Zio" Giulio ("Uncle" Giulio Andreotti), for the same reasons, would step into the breach and take Lima's place. In exchange, a special effort will be made to obtain the objects that he is "crazy" about, such as, for instance, "a particular painting."[180] On the other side of the fence, Falcone was viewed as someone who "wants to be powerful," willing to do anything to avoid seeing the *maxiprocesso* collapse. As is evident in particular from the last instance mentioned, the portrayals of events might well not be false, but they are in any case twisted to fit a simplified schema. There was an assumption that in the overworld, just as in the world of Cosa Nostra, the rules that have been solemnly set forth will be respected only as long as they are useful. There is a certainty that, in comparison with personal relationships and, in the final analysis, the considerations of force, those rules will have no value or importance.

As the tide turned in the 1970s and 1980s, repression began to hit Cosa Nostra, which attempted to persuade its Christian Democratic partner to hinder the machinery of justice. The most obvious point of leverage ran through the control of votes. In his alleged meeting with Andreotti, Bontate is said to have exclaimed:

> In Sicily, we are in charge, and if you do not want to eliminate the Christian Democratic Party entirely, you will have to do as we tell you to do. Otherwise, not only will we take away every vote you have in Sicily, but even the votes in Reggio Calabria and all of southern Italy. You will only be able to count on the votes of northern Italy, where everybody votes Communist, and you had better accept that this is how things are.[181]

The threat was put into effect during the consulship of Riina, during the elections of 1987, when the order went out to vote for the *garantismo* (civil rights concerns) of the socialists and the radicals, and against the unreliability of the Christian Democrats. In the Palermo prison of the Ucciardone, the bloc of votes went as directed, and, apparently, the prisoners self-imposed a tax on behalf of the radicals. In certain lower-class quarters as well, the result was what the Mafia called for, but on the city, provincial, and regional levels the success of the socialists corresponded with the figures for the national vote. Indeed, the vote for the socialists went hand in hand with the success of the Christian Democratic Party, likewise in keeping with the general trend and in defiance of the Cosa Nostra boycott.

One is therefore forced to wonder where, on this occasion, all the votes went. And we are referring not only to the votes of the entire Mezzogiorno, claimed boastfully by Bontate, but the 180,000 votes that in 1988, in Palermo alone, according to the then judge Ayala, were supposedly controlled by the Mafia; or even the fifty or sixty thousand votes that since 1994—after state repression weakened the organization—and even today, according to the progressive members of parliament, have been controlled by Cosa Nostra.[182] The inductive method whereby these estimates were made, by simply multiplying the presumed number of members of the *cosche* by a figure of seventy or eighty votes that were under the influence of each individual mafioso, appears, first and foremost, crude. It is reasonable to suppose that the single most important one of the 2,700 affiliated members (in 1988) or the 780 affiliated members (as of this writing) might influence eighty votes. Or even more; it is fair even to suppose that the second or third is able to do the same, but it is improbable to say the least that the hundredth-ranked member or the thousandth-ranked member, or the 2,700th-ranked affiliated member would be able to find, in the shared milieu in which he and all the others were fishing, in the clientelistic network of the Mafia *cosca*, an extra eighty votes lying around, available to be influenced, and not yet snapped up by his various superiors. To go any further, what is required is open propaganda or publicity, of other means, or a political machine—in other words, solutions that are different from the workings of the Mafia. Moreover, as Falcone noted at the time, criticizing his friend and colleague Ayala, "all this presupposes a unity of intent, let us call it a political supervision of Cosa Nostra that in reality does not exist. There are no meetings and votes of the board of directors of Cosa Nostra that communicate on various occasions what party or what candidate to vote for."[183] Let us suppose that in an exceptional circumstance, such as in 1987, this does happen; then it may still be possible that the political instrument is not sufficiently flexible to change horses in midstream and that the *capi-bastone* neither wish nor are able to manage such a change. Finally, there is no assurance that new and improvised alliances are able to function better than the old ones. For instance, consider the case of Claudio Martelli, elected to parliament that year in Palermo on a *garantista* (civil rights protection) platform; as Italy's minister of justice, Martelli would give Giovanni Falcone, Cosa Nostra's most fearsome and powerful enemy, a very influential Roman office.[184]

This approach seems to open up to discussion the idea of an exchange between Mafia and politics revolving around the electoral process. In order to understand what the Mafia gives to politics, it would first be necessary to examine more closely the way in which each of them interacts with "dirty" business, covering transactions that take place on a territorial basis (such as public works) and financial transactions. Mafiosi certainly do play the role of ward heelers and *capi-elettori* (electoral lieutenants—*translator's note*), they help to guide electoral blocs, and they take part in the implementation of the workings of the political machine. It is questionable, however, whether in a large city or even on a regional scale—the case of individual towns and villages is another matter, as are corrupt neighborhoods or quarters—they could represent the executive function, the motor, the ideational, and decision-making circuits. If we look as well to the past, the Mafia's intervention in the crucial junctures of Sicilian political life comes to relatively little. At a certain point, the Mafia focused on Sicilian separatism but was incapable of procuring major electoral successes on its be-half. It should also be considered that the MIS, although it never had the mass following that some have described, did enjoy a considerable popular vote and through no help from the *cosche*. Later, the mafiosi supported the Italian right, until the convulsive aftermath of Operation Milazzo. Only when the Christian Democratic Party was already triumphant did they flow into it, and even then—as Captain Malausa would have said—out of "personal interest," inaugurating the long phase in which the Mafia and the Christian Democratic Party's destinies were intertwined.

Cosa Nostra is not a political party, and it does not gather votes on its own behalf. That kicks the topic back into the court of politics, opinions, and material and symbolic transactions. For instance, in the success of Forza Italia in Palermo in the political elections of 1994, just a few months before the overwhelming majority victory that ushered Leoluca Orlando in as mayor (certainly under an opposing political trend), the Mafia mobilization followed, just as in the good old days of the Christian Democratic Party, the establishment of an alliance in and of itself capable of producing myths, ideas, projects, tools, and men for the governance of the public interest. The fact that Forza Italia focused part of its electoral campaigns in 1994 and 1996 on a specious platform of defending civil rights (an attack on the legislation rewarding state's witnesses, on the measures for detention and security in the prisons, and on the very concept of Mafia affiliation and association) proves once again that the most important element is the political momentum of a proposal. In a certain sense we might say that many of the areas subject, according to the Palermo investigators, to the illegal, subterranean, and ineffective negotiations between Cosa Nostra and Andreotti over the course of the 1980s are now part of the open, official, and legal program of Forza Italia (Silvio Berlusconi's political party, founded in 1993), targeting the interests of the Italian people and therefore of the Mafia lobbies as well.

Cosa Nostra therefore seemed incapable of properly managing its own electoral influence independently of the input of a political party, and to a far greater degree was incapable of guiding political developments. That explains why in the last fifteen or twenty years the Mafia's obligatory path was unfailingly that of terrorism, as doubtful in its efficacy as it was murderous in its outcomes, and the Mafia chose that path in its attempts both to hinder its adversaries and to influence its allies, both current and potential. Piersanti Mattarella, for instance, is supposed to have been killed because, even though he came out of a family tradition that left him open to Mafia influence, at a certain point he made a clear and decisive alliance against the Mafia. But it was above all the inability of political power to keep firm control over the judiciary power at the time of the definitive confirmation of the outcome of the *maxiprocesso* that triggered the Mafia's ferocious reprisal. Ignazio Salvo and Salvo Lima—the alleged great middlemen between the Mafia and Andreotti—were thus punished for their inability to ensure the protections that Riina and his partners expected. In the end, in 1993, the Corleonese Brusca and Bagarella planned to strike a blow against that *cornuto* ("cuckold") Andreotti, either personally or against one of his children, because he had "turned his back" on his friends.[185] Both episodes may have gone differently from the way they were described by the *pentiti* and hypothesized by the investigating magistrature of Palermo, but in any case, this is the logic. I do not believe, on the other hand, that the "losers" of the Bontate-Inzerillo group truly made use of an opposing methodology—a "traditionalist" method, as the indictment of Andreotti puts it,[186] and as the indictment of the *maxiprocesso* put it earlier—to the one employed by the Corleonese. Indeed, the logic that initially pushed Cosa Nostra toward terrorism was common to the various groups within Cosa Nostra, rendered similar by their competition to control politics and politicians, similar to the competition to control business and smuggling, even before the second Mafia war, or the takeover of the commission. Buscetta, for instance, attributed to Inzerillo the murder of the magistrate Gaetano Costa. When he realized that Rosario Nicoletti (the Sicilian regional secretary for the Christian Democratic Party, who committed suicide in 1984) was negotiating with Riina, Stefano Bontate in person said to Mannoia: "If that *crasto* [cuckold or, less frequently, eunuch; a sexual insult] doesn't start behaving right, we are going to have to kill him."[187]

During the course of the meeting that followed the Mattarella killing, again according to the *pentito* Mannoia, Bontate is said to have "warned the Honorable Andreotti against implementing any special measures or laws, because if that were to happen, there would be very grave consequences."[188] We are not interested in establishing whether or not the meeting ever actually took place. What interests us here is the fact that the strategic line of Cosa Nostra, as it is set forth by the chieftains to the membership, calls for a transition from a relationship (either partnership or intimidation) with administrators for the management of business, contracts, and the like, to a step up, that is, to the level of attempting to influence, with promises and threats, the course of active legislation and, as it were, the larger political sphere. Only this further transition is capable of explaining the corresponding terrorist escalation. There are even clearer examples. Falcone, working in collaboration with Claudio Martelli, launched legislative measures against the Mafia, as well as a regular monitoring of the verdicts handed down by the Court of Cassation, Italy's Supreme Court. It would appear that that effort managed to save the *maxiprocesso* from potential derailing. It was on this higher level of battle that Falcone's adversary played the bloody card of murder. That card, however, did not obtain the Mafia's hoped-for result. For that matter, what concrete result could ever have been achieved by the attacks on the Uffizi in Florence and on Via Fauro (1993), which were so similar to the attacks seen in the realm of political terrorism?

... AND THE MAFIA SEEN FROM THE POINT OF VIEW OF POLITICS

In preparation for his departure for Palermo, where he would soon meet his fate, Carlo Alberto Dalla Chiesa went to see Andreotti, in response to a request from Senator Andreotti himself, which seemed a fairly natural turn of events, "given the fact that his electoral base was in Sicily." "I was very clear with him," noted the general in his diary on 6 April 1981. "I told him in no uncertain terms that I would have no special consideration for that sector of the electorate from which his *grandi elettori* (major electoral lieutenants—*translator's note*) draw their votes. I am convinced that his imperfect understanding of the phenomenon . . . has led him in the past and continues to lead him to make errors in his evaluation of both men and circumstances."[189]

We see here, in extremely concise form, an interpretation of the entire question of the relationship between the major Italian leader and Cosa Nostra. Dalla Chiesa distinguished three different levels. First was the level of Andreotti himself, who carried on a relationship with the Mafia that was mediated, instrumental, and limited to the sphere of electoral issues; next came the level of the *andreottiani*, "the most thoroughly polluted political family on the island,"[190] the *grandi elettori* (Lima; the president of the Sicilian Region, D'Acquisto; the mayor of Palermo, Martellucci) in whom the major leader superficially placed his trust; third came the level of the electorate from which the *grandi elettori* drew their votes, the Mafia families as distinguished, specifically, from the political families. Here we are not very distant from the statement today of the former Communist senator Emanuele Macaluso: "Andreotti does not produce politics. De Gasperi, Fanfani, and Moro actually took on the complex Sicilian political situation. Andreotti didn't. He used what he found or what was offered to him. In 1968 Lima arrived. And Lima was the one who engaged in politics."[191] And so, on the one hand, if Dalla Chiesa and Macaluso identified a multilinked network that tied Andreotti to the Mafia, a network they analyzed in the light of political responsibility rather than penal liability, on the other hand Andreotti himself in all his statements maintained a position of total closure, denying among other things that he had ever summoned Dalla Chiesa for a meeting, and even stating that "there was no mention of any of the topics that are noted on the page in his diary."[192] And he insisted on that point even though the conversation remains in writing, one might even say, carved, into the page of the diary of the man who was fated to die. On that page of Dalla Chiesa's diary we read a description of Andreotti as, urged by Dalla Chiesa to express an opinion on the misdeeds of his own faithful followers, he suddenly turned the topic to Sindona and told the story of a certain Inzerillo, "who died in America, [and] arrived in Italy in a coffin and with a ten-dollar bill in his mouth." Dalla Chiesa noted with some irritation that this point as well "offered further evidence" of Andreotti's superficiality, and that unfortunately in these matters "folklore is still the predominant element."[193] And yet here Andreotti—who now denies that this part of the conversation ever took place— seems to point out a trail, a code of interpretation, in a manner that is finally significant.

The Inzerillo in question was the brother of Salvatore, the great middleman of the trans-Atlantic drug traffic whose murder—accompanied by Bontate's murder—marked the beginning of the offensive of the Corleonese. It would appear that the great Carabiniere investigator knew relatively little about all this, like nearly everyone in April 1981, while Andreotti, if only for the flash of an instant, appears to have been privy to secret matters. For that matter, the issue of conflicts among mafiosi concerning the great prize at stake, the narcotics traffic, immediately led to the figure of Michele Sindona. As we know, Sindona was supported by Andreotti and by the *andreottiani* even after he had been indicted by the Italian justice system, and even after the murder of the lawyer Ambrosoli at Sindona's orders. Sindona came out of age-old ties with the Gambinos of New York, and as we have noted, he had other ties with Rosario Spatola. Sindona therefore was perfectly integrated into the Sicilian American connection that was so much the focus of the second Mafia war. According to the *pentito* Mannoia, Sindona represented for the Bontate-Inzerillo group the financial channel that the head of the P2 Masonic lodge Licio Gelli (and with him, perhaps, Roberto Calvi, president of the Banco Ambrosiano) constituted for the Corleonese. Mutolo instead stated more generically that both of them had invested in Sindona's banks. Now that Sindona's business affairs had turned for the worse, they were demanding "the restitution of their money."[194]

The bloody conflict that pitted the two wings of the militant Mafia in Palermo against each other did not necessarily entail a corresponding opposition between the financial channels utilized by those two wings in Milan or in New York, nor, for that matter, between their political sponsors. It is instead possible that an explosion of violence on this scale and with this degree of obviousness—let us consider the murder of Ambrosoli, the attempt on the life of the vice president of the Banco Ambrosiano, the mysterious murder of Roberto Calvi, and even the "suicide" of Sindona—may have rendered problematic the relations between these business-Mafia groups and their political sponsors. Based on these elements, we might attempt to reconstruct, on an entirely hypothetical basis, a consistent version as offered by Andreotti. When Andreotti suddenly changed the subject with Dalla Chiesa, he might have been trying to tell him that there were two wings of the Mafia, the Sicilian American wing tied to the drug trade and the political wing; that the really dangerous group was the Sicilian American wing; and that it was his responsibility to protect the interests of the second, political wing through Lima and the Salvos. This would explain how the measures taken against the narcotics traffickers, about which Andreotti still boasts today, should have been accompanied and are still accompanied by the defense of Lima. This would also explain Andreotti's cryptic references to the vendetta of the drug traffickers and/or the Americans—which took the form of a terror attack against Lima and Salvo, and a judicial attack against Andreotti himself—as well as his polemic against Buscetta, who knew much more about the American side than he was ever willing to reveal.

Macaluso, setting forth in a certain sense Andreotti's thesis, stated that drugs had created a wedge between the political class and the Mafia, terrorizing the political class and rendering the Mafia even more audacious and bold. This is a plausible, but not ultimately convincing, explanation, both in specific and in general terms. Speaking specifically, in the Mafia war and in the terrorist escalation we see not so much a conflict between narcotics traffickers and politicians as an attempt on the part of the commission to seize control of both drug trafficking and political ties. Speaking in more general terms, the Mafia is never reduced to an association of drug traffickers, or abstract financiers whose assets do their work purely in the virtual world of computers.[195] In recent years, the Mafia has enriched itself through drug dealing, but it has also utilized the increasingly profitable opportunities available in the Italian version of the welfare state; it has strengthened itself through the proliferation of illegal behavior at all levels; and most important, from its contact with a corrupt political machine, it has derived the idea—and it matters little whether that idea had any foundation in reality—that it could act as a protagonist on the stage of the battle for power.

The attempt to put all the blame on narcotics is also an indication of the need that some members of the political class feel to find a way of saving their souls, in bad faith, as I believe is the case with Andreotti, or in good faith, as is the case with Macaluso.[196] The history of relations between the Mafia and politics is not the true history of Italy, as those who published the indictment of Andreotti have claimed. Nor is it even the true history of Sicily. But among the other histories, edifying or less edifying, of civilization or barbarianism, it is one of the histories of Italy, and not the least important one. Part of that history comes out of narcotics, another portion comes out of the depths of Sicilian history and reality, and yet another comes from the political system. Of that history and of the role that he played in it, Andreotti chooses to say nothing, to such a degree that the lack of verisimilitude of his defense constitutes the greatest single piece of evidence of some degree of guilt on his part. He might have said that he supported Sindona in order to safeguard relations between Italy and the Vatican; that he knew the Salvos for electoral reasons; that he allowed Lima to carry on his regional politics and policies without understanding much of what he was doing; that he had talked about certain topics with Dalla Chiesa without assigning much importance to those conversations. But, if he wishes to be at all credible, he would have to admit that he failed to realize to what degree Lima, the Salvos, and Nicoletti were, at the very least, compromised and subject to pressure and extortion; that he failed to understand how dangerous and murky the influences that were growing in their entourage, which was directly or indirectly his own entourage, had come to be for them, and above all, for our common homeland, Italy. Andreotti must necessarily be aware of the role attributed to the Salvos as early as the preliminary investigation of the *maxiprocesso*; nor could he fail to be aware that the murder of Ignazio Salvo, along with the murder of Lima, and the massacres of Capaci and Via d'Amelio, constituted the most audacious and overt of all of Cosa Nostra's offensives. Today, after all that has happened, Andreotti still considers the Salvos to be individuals of mere local importance. And that is the most unpersuasive and astonishing aspect of the entire story, even more than the alleged kiss that he exchanged with Riina.

THE PROBLEM OF FALCONE

The Andreotti case, and more in general the history of the Mafia over the past twenty years, are essential contexts in which to study a number of the interpretive questions from which we initially set out. The Mafia is an organization that links criminals together in an age-old, well-consolidated structure, rendered more compact by the ritual of the oath, capable of surviving, renewing itself, and growing ever stronger over the course of more than a century. From its very beginning, that organization has determined a series of specific internal hierarchies, independent of the more general hierarchies of the economy and of politics. Nevertheless, for the entire first period of its history, the Mafia remained a lesser power in relation to the power of the large landowners and the major notables, a power that could continue to function only if connected to those greater powers through a series of clientelistic networks. Frank Coppola, newly returned to Italy after many years of living in America, immediately declared that he was a "devoted follower" of Vittorio Emanuele Orlando and worked in favor of Orlando's political interests. In turn, Orlando could excite the Mafia's hopes and safeguard its interests, but only alongside the many other interests that Orlando was encouraging and safeguarding, if and when that was in his own best interest. Buscetta mirrored, with a certain degree of nostalgia, the prudent conception of the relationship with politics that "traditional" mafiosi preserved. He claimed that even a corrupt parliamentarian had to be allowed to vote in favor of a law against the Mafia, because any reasonable person will understand that the politician "must preserve that public image even if his actions redounded to the harm of Cosa Nostra."[197] In other words, politicians had to respect the rules of politics, just as mafiosi respect the rules of the Mafia, because the only way for matters to function was to leave them in their natural order. Moreover, I would say, the traditional Mafia—both in the liberal era and in the early period of the Italian republic—had absolutely no notion that it might determine the content of legislation; it tended to leave issues of that sort not merely formally, but substantially as well, in the hands of major notables, or perhaps to the ability of some local lobby or some association of property owners to negotiate. Things, however, changed over time, and much more rapidly outside of Cosa Nostra than on its interior. As we have seen, Cosa Nostra showed signs of surprising stability over the long term. Major landowners vanished as a political and social power with such speed that one is tempted to think that it was Fascism that preserved them in an artificially prolonged existence for twenty years. The notables of Sicily made way for the party machine, as a result of the proportional electoral system, the hegemony of the Christian Democratic Party, and also the disintegration of the "traditional" rural society. This did not mean that the political system became impermeable to the mafiosi; if anything, they enjoyed a greater ability to exert pressure on the realm of politics and were better able to redistribute the swelling stream of resources that the political system was responsible for allocating, as well as having a greater ability to paralyze the administrative, police, and judicial apparatus of the Italian state, let alone the townships and the Sicilian regional governments, where it would be naïve at best to hypothesize any distinction between politics and administration.

At a time in which society in general was no longer rigidly structured by social standing and authority, the Mafia began to think that there was no lid capable of covering what was boiling in its cauldron. In the end, the organization attempted to transport the network within itself, to subordinate to itself all outside contacts, whether with profiteer or politician. Let us remember the answer that Buscetta himself offered when he was asked about Sindona's secrets: "The secrets of Sindona were light as a feather compared with the secrets of Bontate";

perhaps because the latter secrets were weighed down with lead, Sciascia commented.[198] Here is a history in which the hierarchies are inverted: Bontate has weightier secrets than does Sindona, Riina is worth more than Bontate, and the sheepherder Leggio eliminates the notable Navarra.

In this sense, the intellectual battle, above and beyond the judicial battle, that Giovanni Falcone waged was especially important, as was the attempt to extract Cosa Nostra from the network of its external political and business relations, so as to be able to examine the Mafia itself. This was a problem of judicial and repressive strategy that coincided to a certain degree with the problem facing us scholars, inasmuch as that which cannot be distinguished cannot be fought. In particular, Falcone refused to consider the relations between politics and the Mafia according to a hierarchic scheme:

> [I]f it is true that a fair number of Sicilian politicians have been, to all intents and purposes, adepts of Cosa Nostra, it is also true that within the Mafia as an organization they have never enjoyed particular prestige because of their political origins. In short, Cosa Nostra is so strong, compact, and independent that it can speak and make alliances with whomever it chooses, but never from a subordinate position.[199]

Similarly, the mafiosi who boast a particularly rich trove of outside relations, both political and business-linked, do not necessarily enjoy a corresponding degree of power within the organization. Nowadays, when *pentiti* are describing with a wealth of detail the highly placed contacts of Bontate in the "overworld," we still should not forget how easily the boss of S. Maria di Gesù was eliminated. When we analyze the role of the Salvos and of Lima in the system of political and Mafia power, we should also keep in mind that Ignazio Salvo and Salvo Lima were gunned down no differently than any other poor resident of the *borgata*.

"Above the organization's top levels," Falcone insisted, "there are no 'third levels' of any kind, influencing or deciding the direction of Cosa Nostra." Knowing full well that the world of the Mafia involved no marionettes or marionettists, no superagencies controlling the unsuspecting leaders of the cupola, he judged the idea of the *grande vecchio* ("powerful old man"), "who pulled the strings of the Mafia from the very top of the political sphere," nothing more than a sign of great "intellectual crudity."[200] This thesis was later confirmed, not only by the courts but also by the murderous reaction of the Mafia as an organization. Already, it had been the cause of a crescendo of attacks from the "Anti-Mafia" front itself—and in particular from Leoluca Orlando—against Falcone, who was accused of having "sidelined" the most delicate and dangerous trials, the political trials, and of having refrained from attacking the Third Level, the much touted Supercupola. In this connection, we are familiar with Buscetta's position on the subject. From the time of his first confessions, the *pentito* made it clear that he had very important information on this topic and that he was not yet willing to reveal it because Italy was not yet ready to accept it because the ensuing skepticism would have overturned the entire judicial procedure then under way. We may assume that first of all the pool decided to complete the *maxiprocesso*, which would culminate in the essential demonstration of the existence of Cosa Nostra as a centralized and organized entity, a proposition to which few indeed (including experts on the Mafia) might have been willing to agree only a short time before. Under the leadership of Giancarlo Caselli, the Turinese magistrate who took over the supervision of the investigations into Cosa Nostra after the murder of Falcone, the investigating magistrature of Palermo delved intensively into the connection between Mafia and politics, but inevitably focusing on the idea of Cosa Nostra's "sovereignty" that had been so crucial to Falcone.

The political and Mafia-linked murders that still remain particularly obscure are difficult to interpret in this context. The problem has been nicely stated by Nicola Tranfaglia, who wondered whether the intertwining links between Cosa Nostra, terrorist groups, and occult lobbies might express "a coherent political project," or whether they amount to nothing more than "tactical alliances, however frequent."[201] We might view the murder of Dalla Chiesa in light of this second hypothesis if it were proved to be linked to the Moro case. There are observers who have attributed to Cosa Nostra a substantial role in an international front, perhaps originally inspired by an anti-Communist conviction. Mattarella and La Torre, on the other hand, were representatives of the left wing of the Christian Democratic Party and the Communist Party precisely in the historic phase in which these two groups were trying out a conflict-ridden accord; La Torre had been a leader in the struggle against the installation of the cruise missiles in Comiso; both Terranova and Costa were among the few high-ranking "red" magistrates. This is how in 1982 the Catholic-inspired magazine *Segno*, which represented (and still represents) a point of reference in the struggle against the Mafia, commented on those facts: "At a time when democratic institutions—the legal power—are undergoing the growing influence of the left and the various popular forces, the extralegal centers of power, accepting murder and massacres as political weapons, step into the field to have their say on the outcome and results of the political crisis of our country."[202]

Among these right-wing antidemocratic efforts was a plan to take part in the Borghese coup presented in 1970 to Leggio by Salvatore Greco "*chicchiteddu*," accompanied by Buscetta, which might have emerged from Italian and South

American milieux (P2?) and for that reason was rejected. After the unhappy experience with Mori (who enacted a brutal, undemocratic, and largely successful campaign of suppression of the Mafia under Mussolini—*translator's note*), the mafiosi had little fondness for Fascism. Then there was the story of Sindona, who in 1979 is believed to have attempted to organize a separatist revolt, of which, however, there was not the slightest indication in the press or in public opinion: evidently, this was a public mutiny so secret that not even the necessary protagonists of the uprising, the Sicilians, knew anything about it.

Since the Grand Plot remains an inscrutable, unknowable black box, we should point out that in both cases in question, the initiative came from the losing group in the second Mafia war. For those mafiosi, the political relations constituted a substantial portion of their total capital. That means that they were the wealthiest in both this area and in terms of narco dollars. That doesn't necessarily mean that they really believed that they would be able to successfully implement these improbable projects. Rather, we can theorize that by taking them seriously, they would be likely to enhance their own prestige as mediators, both in the eyes of their outside contacts, with whom they were thus able to establish more intimate and profitable contacts, and in the estimation of their counterparts inside Cosa Nostra. This is true, for instance, of Bontate, who attempted to prop up his waning power inside the commission by offering his services to the Christian Democratic Party as a middleman for a negotiated solution to the Moro case. For the opposite reason, that is, to devalue Bontate's prestige, his adversaries inside Cosa Nostra, Riina and Calò, did their best to hinder that project.[203] If this is a plausible interpretation, then it is important to note that an event that was (in our view) absolutely fundamental to Italy's recent history was instead treated by the mafiosi in an instrumental manner, in terms solely of their own internal conflicts. We thus can see clearly how, in their hallucinatory universe, everything is considered solely as a subordinate issue, seen through the filter of the *Cose* (or "things") of Cosa Nostra (which of course means "Our Thing," just as *res publica*, the Latin root of "republic," means "public thing," and a "thing" or "ting" is the name for governing assemblies in Germanic and Scandinavian cultures—*translator's note*). This is a logic that all sectarian organizations seem to share. For instance, it is true of the terrorist organizations with which the Mafia established a relationship of interaction at the end of the 1970s.[204] I would describe that relationship as primarily cultural rather than material. The mafiosi actually met the terrorists in prison, but they measured themselves against the actions of the terrorists. The Brigate rosse (Red Brigades), Prima linea (First Line), and other comparable organizations were actively competing to gain the support and allegiance of the various abettors and adherents.

This rivalry took the form of a race to see who could strike the highest blow, hit the most "excellent" target. That was a crucial element in the killing of Aldo Moro. Cosa Nostra dubbed the assassination of Dalla Chiesa "Operation Carlo Alberto." In the prisons, likewise, the Catanians celebrated and gained in credibility and respect in the eyes of those who believed that the killers of Santapaola had "carried out the assassination, with perfect operational efficiency."[205] When Salvo Lima was assassinated, a mafioso convict said, "Accuminciaru finalmente" ("At last they've begun"),[206] reassured by the fact that his fellow mafiosi were finally beginning to carry out actions outside the prison walls as well. The Mafia does not publish newspapers or broadcast news reports, and therefore many of the actions that the Mafia carries out seem to have been conceived at least in part as messages designed to be amplified by the prison grapevine, by the rumor mill of the Palermo *borgate,* and in the conversation of drug traffickers in hotels throughout the world. It was true, for instance, of Badalamenti and Buscetta, who watched the evening news reports on television in far-off Rio de Janeiro and carefully decoded the message of the spectacular murder.[207] Buscetta himself offered an interpretation of the murder of Costa, seeing it as having been ordered by Inzerillo less as a way to halt the investigation than as a way "merely to display the extent of his power,"[208] that is, to offset the propaganda effect on the attentive audience of Cosa Nostra of the attacks carried out by the Corleonese.

The element of internal conflict between the factions is still overwhelmingly predominant. I believe that following the defeat of the MIS the Mafia had, and continues to have, only slight interest in large-scale politics, in which it is only marginally involved, and that without great enthusiasm. Nonetheless, those affiliated with Cosa Nostra are naturally interested in what happens in the day-to-day management of public affairs, and therefore in politics as machine far more than in politics as project. We have seen that in 1987 Riina was unable to administer a punishment to the Christian Democratic Party by draining away votes, perhaps in part hindered by resistance within the organization. This was true, for example, of Antonio Madonia, who continued to vote for the candidates of the Christian Democratic Party, in part to safeguard well-established relationships of "friendship."[209] More in general, the Madonias, although they continued to form part of the Corleonese alliance, still kept secret even from their allies their "close relations with the 'people who matter' in political, administrative, and economic milieux,"[210] because, evidently, they were reluctant to expose themselves to the risk that others might attempt to use those channels. Let's remember that Pippo Calderone attempted to keep his relationship with Costanzo secret from his fellow mafiosi, just as Calò attempted to force his way into the exclusive relationship that tied Riina (before he became the top-ranking boss) to Ciancimino. Franco Restivo, a major notable in the Christian Democratic Party, was a *compare* (roughly, "godfather") of Antonino Mineo, the Mafia capo of Bagheria, and obviously Restivo afforded him special treatment. For the La Barberas, and later for Stefano Bontate, the relationship with Lima was important. As a result, the ties with major businessmen and major politicians, in brief, with the establishment, do not appear to be subordinate to the rank held within the organization by a given mafioso. On the contrary, those who possess such relations necessarily find themselves in strategic positions as mediators with the outside world. "When a man of honor—even a high-ranking one, such as a *capo-mandamento*—needed to get in touch with a political leader, he had to pass through these channels."[211]

We might say, though strictly limited to the context of this specific point, that the fact that a politician might actually be affiliated with Cosa Nostra, or merely in collusion, does not constitute a crucial difference: the channel of communication remains private, and the organization is not identified with the channels utilized by its members. The undeniable processes of centralization, then, do nothing to change the twofold character of the phenomenon of the Mafia, which we have identified as a feature stretching back to the very origins. Relationships with politicians and with profiteers constitute, along the borders and even in the interior of the organization, an array of fluid networks through which a series of traditional intertwinings are reproduced, linking underworld and overworld. These relationships represent for an individual Mafia capo his personal and private "capital," or assets, comparable to the contacts utilized in narcotics trafficking, and it may even be that this capo considers it more to his advantage to be an integral part of a political machine than to pursue the supposed general interests of the organization.

The question then arises whether Cosa Nostra is capable of taking over (or even aspiring to do so) the direct management of political power. The parasitic conception of the relationship with politics necessarily and inevitably constitutes a daunting obstacle in this sense. In this context, we should also take into consideration the issue of the instruments with which the affiliates and even the capos of the Mafia interpret reality. They remain convinced that, as an old proverb frequently cited in nineteenth-century studies puts it: "If you have money and friends, you can ass-fuck the law" ("Chi ha denari ed amicizia va in culo alla giustizia"); now they add to that belief their faith in the effects of violent reprisals against friends who fail to keep their promises. That, however, is how things look when viewed through a keyhole, a visual angle that does little to allow one to perceive and appreciate the complexity of the mechanisms that regulate the operation of official power, the relationships among the various political groups and those linking the political system, the administration, and the magistrature, as well as the role played by public opinion. It is exceedingly difficult to condition this vast field of forces with a pair of tools as elementary as the carrot of exchanging favors and the stick of terroristic intimidation. Totò Riina believed that he could maintain Andreotti's support by threatening him or by reminding him of his obligations with a reassuring and saccharine demonstration of the famous kiss during the second summit meeting. And if that notorious meeting really did take place, it represented less Andreotti's recognition of the sovereignty of his counterpart,[212] and more another demonstration of his own cynicism, of his ability to manipulate those who, looking at things from the underworld, preserved a naïve faith in the rectitude and loyalty of the powerful in the overworld.

Lastly, there is the question of the effectiveness of the terroristic actions that derived from the processes of centralization within Cosa Nostra. Here we may reasonably introduce the concept of unintended consequences. Just as Sicilian involvement in the world heroin trade tended to decline from the mid-1980s (as a result of the Mafia wars?), likewise it may be (let us hope) that as a result of the "militarist" approach there will be a corresponding decline in the influence of Cosa Nostra in Italian politics. The challenge and the response reinforced one another in a reciprocal dynamic, and surely part of the responsibility for the fact that for the past fifteen years there has been an Anti-Mafia, and that there has been an increasingly lively and powerful resistance to the Mafia on the part of a number of public institutions[213] and from public opinion itself, can be laid to Mafia terrorism itself. At the end of 1996, as I write this chapter, most of the upper echelons and the leaders of the "shadowy partnership" have been found guilty and sentenced to prison. Still, how belatedly, and at what a high price in blood and civilization, and with what (permanent?) deformations of the country's public spirit has Italy finally attained this commendable result!

The heavy cost paid by the nation is a clear demonstration of how unacceptable the cynicism and nonchalance of Italy's political leadership have been over the past thirty years, both in political and ethical terms. "I had read one day," wrote Andreotti in an apparently random point in his self-justifying book, "that a major Mafia figure had been arrested, a certain Michele Greco, better known as *il Papa*—the Pope."[214] And so, Andreotti, then undergoing trial for association with the Mafia, was scarcely able to remember having read in a newspaper the name of the head of the commission during the years of his greatest power. It is here that the two opposing points of view, that of the underworld and that of the overworld, finally intersect and clash. Riina believed that he could control the political world with favors and threats; Andreotti felt that a major politician, and the large world of high-level politics, could brush against such a profoundly vulgar world and people without being substantially besmirched by it, that the Mafia itself was actually not really all that deserving of his attention.

For that matter, a great statesman like Vittorio Emanuele Orlando saw matters in the same light. And the political class of the liberal era of Italian politics and the first quarter century of the Italian republic viewed things similarly, as did the state officials, the notables, and the entrepreneurs of the beautiful island of Sicily. The only problem is that at a certain point this mechanism based on the laudable idea of tolerance began to run out of control, and the Sicilian Mafia increasingly tainted and polluted the consciences and the institutions of democracy, and even the basic possibility of there being such a thing as a democracy. The cases of Calvi and, most importantly, Sindona both demonstrate the degree to which, beginning from the watershed period that we have dated at the end of the 1970s, one of the profiteering Mafia networks grew, and that network came very close to flooding into the heart and nerve center of Italian economic, as well as political, power. (Sindona was a man who came out of nowhere and suddenly and rapidly rose to the highest levels of the financial world, international, Italian, and American. He went on to found "one of the largest, indeed perhaps the largest of all of Europe's financial companies," and ultimately attempted to take control of the fundamental institutions of Italian capitalism[215] through his ties to the Andreotti group, the P2, and the American and Sicilian Cosa Nostra.) From this point of view, no comparison can legitimately be made between the crimes with which Andreotti has been charged and the responsibility of a Crispi or a Giolitti, to which comparison is often, and irresponsibly, made. The exact same distinction can be made with regard to the unprecedented danger that the Mafia has posed over the past thirty years of Italian history.

Cosa Nostra linked itself in an absolutely new manner to high-level politics and business, that is, to the major period (which we hope and trust is over) of the welfare state and "weak" government, disintegrating among ad hoc institutions, laws crafted *ad personam* (for individual interests), lobbies, factions, clientelism and favoritism, local medical boards and regional governments, bribes for everyone, rampant profiteering, and concealed powers. In order to interpret such a system, which is the context within which the Mafia has metastasized, we would need a history of Italy, as a history of Sicily would be inadequate. However, to attempt to resolve the entire question of the Mafia in this context would amount to committing the same error as the anthropologists who believed that it was entirely a product of southern Italian society. Likewise, only someone who believes that the entire story took place between Italy's political power

centers, Palazzo Chigi and Montecitorio, can believe that the Mafia is political.
The organization that today is known as Cosa Nostra, under various variant
names, in different times and under different regimes, has been active for a very
long time; it is old, but it is not afraid of modernity. Let us only hope that this
formidable historical continuity can soon be interrupted.

NOTES

ABBREVIATIONS AND TERMS USED IN THE NOTES

AAGGRR	Affari generali riservati (General Affairs, Secret)
AC	Ministero degli Interni, Ammistrazione civile (Ministry of the Interior, Civil Administration)
ACS	Archivio centrale dello Stato (Central State Archives)
Antimafia: Doc.	*Antimafia, Documentazione allegata alla relazione conclusiva* (Antimafia, Documentation attached to the concluding report), ed. Commissione Parlamentare d'inchiesta sul fenomeno della mafia in Sicilia. Rome: Camera dei Deputati.
Antimafia: Singoli mafiosi	*Antimafia, Relazione sull'indagine riguardante singoli mafiosi* (Antimafia, Report on Investigations Concerning Individual Mafiosi), ed. Commissione Parlamentare d'inchiesta sul fenomeno della mafia in Sicilia. Rome: Camera dei Deputati.
APCD	Atti parlamentari della Camera dei deputati (Parliamentary Proceedings of the Chamber of Deputies)
ASAG	Archivio di Stato di Agrigento (IV) (State Archives of Agrigento)
ASCL	Archivio di Stato di Caltanissetta (State Archives of Caltanissetta)
ASPA	Archivio di Stato di Palermo (State Archives of Palermo)
ASSO	*Archivio Storico per la Sicilia Orientale*
b.	*busta* (envelope)
BCI	Biblioteca Comunale di Imola (Municipal Library of Imola)
bis	second
CPC	Casellario politico centrale (IV) (Central Political Records Office)
CR	Carteggio riservato (Private correspondence of the Secretariat of the Duce)
CS	*Corriere della Sera*
f.	fascicle
fondo	file or collection

GDS	*Giornale di Sicilia*
GP	Gabinetto Prefettura (Cabinet of the Prefecture)
GQ	Gabinetto Questura (Cabinet of the Police Administration)
MAP	Miscellanea affari penali (Miscellaneous, Penal Affairs)
PG	Ministero degli Interni, Polizia Giudiziaria (Ministry of the Interior, Judicial Police)
PS	Ministero degli Interni, Direzione di pubblica sicurezza (Ministry of the Interior, Head Office of the Police)
QAG	Archivio generale Questura (Police Administration, General Archives)
t., tt.	tome, tomes (*Note:* There is a distinction in Italian between volume and tome. A volume can be made up of more than one tome.)
ter.	third

CHAPTER I. INTRODUCTION

1. We should, however, refer to the works of S. F. Romano, *Storia della mafia* (Milan, 1966); F. Brancato, "La Mafia nell'opinione pubblica e nelle inchieste dall'Unità al fascismo," in *AntiMafia: Relazione sui lavori svolti . . . al termine della v legislatura*, pp. 163ff. G. Barone, G. Fiume, R. Mangiameli, P. Pezzino, G. Raffaele, and N. Recupero, who represent the "new" and more aggressive historiography on the topic, will be mentioned as we move forward. Let me cite here my own works, which will be reused in this context: "Nei giardini della Conca d'Oro," *Italia contemporanea*, 1984, 156, pp. 43–53; "Il tenebroso sodalizio," *Studi storici*, 1988, pp. 463–89; "Tra banca e politica: il delitto Notarbartolo," *Meridiana*, 1990, 7–8, pp. 119–55. Let me also mention here the study that I wrote with R. Mangiameli, "Mafia di ieri, Mafia di oggi," *Meridiana*, 1990, pp. 17–44.
2. "Una nuova fase della lotta alla mafia," Interview with Giovanni Falcone, *Segno*, 1990, 116, p. 10.
3. In this connection, see N. Tranfaglia, *La mafia come metodo* (Rome, 1991).
4. L. Galluzzo, F. Nicastro, and V. Vasile, *Obiettivo Falcone: Magistrati e mafia nel palazzo dei veleni* (Naples, 1989), pp. 167–68.
5. The play was produced by the lead actor Giuseppe Rizzotto, but apparently it was written by a certain Gaspare Mosca. See G. G. Lo Schiavo, *100 anni di mafia* (Rome, 1962).
6. Quoted by P. Alatri, *Lotte politiche in Sicilia sotto il governo della Destra (1866–1874)* (Turin, 1954), pp. 92–93. The variant spelling—maffia—remained frequent throughout the rest of the nineteenth century and only disappeared gradually.
7. In a report dated 31 July 1874 to the Ministry of the Interior, published as part of the documentation related to the police law (*legge di PS*) of 1875, in Atti parlamentari della Camera dei deputati (APCD), 1874–1875, Documents, attachment A 1, p. 13.
8. Report dated 4 April 1875, in APCD, 1874–1875, Documents, no. 24 *ter.*, p. 20.
9. L. Franchetti, "Condizioni politiche e amministrative della Sicilia," in L. Franchetti and S. Sonnino, *Inchiesta in Sicilia* (Florence, 1974) (1st ed. 1876). A more recent edition of Franchetti's book exists (Rome, 1991), with an introduction by P. Pezzino.
10. N. Recupero, "Ceti medi e 'homines novi': Alle origini della mafia," *Polis*, 1987, 2, p. 316. See, by the same author, "La Sicilia all'opposizione (1848–74)," in *La Sicilia*, ed. M. Aymard and G. Giarrizzo (Turin, 1987), pp. 41–85. The etymology was fanciful to the point of verging on the surreal: it explained "Mafia" as an acronym made up of the initials of the slogan "Mazzini

Autorizza Ferimenti Incendi Avvelenamenti" (Mazzini Authorizes Assaults, Arson, and Poisonings), reported in Henner Hess, *Mafia*, preface by L. Sciascia (Rome, 1991) (1st ed. 1970), p. 6.

11. Report of the Grand Jury established in New Orleans in 1892, quoted in H. S. Nelli, *The Business of Crime: Italians and Syndicate Crime in the United States* (Chicago, 1981), p. 65.

12. G. Pitrè, *Usi e costumi, credenze e pregiudizi del popolo siciliano* (Palermo, 1978), vol. 2, respectively, pp. 292 and 294.

13. Ibid., pp. 288–93; the *Dizionario siciliano* by G. Traina (1868), cited by Pitrè, hypothesizes that the term might be of Tuscan origin; the *Nuovo dizionario siciliano-italiano* by V. Mortillaro (Palermo, 1875) calls it a "Piedmontese word [*sic!*] introduced to the rest of Italy."

14. An aspect emphasized for the area of Gioia Tauro by P. Arlacchi, *Mafia, contadini e latifondo nella Calabria tradizionale* (Bologna, 1980); F. Piselli and G. Arrighi, "Parentela, clientela e comunità," in *La Calabria*, ed. P. Bevilacqua and A. Placanica (Turin, 1985), pp. 367–494.

15. A. Cutrera, *La mafia e i mafiosi: Saggio di sociologia criminale* (Palermo, 1900), p. 57.

16. Concerning the nineteenth-century Camorra, see the fundamental studies by M. Marmo, "Economia e politica della camorra napoletana nel sec. XIX," in *Quaderni dell'Istituto universitario orientale. Dipartimento di scienze sociali* (Naples, 1989), vol. 2, pp. 103–30; "Ordine e disordine: la camorra napoletana nell'ottocento," *Meridiana*, 1990, 7–8, pp. 157–90; "Tra le carceri e i mercati: Spazi e modelli storici del fenomeno camorrista," in *La Campania*, ed. P. Marcy and P. Villani (Turin, 1990), pp. 691–730. A two-century sketch of the subject is provided in I. Sales, *La camorra le camorre* (Rome, 1988).

17. E. Ciconte, *'Ndrangheta: Dall'Unità a oggi* (Rome, 1992), and E. Ciconte, *Processo alla 'ndrangheta* (Rome, 1996). But concerning the difficulties with a history of the Calabrian Mafia, see P. Bevilacqua, "La mafia e la Spagna," *Meridiana*, 1992, 13, pp. 110–16.

18. Hess, *Mafia*; A. Blok, *La mafia di un villaggio siciliano, 1860–1960* (Turin, 1986) (1st ed. 1974); J. Schneider and P. Schneider, *Classi sociali, economia e politica in Sicilia* (Soveria Mannelli, 1989) (1st ed. 1976); Arlacchi, *Mafia, contadini e latifondo*, and Arlacchi, *La mafia imprenditrice: L'etica mafiosa e lo spirito del capitalismo* (Bologna, 1983). The Schneiders have recently returned to the question with new and persuasive arguments: see their essay "Mafia, antimafia e la questione della cultura," in *La mafia, le mafie*, ed. G. Fiandaca and S. Costantino (Rome, 1994), pp. 299–324 (available in English as *Reversible Destiny: Mafia, Antimafia, and the Struggle for Palermo* [Berkeley, 2003]).

19. According to the interesting theorization by R. Catanzaro, "La mafia come fenomeno di ibridazione sociale," *Italia contemporanea*, 1984, 156, pp. 7–41.

20. See, respectively, in this volume, chapters 2 and 3.

21. Summation by the lawyer G. Russo Perez in *Giornale di Sicilia* (GDS), 8 June 1930.

22. Tribunal of Palermo Verdict vs. Spatola + 119 Others (investigating magistrate, Falcone), p. 485.

23. See chapter 2 in this volume.

24. N. Gentile, *Vita di capomafia, memorie raccolte da F. Chilanti* (Rome, 1993) (1st ed. 1963), p. 201.

25. J. Bonanno, *Uomo d'onore: L'autobiografia di J. B.* (Milan, 1985), passim.

26. Interview with G. Pagano, in *L'Inchiesta sulle condizioni sociali della Sicilia* (1875–76), 2 vols., ed. S. Carbone and R. Grispo (Bologna, 1968), p. 483.

27. In the interview with Indro Montanelli, *Pantheon minore* (Milan, 1958), quoted by Arlacchi, *La mafia imprenditrice*, p. 43.

28. See, respectively, the letter from the bishop of Caltanissetta, G. Jacono, 12 June 1935, quoted in C. Naro, *La Chiesa di Caltanissetta tra le due guerre* (Caltanissetta, 1991), vol. 2, p. 167; and C. Sarauw, *Note e richieste al R. Governo per l'assetto dell'industria zolfifera siciliana* (Catania, 1922), pp. 5–6.

29. See, for example, the critical observations by R. Catanzaro, "Mafia come impresa?" in Various Authors, *L'Italia estrema* (Rome, 1992), vol. 4, pp. 37–43, and Catanzaro, *Il delitto come impresa: Storia sociale della mafia* (Padua, 1988); U. Santino, *La mafia interpretata* (Soveria Mannelli, 1995); and U. Santino and G. La Fiura, *L'impresa mafiosa dall' Italia agli Stati Uniti* (Milan, 1990).

30. See, in this volume, chapter 5, on the apologetic positions held by Buscetta and, on the American side, P. Jenkins, "Narcotics Trafficking and the American Mafia: The Myth of Internal Prohibition," *Crime, Law and Social Change,* November 1992, 18, pp. 303–18.

31. The letter was published in "Diario della settimana," supplement to *L'Unità*, 30 October–5 November 1996, p. 58.

32. D. Gambetta, *La mafia siciliana: Un'industria della protezione privata* (Turin, 1992). In this connection, however, see also Catanzaro, *Il delitto come impresa*, pp. 27–30 and 76–79.

33. This stance emerges clearly in the book by M. Onofri, *Tutti a cena da don Mariano: Letteratura e mafia nella Sicilia della nuova Italia* (Milan, 1996).

34. In particular, see M. Marmo, "Le ragioni della mafia: due recenti letture," *Quaderni storici,* April 1995, 88, pp. 195–211; R. Catanzaro, "Recenti studi sulla mafia," *Polis*, 1993, 2; Santino, *La mafia interpretata*.

35. G. Mosca, *Che cosa è la mafia*, now in Mosca, *Uomini e cose di Sicilia* (Palermo, 1980), p. 12. This locus is referenced by G. Fiandaca and S. Costantino, "La mafia degli anni '80 tra vecchi e nuovi paradigmi," *Sociologia del diritto*, 1990, 3, p. 76.

36. From a verdict handed down by the Tribunal of Locri in 1950, quoted by Ciconte, *'Ndrangheta*, p. 242.

37. Testimony by Vitale in *Maxiprocesso* (Maxitrial), p. 13.

38. Tribunal of Catania, Ordinanza di custodia cautelare nei confronti di V. Aiello e altri (December 1993), passim.

39. Quoted by O. Cancila, *Storia dell'industria in Sicilia* (Rome, 1995), p. 306.

40. *Rapporto Sangiorgi*, ACS, AC, p. 6.

41. Fiandaca and Costantino, Introduction, in *La mafia, le mafie*, pp. x–xi; Santino, *La mafia interpretata*, pp. 37ff.

42. See chapter 5 in this volume for the revelations of Buscetta, which correspond with what we know about a *cosca* (Mafia family), which is quite different, however, from those in Palermo, the Catanian Santapaola-Pulvirenti *cosca*; Tribunal of Catania, Ordinanza, pp. 71ff.

43. A. Block, *East Side, West Side: Organizing Crime in New York* (Cardiff, 1980). I agree with Catanzaro, *Recenti studi,* and Catanzaro, "La struttura organizzativa della criminalità mafiosa in Sicilia," in Various Authors, *La criminalità organizzata* (Milan, 1993), pp. 147ff.; the criticisms raised by Santino, *La mafia interpretata,* concerning the incompatibility of my approach and that of Block are not sufficient to persuade me to renounce the use of this terminology.

44. The distinction between protectors and the protected (see Gambetta, *La mafia siciliana,* pp. 319ff.) is criticized by Santino, *La mafia interpretata,* who, among other matters, references the case of Angelo Siino, who Gambetta considered a client of the Mafia enterprise but who was in fact a fully integrated member of Cosa Nostra (pp. 64–65); see also Marmo, *Le ragioni della mafia*.

45. However, the landing of other Mafia capos (Masseria, Bonanno, Gambino, and Profaci) dates back earlier than the middle of the decade, when the repression had not yet begun and the mafiosi were still on good terms with the government parties.

46. In Chicago we find among the Mafia bosses three Campanians (Torrio, Al Capone, and Ricca), two Calabrians (Colosimo and Nitti), and only two Sicilians (Accardo and Giancana).

However, the fact that the non-Sicilians, both in New York and Chicago, should all have come from Campania and Calabria may be indicative of the intertwining with prior and existing criminal traditions. I take my information from H. Abadinsky, *Organized Crime* (Chicago, 1994), passim.

47. The attempt to identify an authentic Sicilian Mafia in America has legitimized legends such as that of the simultaneous elimination throughout the United States of forty to sixty "old" Sicilian mafiosi, along with Maranzano: see the critique of A. Block, *Space, Time and Organized Crime* (London, 1994), pp. 3ff.

48. R. Scarpinato, a member of the pool of investigative magistrates in Palermo, wrote: "Blood relations must be set aside if necessary. If the organization orders the murder of a man of honor's relative, he must bend to this event as a higher necessity." See "Caratteristiche e dinamiche degli omicidi eseguiti e ordinati da Cosa nostra," *Segno*, 1996, 176, p. 78.

49. Nick Gentile, *Vita di capomafia* (Rome: Editori Riuniti, 1963), passim.

50. I take this information from Block, *Space, Time*, p. 27; I believe that the Italian equivalent of Treasury Police is Guardia di Finanza.

51. J. L. Albini, "L'America deve la mafia alla Sicilia?" in Various Authors, *Mafia e potere*, ed. S. Di Bella (Soveria Mannelli, 1983), vol. 1, p. 189.

52. F. J. Ianni, *Affari di famiglia* (Milan, 1984). (In English: *A Family Business: Kinship and Social Control in Organized Crime*. With Elizabeth Reuss-Ianni.)

53. As noted on the cover of the renowned book *Honor Thy Father*, the biography of Bonanno's son, Bill, by G. Talese (New York, 1981) (1st ed. 1971).

54. G. Hawkins, "God and the Mafia," *Public Interest*, Winter 1969, 14, pp. 24–51; cited in Santino and La Fiura, *L'impresa mafiosa*, p. 257.

55. Concerning Hawkins, see the criticisms by Peter Reuter, *Disorganized Crime: The Economics of the Visible Hand* (Cambridge, MA, 1983), p. 7 and note; also see the declarations by Sciortino in *Antimafia, Bernardinetti Report*, p. 593.

56. Hess, *Mafia*, pp. xii and passim.

57. Arlacchi, *La mafia imprenditrice*, pp. 66–67; Schneider and Schneider, *Classi sociali*, in particular p. 250; in a parallel approach, see Blok, *La mafia di un villaggio siciliano*. In recent political and journalistic speeches and writings, Arlacchi has given evidence of having changed his opinion: see his self-criticism in *Gli uomini del disonore* (Milan, 1992), p. viii.

58. Decree of the investigating magistrate of Agrigento (2 April 1986), published under the title *La mafia di Agrigento*, ed. G. Arnone (Cosenza, 1988), pp. 279–80.

59. G. M. Puglia, "Il mafioso non è un associato per delinquere," *La scuola positiva*, 1930, 1, p. 156.

60. R. T. Anderson, "From Mafia to Cosa Nostra," *American Journal of Sociology*, November 1965, 3, pp. 302–10.

61. *President's Commission on Organized Crime, Report to the President*, vol. 1, *The Impact* (Washington, DC, 1986), pp. 26–27.

62. Hess, *Mafia*, p. 109; G. Alongi, *La maffia nei suoi fattori e nelle sue manifestazioni: Studio sulle classi pericolose della Sicilia* (Turin, 1886). See a second, revised edition of Alongi's text published under the title *La mafia* (Palermo, 1904). Cutrera, *La mafia e i mafiosi*.

63. L. Violante, *Non è la piovra: Dodici tesi sulle mafie italiane* (Turin, 1994), pp. 58–59 and 81ff.

64. We support the views of A. Baratta, "Mafia e Stato: Alcune riflessioni metodologiche," in *La mafia, le mafie*, ed. Fiandaca and Costantino, pp. 95–117. This is the source of the need to link the concept of Mafia to that of the "Mafia bourgeoisie" on which Santino focused, for instance, in "La mafia come soggetto politico," in *La mafia, le mafie*, ed. Fiandaca and Costantino, pp. 122–24, and G. Di Lello, *Giudici* (Palermo, 1994), pp. 10 and passim. I would only observe that in no way can the Mafia be considered as a social class (or vice versa), and that

therefore such an exposition provides no help in making the necessary distinction among the various components of the Mafia network.

65. Mentioned in the report by F. Conti to the Istituto Meridionale di Storia e Scienze Sociali seminar concerning associationism during the liberal era, held in Rome in spring 1996.

66. Gentile, *Vita di capomafia*, p. 55.

67. Testimony by Buscetta, *Dibattimento* (trial hearing), vol. 1, p. 37.

68. W. Natoli, *I Beati Paoli* (Palermo, 1971). See also F. Renda, *I Beati Paoli: Storia, letteratura e leggenda* (Palermo, 1988).

69. Hess, *Mafia*, pp. 134ff.

70. Victor W. Turner, *The Ritual Process: Structure and Anti-Structure* (London: Routledge and Kegan Paul, 1969), p. 103, as noted on p. 38, n. 6 in the Italian edition, *Il processo rituale* (Brescia, 1972); I retranslated the last phrase.

71. G. Ciotti, *I casi di Palermo* (Palermo, 1866), p. 7.

72. Marmo, "Tra le carceri e i mercati," p. 724. But see also the essays by Marmo herself and by P. Pezzino, in Various Authors, *Onore e storia nelle società mediterranee*, ed. G. Fiume (Palermo, 1989).

73. Giuseppe Giarrizzo, "Mafia," in *Enciclopedia italiana* (Rome, 1993), Appendix 5, p. 278.

74. Alongi, *La maffia*, p. 75. But already the report (mentioned above) by the prefect of Trapani (16 May 1874) noted the connection between the concept of humility and the concept of humanity. Also, E. Onufrio, "La mafia in Sicilia," *Nuova Antologia*, 1877, pp. 365–67, harked back to the terminology of the prison Camorra and the *ricottari*, or pimps. Among the historical references, see P. Pezzino, *Una certa reciprocità di favore: Mafia e modernizzazione violenta nella Sicilia post-unitaria* (Milan, 1990), pp. 118 and passim.

75. Quoted in R. Mangiameli, "Gabellotti e notabili nella Sicilia dell'interno," *Italia contemporanea*, 1984, 156, p. 67.

76. S. Romano, *L'ordinamento giuridico* (Florence, 1945) (1st ed. 1918), p. 101; Romano, however, does not use the word "Mafia" in this text.

77. Ibid.

78. G. G. Lo Schiavo, "Nel regno della mafia," in *Processi* (1955), quoted by Galluzzo and others, *Obiettivo Falcone*, p. 75. Equally adulatory is the depiction in Lo Schiavo's novel, *Piccola pretura* (Milan, 1948), on which P. Germi based his film *In nome della legge* (1949). But see also Lo Schiavo, *100 anni di mafia*.

79. Gambetta, *La mafia*, pp. xii–xiii, concerning which see the critical observations of G. Fiandaca, "La mafia come ordinamento giuridico: utilità e limiti di un paradigma," *Segno*, 1994, 155, pp. 23–35.

80. Quoted by C. Mori, *Con la mafia ai ferri corti* (Milan, 1932), pp. 15ff.

81. G. Falcone, *Cose di Cosa nostra*, written with M. Padovani (Milan, 1991), p. 37. See references by Terranova to Giampietro in chapter 5 of this volume.

82. See also the letters by Santapaola, along with the letter by Ferone, in "Diario della settimana," supplement to *L'Unità*, 30 October–5 November 1996, pp. 58–62.

CHAPTER II. THE REVELATION

1. The most solidly supported derivation is from the Arabic *marfud,* whence the Sicilian term *marpiuni* (swindler, crafty person) *marpiusu-mafiusu:* V. Lo Monaco, "Lingua Nostra," 1990, quoted by Giuseppe Giarrizzo, "Mafia," in *Enciclopedia italiana* (Rome, 1993), pp. 277–78.

2. *Poche parole alla Commissione parlamentare* (Palermo, 1867), in appendix to the *Inchiesta Fabrizi*, p. 515. In general, see P. Alatri, *Lotte politiche in Sicilia sotto il governo della Destra*

(1866–1874) (Turin, 1954), and F. Brancato, *La Sicilia nel primo ventennio del Regno d'Italia* (Bologna, 1956).

3. Letter from Pantaleoni to Ricasoli, September–October 1861, quoted by F. Brancato, *La Mafia nell'opinione pubblica e nelle inchieste dall' Unità al fascismo* (Cosenza, 1986).

4. These were the *pugnalazioni* (stabbings) that the *questura* attributed to a plot put together by the opposition on both left and right, including even the moderate prince of Sant'Elia. See the brilliant but unpersuasive treatment by L. Sciascia, *I pugnalatori* (Turin, 1976), and, now, the well-documented book by P. Pezzino, *La congiura dei pugnalatori* (Venice, 1992). Terrorism played a major role in the Palermo of those years in defining the relationship among the democratic forces, and between those forces and the authorities, as demonstrated by the murder of C. Trasselli and the wounding of F. Perroni Paladini, both moderate followers of Garibaldi; see Alatri, *Lotte politiche*, pp. 109 and 137.

5. The most recent version of this historiographic approach is found in Nicola Tranfaglia, *La mafia come metodo* (Rome, 1991), though it is criticized by P. Bevilacqua, "La mafia e la Spagna," *Meridiana*, 1992, 13. More typical of the Sicilian cultural tradition is the variant found in V. Titone, *La società siciliana sotto gli spagnoli e le origini della questione meridionale* (Palermo, 1978).

6. D. Gambetta, in *La Mafia siciliana: Un'industria della protezione privata* (Turin, 1992), and also in "La protezione mafiosa," *Polis*, August 1994, pp. 302–3, states instead that Spain introduced into southern Italy the element of "mistrust" that engendered the Mafia. He considered significant the fact that an endemic violence—which is hardly the same thing as the Mafia—also exists in other former Spanish colonies such as the Philippines. The reasoning is weak and mostly allusive. Why make the comparison to the Philippines but not to China and Japan, both of which have major forms of organized crime? Why should we think that Spanish rule had such negative effects on southern Italy but not on the Netherlands, Lombardy, and even on Spain itself? It should be recalled that Sicily was never a colony, but rather one of the realms of the Aragon crown, and that at the end of the fifteenth century it passed to the crown of Castile, preserving its status, its laws and orderings, and its influence on imperial policy. It should be compared not to the Americas or the Philippines, but rather to Aragon and to the other Iberian possessions of the Hapsburgs, not including Castile. H. G. Koenigsberger, *The Practice of Empire* (Ithaca, NY, 1969); G. Giarrizzo, "La Sicilia dal Cinquecento all'Unità d'Italia," in G. Giarrizzo and V. D'Alessandro, *La Sicilia dal Vespro all'Unità d'Italia* (Turin, 1989).

7. As in O. Cancila, *Così andavano le cose nel secolo sedicesimo* (Palermo, 1984); it seems excessive that the Holy Office should be described here as "a large Mafia organization" (p. 29).

8. L. Franchetti, "Condizioni politiche e amministrative della Sicilia," in L. Franchetti and S. Sonnino, *Inchiesta in Sicilia* (Florence, 1974) (1st ed. 1876), a thesis that was later broadly adopted, for instance, by P. Pezzino, *Una certa reciprocità di favori: Mafia e modernizzazione violenta nella Sicilia post-unitaria* (Milan, 1990).

9. See, for instance, Gambetta's contribution to the debate with Lupo, Pezzino, and Tranfaglia in *Passato e presente*, 1994, 31, pp. 24–25.

10. S. Lupo, "Tra centro e periferia: Sui modi dell'aggregazione politica nel Mezzogiorno contemporaneo," *Meridiana*, 1988, 2, pp. 18–22.

11. Pezzino, *Una certa reciprocità*, and Pezzino, *Il paradiso abitato dai diavoli* (Milan, 1992). See also the writings of E. Iachello and A. De Francesco, in Various Authors, *Elites e potere in Sicilia*, ed. F. Benigno and C. Torrisi (Rome, 1995).

12. G. Fiume, *Le bande armate in Sicilia (1819–1849): Violenza e organizzazione del potere* (Palermo, 1984), p. 117. Sharing this view, among the contemporaries, is L. Bianchini; see Brancato, *La mafia*, p. 172.

13. Fiume, *Le bande armate*, passim.

14. E. Sereni, *Il capitalismo nelle campagne* (Turin, 1980) (1st ed. 1946), pp. 145ff.

15. See G. Cammareri Scurti, *Il latifondo in Sicilia e l'inferiorità meridionale* (Milan, 1909), pp. 8off.; the *Inchiesta parlamentare sulle condizioni dei contadini nelle province meridionali e nella Sicilia* (Rome, 1908), vol. 6; and my own "I proprietari terrieri del Mezzogiorno," in *Storia dell'agricoltura italiana in età contemporanea* (Venice, 1990), vol. 2, pp. 105–50.

16. In *Inchiesta Fabrizi*, p. 117.

17. Fiume, *Le bande armate*, p. 74.

18. Report dated 3 August, in E. Pontieri, *Il riformismo borbonico nella Sicilia del Sette e dell'Ottocento* (Rome, 1945), pp. 222–25.

19. Quoted by Fiume, *Le bande armate*, p. 75.

20. G. Fiume, *La crisi sociale del 1848 in Sicilia* (Messina, 1982), p. 64.

21. G. Fiume, "Il disordine borghese nella Sicilia dei Borbone: il caso di Marineo (1819–1859)," in Various Authors, *Contributi per un bilancio del regno borbonico* (Palermo, 1990); S. Costanza, *La patria armata: Un episodio della rivolta antileva in Sicilia* (Trapani, 1989); and my own "Tra centro e periferia."

22. In *Inchiesta Bonfadini*, p. 277.

23. See A. De Francesco, *La guerra di Sicilia* (Catania, 1992).

24. Fiume, *La crisi sociale del 1848*, as well as R. Romeo, *Il Risorgimento in Sicilia* (Bari, 1950), and Giarrizzo, "La Sicilia dal Cinquecento all'Unità."

25. Among the recent literature, see also Giarrizzo, "La Sicilia dal Cinquecento all'Unità," and P. Pezzino, "La tradizione rivoluzionaria siciliana e l'invenzione della mafia," *Meridiana*, 1990, 7–8. Similarly, in modern-day Colombia the narcotics cartels have established themselves in areas that have experienced a stubborn and endemic civil war; see P. Burin des Rozies, *Cultures mafieuses: L'exemple colombien* (Paris, 1995). Something similar can be said concerning the warlords in the areas bordering China.

26. Stated in December 1860 by the deputy M. Cordero di Montezemolo in a letter to Cavour, in G. Scichilone, *Documenti sulle condizioni della Sicilia dal 1860 al 1970* (Rome, 1952), pp. 62–63.

27. Where armed men emerged "from all the houses" carrying red banners on which was written "Republic"—but relying on the support of reactionary monks—and then headed for Palermo: see *Inchiesta Fabrizi*, p. 347.

28. V. Maggiorani, *Il sollevamento della plebe di Palermo e del circondario nel September 1866* (Palermo, 1866), pp. 82–83; G. Ciotti, *I casi di Palermo* (Palermo, 1866); A. Maurici, *La genesi storica della rivolta del 1866 in Palermo* (Palermo, 1916), pp. 469ff. In historiographic terms, see F. Brancato, "Origine e caratteri della rivolta palermitana del September 1866," *Archivio storico siciliano*, 1955, and the monographic issue of *Nuovi quaderni del Meridione*, 1966, 16.

29. Maggiorani, *Il sollevamento*, p. 6.

30. Maurici, *La genesi*, p. 471.

31. *Inchiesta Bonfadini*, p. 522.

32. Consider, for instance, the confiscation of the property of religious institutes, which interrupted the financial flow from all over Sicily that had made it possible for local society to use those resources locally; or the way in which the new state completed the work of the Bourbon state in the field of public works and the distribution of offices (for instance, judicial offices), helping other cities to the detriment of the capital city. Almost all the interviews in the *Inchiesta Fabrizi* indicate the specific nature of Palermo; in contrast, see Alatri, *Lotte politiche*, pp. 10ff.

33. See the testimony of Commissioner Felzani, in *Processo dei Fratelli: Amoroso e compagni* (Palermo, 1883), p. 53. It was in the Amoroso home that Badia was arrested and that the meetings

of the insurrection committee were held. See Maurici, *La genesi*, p. 337; Alatri, *Lotte politiche*, p. 138. Concerning Miceli, see, among others, Fiume, *Le bande armate*, pp. 102ff.

34. Maggiorani, *Il sollevamento*, p. 69. This renders less believable the thesis that in 1863 Sant'Elia might have been the mastermind behind the *pugnalatori*, or stabbers. Such an individual, collaborating among others with the Gucciones of Alia (Guccione, *Storia di Alia* [Rome, 1991], p. 345)—whom we shall see later among the leading mafiosi *gabellotti* (renters and sublessors of parcels of farmland)—would have needed to expose himself, in order to find the killers, by contacting prospective thugs chosen almost by chance throughout Palermo.

35. *Inchiesta Bonfadini,* p. 406. Among Licata's noteworthy actions is also the denunciation of the fanciful Bourbon-Republican plot of Corrao: Pezzino, *La congiura*, p. 178.

36. Contribution of the duke of Cesarò in *Inchiesta Bonfadini.*

37. G. Petix, *Memorie e tradizioni di Montedoro* (Montedoro, 1984), vol. 1, pp. 241–42.

38. The family was involved in other violent episodes: a Caico was kidnapped around 1874, with the payment of a ransom "followed by the immediate capture of three of the criminals, and by the killing of a fourth"; a Caico, mayor of Montedoro, was arrested in 1897 (and subsequently acquitted) for the murder of the chief of the opposing faction. See L. Hamilton Caico, *Vicende e costumi siciliani* (Palermo, 1983), pp. 161–62; testimony of Senator F. Morillo of Trabonella, in *Inchiesta Bonfadini*, p. 1028; Petix, *Memorie*, pp. 291–94.

39. *Inchiesta Bonfadini,* pp. 462–63.

40. Archivio di Stato di Palermo, Gabinetto Prefettura (ASPA, GP), 1876, b. 35, f. 6, the *questore* to the royal prosecutor, 21 September 1875, respectively, pp. 14–15 and 15–16.

41. See my own *Il giardino degli aranci: Il mondo degli agrumi nella storia del Mezzogiorno* (Venice, 1990), and O. Cancila, *Palermo* (Rome, 1988), passim.

42. L. Franchetti, *Politica e mafia in Sicilia: Gli inediti del 1876*, ed. A. Jannazzo (Naples, 1995), p. 190. Turrisi's letter of protest is in *L'Amico del popolo*, 24 August 1874. The list of the mafiosi of Cefalù is in ASPA, GP, 1877, b. 39.

43. D. Farini, *Diario di fine secolo 1896–1899* (Rome, 1961), vol. 2, p. 909.

44. Interview in *Inchiesta Bonfadini*, p. 473.

45. L. Tirrito, *Sulla città e comarca di Castronovo di Sicilia* (Palermo, 1873), vol. 2, pp. 69–70. Moreover, the Nicolosi were pro-Bourbon. Concerning the Gucciones, see Guccione, *Storia di Alia.*

46. List of the mafiosi of Termini, category I, no. 20, in ASPA, GP, 1877, b. 39. For Leone see G. Alongi, *La mafia* (Palermo, 1904), p. 85; according to Valvo Di Menza, *Le cronache delle assise di Palermo* (Palermo, 1878), p. 74.

47. Mangiameli, "Banditi e mafiosi dopo l'Unità," *Meridiana*, 1990, 7–8, pp. 73–117.

48. Ibid.

49. See the extensive documentation in ASPA, GP, b. 85.

50. Quoted in Mangiameli, "Banditi e mafiosi," p. 104. That same year, Borsani was transferred.

51. *Audizione* (examination of witnesses), in *Inchiesta Fabrizi*, p. 29.

52. In particular, see H. Hess, *Mafia* (Rome, 1991) (1st ed. 1973), and A. Blok, *La mafia di un villaggio siciliano, 1860–1960* (Turin, 1986) (1st ed. 1974).

53. Report dated 31 July 1974, pp. 13–14.

54. C. Fiore, "Il controllo della criminalità organizzata nello Stato liberale," in *Quaderni dell'Istituto universitario orientale: Dipartimento di scienze sociali* (Naples, 1989), vol. 2, p. 132.

55. Quoted by Fiume, *Le bande armate*, p. 75.

56. Summary of the reports (18 January 1875) in APCD, 1874–1875, Documents, attachment 2, p. 57. The reader should recall the analogous role played by the Neapolitan Camorra, though

for only a brief period, until the repression brought about by S. Spaventa: M. Marmo, "Economia e politica della camorra napoletana nel sec. XIX," in *Quaderni dell' Istituto universitario orientale: Dipartimento di scienze sociali* (Naples, 1989), vol. 2, pp. 114ff.

57. N. Turrisi Colonna, *Cenni sullo stato attuale della sicurezza pubblica in Sicilia* (Palermo, 1988) (1st ed. 1864), p. 43.

58. Ibid., p. 48.

59. Privately, he declared to Franchetti that his *campieri* "were obliged" to supply the brigands: "necessarily, because a vendetta can ruin one of my immense olive groves." See Franchetti, *Politica e mafia*, p. 58.

60. Giarrizzo, "La Sicilia," p. 700.

61. Quoted by N. Recupero, "La Sicilia all'opposizione," pp. 48–49.

62. Report of the *questore*, 28 February 1876, in ASPA, GP, b. 35.

63. N. Recupero, "Ceti medi e 'homines novi': Alle origini della mafia," *Polis*, 1987, 2, p. 313.

64. I quote again from the report on the Giammona group.

65. "Corriere giudiziario," appendix of the *Giornale di Sicilia* (GDS), 15 May 1878; descriptions of the rituals in ASPA, Gabinetto Questura (GQ), 1880, b. 7.

66. Respectively, Di Menza, *Cronache,* and testimony by Rudinì, in *Inchiesta Fabrizi,* p. 118. Prison and internal exile brought together Neapolitan and Sicilian organized crime: see also Di Menza, *Cronache,* as well as the report by the prefect of Trapani in APCD, 1874–1875, 16 May 1874, p. 15. Of note is the legend of the Catalonian noblemen who founded regional crime traditions in the south of Italy at Favignana; see E. Ciconte, *'Ndrangheta Dall' Unità a oggi* (Rome, 1992), pp. 6–8. Concerning the prison Camorra, see M. Marmo, "Tra le carceri e i mercati: Spazi e modelli storici del fenomeno camorrista," in *La Campania,* ed. P. Marcy and P. Villani (Turin, 1990). According to a document from 1861 (in G. Machetti, "Camorra e criminalità popolare a Napoli," *Società e storia,* 1991, 51, p. 80), the Bourbon army was the vehicle of importation to Naples from Sicily (where the army recruited ex-convicts) of a "broader, more ferocious, and lower" Camorra than the native one.

67. G. Baglio, *Ricerche sul lavoro e sui lavoratori in Sicilia: il solfaraio* (Naples, 1905), and G. Barone, "Formazione e declino di un monopolio naturale," in S. Addamo et al., *Zolfare di Sicilia* (Palermo, 1989), p. 94.

68. T. V. Colacino, "La Fratellanza," *Rivista di discipline carcerarie,* 1885, cited in Pezzino, *Una certa reciprocità,* pp. 212ff.; another study from the same period is the one by F. Lestingi, "La fratellanza nella provincia di Girgenti," *Archivio di psichiatria,* 1884. Both of them are mentioned by A. Cutrera, *La mafia e i mafiosi: Saggio di sociologia criminale* (Palermo, 1900), p. 125. Concerning the entire episode and the social issues mentioned above, see Pezzino, *Una certa reciprocità,* pp. 202ff.

69. L. Pirandello, *La lega disciolta,* in *Corriere della Sera* (CS), 6 June 1910, now in L. Pirandello, *Novelle per un anno* (Milan, 1990), vol. 3, t. 1, pp. 70–80; this same text and issue were also mentioned in Giarrizzo, "Mafia," in E. J. Hobsbawm, *I ribelli* (Turin, 1966) and *I banditi* (Turin, 1971).

70. The numbers do not include draft-dodgers and deserters: Report of the Depretis Commission in APCD, 1874–1875, Documents, *Progetti di legge* (draft bills), 24 A, p. 21.

71. Another report by Calà Ulloa, 25 April 1838, in E. Pontieri, *Il riformismo borbonico nella Sicilia del Sette e dell'Ottocento* (Rome, 1945), p. 217.

72. Concerning which, see L. Mascilli Migliorini, "Il mondo politico meridionale di fronte alla legge di PS del 1875," *Nuova rivista storica,* 1979; F. Renda, *Storia della Sicilia* (Palermo, 1985), vol. 2, pp. 32ff.

73. The reports by Fortuzzi, dated 4 April and 4 January 1875, in APCD, 1874–1875, Documents, *Progetti di legge* (draft bills), no. 24 *ter.*, pp. 20 and 58.

74. Judgment of the Depretis Commission, no. 24 A, p. 23.

75. Ibid., pp. 3890 and 3886–87.

76. *Relazione*, p. 12.

77. See the controversy in *Inchiesta Bonfadini*; the regulations on the special security regimen of *ammonizione* are in Fiore, "Il controllo della criminalità organizzata," vol. 2, pp. 141ff.

78. Circular letter dated 6 July 1871, cited in Alatri, *Lotte politiche*, p. 363.

79. See G. Giarrizzo, *Catania* (Rome, 1986), in particular pp. 25–26. There were clashes as well between *questura* and Borsani, Tajani's predecessor and future chairman of the parliamentary commission; see Alatri, *Lotte politiche*, pp. 180ff.

80. APCD, 1874–1875, *Discussioni*, 11 June 1875, p. 4124. This and other texts by Tajani are now in Tajani, *Mafia e potere*, ed. P. Pezzino (Pisa, 1993).

81. APCD, *Discorso*, p. 4132.

82. See R. Mangiameli, "Dalle bande alle cosche: La rappresentazione della criminalità in provincia di Caltanissetta," in Various Authors, *Economia e società nell'area dello zolfo*, ed. G. Barone and C. Torrisi (Rome, 1989), pp. 210–11.

83. The materials of the investigation, which can be consulted at ACS, were partially published in 1968 (*Inchiesta Bonfadini*), and another part appeared in E. Iachello, *Stato unitario e disarmonie regionali* (Naples, 1987). Concerning the investigation, see the introduction to Iachello's text, as well as P. Pezzino, *Una certa reciprocità*, pp. 31–80.

84. See now, in the edition edited by F. Barbagallo: Pasquale Villari, *Le lettere meridionali ed altri scritti sulla questione sociale in Italia* (Naples, 1979) (1st ed. 1875).

85. I quote from Bonfadini's draft, session of 25 March 1876, in *Inchiesta*, p. 156, themes that were, of course, included in the final report, in *Inchiesta*, pp. 1135ff.

86. S. Salomone-Marino, *Leggende popolari siciliane in poesia* (Palermo, 1880), p. xxii; but see the handsome reconstruction by Mangiameli, "Banditi e mafiosi dopo l'Unità."

87. Fiume, *Le bande armate*, p. 74.

88. APCD, 1874, Documents, report of Minister Cantelli on the police measures (*provvedimenti di PS*), pp. 2 and 4. Concerning the interaction between criminals on the run and novice criminals, see also the account of Don Peppino il Lombardo in Mangiameli, "Dalle bande alle cosche," p. 197.

89. Quoted by Fiume, *Le bande armate*, p. 75.

90. G. Pagano, *La Sicilia nel 1876–77* (Palermo, 1877), p. 41.

91. See Hess, *Mafia*, passim, and Pezzino, *Una certa reciprocità*, pp. 129–31.

92. Interview with the commanding colonel of Agrigento, p. 580. The episode is also in Pezzino, *Una certa reciprocità*, pp. 60–61.

93. E. Fincati, *Un anno in Sicilia, 1877–1878* (Rome, 1881), p. 76. The judgment is undercut by the improved relations between the state and the governing classes after 1876.

94. Mangiameli, "Banditi e mafiosi," p. 98.

95. APCD, *Discorso*, p. 4126.

96. According to the sarcastic expression of G. Di Menza, *Cronache delle assise di Palermo* (Palermo, 1978), vol. 2, p. 232. See Mangiameli, "Banditi e mafiosi," concerning these episodes and for a profile of Di Menza himself, who was a magistrate and man of the Italian left (p. 75).

97. APCD, *Discorso*, p. 4131.

98. Interview (see note 92 above).

99. Final report, in *Inchiesta Bonfadini*, p. 1158.

100. At least according to the testimony of the baron, pp. 699–702.

101. The summation of Tajani with the testimony of Barraco in *Antologia della mafia,* ed. N. Russo (Palermo, 1964), p. 163.

102. APCD, *Discorso,* p. 4133.

103. See, respectively, the report, p. 5, and the interview in *Inchiesta Bonfadini* (subsequent to his resignation), pp. 969–70.

104. APCD, 11 June 1875, p. 4114.

105. I refer the reader to L. Sandri's introduction to *Inchiesta Bonfadini* and to Iachello's introductory essay, *Stato unitario,* pp. 7–86.

106. S. Sonnino, "I contadini in Sicilia," in Franchetti and Sonnino, *Inchiesta,* vol. 2.

107. Franchetti, "Condizioni politiche," p. 93.

108. Interview with Rudinì, in *Inchiesta Bonfadini,* p. 951; Giuseppe Pitrè, *Usi e costumi, credenze e pregiudizi del popolo siciliano,* facsimile edition (Bologna, n.d.), p. 291.

109. Franchetti, *Politica e mafia,* p. 41.

110. Ibid., pp. 68–69, 37, and 48–49.

111. Ibid., pp. 198 and—for the previous references—34, 32, 62.

112. Ibid., pp. 36, 46, 49.

113. Ibid., p. 196.

114. But among the letters written by Sidney Sonnino to Emilia Peruzzi, now being prepared for publication, and which I was able to consult thanks to the courtesy of the editor Paola Carlucci, there is one (dated from Palermo, 2 March 1876, and numbered CXXX) in which he writes about Turrisi: "Here they say that he is linked to the Mafia—but this is of no importance to us, and we would like to hear what he has to say."

115. Franchetti, "Condizioni politiche," p. 91.

116. Ibid., p. 31.

117. It should be remembered that Franchetti, traveling in 1874 through the mainland of southern Italy, had found not a trace of such a phenomenon: see *Condizioni economiche e amministrative delle province napoletane* (Rome, 1985).

118. In an intentionally misleading manner, Giuseppe Torina, former mayor of and member of parliament for Caccamo, considered (as we shall see) to be an exponent of the *alta maffia,* claimed that the "maffiosi are in the countryside," not in town; see *Inchiesta Bonfadini,* p. 441.

119. Franchetti, "Condizioni politiche," pp. 33–34. The attempt to distinguish between the two types of *manutengolismo* (out of interest and out of necessity) was already mentioned in the report by Rasponi dated 31 July 1874, pp. 13–14.

120. Mangiameli, "Banditi e mafiosi."

121. Franchetti, "Condizioni politiche," p. 55.

122. There is an overvaluing of the antibrigand mobilization referred to by Franchetti: see Mangiameli, "Banditi e mafiosi," pp. 98–99.

123. I can only refer the reader to R. Romanelli, *Il comando impossibile* (Bologna, 1988).

124. Iachello, *Stato unitario,* p. 70, recalls that Fortuzzi was one of Franchetti's sources; see also E. Cavalieri, introduction to the *Inchiesta,* p. xxiii.

125. See pp. 218–39 of Franchetti, "Condizioni politiche," and for the references, see pp. 219, 221, 222, and 224.

126. Title of a pamphlet by R. Conti (Catania, 1877).

127. G. Alongi, *La maffia nei suoi fattori e nelle sue manifestazioni: Studio sulle classi pericolose della Sicilia* (Turin, 1886), p. 9.

128. Pagano, *La Sicilia nel 1876–77,* p. 35.

129. ACS, *Giustizia,* Affari generali riservati (AAGGRR), 1877, b. 37, in particular the *Prospetto dei processi . . . per abusi di autorità;* see also ASPA, GP, 1877, b. 42, with yet another of the long lists of conflicts between the magistracy and the *questura* (police administration).

130. Pagano, *La Sicilia*, p. 41.

131. The lists are found in ASPA, GP, 1877, b. 39; but already in the previously mentioned report, dated 31 July 1874, p. 14, Rasponi announced a coming "list of Maffiosi broken down by rank."

132. File concerning M. Abbate, no. 66 in the Termini list, category II.

133. Respectively, files on A. Di Marco, no. 70, and on L. Crimi, no. 67, Termini.

134. File no. 50, Termini.

135. File on G. Demma, no. 52, Termini.

136. Respectively, report of the *delegato di PS*, dated 10 June 1877, and telegram from Nicotera to the prefect, dated 26 January 1877, in ASPA, GP, 1877, b. 39; file on Torina, category I, Termini, no. 22. The above-mentioned interview with Torina, on pp. 433–42 of the *Inchiesta Bonfadini*, is from start to finish a polemic against the "excesses" of the special security regimen of *ammonizione*.

137. Letter dated 17 February 1877, in ASPA, GP, 1877, b. 39.

138. Report from the *delegato di PS*, October 1872, in ASPA, GP, 1877, b. 39.

139. File no. 3, category I, Termini.

140. Testimony in the Notarbartolo trial reported by G. Marchesano, *Processo contro Raffaele Palizzolo & C. Arringa dell'avv. G.M.* (Palermo, 1902), p. 309. Claims of collaborationist merit on the part of notables-qua-mafiosi in the 1880s are found as well in Hess, *Mafia*, pp. 92–94.

141. "La questione Avellone," in GDS, 3 April 1892, quoted by Cancila, *Palermo*, p. 235.

142. File no. 1, category I, Termini.

143. File no. 4–5, category I, Termini.

144. Report dated 10 June 1877 in ASPA, GP, 1877, b. 39. The Runfola brothers were landowners in Valledolmo, no. 6 and no. 7 on the Termini list, category I; Cerrito is thought to be a member of the family of major leaseholders in Caltavuturo.

145. Information provided by Member of Parliament Girolamo De Luca Aprile and reported in the summary of the first preliminary investigation into the killing of Notarbartolo, in ACS, *Giustizia*, MAP, b. 126. It is noteworthy that De Luca Aprile was among the critics of Malusardi: see Brancato, *La mafia*, p. 230. Marchesano, *Processo*, pp. 348–49, notes that, since Palizzolo was pro-ministerial, the reasons for the special security regimen of *ammonizione* must not have been linked to electoral considerations.

146. *Prospetto dei processi . . . per abusi di autorità*, pp. 1–2.

147. Alongi, *La mafia*, p. 299.

148. Quoted by Pezzino, *Una certa reciprocità*, p. 138.

149. Ibid.

150. APCD, *Discussioni*, session of 8 July 1896, pp. 7315–53 and in particular p. 7347.

151. The letters are quoted by Marchesano, *Processo*, pp. 320–29; the letter concerning Filippello is in ASPA, GQ, 1866–1939, b. 20.

152. APCD, *Discussioni*, session of 8 July 1896, pp. 7315–53.

153. Cutrera, *La Mafia*, p. 91; concerning Li Destri, see the documentation quoted by Hess, *Mafia*, passim.

154. Sonnino, "I contadini," p. 68. But see my own *Il giardino degli aranci: Il mondo degli agrumi nella storia del Mezzogiorno* (Venice, 1990).

155. The interview with Corleo in Iachello, *Stato unitario*, pp. 259–60. Identical tone and emphasis are found in Villari, *Le lettere meridionali*, p. 56; unconvincing, on the other hand, is N. Colajanni, *La delinquenza in Sicilia e le sue cause* (Palermo, 1885), pp. 35ff.

156. Thesis set forth in the final report of the *Inchiesta Bonfadini*, p. 1079.

157. APCD, *Discorso*, p. 4125.

158. Franchetti, "Condizioni politiche," p. 95.

159. Interview in *Inchiesta Fabrizi*, p. 77.

160. Franchetti, "Condizioni politiche," pp. 97–99.
161. *Atti della Giunta per l'inchiesta agraria*, vol. 13 (Rome, 1884–1885), file 1.2, p. 249.
162. Respectively, anonymous, 22 March 1879, pp. 2–3; letter from an adviser to the prefect (the *settembrini* were those who took part in the unrest of September 1866); list of the advisers of 1879: ASPA, GP, b. 61.
163. *Processo Amoroso*, p. 160.
164. G. De Felice, *Maffia e delinquenza in Sicilia* (Milan, 1900), pp. 52–53.
165. Respectively, letter from the *questore* to the prefect, 10 October 1875, in ASPA, GP, 1876, b. 35; Anonymous in ASPA, GP, 1880, b. 51.
166. Testimony of the chief justice of the Corte d'Appello (appeals court) of Palermo, S. Schiavo, in *Inchiesta Bonfadini*, pp. 376–77.
167. Interview in *Inchiesta Bonfadini*, p. 477.
168. This is an expression from Gestivo, interview, whose pro-Mafia ideology is quite clear.
169. I quote from Galati's memoir, "I casi di Malaspina e la mafia nelle campagne di Palermo," in *Inchiesta Bonfadini*, pp. 999–1016, in particular p. 1000; also in ASPA, GP, 1876, b. 5.
170. Summation by the lawyer Siracusa, *Processo Amoroso*, p. 218.
171. The *questore* to the prefect, 10 October 1875, in ASPA, GP, b. 35.
172. Galati, "I casi di Malaspina," p. 1001.
173. The *questore* to the prefect, 18 September 1875, in ASPA, GP, b. 35.
174. *Processo Amoroso*, p. 238.
175. The minister to the prefect, 18 September 1875, p. 3, in ASPA, GP, 1875, b. 35, f. 6.
176. The *questore* to the prefect, 26 October 1875, *fondo* cited above, pp. 11 and 10.
177. Exchange of letters between Codronchi and Gerra, 26 and 30 November 1875, ASPA, GP, 1877, b. 39.
178. Memoir dated 29 December 1875, file cited above.
179. The minister to the prefect, 12 August 1875, pp. 2 and 4.
180. Report of the *questore* to the public prosecutor, 29 September 1876, in ASPA, GQ, 1880, b. 7, with extensive documentation. See also Di Menza, *Le cronache*, pp. 221ff., and Cutrera, *La mafia*, pp. 118ff.
181. As documented by many of the witnesses in the 1878 trial and from the statement of the defendant S. Spinnato, 27 April 1878, in ASPA, GQ, 1880, b. 7.
182. Di Menza, *Le cronache*, p. 232.
183. The *delegato di PS* Bernabò to the *questore*, 16 September 1876, p. 3, in ASPA, GQ, 1880, b. 7. Among the *stoppagghieri*, two claimed that they had been persecuted by Albanese: statements of the defendants, ibid.
184. The royal public prosecutor of Palermo to the minister, 18 January 1879, in ACS, *Giustizia*, MAP, b. 49.
185. Letter to the GDS, 28 May 1878.
186. Concerning the tragic conflict with Mayor Calderone of Marineo, see also the memoir written (1887) by his wife, G. Cirillo Rampolla, *Suicidio per mafia*, introduction by G. Fiume (Palermo, 1986).
187. Report from the *delegato di PS* of Misilmeri, 1 December 1876, together with other reports in ASPA, GQ, *fondo*.
188. Di Menza, *Le cronache*, p. 238.
189. Documentation in ACS, *Giustizia*, MAP, b. 49; the text of the letters is in *Processo Amoroso*, pp. 148–50.
190. Franchetti, "Condizioni politiche," p. 96.
191. ASPA, GP, b. 63.

192. *Processo Amoroso,* p. 56.
193. Trial for wife-murder, attributed to a Palermo mafioso: report by the prefect, 23 August 1914, p. 3, in ACS, Polizia Giudiziaria (judicial police), b. 144.
194. Report by the prefect, 16 June 1912, p. 2, file cited above, b. 374.
195. Testimony and the incident in ASPA, GQ, b. 63, where the trial documentation is found as well.
196. *Processo Amoroso,* p. 41.
197. Ibid., p. 203.
198. See the report, dated 8 March 1880, in ASPA, GQ, *fondo.*
199. Telegram by Marinuzzi in *L'Amico del popolo,* 5 March 1880. An extensive summary of the summation is in ASPA, GQ, *fondo.*
200. *Processo Amoroso,* p. 24.
201. Ibid., p. 251.
202. Ibid., p. 40.
203. "I casi di Malaspina," p. 1000.
204. E. Arnao, *La coltivazione degli agrumi* (Palermo, 1899), p. 373.
205. Respectively, F. Alfonso, *Trattato sulla coltivazione degli agrumi* (Palermo, 1875), p. 463; interview with the exporter F. Puglisi in Iachello, *Stato unitario,* p. 200.
206. Description of the murder of one of these middlemen in Bernabò's report to the *questore,* 24 September 1876, ASPA, GQ, *fondo.* For an in-depth analysis of the transactions peculiar to the citrus trade, however, for which there is not enough space in this context, I refer the reader to my *Il giardino degli aranci.*
207. Interview with Pagano, in *Inchiesta Bonfadini,* p. 483.
208. The *questore* to the royal public prosecutor, 29 September 1876, p. 8.

CHAPTER III. *GUARDIANI* AND PROFITEERS

1. A profile of Notarbartolo, laudatory but accurate in every detail that can be cross-referenced to other sources, was written by his son, L. Notarbartolo, *Memorie della vita di mio padre, Emanuele Notarbartolo di San Giovanni* (Pistoia, 1949). Concerning the period of the *sindacatura,* see O. Cancila, *Palermo* (Rome, 1988), pp. 148–55; concerning the management of the bank, see R. Giuffrida, *Il Banco di Sicilia* (Palermo, 1973), vol. 2, pp. 307–19. See also Giuseppe Barone, "Egemonie urbane e potere locale, 1882–1913," in *Storia d'Italia,* ed. M. Aymard and G. Giarrizzo (Turin, 1987), pp. 307–19; and P. Pezzino, *Una certà reciprocità di favore: Mafia e modernizzazione violenta nella Sicilia post-unitaria* (Milan, 1990).
2. G. Marchesano, *Processo contro Raffaele Palizzolo & C. Arringa dell'avv.* G.M. (Palermo, 1902), p. 213.
3. *Per l'assassinio del comm. Notarbartolo* (24 October 1896), p. 1, in Biblioteca Comunale di Imola (BCI), Carte Codronchi, *Commissariato civile per la Sicilia,* cat. 16, Processo Notarbartolo, b. 8217.
4. Report of the Minister of Justice dated 26 February 1894, p. 1, in ACS, *Giustizia,* MAP, b. 126.
5. Testimony at the trial in Milan by the *questore* of Messina Peruzy, formerly police detective in Palermo, in GDS, 23–24 November 1899.
6. R. Poma, *Onorevole alzatevi!* (Florence, 1976), described the courtroom hearings that I myself read about in the accounts of the *Corriere della Sera* (CS), the GDS, and *L'Avanti!* as well as other daily newspapers.
7. Letter to Codronchi, 5 December 1899, in BCI, file cited in note 3 above.

8. Notarbartolo, *Memorie*, p. 339.

9. *L'Avanti!* 18 November 1899.

10. CS, 4–5 September 1901.

11. Report of the prefect De Seta dated 15 May 1900 in ACS, PS, AAGGRR 1879–1903, b. 1., fasc. 1/11, p. 4, containing a note from Di Blasi.

12. GDS, 3–4 December 1899.

13. GDS, 15–16 December 1899.

14. GDS, 23–24 November 1899.

15. S. Sonnino, *Diario 1866–1912*, ed. B. F. Brown (Bari, 1972), vol. 1, p. 428 and also p. 423.

16. *L'Avanti!* 8 December 1899.

17. Rastignac [V. Morello], "I discorsi del giorno: de malo in pejus," *La Tribuna*, 15 December 1899.

18. G. De Felice, *Maffia e delinquenza in Sicilia* (Milan, 1900), p. 42.

19. Letter to the Minister of Justice, 14 February 1900, p. 6 in ACS, *Giustizia*, MAP, b. 125.

20. Sonnino's speech to the Chamber of Deputies on 6 July 1896 is in S. M. Ganci, *Il commissariato civile per la Sicilia del 1896* (Palermo, 1958), pp. 320–40. A list of the government parliamentarians upon Codronchi's arrival is in BCI, file cited above, cat. 15, b. 8182. Concerning the *commissariato civile*, see Barone's summary, "Egemonie urbane," pp. 285–94.

21. D. Farini, *Diario di fine secolo 1896–1899* (Rome, 1961), vol. 2, p. 908.

22. Speech of 8 July 1896, p. 7349.

23. Notarbartolo, *Memorie*, p. 333.

24. Letter and notes in BCI, file cited above.

25. Undated notes in BCI, file cited above. The investigation into the municipal government of 1900–1901 would describe the period of the Amato-Pojero mayoralty as "one of the saddest and most deplorable periods." Quoted in Cancila, *Palermo*, p. 205.

26. Respectively, De Felice, "Le responsabilità del governo: i consiglieri della maffia," *L'Avanti!* 28 December 1899; Cancila, *Palermo*, pp. 103–4.

27. D. Farini, *Diario di fine secolo 1896–1899*, vol. 2, p. 1188.

28. Ibid., p. 908.

29. "La mafia: sue origini e sue manifestazioni," GDS, 10–11 December 1899.

30. *Sangiorgi Report*, attachment to the XVI report, p. 16.

31. The negotiations among Codronchi, Lucchesi, and Bertolani in BCI, file cited above, cat. 14, b. 7816 *bis*. According to a memorandum from the civil plaintiff (14 January 1900, pp. 4–5), it was allegedly Cosenza who persuaded the ex-convict to refrain from naming the mastermind: ACS, *Giustizia*.

32. Notarbartolo, *Memorie*, pp. 335–38.

33. Letter dated 5 October 1899, pp. 3–4; in the same connection, and in the same file cited above, also a letter from Rudinì to Codronchi, dated 10 October 1899.

34. Letter, p. 1.

35. Ibid., p. 2.

36. Report dated 15 May 1900, p. 5.

37. Cosenza to Gianturco, 1 April 1901, p. 4, in ACS, *Giustizia*, b. 126.

38. Memorandum dated 14 January 1900, p. 14.

39. Notarbartolo, *Memorie*, pp. 351–52.

40. Drago, "La maffia è necessaria," *L'Avanti!* 5 December 1899.

41. Letter dated 8 July 1900 in BCI, file cited above, cat. 16, b. 8223. By G. De Felice; see, for instance, "L'ex-Viceré Codronchi e la mafia," *L'Avanti!* 9 December 1899.

42. In Atti parlamentari della Camera dei deputati (APCD), *Discussioni*, 1 December 1899, pp. 344 and 383.

43. "Attorno al processo Notarbartolo," *Il Tempo*, 2 January 1900, and the comment by G. De Felice, "Sempre le lettere del generale Mirri," *L'Avanti!* 4 January 1900.

44. "La mafia: sue origini."

45. Documents from January 1900 in ACS, *Giustizia*, file cited above, b. 125.

46. Report dated 1 March 1900 in ACS, file cited above.

47. The dense exchange of letters between the pair, summer–fall 1900 (previously utilized by Barone, "Egemonie urbane," pp. 315–16), in ACS, *Giustizia*, file cited above, b. 126.

48. Pietro Rosano et al., *Memoria in difesa di R. Palizzolo* (Palermo, 1904), p. ix.

49. CS, respectively, 28–29 September and 1–2 October 1901.

50. Rosano et al., *Memoria in difesa di R. Palizzolo*, p. ix.

51. G. Mosca, "Palermo e l'agitazione pro-Palizzolo," in Mosca, *Uomini e cose di Sicilia* (Palermo, 1980), p. 52.

52. See Frosini's observations in his introduction to Mosca, *Uomini e cose*, pp. xiv–xv, as well as the obituary of Rudinì, *Uomini e cose*, pp. 89–98. Mosca would later be elected a member of parliament for Caccamo; might he have pulled his punches concerning the followers of Palizzolo?

53. Archivio di Stato di Palermo (ASPA), GP, b. 84; but see also Notarbartolo, *Memorie*, pp. 165–88.

54. Marchesano, *Processo*, p. 417.

55. Respectively, report dated 21 August 1882, pp. 2–3, in ASPA, GP, b. 84; dated 3 August 1875 in ASPA, GP, b. 33; personal file in ASPA, GQ, b. 20; Pezzino, *Una certa reciprocità*, pp. 163–64.

56. *Sangiorgi Report*, XXIV report, pp. 4–5.

57. A. Cutrera, *La mala vita di Palermo* (Palermo, 1900).

58. Marchesano, *Processo*, p. 332.

59. E. Bertola, *Requisitoria pronunciata alla Corte d'Assise di Bologna* (Bologna, 1902). An extensive summary of the matter can also be found in CS, 9–10 September 1901.

60. Bertola, *Requisitoria*, p. 27.

61. Ibid., p. 28.

62. Statement of the witnesses Accardi and Barabbino, in Bertola, *Requisitoria*, pp. 30 and 32; Pezzino, *Una certa reciprocità*, p. 161.

63. *Sangiorgi Report*, pp. 370–72. A case resembling that of the Gentile estate was the case of the Ferreri estate under Tommaso Natale, a base of operations for cattle thieves and "the most greatly feared smugglers": from the commander of the Carabinieri to the prefect, 3 January 1896, in ASPA, GP, b. 148, f. 16.

64. *Per l'assassinio del comm. Notarbartolo: Sunto e impressioni della pratica esistente in questura* (24 October 1896), in BCI, file cited above, cat. 16, b. 8217, p. 23.

65. ACS, Interni, AAGGRR, 1879–1903, b. 1, fasc. 1/11, telegram dated 18 December 1899.

66. The prefect to the prime minister, 24 October 1900, pp. 3 and 4, in ASPA, GQ, b. 20.

67. "La misteriosa scomparsa di 4 persone," GDS, 6–7 and 12–13 November 1897.

68. Undated handwritten note, certainly in the hand of Sangiorgi, in ASPA, GQ, b. 20.

69. *Sangiorgi Report*, p. 47.

70. Ibid., p. 9.

71. Ibid., p. 193.

72. Report of the *questore*, 3 August 1900, in ACS, GQ, b. 20; I do not know whether this Filippo Vitale is the same as the Mafia capo of Altarello and whether this Salvatore Greco is the same as the one identified in the investigation of the *Sangiorgi Report* as a major leader of the Ciaculli group.

73. Calpurnio, *Dai ricordi dal carcere del comm. Raffaele Palizzolo* (Rome, 1908), p. 142.

74. Report dated 24 October 1900.

75. CS, 30–31 October 1901.

76. See, for instance, the concerns of Sangiorgi himself in *Rapporto,* p. 369.

77. See, for instance, the episode: *Rapporto,* pp. 89–90.

78. Ibid., pp. 84ff.

79. Ibid., p. 37.

80. Ibid., p. 38.

81. Ibid., pp. 335–36.

82. G. Alongi, *La maffia nei suoi fattori e nelle sue manifestazioni: Studio sulle classi pericolose della Sicilia* (Turin, 1886), p. 301.

83. Respectively, Anonymous, p. 1, and XXVII report; in *Sangiorgi Report.*

84. *Sangiorgi Report,* p. 10.

85. Drago, "La maffia è necessaria."

86. G. Mosca, "Che cosa è la mafia," in Mosca, *Uomini et cose.*

87. Report that resulted from the ingenuity of Inspector Alongi, 13 May 1904, in ASPA, QAG, b. 1434, Associazione a delinquere, Camastra Giovanni + 75, which described as mafiosi the heads of the organization. In contrast, Cutrera, *La mala vita di Palermo,* tends to distinguish *ricottari,* or pimps, from mafiosi.

88. *Sangiorgi Report,* p. 6.

89. Respectively, ibid., pp. 382ff.; the *delegato di PS* of Villabate to the *questore,* 14 December 1901, in ASPA, GP, b. 20.

90. The *delegato di PS* of Villabate to the *questore,* 29 December 1901, in ASPA, file cited above.

91. See a case of purse snatching and another case of extortion against a street peddler in ACS, PG 1912, b. 374. Concerning the urban Camorra, see Marcella Marmo, "Tra le carceri e i mercati: Spazi e modelli storici del fenomeno camorrista," in *La Campania,* ed. P. Marcy and P. Villani (Turin, 1990), pp. 711ff., and concerning the Camorra of the hinterland, pp. 726ff. For a more general comparison, see Introduction, in *Quaderni dell'Istituto universitario orientale. Dipartimento di scienze sociali* (Naples, 1989), vol. 2, pp. 9–30.

92. *Sangiorgi Report,* XXVI report.

93. See the case of the two *gabellotti* of the Politi estate, subsequently murdered, the Oliveri estate, and the damaging attacks, in *Sangiorgi Report,* pp. 221ff.; XXV report, p. 39.

94. "La misteriosa scomparsa . . . D'Alba, vittima o complice?" GDS, 12–13 November 1897.

95. "Uno strascico delle bombe sparate ai mercanti di limoni," GDS, 24–26 October 1897; concerning these disagreements, I refer the reader to my own *Il giardino degli aranci: Il mondo degli agrumi nella storia del Mezzogiorno* (Venice, 1990), p. 162.

96. *Sangiorgi Report,* pp. 92ff.

97. Ibid., pp. 17ff.; pp. 135ff.

98. Ibid., p. 18.

99. Ibid., p. 43.

100. Ibid., pp. 137, 143ff., attachments 1 and 2 with the signed statements of the two widows.

101. Ibid., p. 149.

102. Ibid., p. 140.

103. Summary of the first preliminary investigation, on p. 126.

104. Ibid. Concerning the fall of the regionalist administration, see Cancila, *Palermo,* pp. 145ff.

105. Notarbartolo to Gerra, 30 March 1876, quoted in Giuffrida, *Il Banco,* p. 145. See also Barone, "Egemonie urbane," pp. 309–11.

106. Notarbartolo to Detective A. Quarta, 30 June 1889, quoted in Giuffrida, *Il Banco,* p. 161.

107. ACS, Carte Crispi, b. 420, letter dated 8 April 1889, reproduced in the appendix of Giuffrida, *Il Banco,* pp. 320–28.

108. Notarbartolo, *Memorie,* pp. 223–24.

109. Marchesano, *Processo,* p. 391.

110. According to Marchesano, *Processo,* p. 394, Palizzolo was in the same situation; the fact was not mentioned by Notarbartolo in his letters, nor do I find evidence of it from other sources.

111. Also, the second letter in ACS, file cited above, is reproduced in the appendix of Giuffrida, *Il Banco,* pp. 329–32.

112. Summary of the first preliminary investigation.

113. Quoted by L. De Rosa, "Il Banco di Napoli e la crisi economica del 1888–1894: Tramonto e crisi della gestione Giusso," *Rassegna economica,* 1963, 2, pp. 349–431, and in particular p. 430.

114. See the analysis by De Rosa, ibid.

115. Quoted by G. Barone, "Crisi economica e marina mercantile nel Mezzogiorno d'Italia (1888–1894)," in *Archivio storico per la Sicilia orientale,* 1974, vol. 1, pp. 45–111, and in particular p. 82; I would refer the reader to this article for the history of the Italo-British company.

116. Ibid., p. 83. Concerning the Florio empire, see S. Candela, *I Florio* (Palermo, 1986).

117. G. Barone, "Lo Stato e la marina mercantile in Italia," *Studi storici,* 1974, 3.

118. Speech dated 29 April 1885 in APCD, *Discussioni,* pp. 13203–21, in particular p. 13219.

119. R. Palizzolo, *Sulle convenzioni marittime* (Rome, 1893), p. 30.

120. Testimony of P. Bazan in Milan in GDS, 25–26 November 1899; but see the clear reconstruction by Marchesano, *Processo,* pp. 452ff.

121. *L'Epoca,* 8 June 1890, quoted by Giuffrida, *Il Banco,* p. 256.

122. Summary of the first preliminary investigation.

123. CS, 6–7 September 1899.

124. Cutrera to the *questore,* 26 and 27 January 1900, in ASPA, GQ, 1866–1939, b. 20. But concerning the financing of citrus exports, I refer the reader to my own *Il giardino degli aranci.*

125. See the personal files found in ASPA, file cited above, and the reports dated 24 and 25 January 1900, in ASPA, GQ, 1866–1939, b. 20.

126. Respectively, *Processo dei Fratelli Amoroso e compagni* (Palermo, 1883), p. 28; and ACS, PS, AAGGRR, 1879–1903, b. 1, fasc. 1/11, telegram from the prefect of Agrigento, 13 December 1899.

127. Account by G. Blandini, June 1909, quoted by G. Barone, "Lo Stato e le opere pie in Sicilia," in Various Authors, *Chiesa e società urbana in Sicilia* (Acireale, 1990), p. 52.

128. *Sangiorgi Report,* pp. 314–15.

129. Respectively, letter dated 9 March and report dated 4 April 1898 in ASPA, GP, b. 172. In more general terms, see my own *Il giardino degli aranci,* pp. 159ff.

130. GDS, 30 November–1 December 1899.

131. Notarbartolo, *Memorie,* p. 394.

132. *Sangiorgi Report,* attachment to the XIV report.

133. Calpurnio, *Dai ricordi del comm. R. Palizzolo,* p. 10; of these alleged *Ricordi* or "memoirs" I have found no other traces.

134. Mosca, "Perché offende l'assoluzione di Palizzolo," in Mosca, *Uomini e cose,* p. 58.

135. Of course, these are recurring themes: note, for instance, the coincidental timing of the presentation of Nitti's book and the opening of the Milan trial, in GDS, 8–9 November 1899.

136. Concerning the "Pro-Sicilia," I refer the reader to Francesco Renda, *Socialisti e cattolici in Sicilia, 1900–1904: le lotte agrarie* (Caltanissetta, 1972).

137. Cancila, *Palermo,* pp. 237–40; Candela, *I Florio;* G. Barone, "Il tramonto dei Florio," *Meridiana,* 1991, 11–12, pp. 15–46.

138. *La Battaglia,* 10 November 1901, quoted in Renda, *Socialisti e cattolici,* p. 405.

139. See, for instance, the previously cited parliamentary speech by De Felice on 1 December 1899, pp. 350–51, and De Felice, *Maffia e delinquenza*, p. 37.

140. See the letter from V. E. Orlando to Giolitti in 1909 quoted by Barone, "Il tramonto dei Florio," p. 34.

141. Electoral platform quoted in Renda, *Socialisti e cattolici*, p. 116, to which I refer the reader for a reconstruction of these events.

142. *L'Ora*, 24–26 July 1904; likewise the rest of the pro-Palizzolo press: "Il caso Palizzolo," *Il Gazzettino rosa*, 11–18 January 1900; Spartachus, "Tasca, Drago e Palizzolo," *La Forbice*, 7 January 1900.

143. De Felice, *Maffia e delinquenza*, p. 43.

144. See the observations by M. Marmo, *Il proletariato industriale a Napoli in età liberale* (Naples, 1978), pp. 223ff., and by F. Barbagallo, *Stato, Parlamento e lotte politico-sociali nel Mezzogiorno* (Naples, 1976), pp. 70ff.

145. In *L'Avanti!* 1 August 1902.

146. "Saprofiti politici," *Critica sociale*, 1895, 13, pp. 194–95.

147. A. Labriola, "Nord e Sud," *Critica sociale*, 1896, 15, p. 234.

148. In *Il Giorno*, 8 January 1900.

149. Napoleone Colajanni, *Nel regno della mafia: dai Borboni ai Sabaudi* (Rome: Rivista populare, 1900), p. 39.

150. In *Il Mattino*, 13 November 1903, quoted in Barbagallo, *Stato, Parlamento*, p. 169. Previously, Rosano had engaged in polemics with the extreme over his decision to defend Palizzolo.

151. L. Pirandello, *I vecchi e i giovani* (Milan, 1913) (1st ed. 1905), p. 7.

152. Article dated 1 August 1902, quoted in CS, 2–3 August 1902.

153. CS, 2–4 October 1901.

154. "La mafia: sua natura e sue manifestazioni," GDS, 10 December 1899.

155. Alongi, *La mafia*, p. 112.

156. In *L'Ora* and in GDS, 31 March, 1 April 1902.

157. APCD, Session of 1874–75, *Discussione*, meeting of 7 June, p. 3966.

158. Mosca, *Che cosa è la mafia*. In this connection, see R. Salvo, "Mosca, la mafia e il caso Palizzolo," *Nuovi quaderni del Meridione*, 1982, pp. 233–45.

159. Marchesano, *Processo*, p. 292.

160. See, respectively, the previously cited deposition in Bologna; the testimony of the daughter in G. Bonomo, *Pitrè, la Sicilia e i siciliani* (Palermo, 1898), p. 345; and the books quoted by Barone and Renda. See also Pitrè, "Per la Sicilia," GDS, 7–8 August 1902.

161. Pitrè, *Usi e costumi, credenze e pregiudizi del popolo siciliano* (Bologna, n.d.), p. 289.

162. *Processo Amoroso*, p. 39.

163. In L. Sciascia, *A futura memoria* (Milan, 1989). Moreover, Hess erroneously attributes the phrase to the defendant Minì; Sciascia, adding one mistake to another, states that "Mini [*sic*] is an expression meaning a fellow; a mid-level or major Mafioso": this is a typical extension toward a symbolic empyrean made up of easily identified events and people. H. Hess, *Mafia*, preface by L. Sciascia (Rome, 1991) (1st ed. 1970), esp. p. vi.

164. *Processo Amoroso*, respectively, pp. 34, 69, 30.

165. Ibid., p. 120.

166. Hess, *Mafia*, p. 44.

167. Summation by Lucifora, in ASPA, GQ, b. 7; summation by Cuccia, in *Processo Amoroso*, p. 250.

168. This thesis was demolished by Marchesano, *Processo*, pp. 69–70.

169. Ibid., pp. 294–95.

170. Pitrè, *Usi e costumi, credenze e pregiudizi*, vol. 2, p. 292.
171. "The man who talks too much destroys himself with his own mouth."
172. This is the opinion of the anonymous source cited above.
173. *Sangiorgi Report*, pp. 277ff., 349ff.
174. Ibid., p. 191; but see also Alongi, *La guardianìa*, p. 354.
175. The *questore* to the prefect, 18 September 1875, p. 5.
176. J. Schneider and P. Schneider, *Classi sociali, economia e politica in Sicilia* (Soveria Mannelli, 1989) (1st ed. 1976), pp. 103ff.
177. "Il processo contro i rapinatori di carrozze," GDS, 7 July 1928. For a case of this sort, see the report for the prefecture, 11 October 1916, in ACS, PG 1916–18, b. 236.
178. Report, cited by Alongi, dated 13 May 1904, p. 12.
179. J. Amery, *Sons of the Eagle: A Study in Guerrilla War* (London, 1948), quoted by Schneider and Schneider, *Classi sociali*, p. 121.
180. G. E. Nuccio, *Il giardino dei limoni* (Palermo, 1926), quoted by S. F. Romano, *La Sicilia nell'ultimo ventennio del secolo XIX* (Palermo, 1958), p. 118.
181. *Sangiorgi Report*, XXVIII report, p. 9.
182. The *questore* to the prefect, 10 October 1875.
183. Report of the prefect of Palermo, 16 March 1916, in ACS, PG 1916–18, b. 236.
184. ASPA, GP, b. 148, f. 16, the commander of the legion of the Carabinieri to the prefect, 3 January 1896, but also *Sangiorgi Report*, p. 253.
185. G. G. Lo Schiavo, *100 anni di mafia* (Rome, 1962).
186. *Processo Amoroso*, p. 47; E. Scalici, *Cavalleria di Porta Montalto* (Naples, 1885), p. 81 of the reprint with the title *La Mafia siciliana*, ed. A. D'Asdia (Palermo, 1980).
187. E. Onufrio, "La mafia in Sicilia," *Nuova Antologia*, 1877, p. 367.
188. P. Arlacchi, *La mafia imprenditrice: L'etica mafiosa e lo spirito del capitalismo* (Bologna, 1983), pp. 26–27. Far more persuasive is the analysis by Catanzaro, *Il delitto come impresa: Storia sociale della mafia* (Padua, 1988), pp. 38–41.
189. Terms used by Francesco Siino, in *Sangiorgi Report*, p. 45.
190. Ibid., p. 95.

CHAPTER IV. DEMOCRATIZATION, TOTALITARIANISM, DEMOCRACY

1. E. Reid, *La mafia* (Florence, 1956), pp. 152ff.; J. L. Albini, *The American Mafia: Genesis of a Legend* (New York, 1971), pp. 159ff.; H. S. Nelli, *The Business of Crime: Italians and Syndicate Crime in the United States* (Chicago, 1981), pp. 27ff.
2. This is a reference to the brigand Leone and was adopted by H. Asbury, *The French Quarter* (New York, 1938), quoted in Albini, *The American Mafia*, p. 160.
3. Quoted by A. Paparazzo, *Italiani del Sud in America* (Milan, 1990), p. 12, to which I refer the reader for this topic.
4. E. Sori, *L'emigrazione italiana dall'Unità alla seconda guerra mondiale* (Bologna, 1979), pp. 330–36.
5. *Plunkitt di Tammany Hall, una serie di conservazioni . . . raccolte da W. L. Riordon*, ed. A. Testi (Pisa, 1991) (1st ed. 1905).
6. Albini, *The American Mafia*, p. 154, my translation. From the literature between the two world wars, I would cite J. Landesco, *Organized Crime in Chicago* (Chicago, 1979) (1st ed. 1929), and F. W. White, *Little Italy: Uno slum italo-americano* (Bari, 1968) (1st ed. 1943). There is a reference

to this debate in P. Arlacchi and N. Dalla Chiesa, *La palude e la città* (Milan, 1987), and in U. Santino and G. La Fiura, *L'impresa mafiosa dall'Italia agli Stati Uniti* (Milan, 1990), pp. 516ff.

7. See my own *Il giardino degli aranci: Il mondo degli agrumi nella storia del Mezzogiorno* (Venice, 1990), pp. 128ff.

8. See chapter 2 in this volume.

9. Letter from the brigand quoted by L. Lumia, *Villalba, storia e memoria* (Caltanissetta, 1990), vol. 2, p. 234.

10. I cite only the case of P. Pollara, *consigliere comunale* (town councilman) of Ficarazzi: report of the prefect of Palermo, 4 February 1916, in ACS, PG, 1916–1918, b. 236.

11. The document is quoted by A. Petacco, *Joe Petrosino* (Novara, 1983), pp. 111–17; the quote is on p. 111.

12. I have reconstructed this episode based primarily on the book by Petacco mentioned in the previous note and another book by N. Volpes, *Tenente Petrosino, missione segreta in Sicilia* (Palermo, 1972). Both of these books reproduce extensive first-hand documentation, part of which is taken from a file from the *questura* of Palermo that cannot be consulted through the normal archival channels.

13. The *Report of Immigration Commission* of the Parlamento federale (Congress) from 1911 instead signaled a cooperative stance to the Italian government. Other difficulties can be attributed to American legislation: see Albini, *The American Mafia*, pp. 168–69.

14. Report quoted by Petacco, *Joe Petrosino*, pp. 138–39.

15. Verdict from the *sezione d'accusa* (prosecution section) of the Palermo Court of Appeals, 22 July 1911, quoted by Volpes, *Tenente Petrosino*, pp. 146–53, and in particular p. 148.

16. Report by Ceola, 2 April, in Petacco, *Joe Petrosino*, pp. 166–70.

17. An interesting opinion because, being that of a fellow townsman born in 1901 (the magistrate M. Margiotta), it reflects the "public opinion" of the time: quoted in L. Sciascia, *A futura memoria* (Milan, 1989), pp. 37–38.

18. Respectively, letter to Ceola from the *questore* of Rome dated 19 March, in Volpes, *Tenente Petrosino*, p. 118, and A. Block, *East Side, West Side: Organizing Crime in New York* (Cardiff, 1980), p. 8.

19. Michele Pantaleone, *Mafia e politica, 1943–1962* (Turin, 1962), information that is not supported by documents, such as the report that Cascio-Ferro was the inventor of the "pizzo," or levying of protection money, organized in Palermo (pp. 29–30). The route through Marseilles was utilized to avoid Italian American border controls: *Report of Immigration Commission* (1911). In 1924 Bonanno left his country along the Tunis–Le Havre–Cuba–Florida route (the last stretch by fishing boat); see J. Bonanno, *Uomo d'onore: L'autobiografia di J. B.* (Milan, 1985), pp. 54–55.

20. I take this information from ACS, Casellario politico centrale (CPC), b. 1141, integrating it with the documentation reported in the volumes quoted by Petacco and Volpes.

21. Pantaleone, *Mafia e politica*, p. 31.

22. Trial, concerning which see Giuseppe Barone, "Egemonie urbane e potere locale, 1882–1913," in *Storia d'Italia*, ed. M. Aymard and G. Giarrizzo (Turin, 1987), pp. 215–16.

23. See account by G. Blandini, June 1909, quoted by G. Barone, "Lo Stato e le opere pie in Sicilia," in Various Authors, *Chiesa e società urbana in Sicilia* (Acireale, 1990), p. 52.

24. See below.

25. Personal file in ACS, CPC, b. 1141.

26. Report by the prefect of Palermo, 12 December 1908, in ACS, file cited above.

27. Summation by Lieutenant Palizzolo, defender of the *fascianti* of Partinico, in G. Casarrubea, *I fasci contadini e le origini delle sezioni socialiste della provincia di Palermo* (Palermo, 1978), vol. 2, p. 257.

28. This is true of, among other cases, the massacre of Caltavuturo, regarding which I refer the reader to the reconstruction by F. Turati, "Il 'trionfo dell'ordine' a Caltavuturo," *Critica sociale*, 1893, 6.

29. A. Drago, "La maffia è necessaria," *L'Avanti!*, 5 December 1899.

30. Casarrubea, *I fasci*, passim.

31. Printed document entitled *Il municipio di Misilmeri* (Palermo, 1901), p. 11, in ACS, AC, *Comuni*, b. 172.

32. I refer the reader to the fundamental work by Barone, "Egemonie urbane."

33. Report from the *delegato di PS*, 20 December 1899, in ACS, file cited above.

34. Respectively, the article "Cose di Monreale," in *La provincia*, 1908, and the manifesto of the municipal administration, 18 June 1908, in ACS, file cited above.

35. Complaint signed by M. Costanzo, 20 March 1908, in ACS, file cited above.

36. Report dated 20 December 1899.

37. Report from the prefect, 4 October 1906, in ACS, AC, *Comuni*, b. 173.

38. Respectively, telegram from Di Pisa to Zanardelli, 29 June 1906, and petition from the *circolo dei civili*, undated, pp. 6 and 7, ACS, file cited above.

39. Prefectorial report dated 16 July 1906 in ACS, file cited above, b. 173.

40. ACS, PG, 1912, b. 374; but see chapter 2.

41. Giuseppe Guido Lo Schiavo, *Il reato di associazione per delinquere nelle provincie siciliane* (Selci Umbro, 1933), p. 145.

42. Claim signed by G. Fiducia Morana, p. 4, and Report of the *Direzione Generale di PS*, 8 June 1906, in ACS, file cited above, b. 172.

43. Fiume, Introduction to G. Cirillo Rampolla, *Suicidio per mafia* (Palermo, 1986).

44. Archivio di Stato di Agrigento (ASAG), Underprefecture of Bivona, b. 107.

45. A. Rossi, *L'agitazione in Sicilia* (Palermo, 1988) (1st ed. 1894), p. 64.

46. See also A. Blok, *La mafia di un villaggio siciliano, 1860–1960* (Turin, 1986) (1st ed. 1974), pp. 122ff. Here, as elsewhere, I use the real names, rather than the conventional names used by the author.

47. I refer the reader to the analysis by G. Procacci, "Movimenti sociali e partiti politici in Sicilia," in *Annuario dell'Istituto italiano per l'età moderna e contemporanea* (Pisa, 1959), pp. 109–214.

48. R. Ciuni, "Un secolo di mafia," in Various Authors, *Storia della Sicilia* (Palermo, 1978), vol. 9, p. 393.

49. Quoted by C. Messina, *Il caso Panepinto* (Palermo, 1977), p. 40.

50. *La Plebe*, 5 January 1905, quoted in *In giro per la Sicilia con "La plebe,"* ed. C. Messina (Palermo, 1985), pp. 71–74.

51. *Relazione prefettizia* dated 11 February 1902 in ACS, AC, *Comuni*, b. 173 (Prizzi).

52. Messina, *Il caso Panepinto*, p. 77.

53. Quoted by G. Barone, "Gruppi dirigenti e lotte politiche," in Various Authors, *Lorenzo Panepinto: democrazia e socialismo nella Sicilia del latifondo*, ed. Giuseppe Barone (Palermo, 1990), p. 61.

54. Report by the prefect of Palermo, 24 November 1915, in ACS, PG, 1916–1918, b. 236.

55. Verro to Colajanni, 27 May 1912, in G. Barone, "La cooperazione agricola dall'età giolittiana al fascismo," in Various Authors, *Storia della cooperazione siciliana*, ed. O. Cancila (Palermo, 1993), pp. 255–56.

56. A. Tasca, "Un apostolo troncato," *L'Avanti!*, 31 May 1911.

57. *L'Ora*, 19–20 May 1911, quoted by Messina, *Il caso Panepinto*, pp. 189ff.

58. Verro to Colajanni, 12 May 1911, in Barone, "La cooperazione."

59. Letter quoted by S. Mangano, *Bernardino Verro socialista corleonese* (Palermo, 1974).

60. Speech to the conference of peasants in Palermo, February 1920, quoted by G. C. Marino, *Partiti e lotta di classe in Sicilia, da Orlando a Mussolini* (Bari, 1976), p. 143. But concerning the awareness of Alongi, see also the report dated 4 March 1920, in ACS, CPC, b. 76, p. 2.

61. Report, pp. 3 and 6.

62. Marino, *Partiti e lotta di classe*, p. 140.

63. S. Centinaro, "La reazione dell'opinione pubblica alla morte di Lorenzo Panepinto," in Various Authors, *Lorenzo Panepinto*, p. 146. The trial, held in Catania *per legittima suspicione,* or recusal of venue, concluded in a *nulla di fatto,* roughly, an acquittal or mistrial or decision not to proceed.

64. Opinion of Verro in the letter cited in note 58 above, dated 12 May 1911.

65. {Relazione prefettizia} cit., 24 November 1915.

66. Lumia, *Villalba*, vol. 2, p. 271.

67. Report of the Rural Savings and Loan (Cassa rurale) of Villalba, in *Commissione parlamentare d'inchiesta sulle condizioni dei contadini nelle province meridionali e nella Sicilia,* vol. 6, *Sicilia* (Rome, 1910), t. I, p. 717.

68. I refer the reader again to Lumia, *Villalba*, vol. 2, pp. 273ff.

69. See the report by G. Alongi, 14 November 1902, published in the appendix of Alongi, *La mafia* (Palermo, 1904), pp. 363–87; and Cutrera, *Varsalona, il suo regno e le sue gesta delittuose* (Rome, 1904).

70. See the report of the investigating magistrate F. U. Di Blasi, 2 October 1928, vol. 4, in *Antimafia: Doc.*, vol. 4, t. V, pp. 423–33.

71. See also the anonymous letter dated Buenos Aires, 9 March 1913, and the report of the prefect, 6 May 1913, in ACS, PG, 1913, b. 103.

72. Alongi, *Relazione,* p. 366. Here as elsewhere the author places perhaps excessive emphasis on the innovative nature of this fin-de-siècle brigandage compared with the "classical" brigandage.

73. An anonymous "threatened landowner" to the prefect, June 1912, in ACS, PG, 1913, b. 374.

74. Di Blasi report, 15 September 1926, I, in *Antimafia: Doc.*, vol. 4, t. V, p. 339. See also the testimony of Candino himself, in A. Spanò, *Faccia a faccia con la mafia* (Milan, 1978), p. 20; the author, the son of the inspector Francesco Spanò serving in the area from 1912 on, makes use of his father's documentation.

75. Alongi, *Relazione*, p. 376.

76. The protest of the mayor, 4 October 1915, in ACS, PG, 1916–1918, b. 236. The pitched battle between the Grisafi gang and one of the Lo Jaconos, following the slaughter of sixteen head of cattle (1912), in ACS, PG, 1912, b. 374. See also Blok, *La mafia*, pp. 131ff.

77. See the network that supports Raffaele Ballo, "acknowledged chief of the criminals, low and high, of the countryside around Palermo and Trapani," in the reports dated 24 February and 4 March 1911, in ACS, PG, 1914, b. 144.

78. The relatives of Varsalona exerted a sort of monopoly over the area mills. See Alongi, *Relazione,* p. 371.

79. Report of the under-prefect of Corleone, 12 September 1913, p. 2, in ACS, PG, 1913, b. 103.

80. Letter from the company Malato & C., 17 February 1913; reply from the prefecture, 29 March, in ACS, PG, 1913, b. 103.

81. M. Genco, *Il delegato* (Palermo, 1991), p. 55; the reference is to the volume cited, *Varsalona*.

82. Letter dated Palermo, 15 August 1914, in ACS, PG, 1914, b. 144.

83. Alongi, *Relazione*, p. 373.

84. Letter from the prince of Camporeale, 30 November 1916, in *Quarant'anni di vita politica italiana: Dalle carte di Giovanni Giolitti* (Milan, 1961), vol. 3, pp. 202–3.

85. Summation of the lawyer Restivo during the Ortoleva trial, in GDS, 28 March 1929.

86. C. Mori, *Con la mafia ai ferri corti* (Milan, 1932), p. 212 and passim.

87. Di Blasi report, vol. 1, pp. 339 and 317.

88. The association of cattle rustlers led by the mayor of Godrano, Giuseppe Barbaccia, was denounced with a prefectorial reaction on 11 May 1916 in ACS, PG, 1916–1918, b. 236. Especially concerning the bloody aftermath of the second postwar period, see the report on the Bosco della Ficuzza, in *Antimafia: Doc.*, vol. 4, t. III, pp. 1223–33.

89. GDS, 22 January 1926.

90. GDS, 6 September and, in general, July–September 1930.

91. Di Blasi report, 26 February 1928, vol. 2, in *Antimafia: Doc.*, vol. 4, t. III, p. 371.

92. Letter cited in the Di Blasi report, vol. 3, p. 378.

93. Concerning the cases of Mistretta, see the extensive reconstruction by G. Raffaele, *L'ambigua tessitura: Mafia e fascismo nella Sicilia degli anni venti* (Milan, 1993); Spanò, *Faccia a faccia*; the cited Di Blasi report; and the judicial accounts cited above.

94. See also the testimony of the priest I. Strano, in GDS, 14 November 1928.

95. Testimony of B. Tusa and L. Seminara in GDS, 11 September 1928.

96. A number of the people I interviewed in Ramacca, aside from the case of the Tusas, also referred to the cases of the Pollacis, who came from Nicosia in the 1920s, and to the Andolinas, who came from Enna in the 1930s.

97. GDS, 28 December 1928.

98. But sentenced to four years during the trial of Nicosia in 1929.

99. Testimony by Calderone and Arlacchi, pp. 10–11.

100. Testimony of the baron in GDS, 15 October 1930.

101. GDS, 11 January 1929.

102. Raffaele, *L'ambigua tessitura*, p. 237.

103. Not very different was the thesis of the lawyer Villasevaglios, in GDS, 19 January 1929, according to which from the Madonie-Caronie mountain massif, the organization extended "into the neighboring river valleys."

104. *La mafia*, p. 143. Blok does not find it contradictory to describe Cascio-Ferro planning cattle thefts in both Bisacquino and Sambuca (p. 147), or to admit (p. 144) that he imposed himself "as a Mafia capo in larger districts." To claim that the "so-called conspiracy to commit crimes" should be defined in terms of "networks of relations" does not resolve the question of the extent and stability of these networks.

105. G. Molè, *Studio-inchiesta sui latifondi siciliani* (Rome, 1929); N. Prestianni, *Inchiesta sulla piccola proprietà coltivatrice formatasi nel dopoguerra*, vol. 6 of the *Inchiesta Inea* (Rome, 1931).

106. Respectively, Barone, "Lo Stato e le opere pie in Sicilia," p. 55; ACS, AC, Podestà: Catania.

107. Raffaele, *L'ambigua tessitura*, pp. 226ff.

108. Documentation in ACS, PS, 1920, b. 87; but see also A. Cicala, "Il movimento contadino in Sicilia nel primo dopoguerra," *Incontri meridionali*, 1978, 3–4, pp. 61–78.

109. File concerning the cooperatives of Ribera in ACS, PS, G1, b. 35: Agrigento.

110. Concerning Genco Russo, see *Antimafia: Biografie*, pp. 39–64; concerning the cases of the Polizzello estate, see *Antimafia: Doc.*, vol. 4, tt. II and III. Concerning the judicial episodes, see "Cooperativa tra i combattenti di Mussomeli," GDS, 9 October 1929, and the Verdict vs. Termini + 20 in ASCL, *Corte d'Assise, Sentenza*, b. 35.

111. The episode is reconstructed with the usual clarity by Lumia, *Villalba*, pp. 340ff.

112. Di Blasi report, vol. 2, p. 370.

113. Letter from the bishop of Caltanissetta, G. Jacono, 12 June 1935, quoted in C. Naro, *La Chiesa di Caltanissetta tra le due guerre* (Caltanissetta, 1991), vol. 2, p. 167.

114. I refer the reader to my own "La crisi del monopolio naturale," in Various Authors, *Economia e società nell'area dello zolfo,* ed. G. Barone and C. Torrisi (Caltanissetta, 1989), p. 354. Concerning the prior affairs of Don Calò see Lumia, *Villalba,* pp. 313ff.

115. Parliamentary speech in May 1949 quoted by O. Barrese, *I complici* (Soveria Mannelli, 1988), p. 18.

116. In GDS, 28 July 1925.

117. APCD, *Discussioni,* 7 February 1923, p. 1516.

118. October 1925; the competition was for piecework in the Trabia mine: GDS, 15 January 1928 and the days following.

119. Telegram dated 3 July in ACS, AC, *Ufficio elettorale,* b. 18. More can be said about Fascism than space allows here; I refer the reader to my own "L'utopia totalitaria del fascismo," in Various Authors, *La Sicilia,* ed. M. Aymard and G. Giarrizzo (Turin, 1987), pp. 371–482.

120. But see Marino, *Partiti e lotta di classe,* pp. 282–88, with the documentation cited in that work.

121. See the list in GDS, 27 February 1926.

122. In GDS, 3 December 1927.

123. Letter from V. Franco quoted by Spanò, *Faccia a faccia,* p. 33.

124. Letter from G. Faraci, 5 April 1923, in ACS, *Carte Bianchi,* b. 2.

125. Speech in Agrigento on 9 May, in B. Mussolini, *Opera omnia* (Florence, 1959), vol. 20, p. 264.

126. The Mori episode is perhaps the most extensively studied case in the history of the Mafia. Aside from the works cited above, see A. Petacco, *Il prefetto di ferro* (Milan, 1976); S. Porto, *Mafia e fascismo* (Palermo, 1977); and C. Duggan, *La mafia durante il fascismo* (Soveria Mannelli, 1986), published in English as *Fascism and the Mafia* (New Haven, 1989). Mori's book, *Con la mafia ai ferri corti,* is as poor in information as it is rich in ideology.

127. C. Mori, *Tra le zagare oltre la foschia* (Florence, 1923).

128. Marino, *Partiti e lotta di classe,* pp. 166–75; "La situazione in provincia di Trapani," *Bollettino della Confederazione dell'agricoltura siciliana,* 16 November 1920.

129. A. Infranca, "Il periodo trapanese del prefetto Mori nel giudizio della stampa locale," *Nuovi quaderni del Meridione,* 1982, 78, pp. 227–61.

130. Letter quoted by G. Faraci, p. 8.

131. Mori, *Con la mafia ai ferri corti,* p. 242.

132. Ibid., p. 244.

133. Ibid., p. 338.

134. Speech delivered in Alcamo in Mori, *Con la mafia ai ferri corti,* pp. 268–71.

135. Opinion of Mussolini, as General Di Giorgio reminded the Duce himself in a letter dated 19 March 1928, quoted by G. Caprì, "Di Giorgio e Mori ai ferri corti," *Osservatore politico-letterario,* January 1977, p. 48; the number does not include those in internal exile.

136. GDS, 4 June 1926.

137. Spanò, *Faccia a faccia,* pp. 42ff.

138. If we are to believe Cucco's autobiography, quoted by Duggan, *La mafia,* p. 50. The press of the time describes adoring crowds.

139. Letter to Scelba quoted by Spanò, *Faccia a faccia,* p. 147.

140. Mori, *Con la mafia ai ferri corti,* p. 365. But see the episode in the report of the vice prefect quoted by Duggan, *La mafia,* p. 87.

141. C. Gower Chapman, *Milocca, un villaggio siciliano* (Milan, 1985), pp. 29–31.

142. Poem reported and published in Naro, *La Chiesa di Caltanissetta,* vol. 2, pp. 62–63.

143. Report from the inspector dated 9 April 1928 in Spanò, *Faccia a faccia*, pp. 62–64, indicative as well of disagreements between the police and the Carabinieri.

144. Report of a police informer, 13 April 1931, in ACS, *Segreteria*, CR, b. 39, personal file of Cucco. For the similar case of the Caltanissetta *federale* D. Lipani, see G. Barone, "Notabili e partiti a Caltanissetta," in Various Authors, *Economia e società nell'area dello zolfo*, pp. 318–20.

145. See my treatment of the history of Sicilian Fascism in "L'utopia totalitaria."

146. Mori, *Con la mafia ai ferri corti*, p. 84.

147. See reports and documents in ACS, PS, AAGGRR, G1, 1920–1945, b. 138; and in ACS, *Polizia politica*, b. 195. A more analytical treatment can be found in my own "L'utopia totalitaria."

148. See his diary for 23 January 1927 in R. Trevelyan, *Principi sotto il vulcano* (Milan, 1977), p. 357.

149. Complaint of April 1927, in ACS, *Segreteria*, p. 2; but see also Spanò, *Faccia a faccia*, p. 38.

150. Mori, *Con la mafia ai ferri corti*, pp. 88–89.

151. GDS, 8 September 1928. Another brother, Gaetano, managed estates in the province of Palermo.

152. The letter is in the Di Blasi report, vol. 1, p. 327.

153. Quoted by Di Blasi, "Il reato di associazione per delinquere," in *Giurisprudenza penale*, 1930, part II, col. 228; see also Lo Schiavo, *Il reato di associazione*, pp. 146–47; both were magistrates working in the field.

154. For the mining Mafia, see GDS, 10 August 1929 and days following; for the Mafia of the latifundium, see the Verdict vs. Alfano + 30 in ASCL, *Corte d'Assise*, 1931, b. 35. Don Calò was acquitted in both cases.

155. Quoted by Blok, *La mafia*, p. 163; the text, censored, appeared in GDS, 30 July 1929.

156. Spanò, *Faccia a faccia*, p. 41.

157. Indro Montanelli, *Pantheon minore* (Milan, 1958), p. 284; perhaps as a result of this renunciation, the bandit managed to remain a fugitive from the law indefinitely.

158. Report of August 1928, quoted by Duggan, *La mafia*, p. 203.

159. Letter dated 21 October in ACS, AC, Podestà: Palermo, Gangi.

160. See the accounts of the trial in GDS, 12 March 1928 and days following.

161. See the harsh exchange between Carella, Sr., and Don Cola in GDS, 15 and 16 March 1928.

162. GDS, 31 March 1928.

163. GDS, 26 March 1928.

164. Mori, *Con la mafia ai ferri corti*, pp. 351ff.

165. What was unrealistic was the ambition to revise the sales contracts, "full-fledged documents of plunder that alone can explain certain 'sudden' explosions of wealth": the property purchased is in any case sacred. S. Sirena, "L'azione della Commissione per le affittanze agrarie," GDS, 18 February 1928.

166. Banco di Sicilia, *Notizie sull'economia siciliana, anno 1928* (Palermo, 1929), pp. 226ff.; Molè, *Studio-inchiesta*, p. 24.

167. Responsibility should be attributed to Inspector Belfiore, "overwhelmed by the dream of creating the largest association": closing statement of the lawyer F. Trigona della Foresta in GDS, 25 December 1930. But see also the admissions of the prosecuting attorney, GDS, 27 November 1930. The opinion of the ambassador is found in a report from 1927, collected in *Memorandum on Sicily under Italian Rule*, in Public Record Office, Foreign Office, 371/33251. Among the references to torture, see that by Abisso (because it was favorable to Mori), in GDS, 11 January 1929.

168. Testimony of C. Soldano, whose father had been murdered, in GDS, 7 August 1930.

169. Member of Parliament Grisafi in GDS, 2 August 1929.

170. Summation of the lawyer, Hon. Ungaro, in GDS, 20 August 1929.

171. Naro, *La Chiesa,* pp. 66–67.

172. Quoted from report in Spanò, *Faccia a faccia,* p. 63.

173. Testimony by Petrusa in GDS, 23 August 1930.

174. Di Giorgio to Mussolini, letter dated 19 March 1928, p. 47 (see note 135 on page 302).

175. Again, see Lupo, "L'utopia totalitaria."

176. Appeal of 19 October 1927 in ACS, PS, G1, b. 141; in the same collection, see b. 33 (Ribera), 56 (Sommatino), 107 (Mistretta); regarding Corleone, see Duggan, *La mafia,* p. 96.

177. Letter from G. Guarino-Amella to Mori quoted by Duggan, *La mafia,* pp. 202–3.

178. Statement by I. Messina, preliminary investigator for the trials against the Mafia families of Bisacquino and Corleone, in *Antimafia: Doc.,* vol. 3, t. I, p. 367.

179. Mori, *Con la mafia ai ferri corti,* pp. 313–14.

180. Summation of the lawyer G. Russo Perez in GDS, 8 June 1930.

181. G. M. Puglia, "Il mafioso non è un associato per delinquere," *La scuola positiva: Rivista di criminologia e diritto criminale,* 1930, 1, p. 156.

182. Quoted by Mori, *Con la mafia ai ferri corti,* pp. 15ff.

183. GDS, 6 May and 7 June 1929. Similar dynamics were seen in the proceedings against the associations of Roccella and Porta Nuova.

184. GDS, 13 January 1928. The law is no. 1254, dated 15 July 1926.

185. GDS, 23 November 1928.

186. Testimony by Calderone and Arlacchi, pp. 14–15 and passim.

187. In the immediate aftermath of both the First World War and the Second World War, there was a sudden rise in crime that ended with the end of the postwar situation; that was a national trend, not merely a regional trend.

188. It is unclear what this belief is based on, given Mori's pro-property position. It is true, however, that the regime did not like to see outlying figures consolidating power. In any case, the prefect remained in power for five years, a much longer period of time than was common.

189. I do not explore the varying impact of the form of repression (prison and/or internal exile) from case to case, which affected the further development of the careers of mafiosi.

190. These were, respectively, among the defendants of the trials against the Mafia in Mazzarino, Partinico, Termini, Corleone, Bagheria, and Monreale.

191. Bonanno, *Uomo d'onore,* p. 70. The statistics are from an official American source: *President's Commission on Organized Crime, Report to the President,* vol. 1, *The Impact* (Washington, DC, 1986), p. 52.

192. In the literature references in R. Candida, *Questa mafia* (Caltanissetta, 1966); Spanò, *Faccia a faccia,* pp. 72–73. Extensive documentation is instead in ACS, PS, FM; references are from b. 138 and 85, respectively.

193. The account of Pantaleone, *Mafia e politica,* pp. 48ff., is reproduced in a countless number of passages of works published about the Mafia.

194. This is the version of Luciano accepted by G. Gellért, *Maffia* (Soveria Mannelli, 1987), p. 78. E. Kefauver, *Il gangsterismo in America* (Turin, 1953), instead described a more straightforward quid pro quo.

195. Also in Gellért, *Maffia,* p. 80.

196. Even as skeptical a scholar as Block, *East Side, West Side,* p. 8, believes that this may be the turning point.

197. *The Problem of Mafia in Sicily,* 29 October 1943, a report by the American captain W. E. Scotten, published by R. Mangiameli in *"Annali" del Dipartimento di scienze storiche della Facoltà di scienze politiche* (Catania, 1980), p. 629.

NOTES

305

198. For which I am indebted to R. Mangiameli, "La regione in guerra (1943–50)," in Various Authors, *La Sicilia*, pp. 485–600.

199. Testimony by Calderone and Arlacchi, p. 46.

200. Note written by the detective in Spanò, *Faccia a faccia*, p. 89.

201. Concerning the deterioration of relations between landowners and the regime in the late 1930s, see Lupo, "L'utopia totalitaria," pp. 457ff.

202. S. Gentile, *Mafia e gabellotti in Sicilia; il PCI dai decreti Gullo al lodo De Gasperi*, in ASSO, 1973, pp. 491–508. We need to go back to "Tesi sul lavoro contadino nel Mezzogiorno" by R. Grieco (1926), in Grieco, *Introduzione alla riforma agraria* (Turin, 1946); and E. Sereni, *La questione agraria nella rinascita nazionale* (Turin, 1975 [but written in 1943]), pp. 239ff.

203. This is the reconstruction of the separatist view quoted by Mangiameli, "La regione," pp. 552ff. But see also Pantaleone, *Mafia e politica*, pp. 89ff., and Lumia, *Villalba*, vol. 2, pp. 448ff.

204. Mangiameli, "La regione," p. 554, to which I refer the reader for the references as well (pp. 553 and 555).

205. Concerning this episode, see *Antimafia: Bernardinetti Report*. Of the specific journalism, I cite only L. Galluzzo, *Meglio morto: Storia di Salvatore Giuliano* (Palermo, 1985). Among the general works on the subject, some good treatments are found in Gellért, *Maffia*, and in particular Spanò, *Faccia a faccia*.

206. Lumia, *Villalba*, vol. 2, p. 447.

207. This plot has been hypothesized more than once by the left and later confirmed by a leading right-wing figure in the separatist movement; see G. di Carcaci, *Il movimento per l'indipendenza della Sicilia* (Palermo, 1977).

208. When the bandit Labruzzo was mysteriously assassinated, Luca emphasized that the "hardworking populace" "were praying for a similar fate to befall the bandit Lombardo": report dated 1 February 1950, in *Antimafia: Doc.*, vol. 4, t. I, p. 75.

209. S. Gatto, *La Sicilia tra autonomia e sviluppo* (1948), later republished in Gatto, *Lo Stato brigante* (Palermo, 1978), p. 53.

210. Spanò, *Faccia a faccia*, p. 113. According to the magistrate G. Bellanca, Rimi was "one of the leading abettors of Giuliano": testimony in *Antimafia: Doc.*, vol. 3, t. I, p. 508.

211. Quoted in L. Galluzzo, F. Nicastro, and V. Vasile, *Obiettivo Falcone: Magistrati e mafia nel palazzo dei veleni* (Naples, 1989), pp. 167–68.

212. See his reports in *Antimafia: Doc.*, vol. 4, t. I.

213. See chapter 1 and earlier in this chapter in this volume.

214. This, at least, is his account in Various Authors, *Chiesa e società a Caltanissetta all'indomani della seconda guerra mondiale* (Caltanissetta, 1984), pp. 358–60.

215. See the episode narrated by the magistrate S. Mercadante of the *campiere* in Enna, who had in the past rendered services to the police and replaced mafioso "in the immediate aftermath of the liberation," following the murder of his brother, which was carried out as an example to others; see *Antimafia: Doc.*, vol. 3, t. I, p. 130.

216. This expression was used by the magistrate A. Di Giovana in relation to the allotment of the estates of the Agrigento baron Cannarella, in *Antimafia: Doc.*, vol. 4, t. I, p. 524.

217. In this regard, see *Antimafia: Singoli mafiosi*, pp. 39ff. Concerning the Polizzello estate, see *Antimafia: Doc.*, vol. 4, tt. II and III.

218. Indictment against Leggio and others, 13 October 1967, in *Antimafia: Doc.*, vol. 4, t. XVI, p. 87 and passim. The fact that two generations should have been considered mafiosi during three different regimes should rule out Duggan's thesis of persecution for the major Fascist *processone* (maxitrial) in Corleone; see Duggan, *La mafia*, pp. 95ff. The Vignali report is in *Antimafia: Doc.*, vol. 4, t. XVI, p. 164. Concerning Navarra, see also *Antimafia: Singoli mafiosi*, pp. 65ff.

219. Anonymous letter received by Li Causi, quoted by Chilanti and Farinella, *Rapporto*, p. 45.

220. Testimony by Streva in *Corte d'Appello di Bari*, Verdict vs. Leggio and others, 23 December 1970, in *Antimafia: Doc.*, vol. 4, t. XVI, p. 1135. For the verdict in the Comajanni case, see *Antimafia: Doc.*, vol. 4, t. XV.

221. Testimony by C. Terranova in *Antimafia: Doc.*, vol. 3, t. I, p. 1188.

222. Testimony of the deputy *questore* A. Mangano in *Antimafia: Doc.*, vol. 3, t. I, p. 1147.

223. See *Antimafia: Singoli mafiosi;* the Giuseppe Greco mentioned there might be the son of Salvatore, born in 1887, head of the family in 1945: see the genealogy in ibid., pp. 135–36, according to which the families have the same name and are linked by ties on the female side, since this Giuseppe Greco of Ciaculli married a Santa Greco, the sister of the "lieutenant." However, I would not rule out a common family tree, given the recurrence of specific first names on both sides.

224. Because his daughter Maria married Salvatore Greco "il senatore."

225. Whence originated the future Mafia capo Michele Greco, son of *Piddu u tenenti*. See the episodes described in *Antimafia: Singoli mafiosi*, pp. 137ff.; see also the indictment against P. Torretta and others, 31 May 1965, in *Antimafia: Doc.*, vol. 4, t. XVII, pp. 720–21.

226. Chilanti and Farinella, *Rapporto*, p. 90.

CHAPTER V. *LA COSA LORO*—THEIR THING

1. Speech in the Italian Senate, 25 June 1949, quoted by O. Barrese, *I complici* (Soveria Manelli, 1988), p. 7.

2. See chapter 1. But concerning this phase, in particular concerning the magistrature, see G. Di Lello, *Giudici* (Palermo, 1994).

3. "Ne hai ancora per poco di questa malandrineria," that is, "this criminal behavior won't last long": testimony of the mother of Carnevale from the extract of the verdict in *Antimafia: Doc.*, vol. 3, t. I, pp. 276–78.

4. Report from the *questura* of Agrigento, 16 April 1947, in *Antimafia: Doc.*, vol. 3, t. VII. 1, pp. 225–27.

5. E. Kefauver, *Il gangsterismo in America* (Turin, 1953).

6. Piero Calamandrei, preface to E. Reid, *La mafia* (Florence, 1956), p. xi.

7. F. Renda, *Un libro sulla mafia negli USA* (1956), now in Renda, *La Sicilia degli anni '50* (Naples, 1987), p. 403.

8. Vittorio Nisticò, Preface to Chilanti and Farinella, *Rapporto*, p. 23. See also Nisticò's testimony in *Antimafia: Doc.*, vol. 3, t. I, pp. 751ff., and the dossier reported in that context.

9. Danilo Dolci's most interesting works are *Banditi a Partinico* (Bari, 1955) and *Spreco* (Turin, 1960).

10. Gatto's articles from 1948–1976 are gathered in the volume *Lo stato brigante* (Palermo, 1978). Michele Pantaleone, one of the contributors to *L'Ora*, published *Mafia e politica 1943–1962* in Turin in 1962.

11. L. Sciascia, *Il giorno della civetta* (Turin, 1968) (1st ed. 1961), p. 99 (English edition: *The Day of the Owl* [Manchester, 1984], p. 101).

12. *Istruttoria maxiprocesso* (preliminary investigation of the Maxitrial), pp. 344ff., and therein the statements of the Honorable C. Mannino. See also G. Giarrizzo, "Sicilia oggi," in Various Authors, *La Sicilia*, ed. M. Aymard and G. Giarrizzo (Turin, 1987), pp. 633ff.

13. Examination of Calderone quoted in the document *Mafia e politica dell'Antimafia*, in a supplement to *La Repubblica*, 10 April 1993, p. 13; see also Testimony by Calderone, pp. 223–24. Concerning the functionality between regional politics and the "reconstitution of the hu-

mus of the Mafia," see Catanzaro's fine summary, *Il delitto come impresa: Storia sociale della mafia* (Padua, 1988), pp. 179ff.

14. That is the title of Pantaleone's book, *Antimafia occasione mancata* (Turin, 1969). Concerning the Anti-Mafia, see also Barrese, *I complici*, and now an anthology of the reports, edited and with an introduction by N. Tranfaglia, *Mafia, politica e affari* (Rome, 1992).

15. Pantaleone, *Antimafia*, p. 18.

16. U. Santino and G. La Fiura, *L'impresa mafiosa* (Milan, 1990), p. 133.

17. For which I refer the reader to Tranfaglia, *La mafia come metodo* (Rome, 1991), pp. 48ff., which rightly emphasizes the contradictions in which Carraro found himself, not only with his *Relazioni di minoranza* (minority reports), but also with Zuccalà's report, which, "sectorial" though it was, appears to be the one best focused on an analysis of the fundamental lines of the problem.

18. See also the evaluation offered by La Torre himself in the introduction to the edition of the minority report, published under the title *Mafia e potere politico* (Rome, 1976).

19. Formulations that already appeared in the Bernardinetti Report and that reappear in the Cattanei Report (for instance, on p. 101) and in the La Torre Report. The *Commissione* was not helped much by its consultants. Note that the opening of Brancato, "La mafia nell'opinione pubblica e nelle inchieste dall'Unità al fascismo" in *AntiMafia: Relazione sui lavori svolti . . . al termine della v. legislatura*, p. 163, states that, now that everything was known about the Mafia, all that mattered was to identify its influence on public opinion!

20. *Rel. La Torre*, pp. 569ff.

21. *Antimafia: Doc.*, vol. 1, p. 94.

22. Pantaleone, *Mafia e politica*.

23. Chilanti, "La mafia 'prefettizia,'" *L'Ora*, 19 April 1963.

24. As emphasized as well for the previous period by R. Mangiameli, *Le allegorie del buon governo: sui rapporti tra mafia e americani in Sicilia nel 1943* (dissertation, University of Catania, 1981).

25. Discussed later in this chapter.

26. Albini, "L'America deve la mafia alla Sicilia?" in Various Authors, *Mafia e potere*, ed. S. Di Bella (Soveria Mannelli, 1983), vol. 1, p. 189.

27. A. Blok, *La mafia di un villagio siciliano, 1860–1960* (Turin, 1986) (1st ed. 1974), p. 207.

28. Arlacchi, *La mafia imprenditrice: L'etica mafiosi e lo spirito del capitalismo* (Bologna, 1983), p. 12.

29. In *Antimafia: Doc.*, vol. 1, pp. 765, 767, and 753.

30. Malausa Report, in *Antimafia: Relazione sulle risultanze acquisite al Comune di Palermo*, p. 47. The continuity of the Vitale family of Altarello is suggested by the recurrence of first names that were not particularly common. In 1930, the trial for criminal conspiracy for the Porta Nuova–Altarello association involved Francesco Paolo Vitale, son of Giovanni Battista; Francesco Paolo, son of Filippo; Leonardo, son of Francesco Paolo; Giovanni Battista, son of Filippo; and so on. See GDS, 19 April 1930.

31. See, however, the similar warning that his elderly mafioso uncle offered to Calderone prior to his induction, in Testimony by Calderone and Arlacchi, p. 41. The minutes of Vitale's interrogations are reproduced in large extracts by L. Galluzzo, F. Nicastro, and V. Vasile, *Obiettivo Falcone: magistrati e mafia nel palazzo dei veleni* (Naples, 1989), pp. 95ff. The citations are on pp. 107, 99, 101, and 109.

32. H. Hess, *Mafia* (Rome, 1991), p. 116; others ignore the question.

33. The text of the confession is in *L'Ora*; but see also the case of the affiliation of the Palermitan doctor, revealed in 1937, in D. Gambetta, *La mafia siciliana: Un'industria della protezione privata* (Turin, 1992), p. 367.

34. Respectively, text by G. Servadio in Various Authors, *Mafia e potere*, ed. S. Di Bella (Soveria Mannelli, 1983), vol. 1, p. 118; Ciuni, "Un secolo di Mafia," in Various Authors, *Storia della Sicilia* (Palermo, 1978), p. 394.

35. Interview in *Antimafia: Doc.*, vol. 1, p. 730. Here too I emphasize my conceptual disagreement with the idea of ad hoc, unstable groups that social scientists focused on during these same years.

36. Tribunal of Palermo, Order of Indictment against L. Leggio + 115, 14 August 1965, in *Antimafia: Doc.*, vol. 4, t. XVI, pp. 208–9.

37. Tribunal of Palermo, Order of Indictment against A. La Barbera + 42, 23 June 1964, *Antimafia: Doc.*, vol. 4, t. XVII, pp. 506ff.

38. Tribunal of Palermo, Order of Indictment against P. Torretta + 120, 8 May 1965 (Justice Terranova), in *Antimafia: Doc.*, vol. 4, t. XVII, p. 627.

39. Cited in *Antimafia*. Rel. Carraro, p. 169.

40. GDS, 6 June 1929.

41. Testimony by Buscetta, *Dibattimento* (trial hearing), vol. 1, p. 104.

42. Testimony by Calderone and Arlacchi, p. 148.

43. Malausa Report, p. 40 (as cited in note 30, above).

44. Respectively, Testimony in *Antimafia: Doc.*, vol. 3, t. I, p. 1053; Verdict vs. La Barbera and others, p. 543.

45. Malausa Report, p. 42.

46. Tribunal of Palermo, Finding of the preliminary investigation vs. Spatola + 119 (preliminary magistrate G. Falcone), pp. 493ff.

47. *Istruttoria maxiprocesso* (Preliminary Investigation of the Maxitrial), p. 86.

48. Ibid., p. 90.

49. One immediately thinks of E. and G. La Loggia from Agrigento, Alessi from Caltanissetta, and Milazzo from Caltagirone.

50. Testimony by Buscetta, *Dibattimento*, vol. 1, p. 37.

51. Chilanti and Farinella, *Rapporto*, pp. 47–49.

52. Vignali Report, p. 163.

53. For all this, see the summation by the public prosecutor G. Pizzillo vs. Vitale and others, 4 December 1974, in *Antimafia: Doc.*, vol. 1, pp. 809–36; but see also the *Istruttoria Maxiprocesso*, pp. 6ff.

54. Verdict vs. Torretta and others, pp. 724ff.; Malausa Report, pp. 43–44; petition of the Palermo Federation of the Italian Communist Party (PCI), attached to the *Rel. La Torre*, p. 850.

55. *Antimafia: Singoli mafiosi*, p. 163.

56. *Corte di Assise* (Court of Assizes) of Catanzaro, verdict vs. A. La Barbera + 114, in *Antimafia: Doc.*, vol. 4, t. XVII, p. 992, and, ibid., also the mentioned verdict of indictment; concerning the La Barberas, see also Chilanti and Farinella, *Rapporto*, pp. 125ff.

57. "Per l'esportazione agrumaria," *Sicilia Nuova*, 19 March 1926; see also the account of the confiscation of 100 kilograms of morphine about to be shipped from Palermo to New York in GDS, 24 July 1926.

58. Tribunal of Palermo, Verdict vs. F. Garofalo and others, 31 January 1966, in *Antimafia: Doc.*, vol. 4, t. XIV.

59. *Antimafia: Rel. Zuccalà*, pp. 353 and 343.

60. Testimony of the American police officer C. Siragusa, quoted in ibid., p. 343.

61. Report of the Comando Generale of the Guardia di Finanza (financial police), 1955–1963, in *Antimafia: Doc.*, vol. 4, t. XIV, part 1, p. 185.

62. *Antimafia: Rel. Zuccalà*, p. 367. Concerning Mancino, see also *Antimafia: Singoli mafiosi*, pp. 203ff.

63. Report of the Guardia di Finanza, 1958, p. 232.

64. A. Block, *East Side, West Side: Organizing Crime in New York* (Cardiff, 1980), p. 129.

65. Report of the Guardia di Finanza, p. 184.

66. Ibid., pp. 248–49.

67. Report of the Guardia di Finanza, 1963, pp. 287–88.

68. Letter from M. Bergez, dated from Tangiers, 16 April 1960, in Report of the Guardia di Finanza, pp. 266–67.

69. Testimony by Buscetta, *Dibattimento*, vol. 1, p. 41.

70. Ibid., p. 218.

71. *President's Commission on Organized Crime: Report to the President*, vol. 1, *The Impact* (Washington, DC, 1986), p. 52.

72. Gambetta, *La mafia siciliana*, p. 319.

73. Report dated 5 April 1971, in *Antimafia: Doc.*, vol. 4, t. XIV, p. 993.

74. P. Reuter, *Disorganized Crime* (Cambridge, MA, 1983); see in particular the case histories on pp. 16off.

75. Letter in Verdict vs. F. Garofalo and others, p. 644.

76. Similarly, Frank Coppola, while preserving close ties in Partinico, took up residence in Pomezia.

77. Testimony by Calderone and Arlacchi, p. 27.

78. Verdict vs. Garofalo and others, p. 908. Sorge, often traveling back and forth between Italy and America, seems like a typical figure out of the enterprise syndicate: Valachi and the other American informer (*pentiti*) were unable to place him in a family, even though they knew him as a powerful individual: ibid., pp. 898–99.

79. Verdict vs. Garofalo and others, p. 625; the previously cited report, *President's Commission on Organized Crime*, pp. 52–53, also mentions the presence of Badalamenti and Buscetta, however.

80. Who claims for himself the role of interlocutor with Bonanno: E. Biagi, *Il boss è solo* (Milan, 1986), pp. 147ff.; and the testimony given to the DEA, cited by C. Sterling, *Cosa non solo nostra: La rete mondiale della mafia siciliana* (Milan, 1990), pp. 82–83.

81. L. Galluzzo, *Tommaso Buscetta, l'uomo che tradì se stesso* (Aosta, 1984), p. 30.

82. Verdict vs. Torretta and others, pp. 659 and 627.

83. J. Bonanno, *Uomo d'onore: L'autobiografia di J. B.* (Milan, 1985), p. 172.

84. Verdict of the Court of Catanzaro, pp. 975–76.

85. Verdict vs. L. Vitale and others, p. 834. This was the period when the *Commissione* had been dissolved and power was held by a triumvirate consisting of Riina himself, Badalamenti, and Stefano Bontate.

86. *Istruttoria maxiprocesso*, pp. 79–80.

87. Verdict vs. Spatola and others, pp. 599 and 787; in Catania as well, the collection of debts was a major activity of Mafia groups.

88. *Antimafia: Rel. sui mercati all'ingrosso*, report of the *questore*, pp. 48ff.

89. Ibid., pp. 12–13.

90. Gambetta, "La mafia elimina la concorrenza: Ma la concorrenza può eliminare la mafia?" *Meridiana*, 1989–1990, 7–8, pp. 319–36; the thesis is very much understated in Gambetta, *La mafia siciliana*, pp. 291ff.

91. Testimony by Buscetta, pp. 102ff.; Testimony by Calderone, p. 81.

92. Testimony by Calderone and Arlacchi, p. 72.

93. Testimony by Calderone, pp. 52ff.

94. Testimony given to the *Antimafia*, XI legislature, 4 December 1992, p. 513. In the events of Sommatino in 1925 (see chapter 3), one of the most important characters was a certain Leonardo Messina of San Cataldo. Concerning the use of the term *Cosa Nostra* with reference to the distant past, I refer the reader to what is stated in chapter 4. For that matter, the *pentito* himself, referring to his own family tradition, emphatically states: "This is not the first time that Cosa Nostra has changed name and skin . . . it has done it in the past as well," Testimony given to the *Antimafia*, XI legislature, 4 December 1992, p. 520.

95. Testimony given to the *Antimafia*, XI legislature, 4 December 1992, p. 519.

96. *Istruttoria maxiprocesso*, pp. 266ff.; in general, G. Martorana and S. Negrelli, *Così ho tradito Cosa Nostra* (Quart, 1993), pp. 61ff. This Madonia should not be confused with the family in Palermo with the same surname.

97. R. Catanzaro, *Il delitto come impresa: Storia sociale della mafia* (Padua, 1988), pp. 184ff.

98. Here I am utilizing Calderone's testimony, integrating it with information from other sources.

99. As early as 1957, for instance, G. B. Ercolano, another member of the *cosca*, was arrested in Pozzillo with Badalamenti: Report of the Guardia di Finanza, p. 224.

100. M. Caciagli, *Democrazia cristiana e potere nel Mezzogiorno* (Rimini, 1977); Giarrizzo, *Catania* (Rome, 1986); C. Fava, *La mafia comanda a Catania* (Rome, 1992).

101. The statistics come from Falcone's estimate, in an interview with G. Fiume, "La mafia tra criminalità e cultura," *Meridiana*, 1989, 5, p. 202.

102. Testimony by Calderone and Arlacchi, pp. 225–26.

103. *Antimafia*, XI legislature, testimony by T. Buscetta, 16 November 1992, p. 355.

104. Concerning the complex intersection between local society and rackets in one of these areas, however, see S. Costantino, *A viso aperto: La resistenza antimafiosa a Capo d'Orlando* (Palermo, 1993).

105. Testimony by Calderone, p. 5.

106. *Antimafia*, testimony by Messina, p. 531.

107. *Istruttoria maxiprocesso*, p. 69.

108. *Antimafia*, XI legislature, 9 February 1993, testimony by Mutolo, p. 1231.

109. Testimony by Calderone, p. 41.

110. Sterling, *Cosa non solo nostra*, pp. 127–42.

111. Testimony by Buscetta, p. 50.

112. Statements at the time of arrest (1986) in S. Lodato, *Dieci anni di mafia* (Milan, 1992), p. 194. In reality Michele, who had the same surname as the Grecos of Ciaculli, was a cousin of *chicchiteddu*. Concerning the charges against Don Piddu, see Testimony by Calderone, pp. 8–9.

113. Testimony by Buscetta, p. 12.

114. Testimony by Calderone and Arlacchi, p. 27.

115. Testimony by Calderone, p. 51.

116. Testimony by Calderone and Arlacchi, p. 94.

117. Testimony by Calderone, p. 248.

118. Quoted in *Istruttoria maxiprocesso*, p. 351. Documents concerning the funds intended by the Salvos for use in payments to politicians, ibid., pp. 352–54.

119. *Istruttoria maxiprocesso*, p. 340.

120. Ibid., p. 32.

121. Verdict vs. La Barbera and others, p. 523.

122. *Istruttoria maxiprocesso*, p. 8.

123. Ibid., p. 328.

124. I quote from an extract from the verdict published in *Città d'utopia*, 1 January 1992, p. 29, and for other references, pp. 27 and 26.

125. Verdict vs. La Barbera and others, p. 25.

126. Testimony by Buscetta, p. 84; but also Testimony by Calderone, p. 116.

127. Biagi, *Il boss è solo*, p. 125.

128. Quoted in S. Turone, *Partiti e mafia, dalla P2 alla droga* (Rome, 1985), p. 78; but see also Sterling, *Cosa non solo nostra*, passim.

129. *President's Commission*, p. 51. Concerning the relationships between the Mafia and narcotics trafficking, see A. Becchi and M. Turvani, *Proibito? Il mercato mondiale della droga* (Rome, 1993), pp. 138ff.

130. As Sterling believes, *Cosa non solo nostra*.

131. Verdict vs. Spatola and others, pp. 480, 506, and 488.

132. Gambetta, *La mafia*, p. 339.

133. *Antimafia*, Testimony by Buscetta.

134. Verdict vs. Spatola and others, p. 510.

135. G. Falcone and M. Padovani, *Cose di Cosa nostra* (Milan, 1991), p. 28.

136. Testimony by Buscetta, p. 1231.

137. Testimony by Buscetta, *Dibattimento* (trial hearing), p. 28.

138. Testimony by Buscetta, p. 268.

139. Testimony by Buscetta, *Dibattimento*, p. 28.

140. Ibid., pp. 218, 243, 89, 178–79.

141. Testimony by Buscetta, p. 299.

142. This is also Sterling's opinion in *Cosa non solo nostra*.

143. Testimony by Buscetta, p. 60.

144. *Istruttoria maxiprocesso*, pp. 324–25.

145. Testimony by Buscetta, pp. 1272–74. For the wiretap on Badalamenti's phone conversation, see Sterling, *Cosa non solo nostra*, p. 96.

146. A use of which the general seems to have been well aware, as shown by passages from his diary, quoted in *Istruttoria maxiprocesso*, pp. 228–30. But see also the book by his son, N. Dalla Chiesa, *Delitto imperfetto* (Milan, 1984).

147. See the testimony by Terranova himself in *Antimafia: Doc.*, vol. 3, t. I, p. 1188.

148. Interview-narrative with/by Falcone in *Rapporto sulla mafia degli anni '80* (Palermo, 1986), p. 27.

149. Falcone and Padovani, *Cose di Cosa nostra*, p. 157.

150. Interview with Cassarà a few days before his death; see Lodato, *Dieci anni*, p. 167.

151. Lodato, *Dieci anni*, p. 172.

152. Concerning which I refer the reader to Galluzzo, Nicastro, and Vasile, *Obiettivo Falcone*.

153. G. Pansa, *Carte false* (Milan, 1986); P. Arlacchi and N. Dalla Chiesa, *La palude e la città: Si puo sconfiggere la mafia* (Milan, 1987), pp. 78ff.

154. Article published in CS, 26 January 1987, now in L. Sciascia, *A futura memoria* (Milan, 1989), p. 139.

155. C. Duggan, *La mafia durante il fascismo* (Soveria Manelli, 1986); the book review in CS, 10 January 1987, now in Sciascia, *A futura memoria*, pp. 123–30.

156. Of which there is ample evidence in the articles republished in the referenced *A futura memoria*; I would remind the reader that these were the years of the Tortora case and the "Calogero theorem."

157. Introduction to Hess, *Mafia*.

158. *Antimafia: Doc.*, vol. 1, p. 872. But also see the analysis set forth by Di Lello in the interview given to V. Villa, "Magistratura e maxiprocesso," in *Area metropolitana*, January 1986, p. 15.

159. Concerning Vitale, however, see not only Rizzo's quoted notations, but also those by La Torre and Terranova in *Antimafia: Doc.*, vol. 1, pp. 716 and 873.

160. Di Lello, "Magistratura," p. 13.

161. *Istruttoria maxiprocesso*, pp. 17ff.

162. It is significant that Blok (*La mafia*), even though he was working on the trial, passed over this defection (*pentimento*), evidently because it did not fit in with his rigid and schematic approach.

163. Testimony by Buscetta, *Dibattimento* (trial hearing), vol. 3, pp. 62–63; the objection is from the lawyer Fragalà.

164. Sciascia, Introduction, in L. Jannuzzi, *Così parlò Buscetta* (Milan, 1986), p. 9.

165. On this point, however, I refer the reader to the opinion of Chief Justice Giordano, according to whom the final verdict was not the product of deductive logic derived from the so-called Buscetta theorem (Lodato, *Dieci anni*, p. 221); and to Sciascia's acknowledgment of the fairness of the verdict, in CS, 27 December 1987, and now in *A futura memoria*, pp. 147–49.

166. In Jannuzzi, *Così parlò Buscetta*, p. 151.

167. Testimony by Calderone and Arlacchi, pp. 56–61.

168. Sciascia, Introduction, in Jannuzzi, *Così parlò Buscetta*, p. 8.

169. P. Maas, *La mela marcia* (Milan, 1972), p. 39. (This is the Italian version of *The Valachi Papers* [New York, 1968].)

170. Testimony by Buscetta, p. 2.

171. Falcone and Padovani, *Cose di Cosa nostra*.

172. Sentenza Spatola (verdict), p. 485. But I refer the reader to what I wrote in chapter 1.

173. Lodato, *Dieci anni*, pp. 202–5.

174. Testimony by Calderone and Arlacchi, p. 159.

175. Testimony at the *Maxiprocesso* (Maxitrial) in Jannuzzi, *Così parlò Buscetta*, p. 166.

176. *Istruttoria maxiprocesso*, p. 14.

177. Testimony by Terranova in *Antimafia: Doc.*, Vol. 1, p. 1188.

178. Verdict vs. La Barbera and others, p. 1090.

179. F. Bartolotto Impastato, *La mafia in casa mia*, interview with A. Puglisi and U. Santino (Palermo, 1987), pp. 60–61.

180. Statement of F. M. Mannoia, in *Processo Andreotti*, p. 110.

181. *Processo Andreotti*, p. 737.

182. Respectively, see G. Ayala, "La lobby mafiosa," *Micromega*, 1988, 4, p. 15, and the estimates for 1994 in *L'Espresso*, 19 November 1995, p. 61.

183. See G. Fiume's interview of Falcone, *La mafia tra criminalità e cultura*, p. 202.

184. Martelli now understands that in 1987 he was the unwitting target of a Mafia approach: *Processo Andreotti*, pp. 221ff.

185. Testimony of Gioacchino La Barbera, *Processo Andreotti*, pp. 215–18.

186. Ibid., p. 757.

187. Ibid., p. 735.

188. Ibid., p. 737.

189. *Istruttoria maxiprocesso*, p. 229.

190. This is the expression used in the well-known letter to Spadolini.

191. E. Macaluso, *Giulio Andreotti tra Stato e mafia* (Soveria Mannelli, 1995), p. 16.

192. *Processo Andreotti*, p. 156.

193. *Istruttoria maxiprocesso*, p. 229.

194. *Processo Andreotti*, pp. 28 and 48.

195. Already, many years ago, Catanzaro, *Il delitto*, p. 249, noted that the recycling of profits from narcotics smuggling entailed a strengthening, not a relaxation, of ties with politics.

196. It is impossible to overlook the parallelism of this attempt with the effort of the mafiosi themselves, that is, the *pentiti,* to blame the drug business for the deterioration of their once beneficent customs.

197. *Antimafia,* testimony by Buscetta, p. 428.

198. Sciascia, *A futura memoria,* p. 109.

199. Lecture by Falcone in the summer of 1989, reported in *L'Unità,* 31 May 1992.

200. Respectively, Falcone lecture, and Falcone and Padovani, *Cose di Cosa nostra,* p. 169. See also the collection of writings by Falcone, *Interventi e proposte (1982–1992)* (Florence, 1994).

201. Tranfaglia, *La Mafia,* p. 102.

202. "Il modello mafia," *Segno,* 1982, 33, p. 6.

203. Testimony by Mannoia, in Tribunal of Palermo, Decree by Judge A. Giardina concerning the Lima Murder, 20 October 1992, published in *Segno,* October–November 1992, 139, pp. 56–57.

204. See also the considerations by P. La Torre, "Se terrorismo e mafia si scambiano le tecniche," *Rinascita,* 16 November 1979, now in La Torre, *Le ragioni di una vita* (Bari, 1982), pp. 125–29.

205. *Istruttoria maxiprocesso,* p. 293. This, of course, is a separate issue, unrelated to the question of whether Santapaola was really responsible for the events in question.

206. In Decree . . . concerning the Lima Murder, p. 19.

207. Testimony by Buscetta, p. 72.

208. Ibid., p. 269. But we should also note the parallel between the murder of Costa and the assassination of Judge Coco by the Red Brigades drawn by Dalla Chiesa in an interview with G. Bocca, in *La Repubblica,* 10 August 1982.

209. *Processo Andreotti,* p. 49.

210. Decree . . . concerning the Lima Murder, testimony by G. Mutolo and G. Marchese, pp. 15–23.

211. Testimony by Mutolo, Decree . . . concerning the Lima Murder, p. 15. A *mandamento* is a group of three families that has a right to send a representative to sit on the *Commissione.*

212. According to the questionable interpretation of the prosecution, *Processo Andreotti,* pp. 761–68, concerning which see also the considerations of U. Santino, "Guida al processo Andreotti," in *Città d'utopia,* November 1995, p. 4.

213. In the context of the magistracy, see, aside from Falcone's writings, the fine work and views of Di Lello, *Giudici.*

214. Andreotti, *Cosa loro: Mai visti da vicino* (Milan, 1995), p. 35.

215. See, among other items, the testimony of G. Carli, in *Relazione di minoranza della Commissione parlamentare d'inchiesta sul caso Sindona,* VIII legislature, Doc. XXIII, no. 2 VI, p. 222.

INDEX

▼▼▼